# BLUE PERIOD

TSUBASA YAMAGUCHI

8



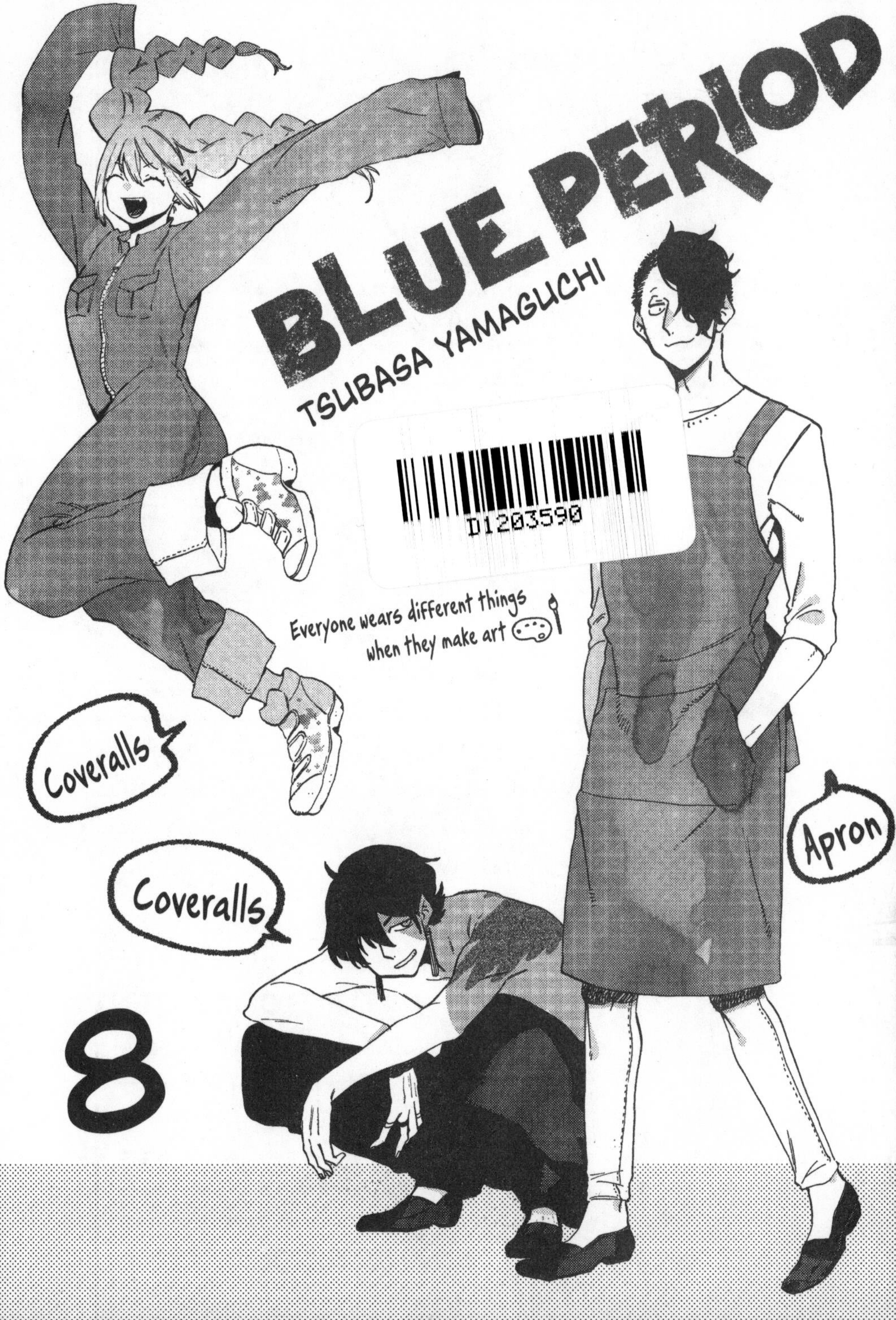
Everyone wears different things when they make art
Coveralls
Apron
Coveralls

# CHARACTERS

**Kinemi Miki**
The one who broke Yatora's mirror during TUA's first exam. She failed the exams twice before getting into TUA.

**Yotasuke Takahashi**
After quitting the prep school that Yatora was attending, he studied on his own and passed TUA's exams on his first attempt. His talent, skills, and unsociable character inspire Yatora to be a better artist.

**Yatora Yaguchi**
After getting hooked on the joy of making art, he studied to get into Tokyo University of the Arts, the most competitive of all Japanese art colleges, and passed on his first attempt. He's a hardworking normie.

**Ryuji Ayukawa**
Goes by the name Yuka. A boy who dresses in women's clothing. Yuka invited Yatora to the Art Club when they were in high school.

**Haruka Hashida**
He used to attend the same prep school as Yatora. He currently attends Tama Art University. As an art connoisseur of sorts, he enjoys museums and the like.

**Maki Kuwana**
Her parents are TUA alumni, and her older sister, who is a bit of a "campus celebrity," currently attends TUA. She changed courses at her prep school and has been studying sculpture for a few months.

# TABLE OF CONTENTS

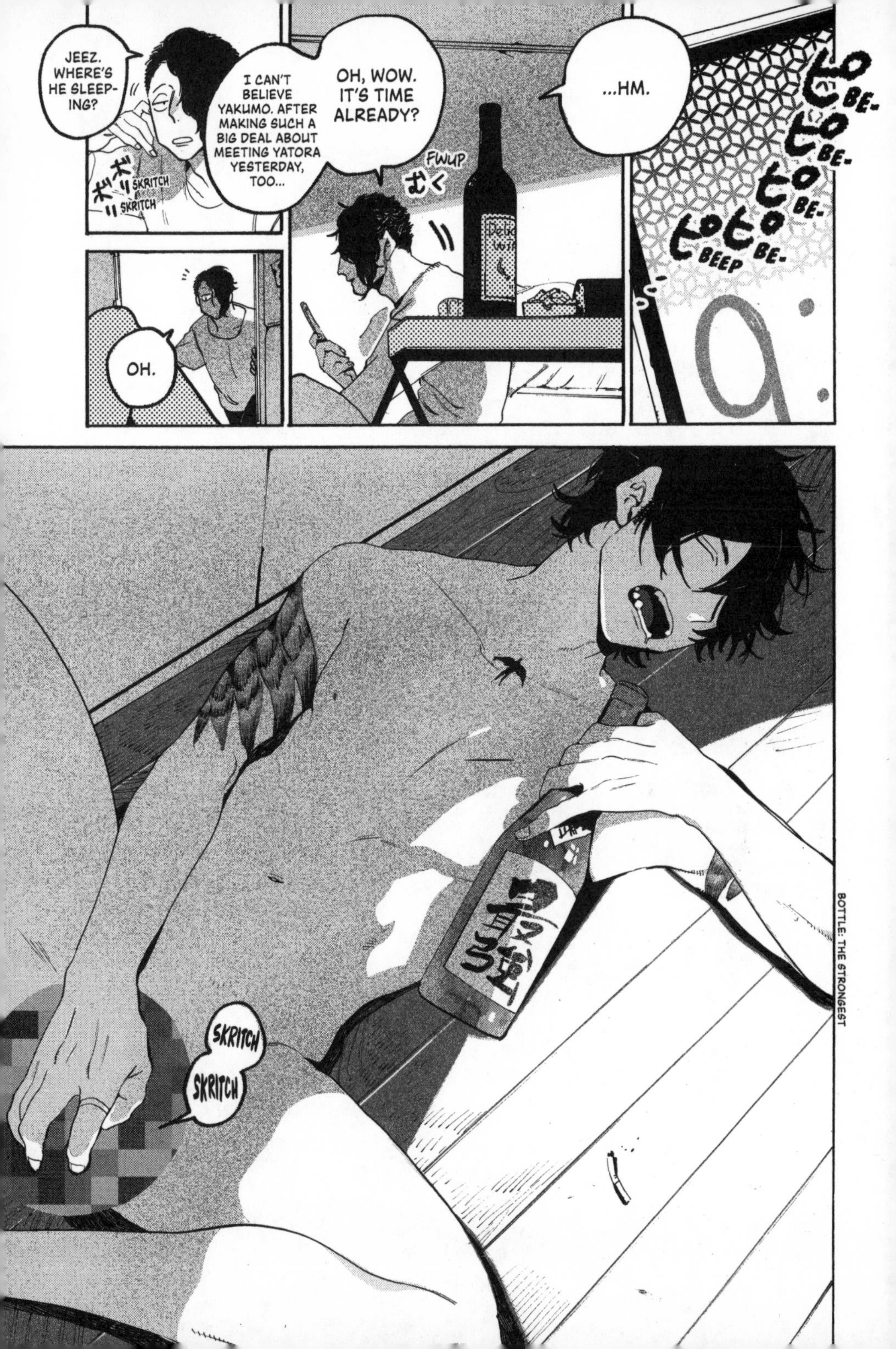
BE-
BE-
BE-
BE-
BEEP
...HM.
OH, WOW. IT'S TIME ALREADY?
FWUP
I CAN'T BELIEVE YAKUMO. AFTER MAKING SUCH A BIG DEAL ABOUT MEETING YATORA YESTERDAY, TOO...
JEEZ. WHERE'S HE SLEEP-ING?
SKRITCH
SKRITCH
OH.
SKRITCH
SKRITCH
BOTTLE: THE STRONGEST

# STROKE 30

## CAN'T JUDGE A BOOK BY ITS COVER

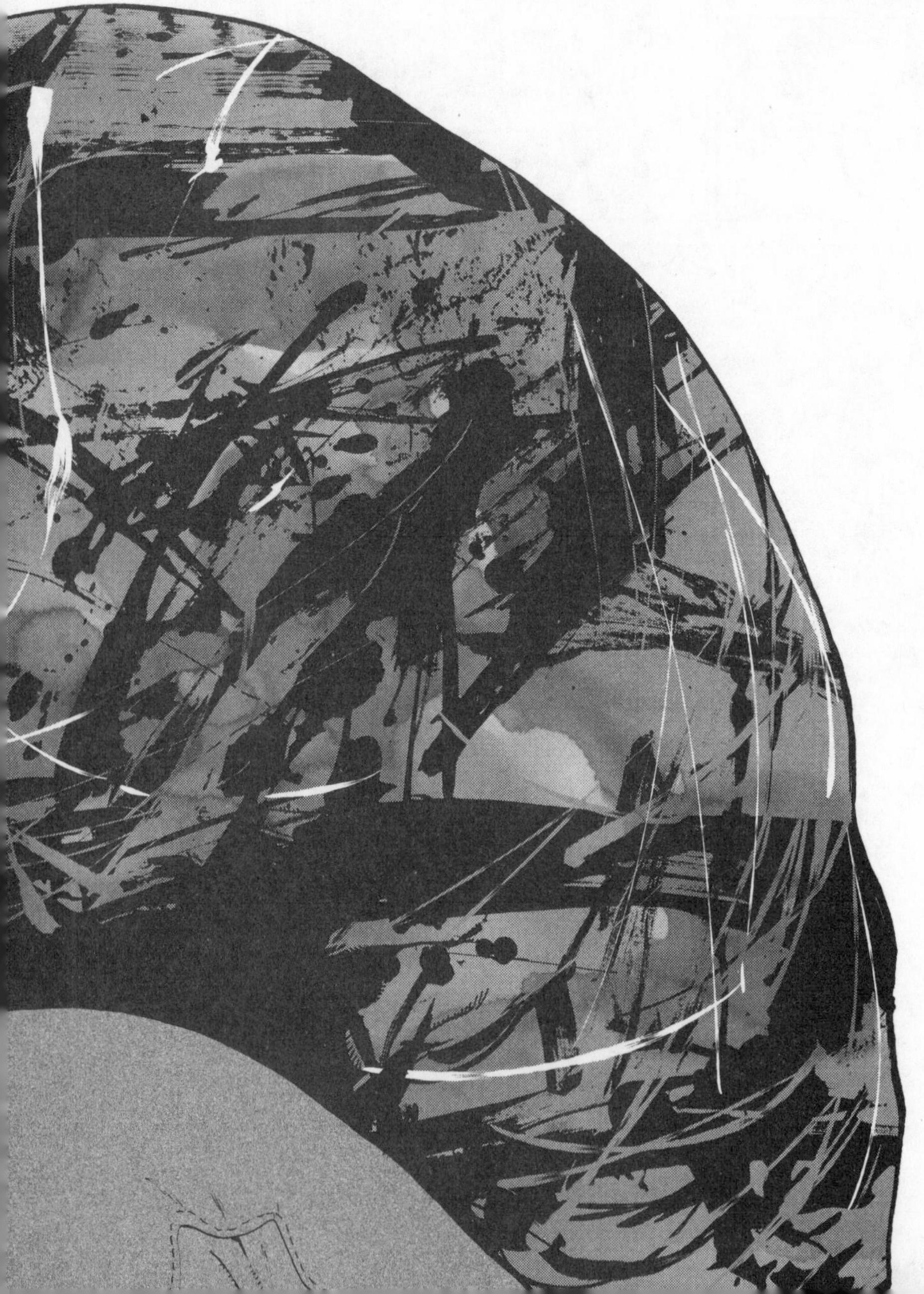

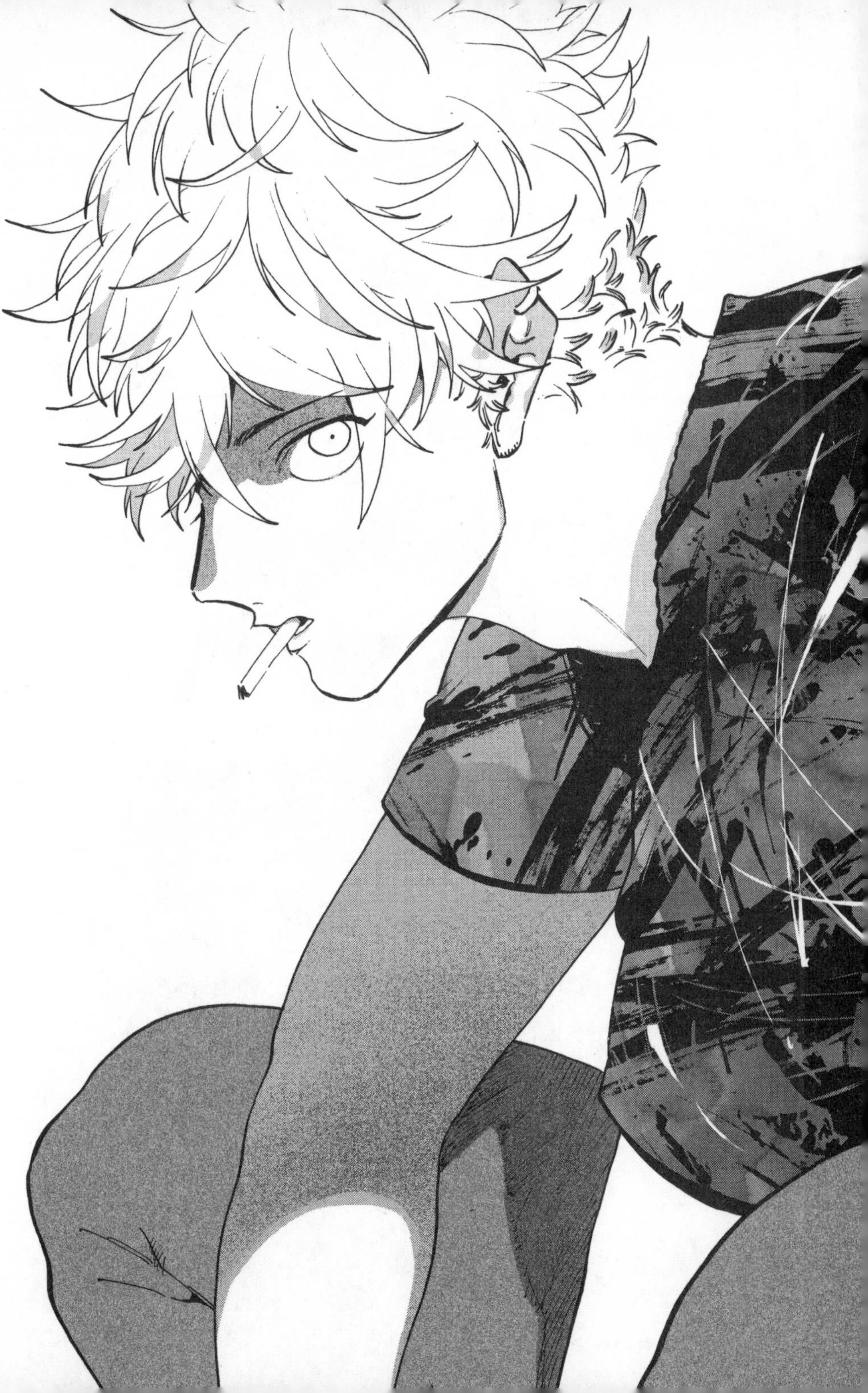

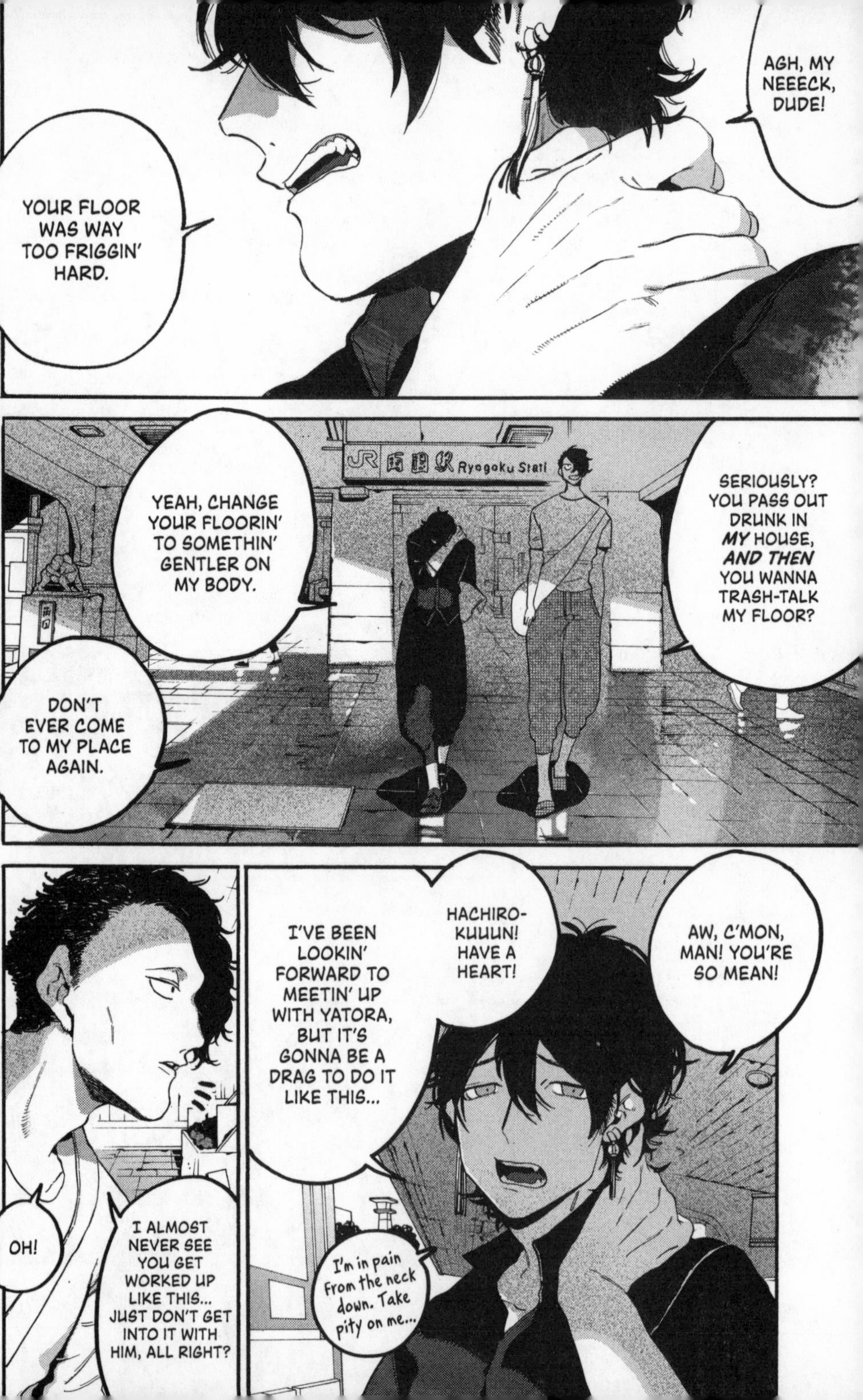
AGH, MY NEEECK, DUDE!
YOUR FLOOR WAS WAY TOO FRIGGIN' HARD.
SERIOUSLY? YOU PASS OUT DRUNK IN *MY* HOUSE, ***AND THEN*** YOU WANNA TRASH-TALK MY FLOOR?
YEAH, CHANGE YOUR FLOORIN' TO SOMETHIN' GENTLER ON MY BODY.
DON'T EVER COME TO MY PLACE AGAIN.
AW, C'MON, MAN! YOU'RE SO MEAN!
HACHIRO-KUUUN! HAVE A HEART!
I'VE BEEN LOOKIN' FORWARD TO MEETIN' UP WITH YATORA, BUT IT'S GONNA BE A DRAG TO DO IT LIKE THIS...
I'm in pain from the neck down. Take pity on me...
OH!
I ALMOST NEVER SEE YOU GET WORKED UP LIKE THIS... JUST DON'T GET INTO IT WITH HIM, ALL RIGHT?

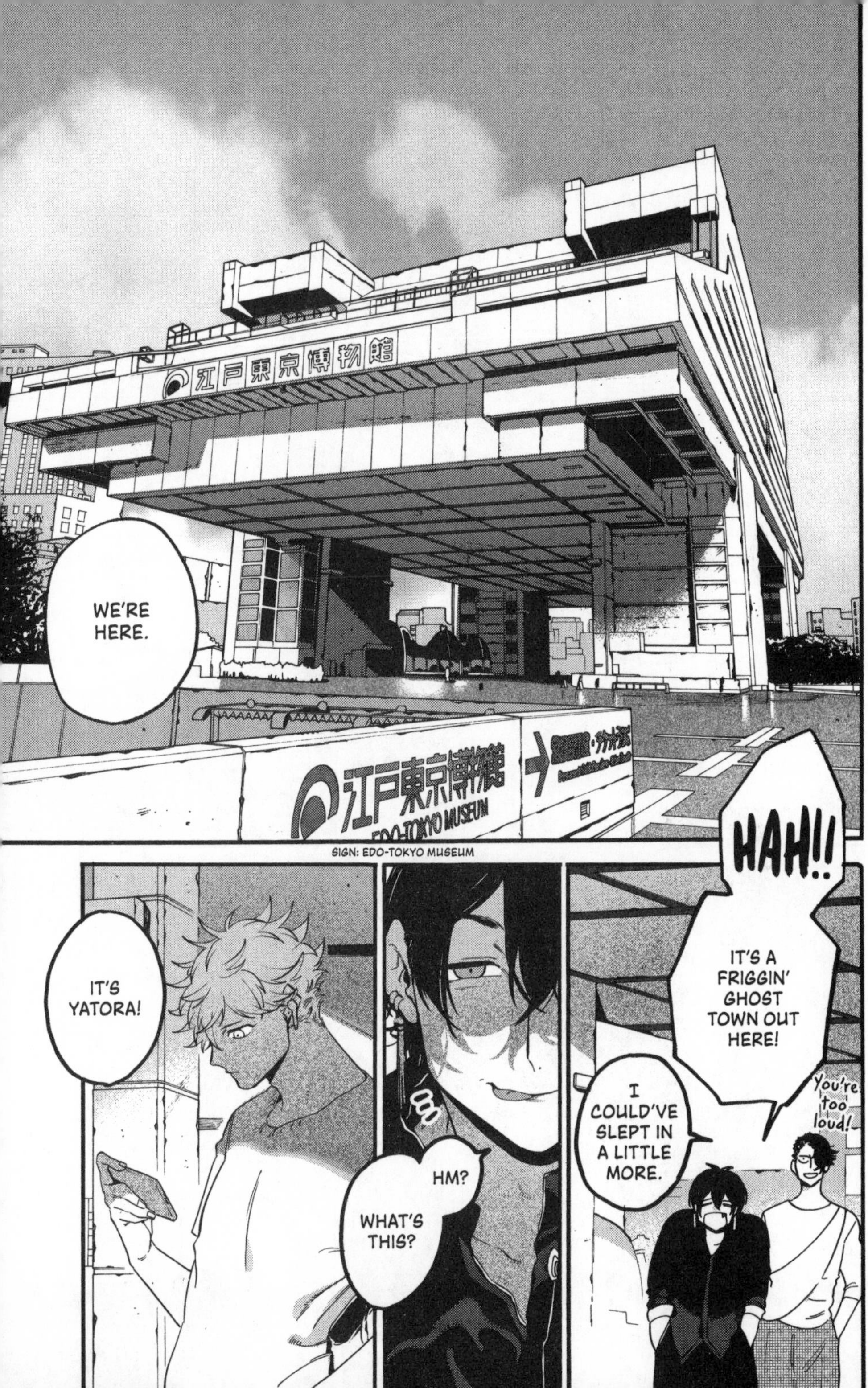
江戸東京博物館
WE'RE HERE.
江戸東京博物館
EDO-TOKYO MUSEUM
SIGN: EDO-TOKYO MUSEUM
HAH!!
IT'S A FRIGGIN' GHOST TOWN OUT HERE!
I COULD'VE SLEPT IN A LITTLE MORE.
You're too loud!
HM?
WHAT'S THIS?
IT'S YATORA!

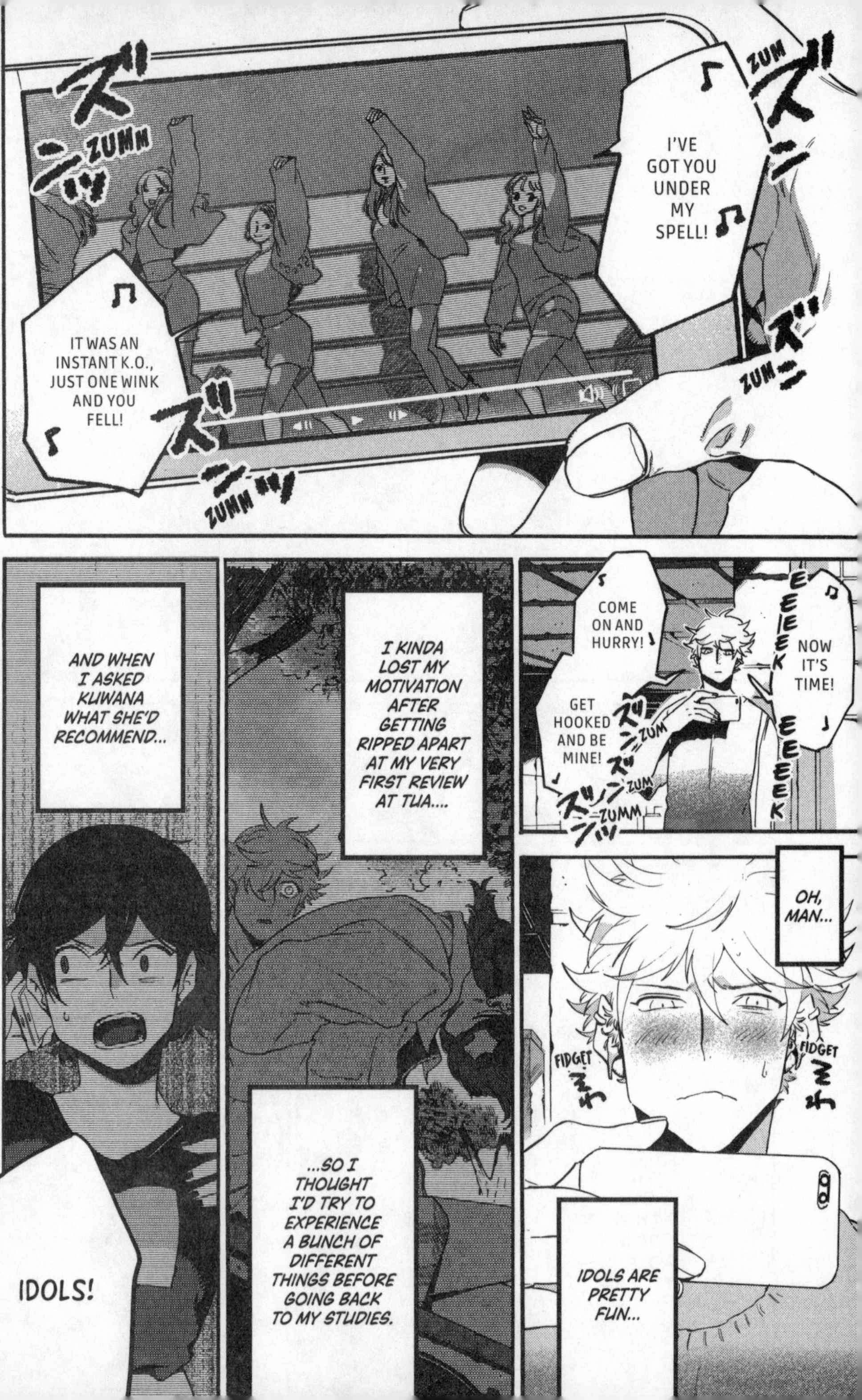
ZUM
I'VE GOT YOU UNDER MY SPELL!
ZUM
ZUMM
IT WAS AN INSTANT K.O., JUST ONE WINK AND YOU FELL!
ZUMM
NOW IT'S TIME!
EEEEK
EEEEK
COME ON AND HURRY!
GET HOOKED AND BE MINE!
ZUM
ZUM
ZUMM
OH, MAN...
FIDGET
FIDGET
IDOLS ARE PRETTY FUN...
I KINDA LOST MY MOTIVATION AFTER GETTING RIPPED APART AT MY VERY FIRST REVIEW AT TUA....
...SO I THOUGHT I'D TRY TO EXPERIENCE A BUNCH OF DIFFERENT THINGS BEFORE GOING BACK TO MY STUDIES.
AND WHEN I ASKED KUWANA WHAT SHE'D RECOMMEND...
IDOLS!

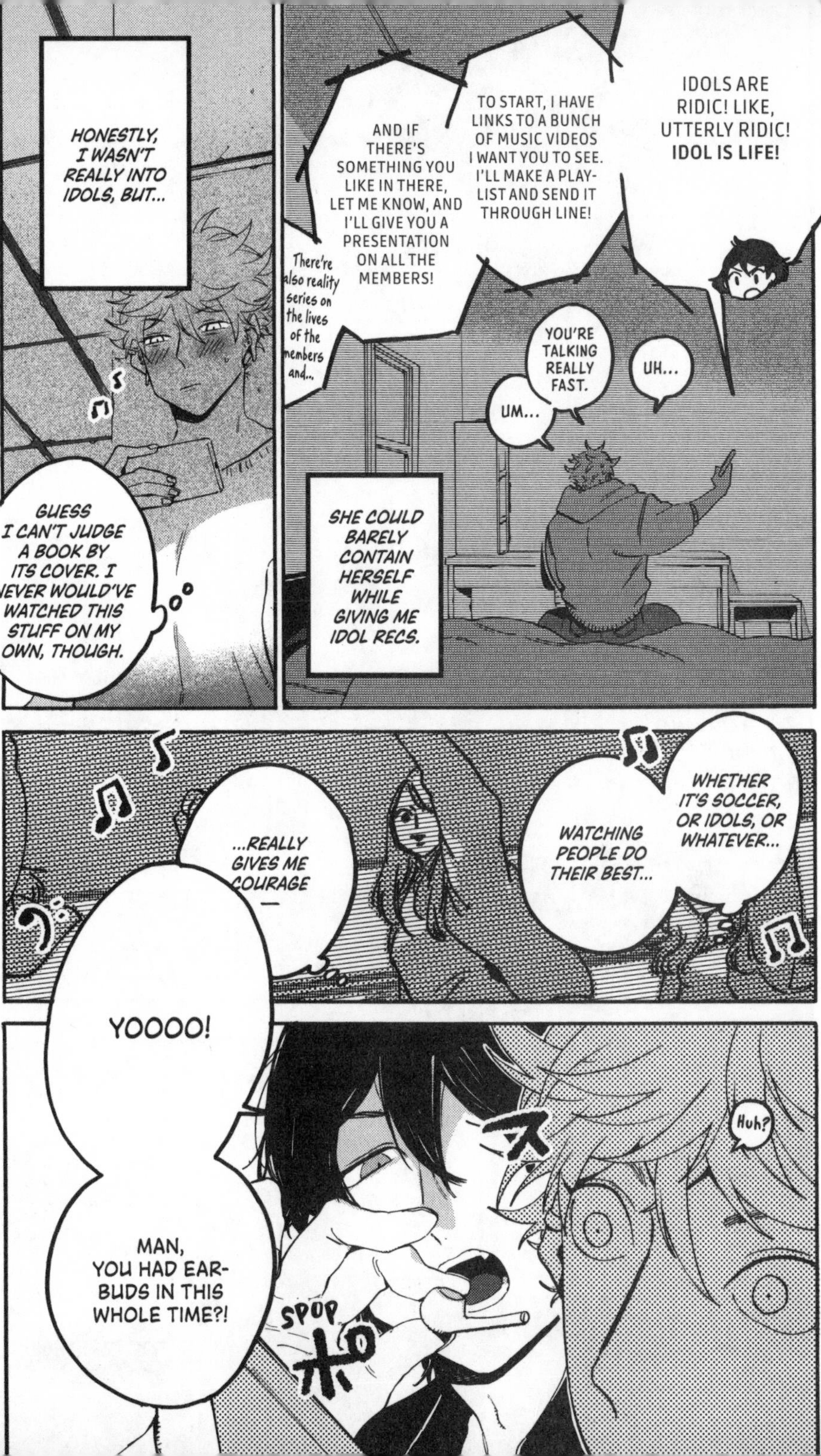
IDOLS ARE RIDIC! LIKE, UTTERLY RIDIC! **IDOL IS LIFE!**
TO START, I HAVE LINKS TO A BUNCH OF MUSIC VIDEOS I WANT YOU TO SEE. I'LL MAKE A PLAY-LIST AND SEND IT THROUGH LINE!
AND IF THERE'S SOMETHING YOU LIKE IN THERE, LET ME KNOW, AND I'LL GIVE YOU A PRESENTATION ON ALL THE MEMBERS!
There're also reality series on the lives of the members and...
UH...
YOU'RE TALKING REALLY FAST.
UM...
SHE COULD BARELY CONTAIN HERSELF WHILE GIVING ME IDOL RECS.
HONESTLY, I WASN'T REALLY INTO IDOLS, BUT...
GUESS I CAN'T JUDGE A BOOK BY ITS COVER. I NEVER WOULD'VE WATCHED THIS STUFF ON MY OWN, THOUGH.
WHETHER IT'S SOCCER, OR IDOLS, OR WHATEVER...
WATCHING PEOPLE DO THEIR BEST...
...REALLY GIVES ME COURAGE—
Huh?
YOOOO!
MAN, YOU HAD EAR-BUDS IN THIS WHOLE TIME?!
SPOP

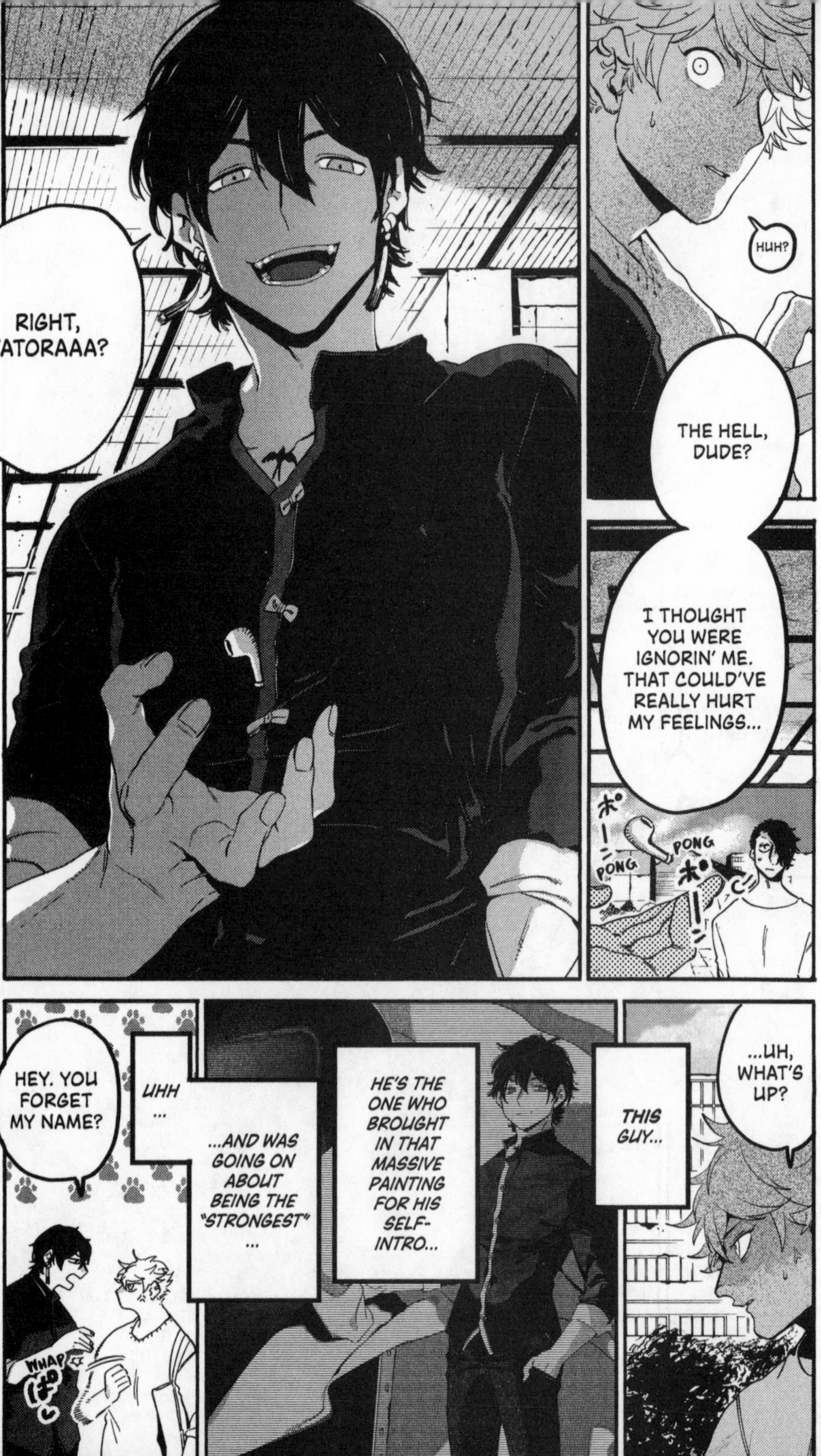
HUH?
THE HELL, DUDE?
I THOUGHT YOU WERE IGNORIN' ME. THAT COULD'VE REALLY HURT MY FEELINGS...
PONG
PONG
RIGHT, YATORAAA?
...UH, WHAT'S UP?
THIS GUY...
HE'S THE ONE WHO BROUGHT IN THAT MASSIVE PAINTING FOR HIS SELF-INTRO...
UHH ...
...AND WAS GOING ON ABOUT BEING THE "STRONGEST" ...
HEY. YOU FORGET MY NAME?
WHAP

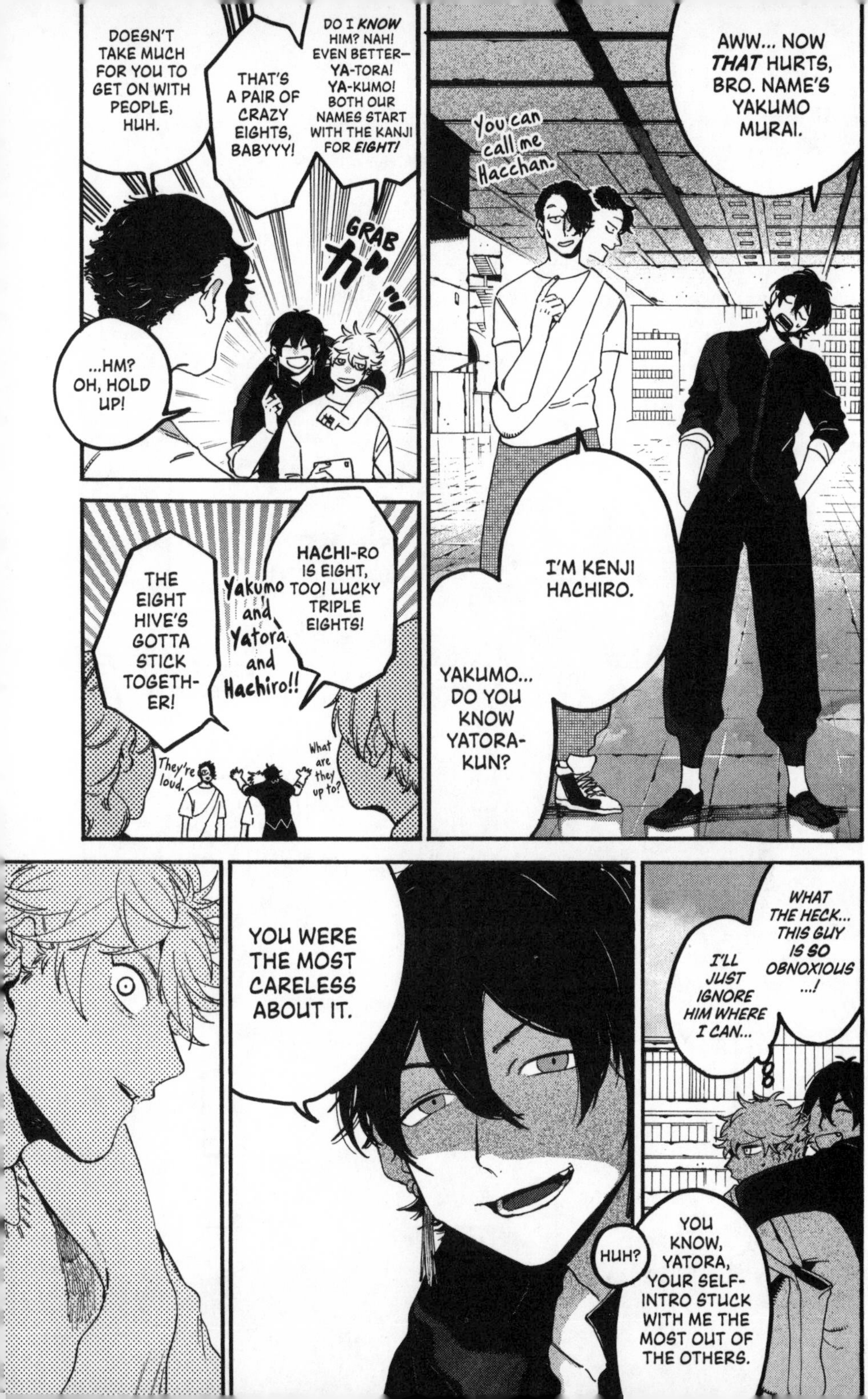
AWW... NOW *THAT* HURTS, BRO. NAME'S YAKUMO MURAI.
You can call me Hacchan.
I'M KENJI HACHIRO.
YAKUMO... DO YOU KNOW YATORA-KUN?
DO I *KNOW* HIM? NAH! EVEN BETTER— YA-TORA! YA-KUMO! BOTH OUR NAMES START WITH THE KANJI FOR *EIGHT!*
THAT'S A PAIR OF CRAZY EIGHTS, BABYYY!
DOESN'T TAKE MUCH FOR YOU TO GET ON WITH PEOPLE, HUH.
GRAB
...HM? OH, HOLD UP!
HACHI-RO IS EIGHT, TOO! LUCKY TRIPLE EIGHTS!
Yakumo and Yatora and Hachiro!!
THE EIGHT HIVE'S GOTTA STICK TOGETHER!
What are they up to?
They're loud.
WHAT THE HECK... THIS GUY IS SO OBNOXIOUS ...!
I'LL JUST IGNORE HIM WHERE I CAN...
YOU KNOW, YATORA, YOUR SELF-INTRO STUCK WITH ME THE MOST OUT OF THE OTHERS.
HUH?
YOU WERE THE MOST CARELESS ABOUT IT.

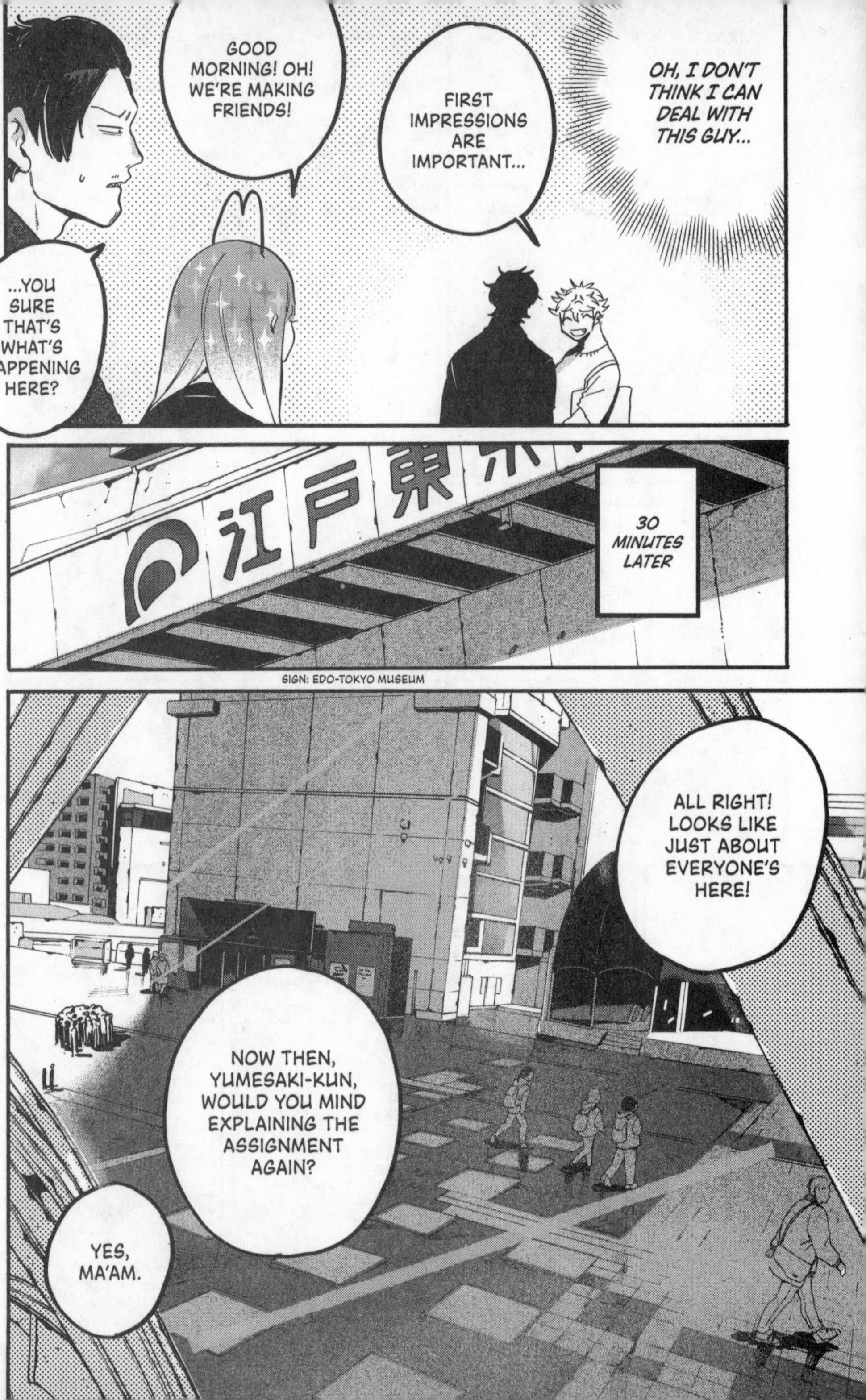
OH, I DON'T THINK I CAN DEAL WITH THIS GUY...
FIRST IMPRESSIONS ARE IMPORTANT...
GOOD MORNING! OH! WE'RE MAKING FRIENDS!
...YOU SURE THAT'S WHAT'S HAPPENING HERE?
30 MINUTES LATER
SIGN: EDO-TOKYO MUSEUM
ALL RIGHT! LOOKS LIKE JUST ABOUT EVERYONE'S HERE!
NOW THEN, YUMESAKI-KUN, WOULD YOU MIND EXPLAINING THE ASSIGNMENT AGAIN?
YES, MA'AM.

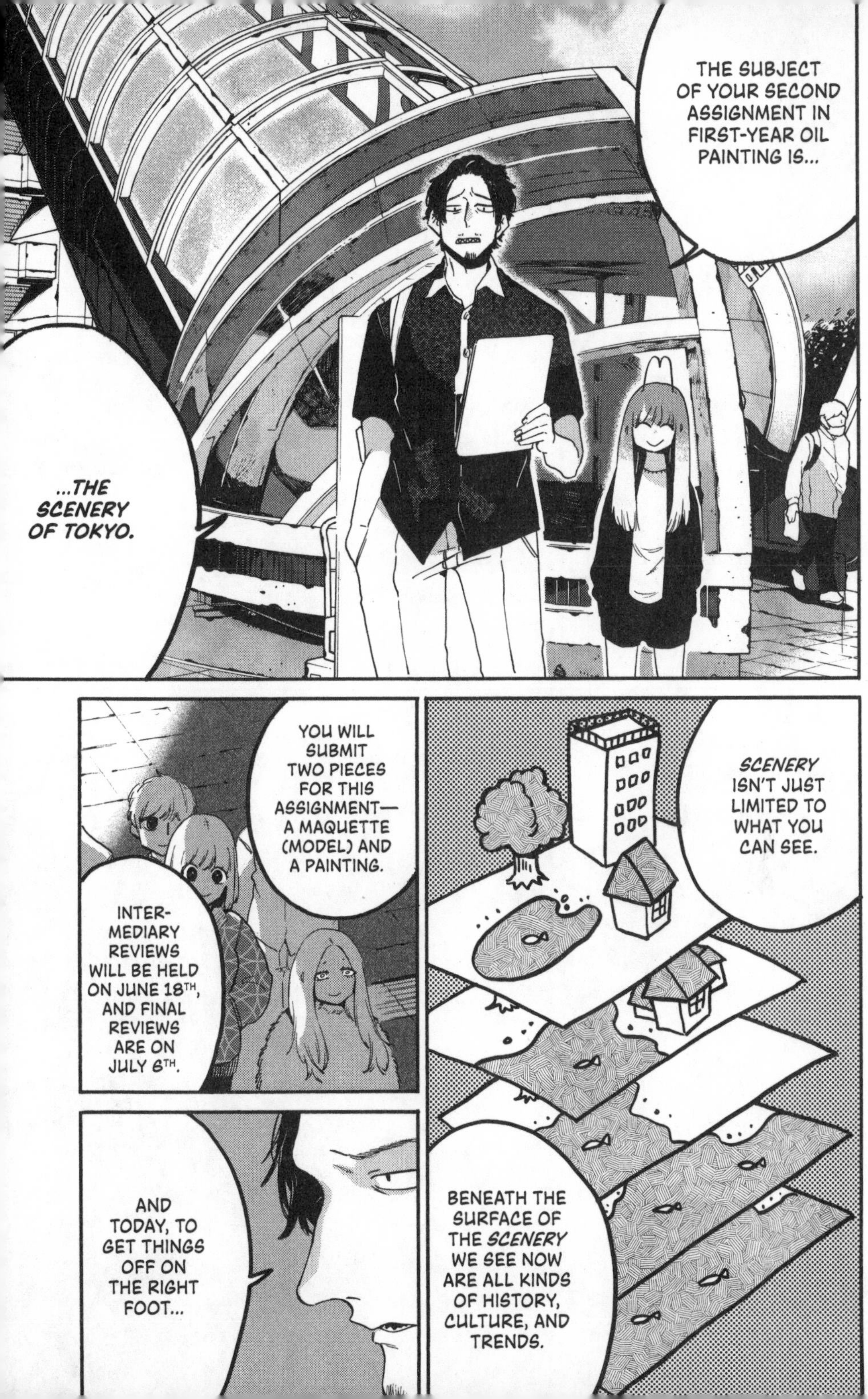
THE SUBJECT OF YOUR SECOND ASSIGNMENT IN FIRST-YEAR OIL PAINTING IS...
...THE SCENERY OF TOKYO.
*SCENERY* ISN'T JUST LIMITED TO WHAT YOU CAN SEE.
BENEATH THE SURFACE OF THE *SCENERY* WE SEE NOW ARE ALL KINDS OF HISTORY, CULTURE, AND TRENDS.
YOU WILL SUBMIT TWO PIECES FOR THIS ASSIGNMENT—A MAQUETTE (MODEL) AND A PAINTING.
INTER-MEDIARY REVIEWS WILL BE HELD ON JUNE 18TH, AND FINAL REVIEWS ARE ON JULY 6TH.
AND TODAY, TO GET THINGS OFF ON THE RIGHT FOOT...

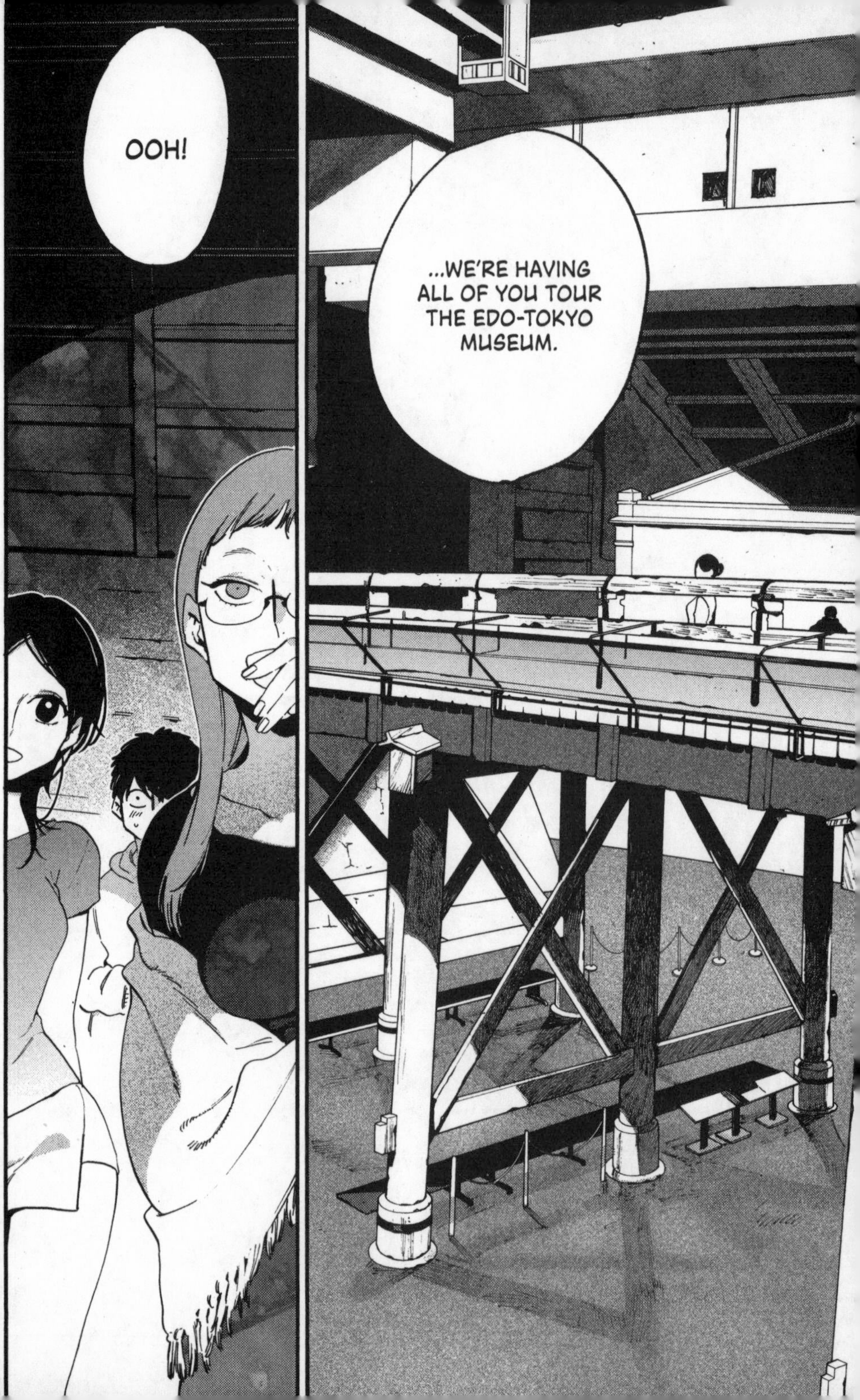
...WE'RE HAVING ALL OF YOU TOUR THE EDO-TOKYO MUSEUM.
OOH!

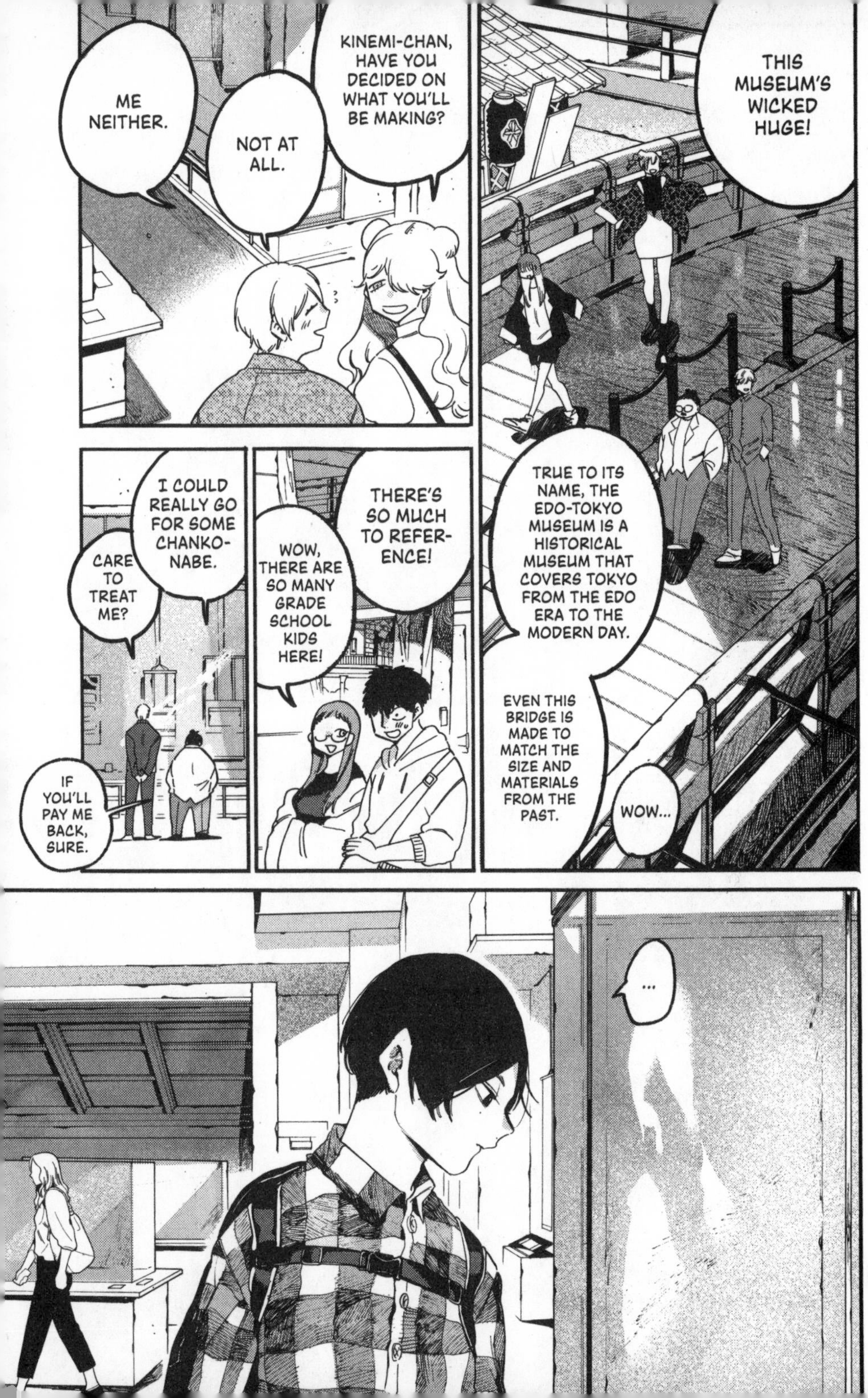
THIS MUSEUM'S WICKED HUGE!
TRUE TO ITS NAME, THE EDO-TOKYO MUSEUM IS A HISTORICAL MUSEUM THAT COVERS TOKYO FROM THE EDO ERA TO THE MODERN DAY.
EVEN THIS BRIDGE IS MADE TO MATCH THE SIZE AND MATERIALS FROM THE PAST.
WOW...
KINEMI-CHAN, HAVE YOU DECIDED ON WHAT YOU'LL BE MAKING?
NOT AT ALL.
ME NEITHER.
THERE'S SO MUCH TO REFER-ENCE!
WOW, THERE ARE SO MANY GRADE SCHOOL KIDS HERE!
I COULD REALLY GO FOR SOME CHANKO-NABE.
CARE TO TREAT ME?
IF YOU'LL PAY ME BACK, SURE.
...

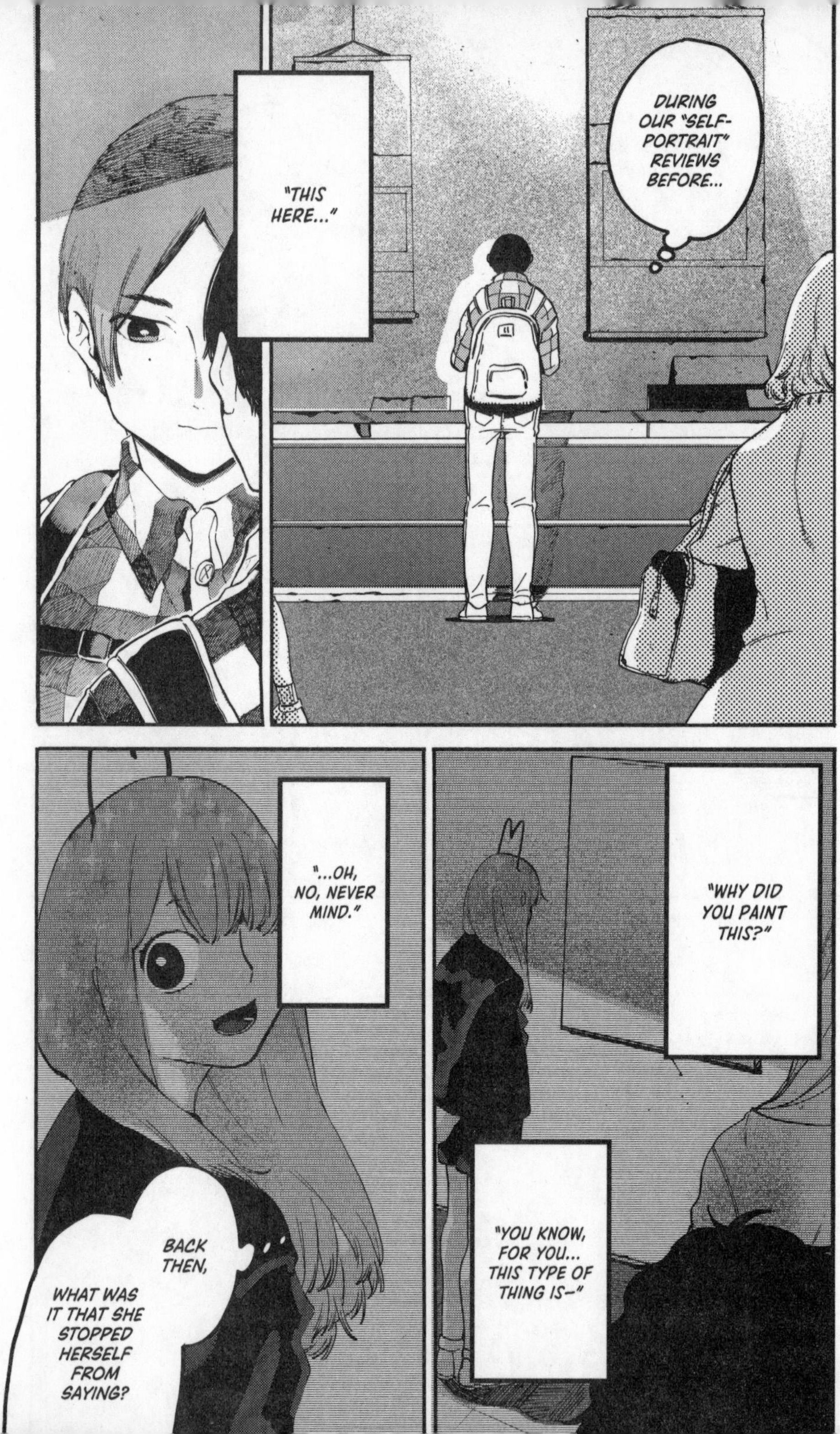
DURING OUR "SELF-PORTRAIT" REVIEWS BEFORE...
"THIS HERE..."
"WHY DID YOU PAINT THIS?"
"YOU KNOW, FOR YOU... THIS TYPE OF THING IS—"
"...OH, NO, NEVER MIND."
BACK THEN,
WHAT WAS IT THAT SHE STOPPED HERSELF FROM SAYING?

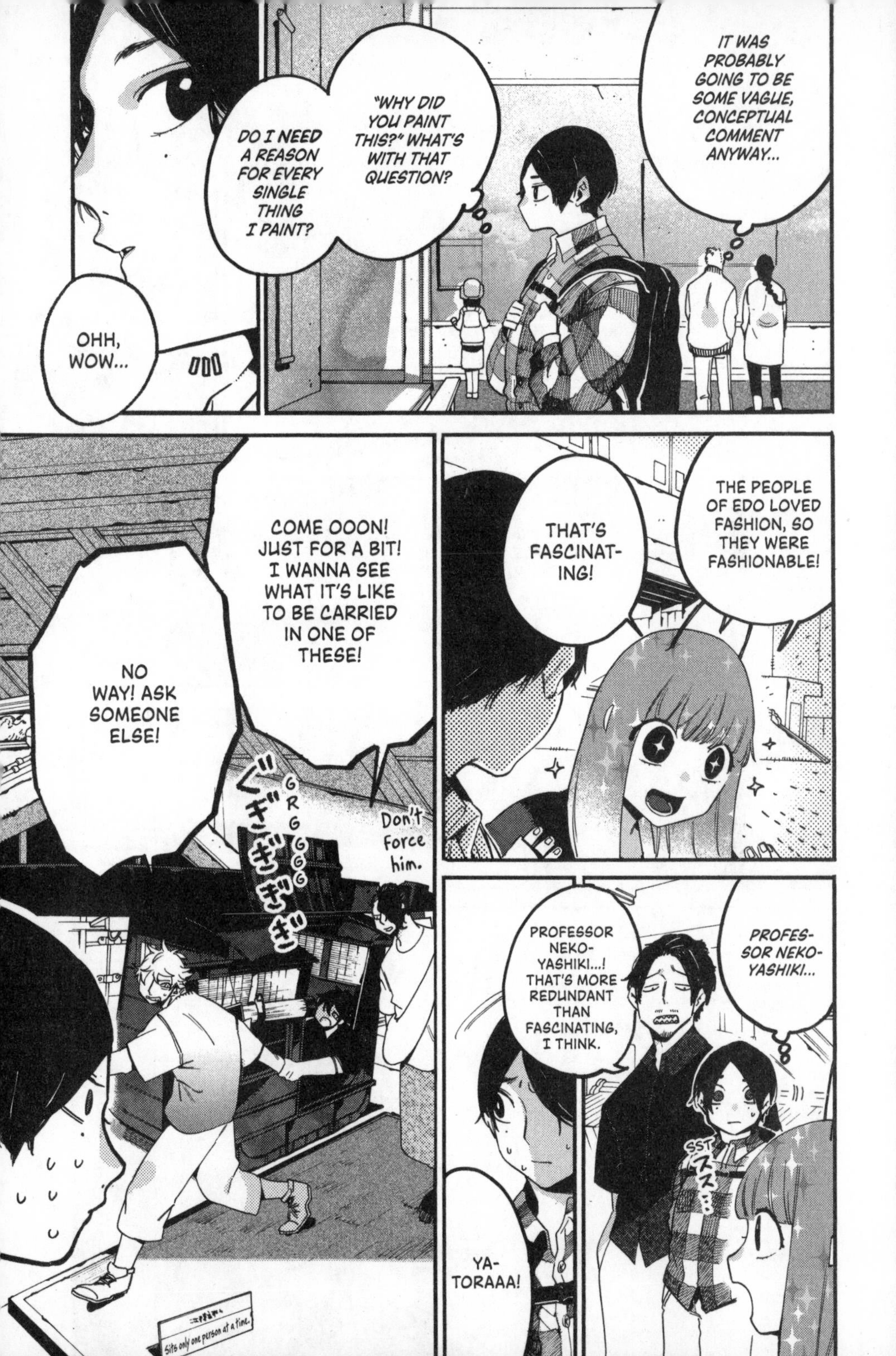
IT WAS PROBABLY GOING TO BE SOME VAGUE, CONCEPTUAL COMMENT ANYWAY...
"WHY DID YOU PAINT THIS?" WHAT'S WITH THAT QUESTION?
DO I NEED A REASON FOR EVERY SINGLE THING I PAINT?
OHH, WOW...
THE PEOPLE OF EDO LOVED FASHION, SO THEY WERE FASHIONABLE!
THAT'S FASCINAT-ING!
PROFES-SOR NEKO-YASHIKI...
PROFESSOR NEKO-YASHIKI...! THAT'S MORE REDUNDANT THAN FASCINATING, I THINK.
SST
YA-TORAAA!
COME OOON! JUST FOR A BIT! I WANNA SEE WHAT IT'S LIKE TO BE CARRIED IN ONE OF THESE!
NO WAY! ASK SOMEONE ELSE!
GRGGGG
Don't force him.
Sits only one person at a time.

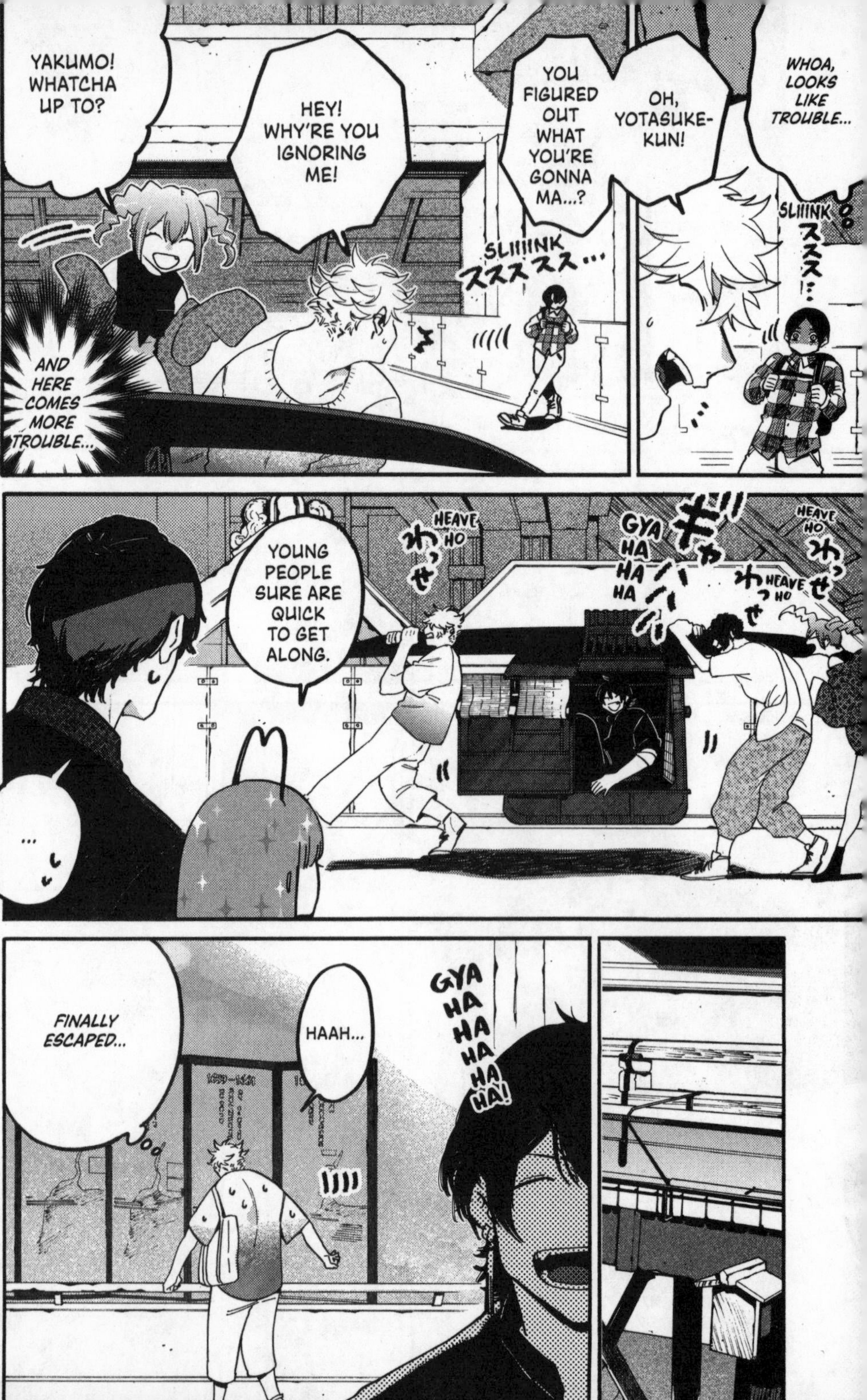
WHOA, LOOKS LIKE TROUBLE...
SLIIINK ススス!!
OH, YOTASUKE-KUN!
YOU FIGURED OUT WHAT YOU'RE GONNA MA...?
SLIIIINK スススス...
HEY! WHY'RE YOU IGNORING ME!
YAKUMO! WHATCHA UP TO?
AND HERE COMES MORE TROUBLE...
HEAVE HO わっせ
HEAVE HO わっせ
GYA HA HA HA ギャハハハ
HEAVE HO わっせ
YOUNG PEOPLE SURE ARE QUICK TO GET ALONG.
...
GYA HA HA HA HA HA HA!
HAAH...
FINALLY ESCAPED...

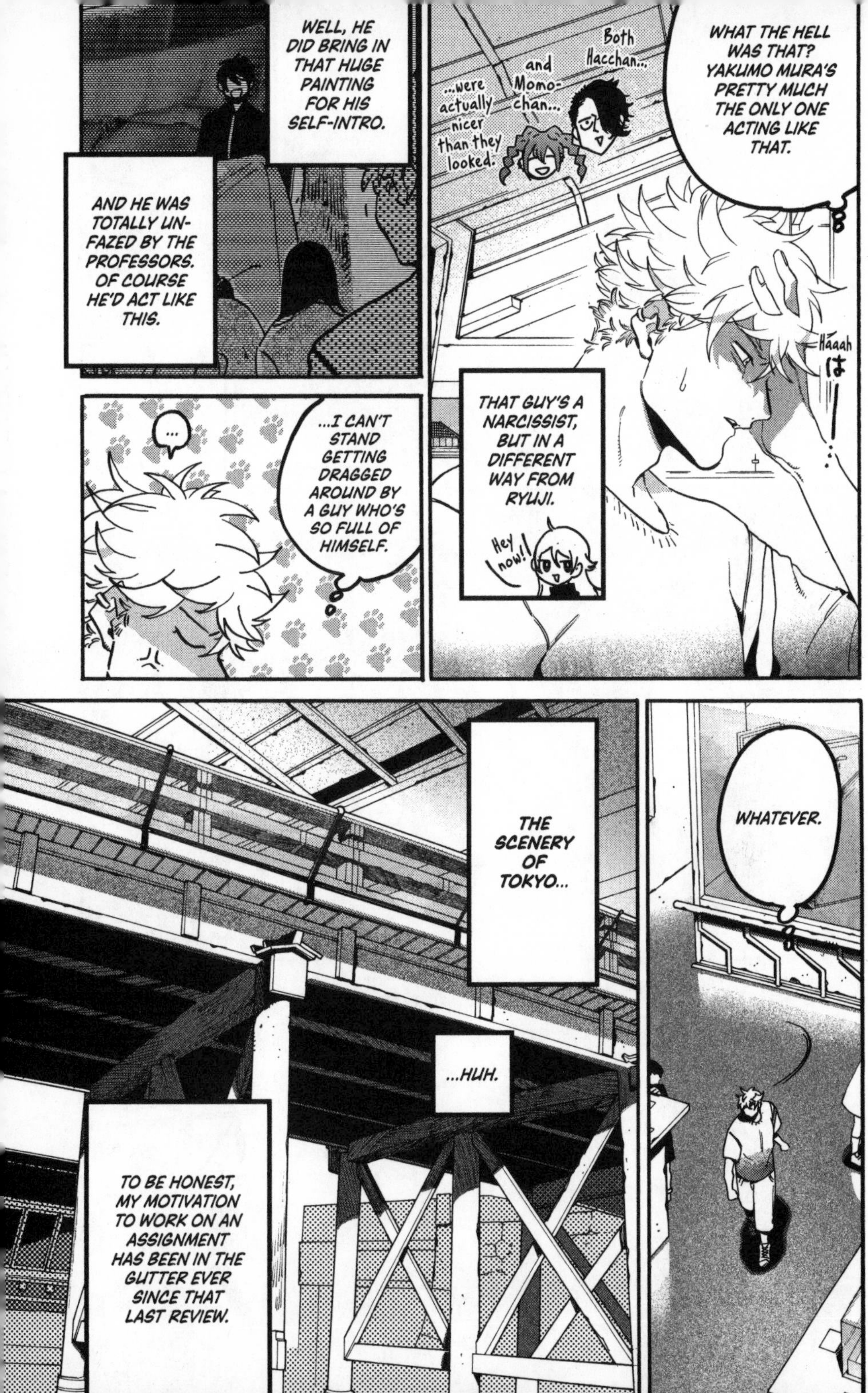
WHAT THE HELL WAS THAT? YAKUMO MURA'S PRETTY MUCH THE ONLY ONE ACTING LIKE THAT.
Both Hacchan...
and Momo-chan...
...were actually nicer than they looked.
Haaah
は
THAT GUY'S A NARCISSIST, BUT IN A DIFFERENT WAY FROM RYUJI.
Hey now!
WELL, HE DID BRING IN THAT HUGE PAINTING FOR HIS SELF-INTRO.
AND HE WAS TOTALLY UNFAZED BY THE PROFESSORS. OF COURSE HE'D ACT LIKE THIS.
...I CAN'T STAND GETTING DRAGGED AROUND BY A GUY WHO'S SO FULL OF HIMSELF.
...
WHATEVER.
THE SCENERY OF TOKYO...
...HUH.
TO BE HONEST, MY MOTIVATION TO WORK ON AN ASSIGNMENT HAS BEEN IN THE GUTTER EVER SINCE THAT LAST REVIEW.

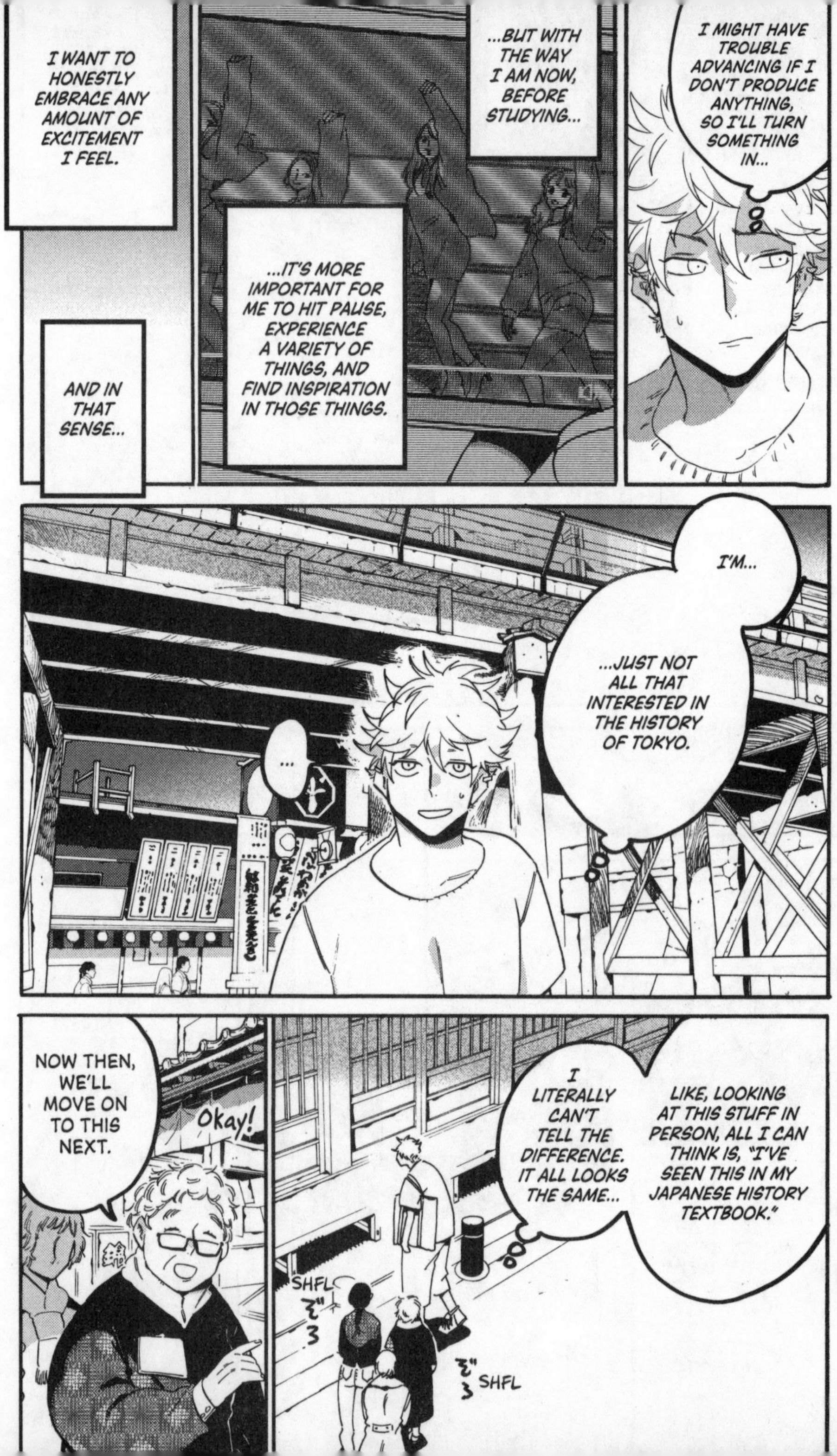
I MIGHT HAVE TROUBLE ADVANCING IF I DON'T PRODUCE ANYTHING, SO I'LL TURN SOMETHING IN...
...BUT WITH THE WAY I AM NOW, BEFORE STUDYING...
...IT'S MORE IMPORTANT FOR ME TO HIT PAUSE, EXPERIENCE A VARIETY OF THINGS, AND FIND INSPIRATION IN THOSE THINGS.
I WANT TO HONESTLY EMBRACE ANY AMOUNT OF EXCITEMENT I FEEL.
AND IN THAT SENSE...
I'M...
...JUST NOT ALL THAT INTERESTED IN THE HISTORY OF TOKYO.
...
LIKE, LOOKING AT THIS STUFF IN PERSON, ALL I CAN THINK IS, "I'VE SEEN THIS IN MY JAPANESE HISTORY TEXTBOOK."
I LITERALLY CAN'T TELL THE DIFFERENCE. IT ALL LOOKS THE SAME...
SHFL
SHFL
NOW THEN, WE'LL MOVE ON TO THIS NEXT.
Okay!

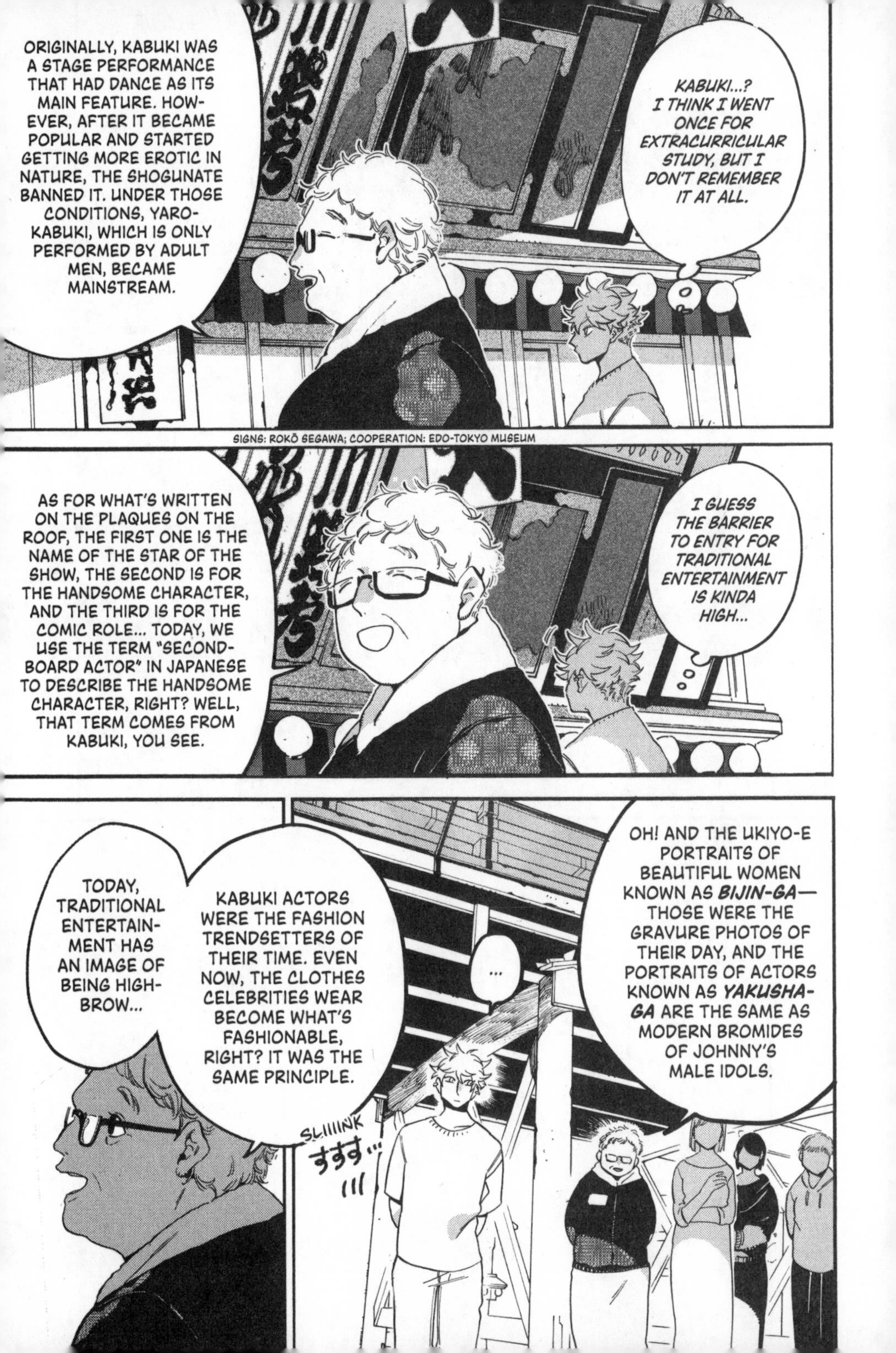
ORIGINALLY, KABUKI WAS A STAGE PERFORMANCE THAT HAD DANCE AS ITS MAIN FEATURE. HOW-EVER, AFTER IT BECAME POPULAR AND STARTED GETTING MORE EROTIC IN NATURE, THE SHOGUNATE BANNED IT. UNDER THOSE CONDITIONS, YARO-KABUKI, WHICH IS ONLY PERFORMED BY ADULT MEN, BECAME MAINSTREAM.
KABUKI...? I THINK I WENT ONCE FOR EXTRACURRICULAR STUDY, BUT I DON'T REMEMBER IT AT ALL.
AS FOR WHAT'S WRITTEN ON THE PLAQUES ON THE ROOF, THE FIRST ONE IS THE NAME OF THE STAR OF THE SHOW, THE SECOND IS FOR THE HANDSOME CHARACTER, AND THE THIRD IS FOR THE COMIC ROLE... TODAY, WE USE THE TERM "SECOND-BOARD ACTOR" IN JAPANESE TO DESCRIBE THE HANDSOME CHARACTER, RIGHT? WELL, THAT TERM COMES FROM KABUKI, YOU SEE.
I GUESS THE BARRIER TO ENTRY FOR TRADITIONAL ENTERTAINMENT IS KINDA HIGH...
TODAY, TRADITIONAL ENTERTAIN-MENT HAS AN IMAGE OF BEING HIGH-BROW...
KABUKI ACTORS WERE THE FASHION TRENDSETTERS OF THEIR TIME. EVEN NOW, THE CLOTHES CELEBRITIES WEAR BECOME WHAT'S FASHIONABLE, RIGHT? IT WAS THE SAME PRINCIPLE.
...
OH! AND THE UKIYO-E PORTRAITS OF BEAUTIFUL WOMEN KNOWN AS *BIJIN-GA*—THOSE WERE THE GRAVURE PHOTOS OF THEIR DAY, AND THE PORTRAITS OF ACTORS KNOWN AS *YAKUSHA-GA* ARE THE SAME AS MODERN BROMIDES OF JOHNNY'S MALE IDOLS.
SLIIIINK
すすす…
SIGNS: ROKŌ SEGAWA; COOPERATION: EDO-TOKYO MUSEUM

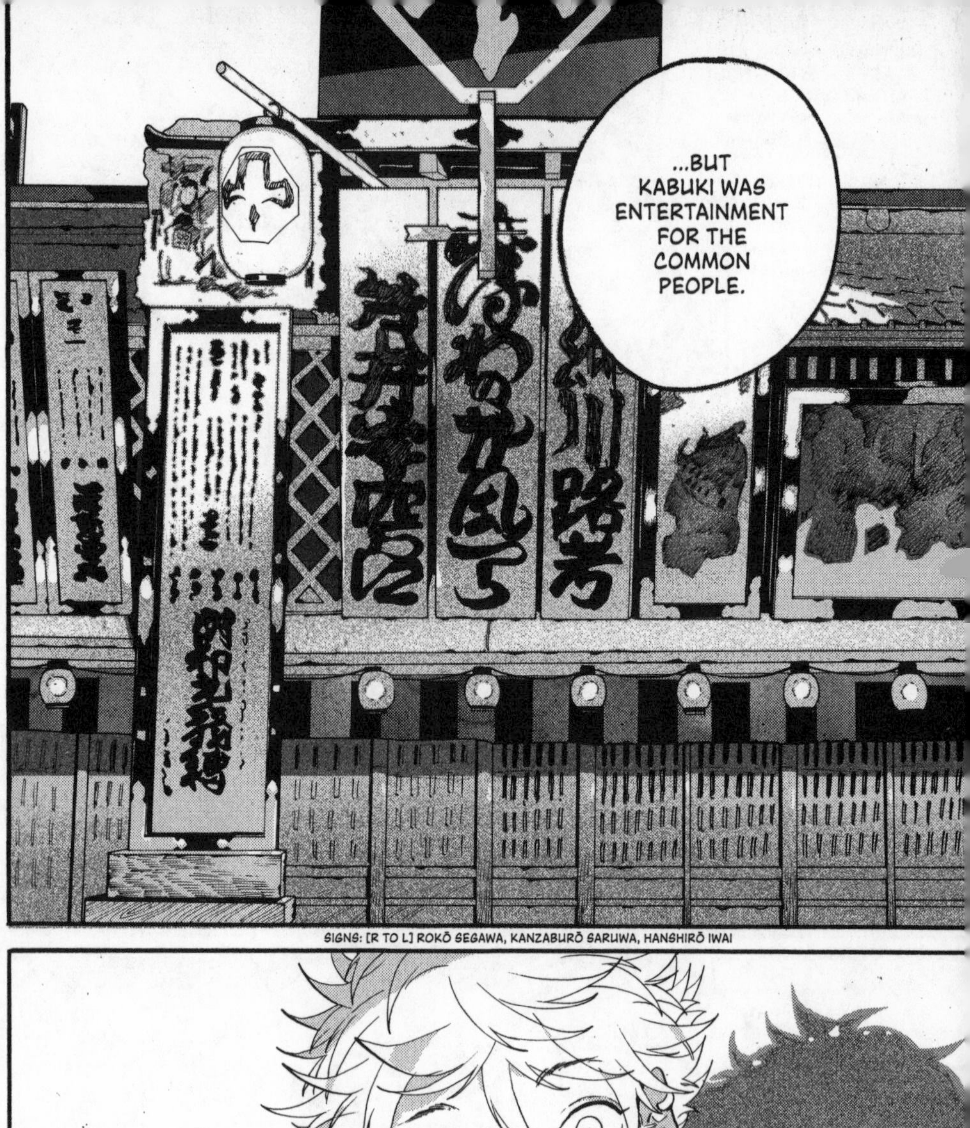
...BUT KABUKI WAS ENTERTAINMENT FOR THE COMMON PEOPLE.
SIGNS: [R TO L] ROKŌ SEGAWA, KANZABURŌ SARUWA, HANSHIRŌ IWAI

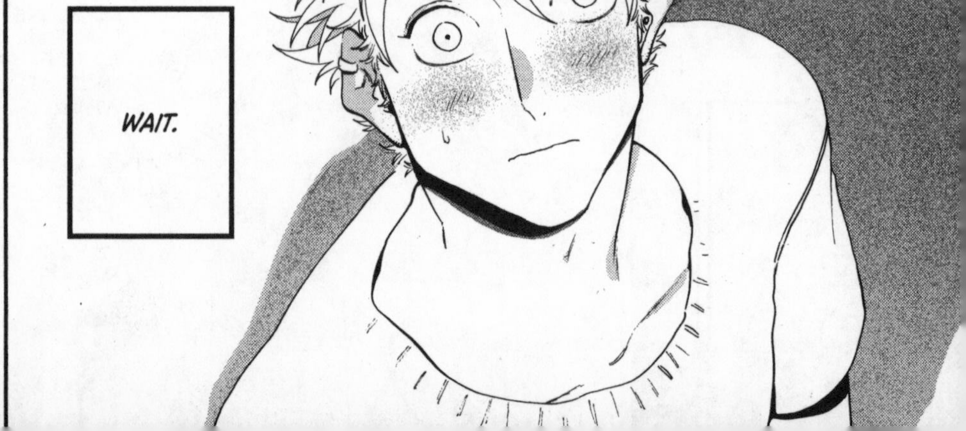
WAIT.

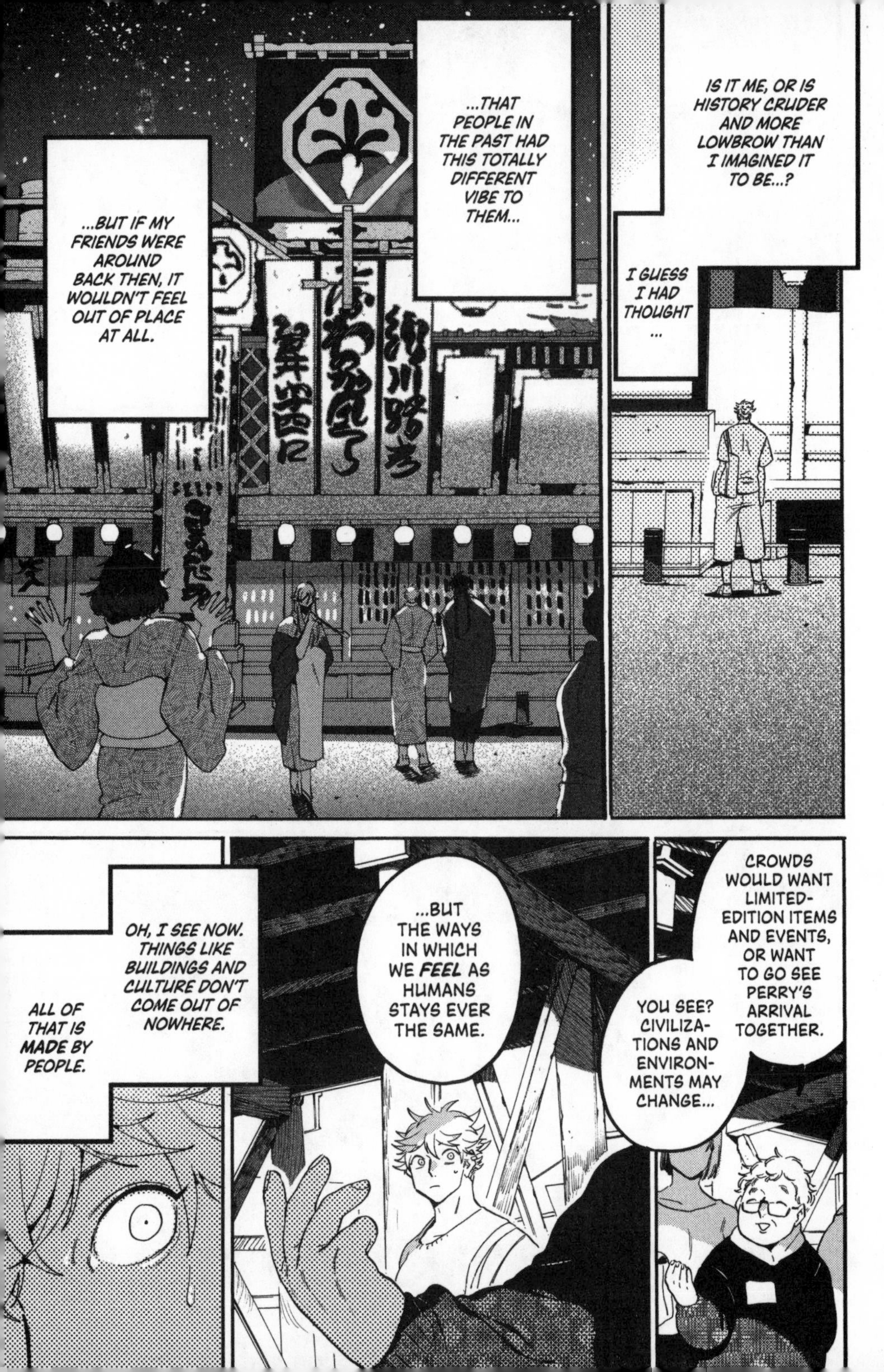
IS IT ME, OR IS HISTORY CRUDER AND MORE LOWBROW THAN I IMAGINED IT TO BE...?
I GUESS I HAD THOUGHT ...
...THAT PEOPLE IN THE PAST HAD THIS TOTALLY DIFFERENT VIBE TO THEM...
...BUT IF MY FRIENDS WERE AROUND BACK THEN, IT WOULDN'T FEEL OUT OF PLACE AT ALL.
CROWDS WOULD WANT LIMITED-EDITION ITEMS AND EVENTS, OR WANT TO GO SEE PERRY'S ARRIVAL TOGETHER.
YOU SEE? CIVILIZATIONS AND ENVIRONMENTS MAY CHANGE...
...BUT THE WAYS IN WHICH WE FEEL AS HUMANS STAYS EVER THE SAME.
OH, I SEE NOW. THINGS LIKE BUILDINGS AND CULTURE DON'T COME OUT OF NOWHERE.
ALL OF THAT IS MADE BY PEOPLE.

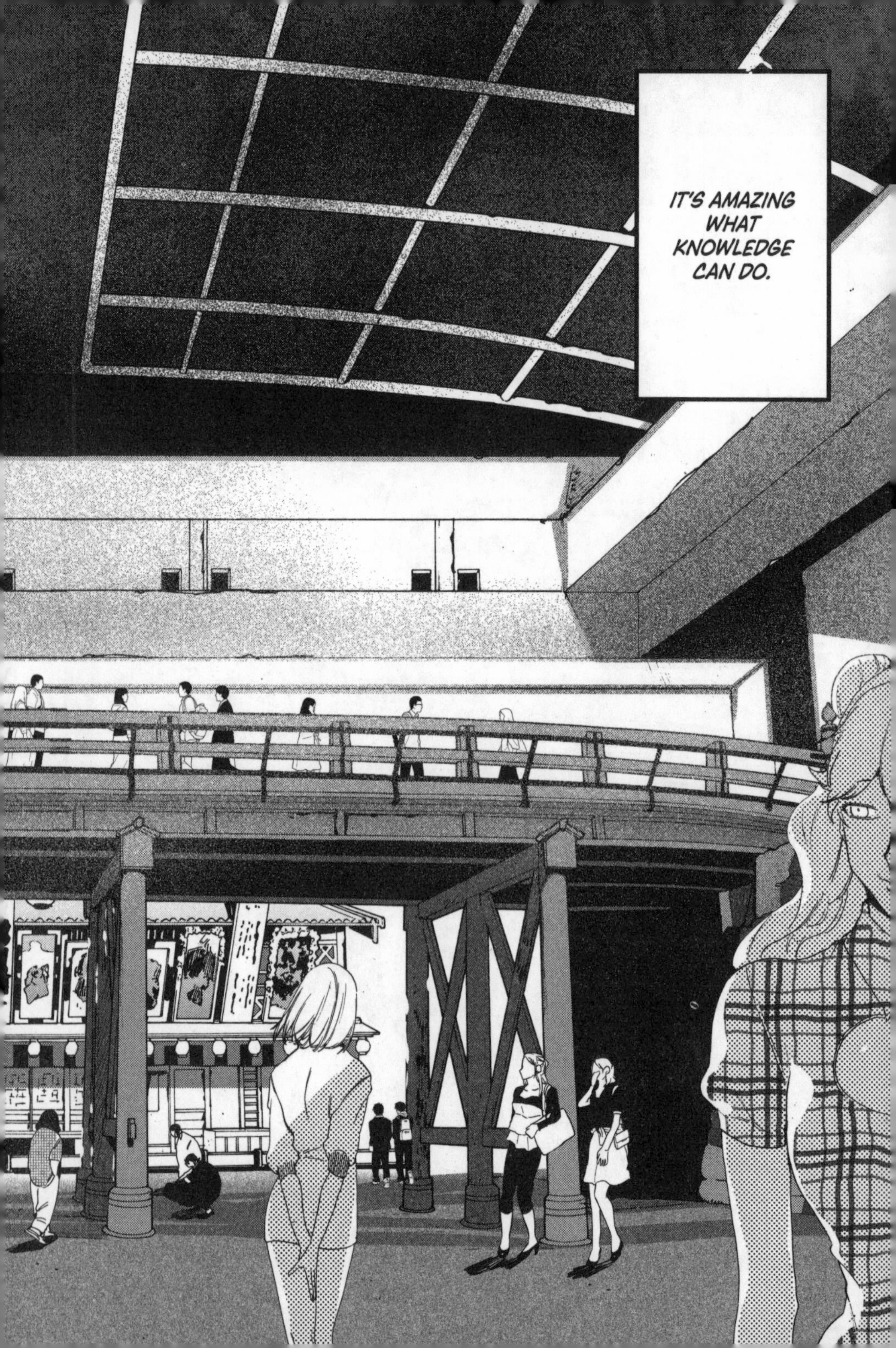
IT'S AMAZING WHAT KNOWLEDGE CAN DO.

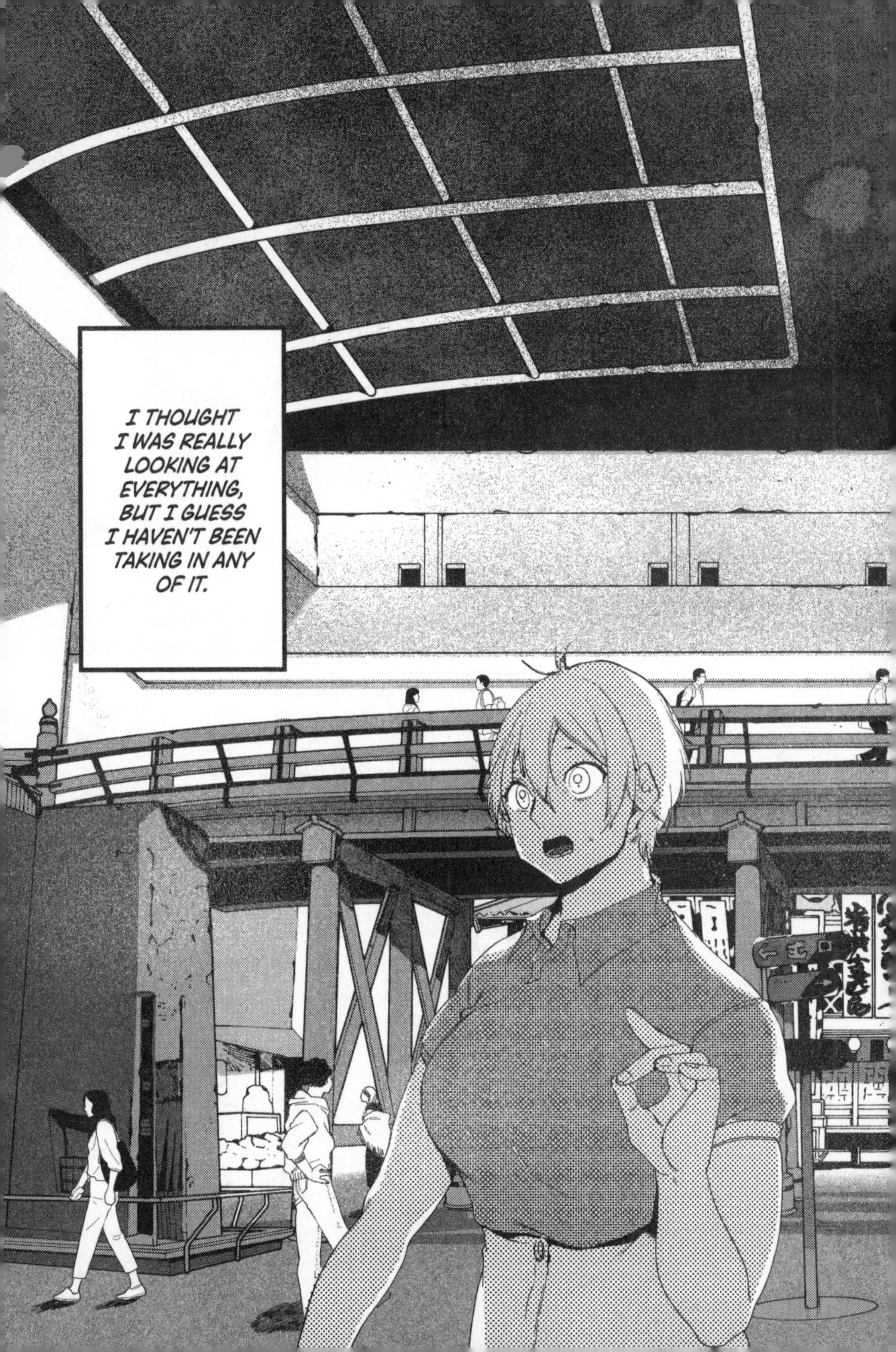
I THOUGHT I WAS REALLY LOOKING AT EVERYTHING, BUT I GUESS I HAVEN'T BEEN TAKING IN ANY OF IT.

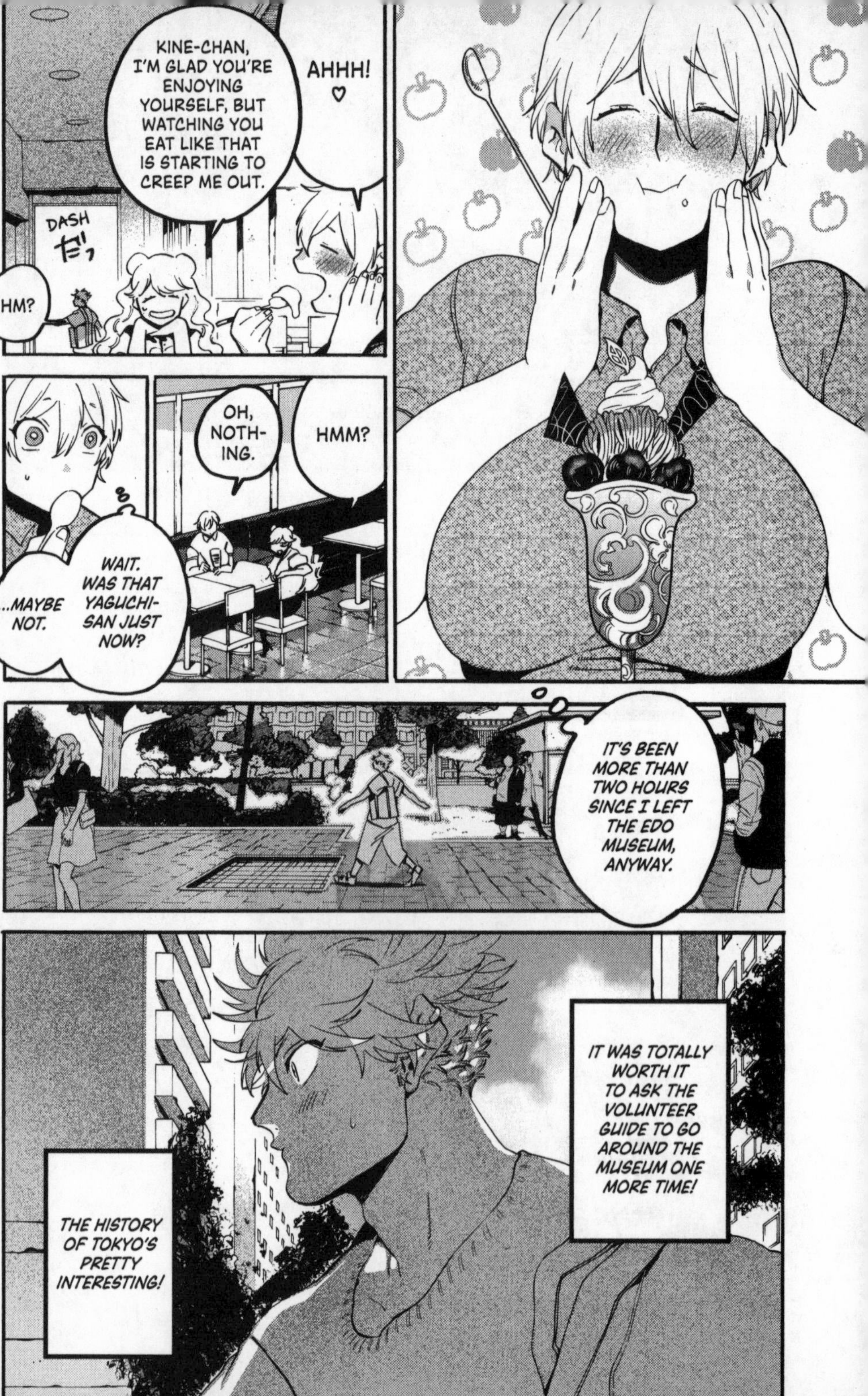
AHHH! ♡
KINE-CHAN, I'M GLAD YOU'RE ENJOYING YOURSELF, BUT WATCHING YOU EAT LIKE THAT IS STARTING TO CREEP ME OUT.
DASH
HM?
HMM?
OH, NOTHING.
WAIT. WAS THAT YAGUCHI-SAN JUST NOW?
...MAYBE NOT.
IT'S BEEN MORE THAN TWO HOURS SINCE I LEFT THE EDO MUSEUM, ANYWAY.
IT WAS TOTALLY WORTH IT TO ASK THE VOLUNTEER GUIDE TO GO AROUND THE MUSEUM ONE MORE TIME!
THE HISTORY OF TOKYO'S PRETTY INTERESTING!

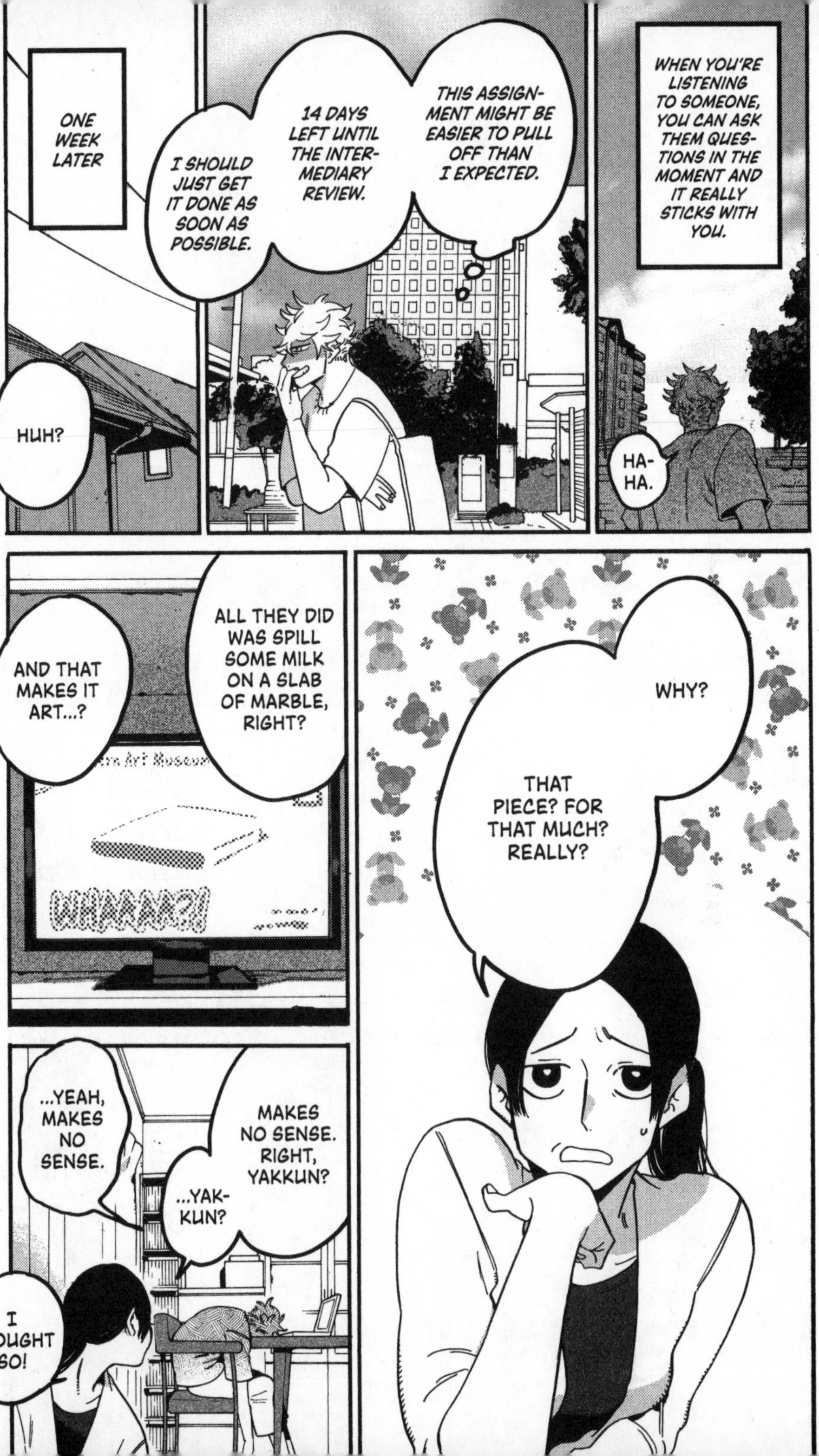

WHEN YOU'RE LISTENING TO SOMEONE, YOU CAN ASK THEM QUESTIONS IN THE MOMENT AND IT REALLY STICKS WITH YOU.
HA-HA.
THIS ASSIGNMENT MIGHT BE EASIER TO PULL OFF THAN I EXPECTED.
14 DAYS LEFT UNTIL THE INTERMEDIARY REVIEW.
I SHOULD JUST GET IT DONE AS SOON AS POSSIBLE.
ONE WEEK LATER
HUH?
WHY?
THAT PIECE? FOR THAT MUCH? REALLY?
ALL THEY DID WAS SPILL SOME MILK ON A SLAB OF MARBLE, RIGHT?
AND THAT MAKES IT ART...?
MAKES NO SENSE. RIGHT, YAKKUN?
...YEAH, MAKES NO SENSE.
...YAKKUN?
I THOUGHT SO!

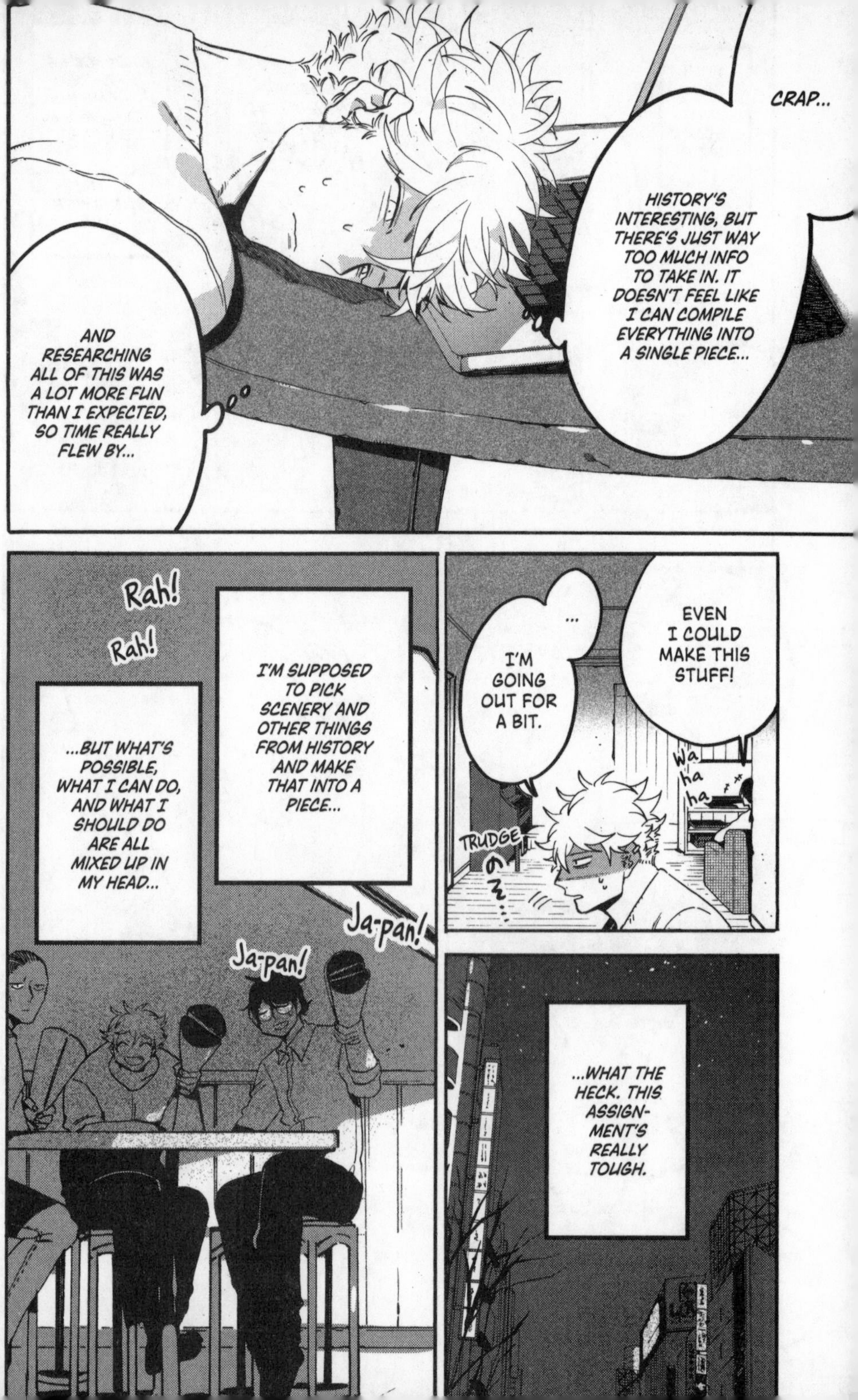
CRAP...
HISTORY'S INTERESTING, BUT THERE'S JUST WAY TOO MUCH INFO TO TAKE IN. IT DOESN'T FEEL LIKE I CAN COMPILE EVERYTHING INTO A SINGLE PIECE...
AND RESEARCHING ALL OF THIS WAS A LOT MORE FUN THAN I EXPECTED, SO TIME REALLY FLEW BY...
EVEN I COULD MAKE THIS STUFF!
Wa ha ha
...
I'M GOING OUT FOR A BIT.
TRUDGE
...WHAT THE HECK. THIS ASSIGNMENT'S REALLY TOUGH.
Rah!
Rah!
I'M SUPPOSED TO PICK SCENERY AND OTHER THINGS FROM HISTORY AND MAKE THAT INTO A PIECE...
...BUT WHAT'S POSSIBLE, WHAT I CAN DO, AND WHAT I SHOULD DO ARE ALL MIXED UP IN MY HEAD...
Ja-pan!
Ja-pan!

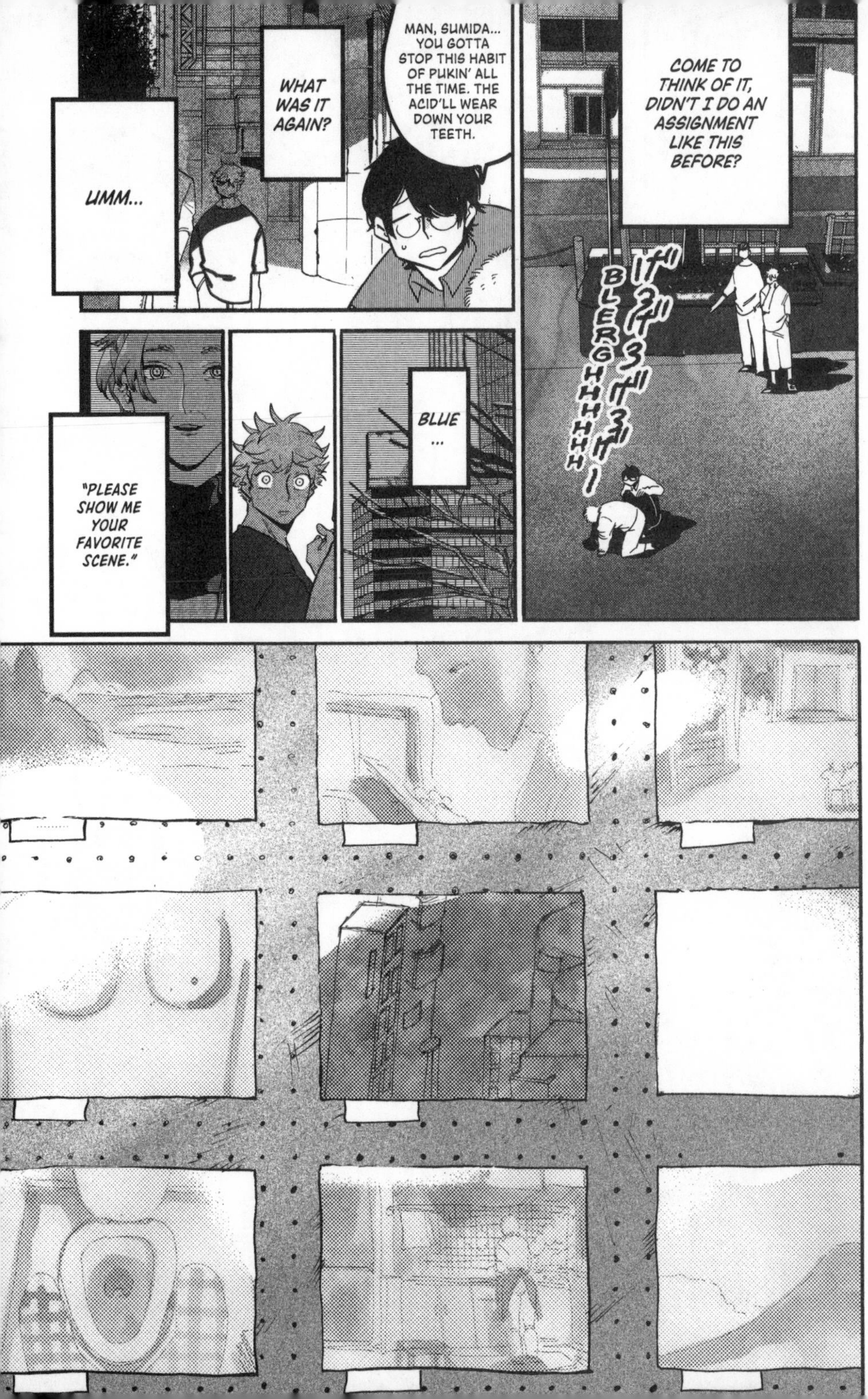
COME TO THINK OF IT, DIDN'T I DO AN ASSIGNMENT LIKE THIS BEFORE?
BLERGHHHHHH
MAN, SUMIDA... YOU GOTTA STOP THIS HABIT OF PUKIN' ALL THE TIME. THE ACID'LL WEAR DOWN YOUR TEETH.
WHAT WAS IT AGAIN?
UMM...
BLUE ...
"PLEASE SHOW ME YOUR FAVORITE SCENE."

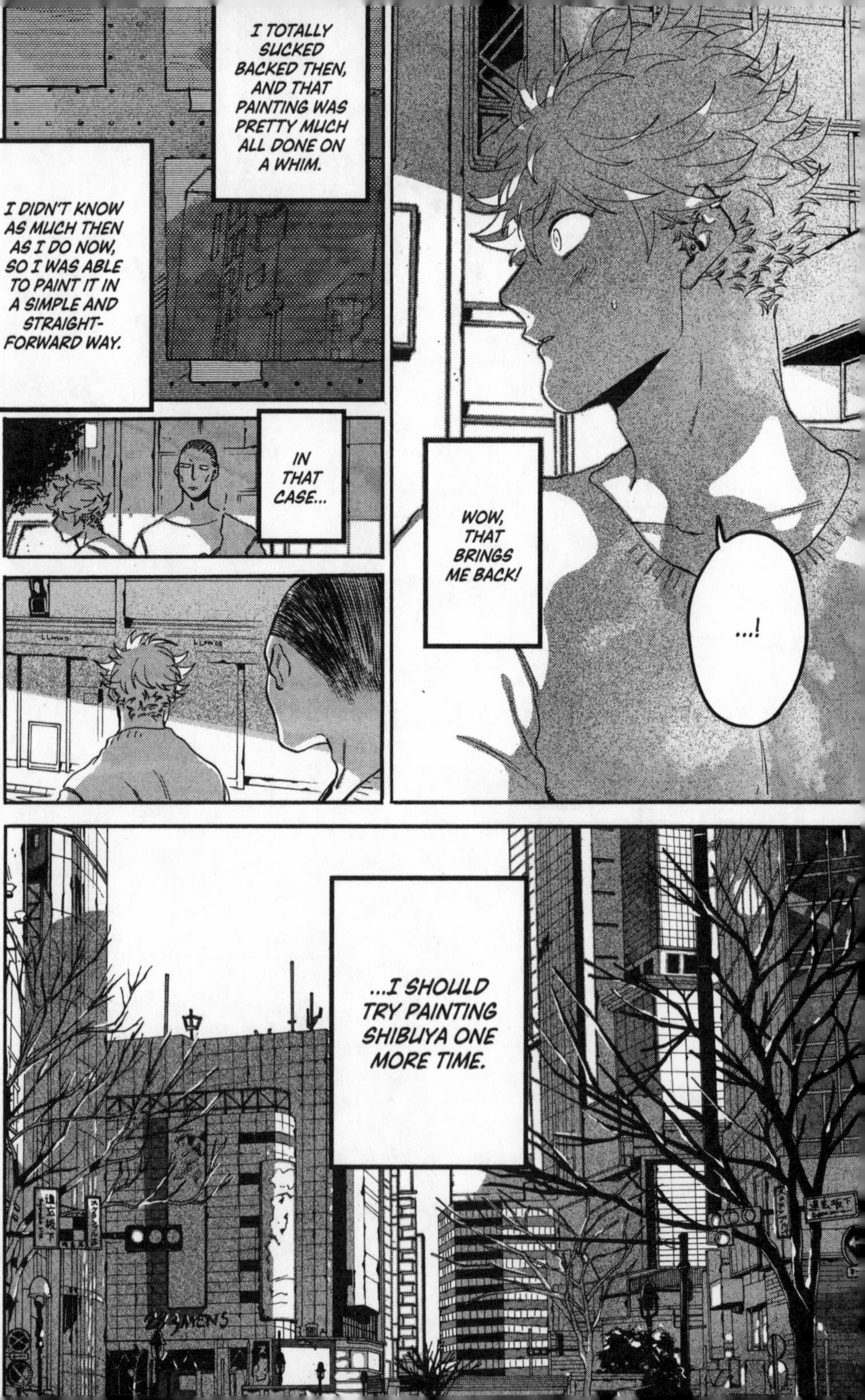
WOW, THAT BRINGS ME BACK!
...!
I TOTALLY SUCKED BACKED THEN, AND THAT PAINTING WAS PRETTY MUCH ALL DONE ON A WHIM.
I DIDN'T KNOW AS MUCH THEN AS I DO NOW, SO I WAS ABLE TO PAINT IT IN A SIMPLE AND STRAIGHT-FORWARD WAY.
IN THAT CASE...
...I SHOULD TRY PAINTING SHIBUYA ONE MORE TIME.

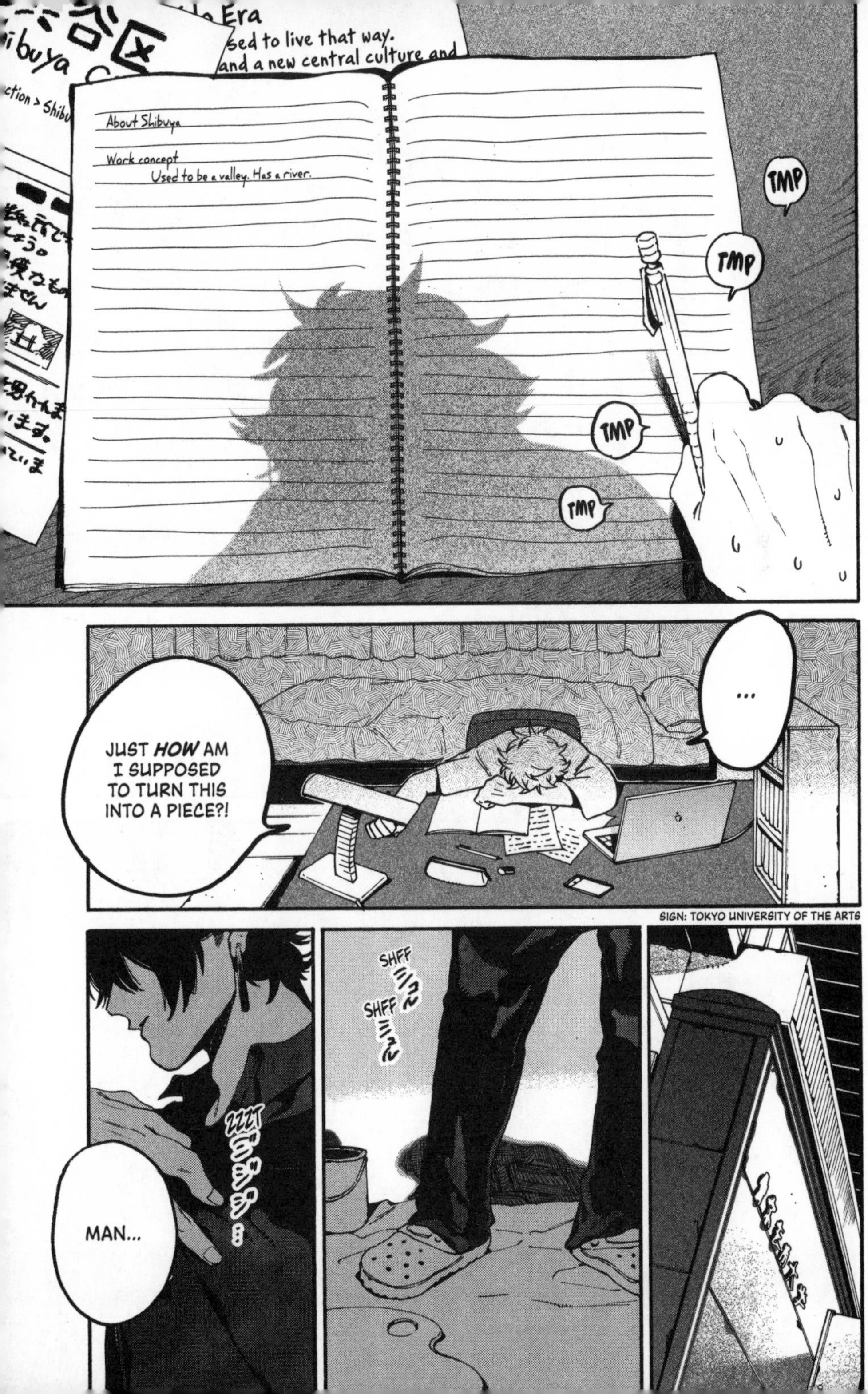

Era
sed to live that way.
and a new central culture and
ibuya
ction > Shibu
About Shibuya
Work concept
Used to be a valley. Has a river.
TMP
TMP
TMP
TMP
...
JUST *HOW* AM I SUPPOSED TO TURN THIS INTO A PIECE?!
SIGN: TOKYO UNIVERSITY OF THE ARTS
SHFF
SHFF
ZZZT
MAN...

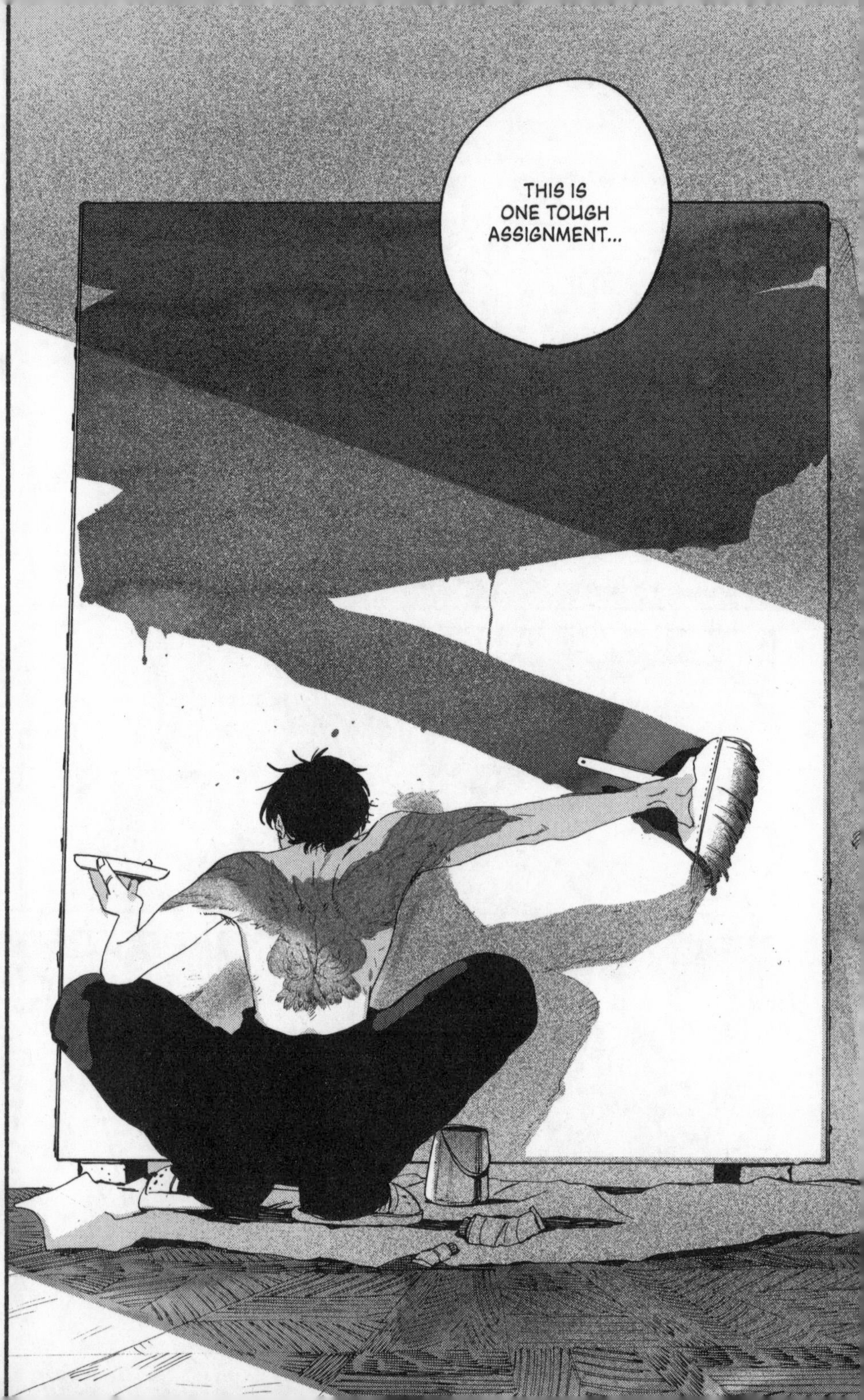
THIS IS ONE TOUGH ASSIGNMENT...

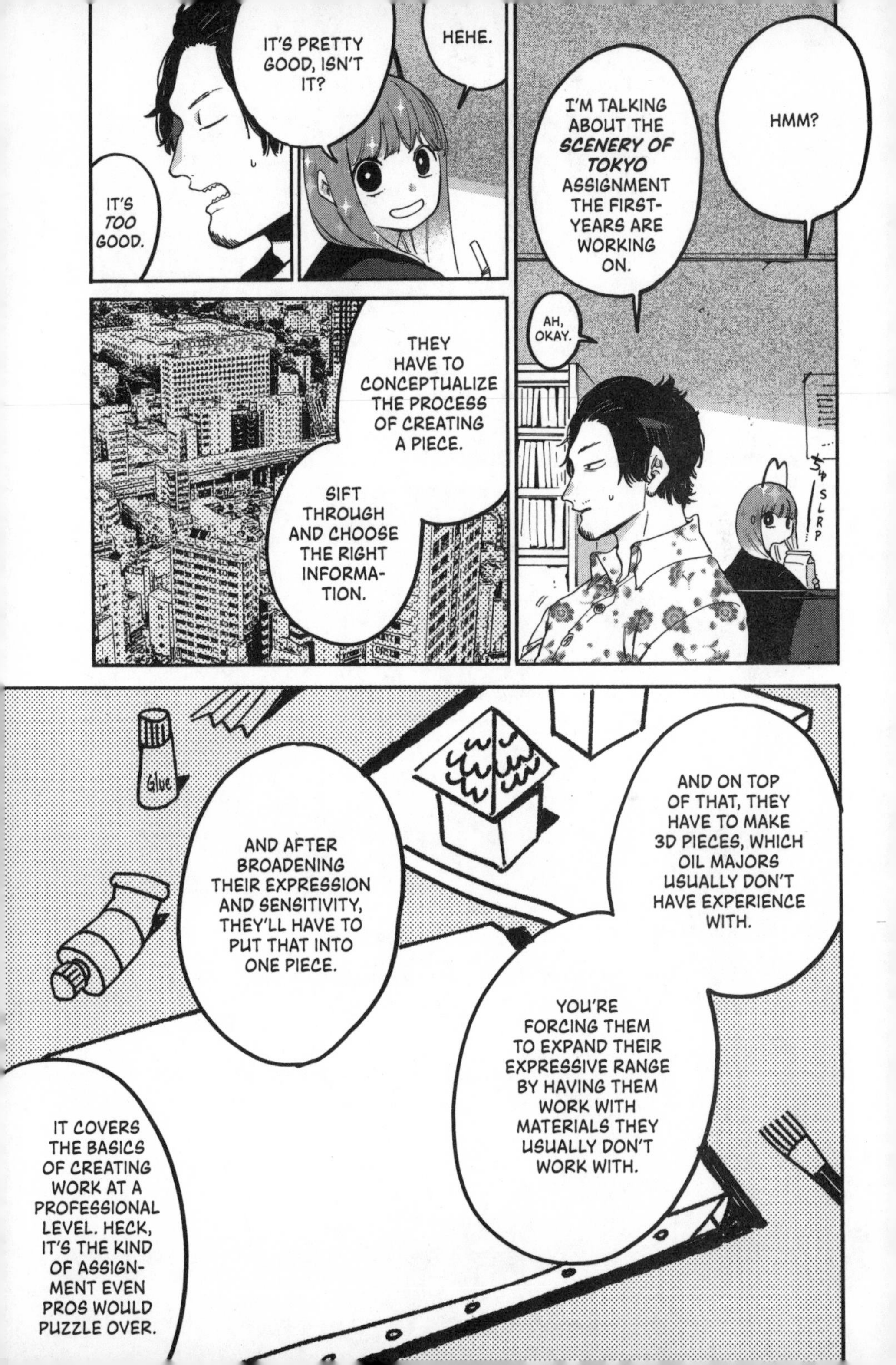
HMM?
I'M TALKING ABOUT THE *SCENERY OF TOKYO* ASSIGNMENT THE FIRST-YEARS ARE WORKING ON.
AH, OKAY.
SLRP
HEHE.
IT'S PRETTY GOOD, ISN'T IT?
IT'S *TOO* GOOD.
THEY HAVE TO CONCEPTUALIZE THE PROCESS OF CREATING A PIECE.
SIFT THROUGH AND CHOOSE THE RIGHT INFORMATION.
AND ON TOP OF THAT, THEY HAVE TO MAKE 3D PIECES, WHICH OIL MAJORS USUALLY DON'T HAVE EXPERIENCE WITH.
AND AFTER BROADENING THEIR EXPRESSION AND SENSITIVITY, THEY'LL HAVE TO PUT THAT INTO ONE PIECE.
Glue
YOU'RE FORCING THEM TO EXPAND THEIR EXPRESSIVE RANGE BY HAVING THEM WORK WITH MATERIALS THEY USUALLY DON'T WORK WITH.
IT COVERS THE BASICS OF CREATING WORK AT A PROFESSIONAL LEVEL. HECK, IT'S THE KIND OF ASSIGNMENT EVEN PROS WOULD PUZZLE OVER.

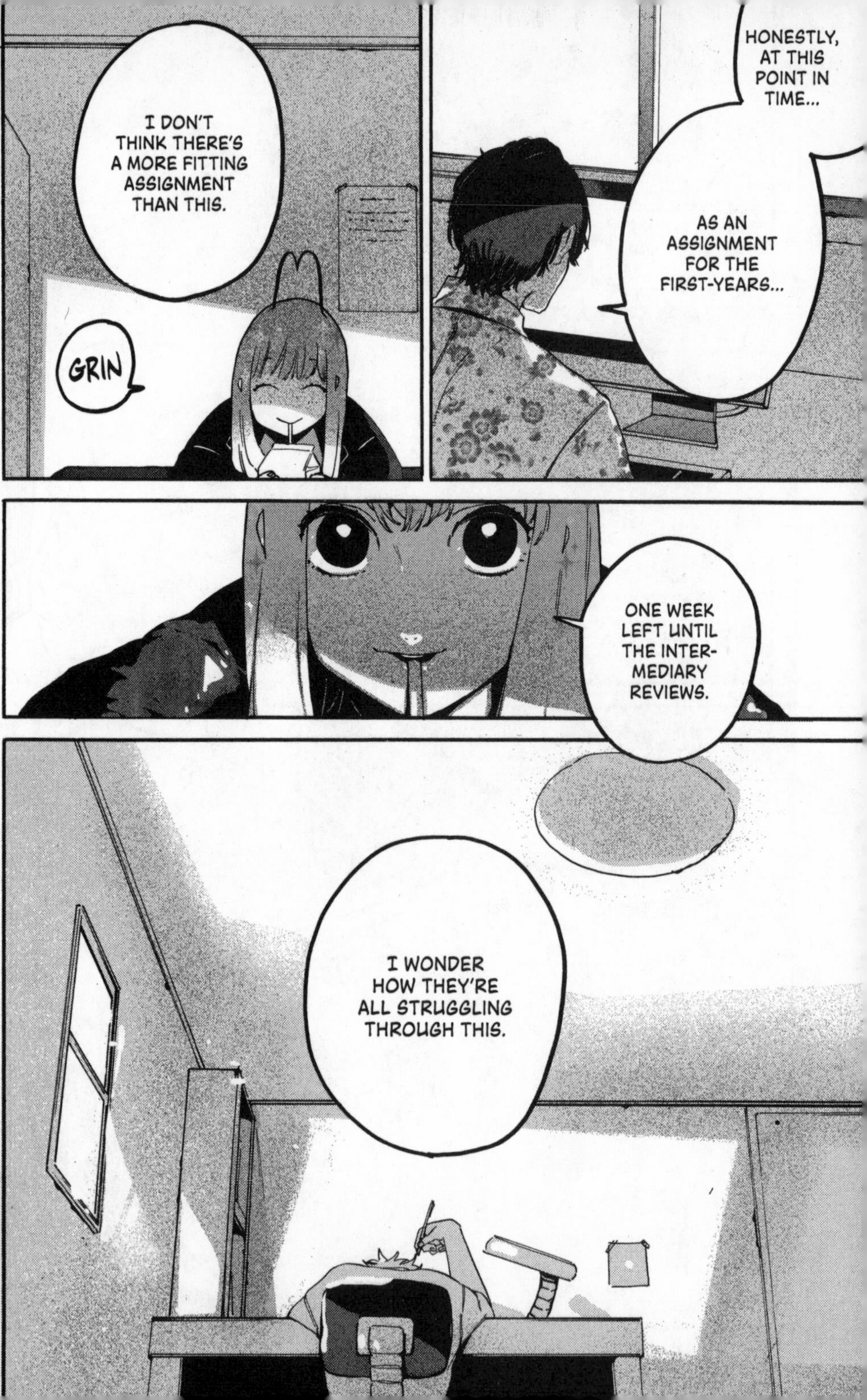
HONESTLY, AT THIS POINT IN TIME...
AS AN ASSIGNMENT FOR THE FIRST-YEARS...
I DON'T THINK THERE'S A MORE FITTING ASSIGNMENT THAN THIS.
GRIN
ONE WEEK LEFT UNTIL THE INTER-MEDIARY REVIEWS.
I WONDER HOW THEY'RE ALL STRUGGLING THROUGH THIS.

STROKE 30 END

# STROKE 31 SHIBUYA WASN'T BUILT IN A DAY

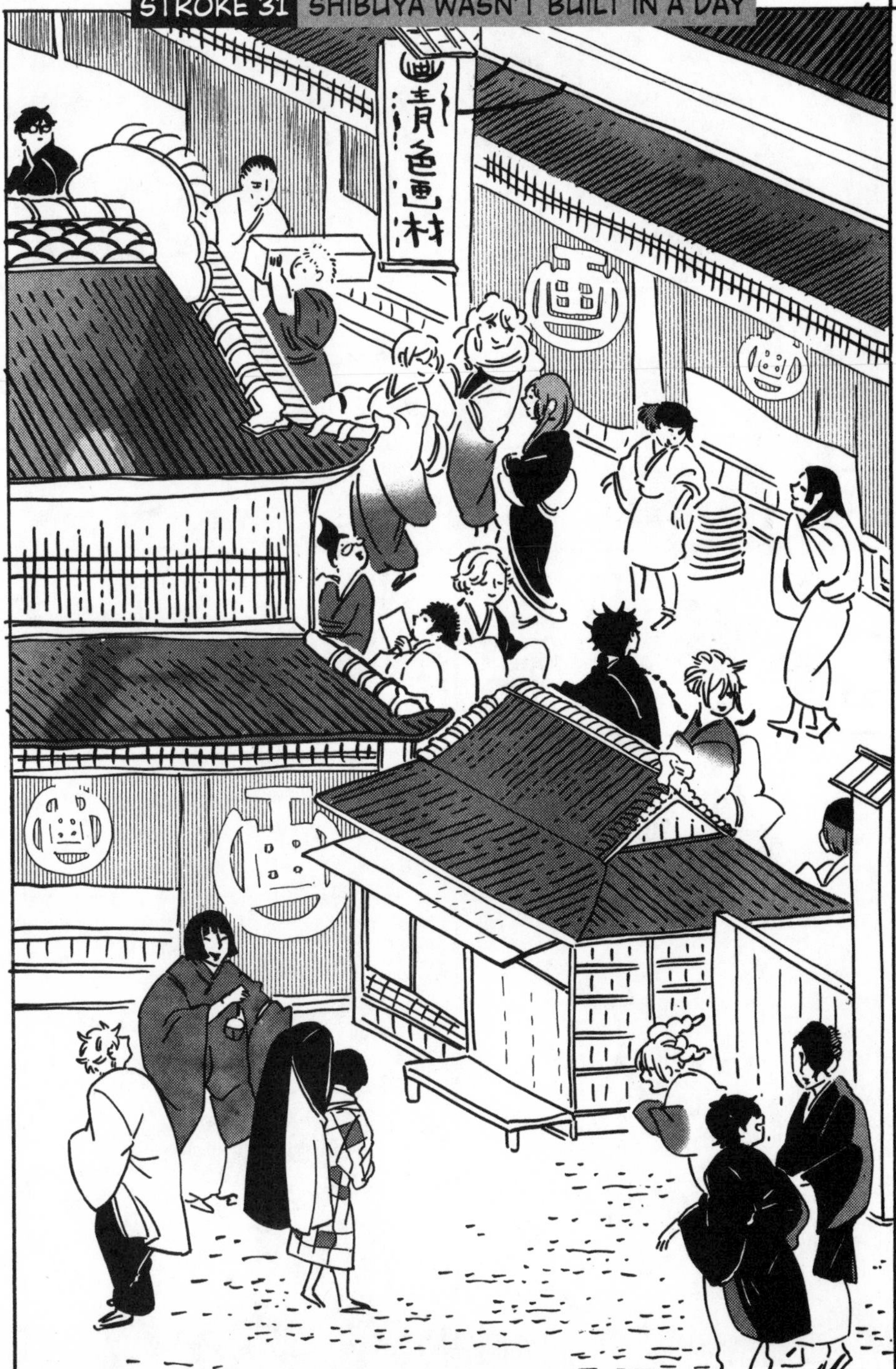
青色画材
SIGN: (ART) BLUE ART SUPPLIES

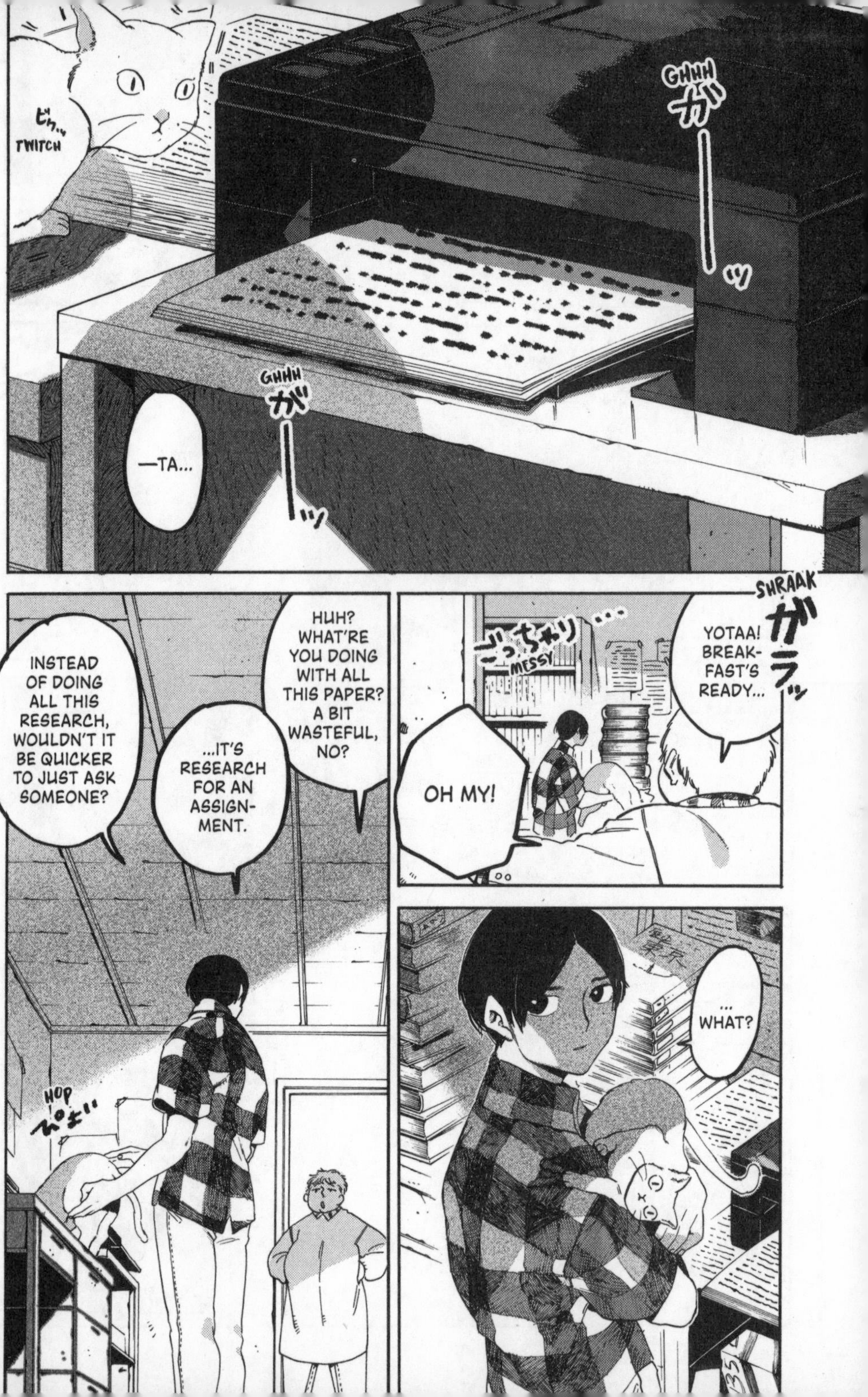
GHHH
がーッ
TWITCH
GHHH
がーッ
—TA...
SHRAAK
ガラッ
YOTAA! BREAK-FAST'S READY...
ごっちゃり...
MESSY
OH MY!
... WHAT?
HUH? WHAT'RE YOU DOING WITH ALL THIS PAPER? A BIT WASTEFUL, NO?
...IT'S RESEARCH FOR AN ASSIGN-MENT.
INSTEAD OF DOING ALL THIS RESEARCH, WOULDN'T IT BE QUICKER TO JUST ASK SOMEONE?
HOP

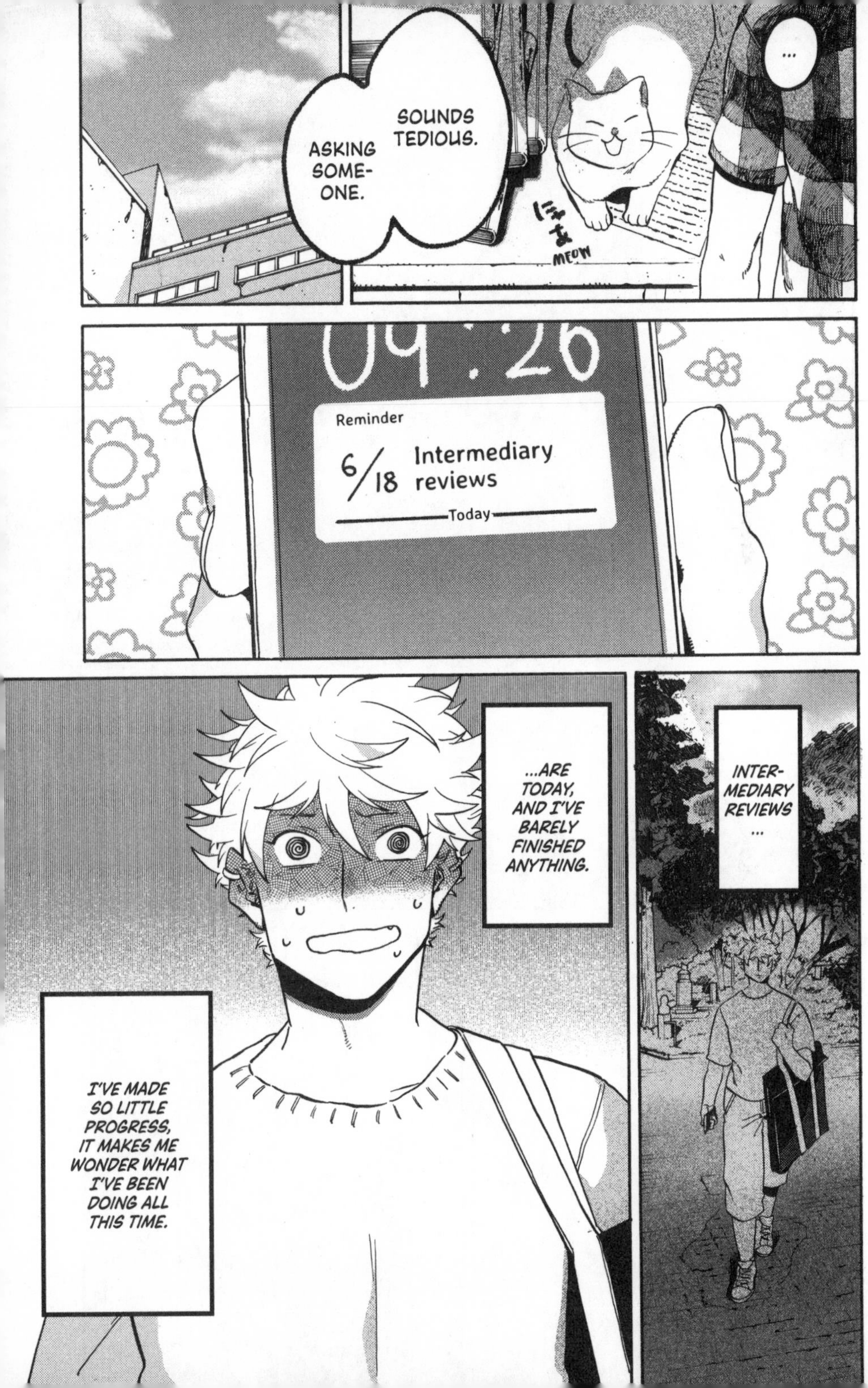
...
にゃ
MEOW
ASKING SOME-ONE.
SOUNDS TEDIOUS.
09:26
Reminder
6/18 Intermediary reviews
Today
INTER-MEDIARY REVIEWS...
...ARE TODAY, AND I'VE BARELY FINISHED ANYTHING.
I'VE MADE SO LITTLE PROGRESS, IT MAKES ME WONDER WHAT I'VE BEEN DOING ALL THIS TIME.

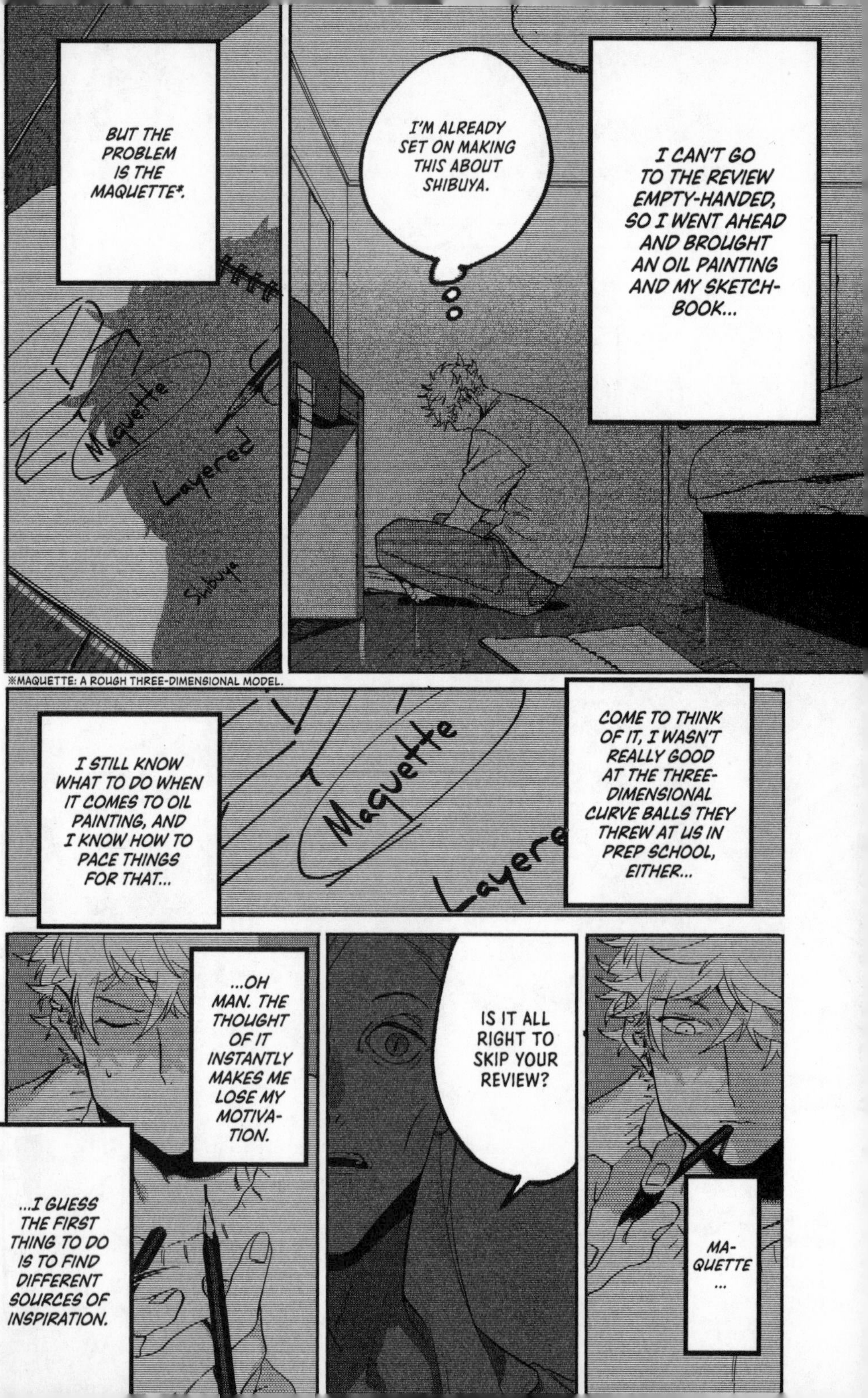
I CAN'T GO TO THE REVIEW EMPTY-HANDED, SO I WENT AHEAD AND BROUGHT AN OIL PAINTING AND MY SKETCH-BOOK...
I'M ALREADY SET ON MAKING THIS ABOUT SHIBUYA.
BUT THE PROBLEM IS THE MAQUETTE*.
Maquette
Layered
Shibuya
COME TO THINK OF IT, I WASN'T REALLY GOOD AT THE THREE-DIMENSIONAL CURVE BALLS THEY THREW AT US IN PREP SCHOOL, EITHER...
Maquette
Layere
I STILL KNOW WHAT TO DO WHEN IT COMES TO OIL PAINTING, AND I KNOW HOW TO PACE THINGS FOR THAT...
MA-QUETTE ...
IS IT ALL RIGHT TO SKIP YOUR REVIEW?
...OH MAN. THE THOUGHT OF IT INSTANTLY MAKES ME LOSE MY MOTIVA-TION.
...I GUESS THE FIRST THING TO DO IS TO FIND DIFFERENT SOURCES OF INSPIRATION.

※MAQUETTE: A ROUGH THREE-DIMENSIONAL MODEL.

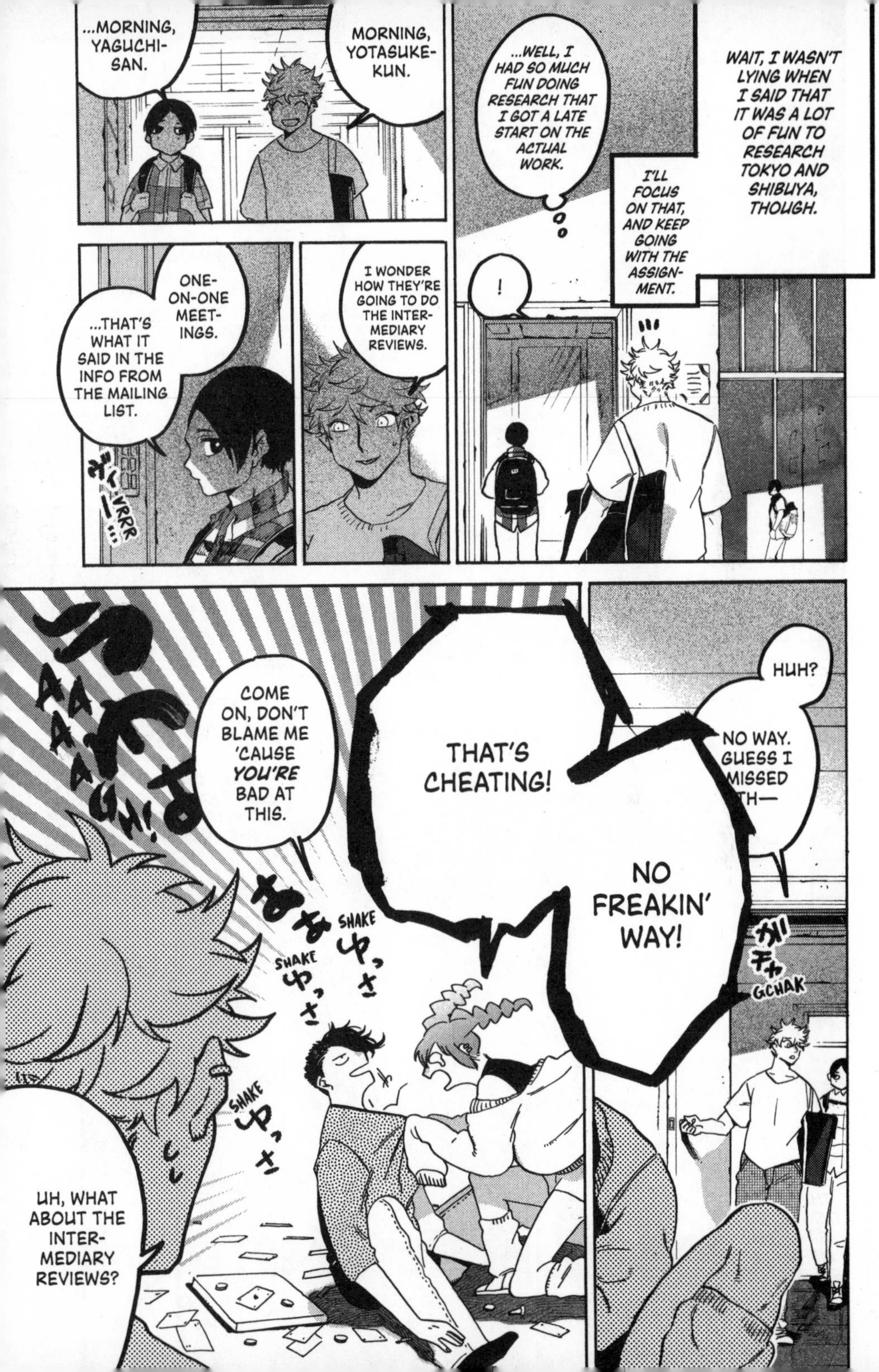
WAIT, I WASN'T LYING WHEN I SAID THAT IT WAS A LOT OF FUN TO RESEARCH TOKYO AND SHIBUYA, THOUGH.
I'LL FOCUS ON THAT, AND KEEP GOING WITH THE ASSIGNMENT.
...WELL, I HAD SO MUCH FUN DOING RESEARCH THAT I GOT A LATE START ON THE ACTUAL WORK.
!
MORNING, YOTASUKE-KUN.
...MORNING, YAGUCHI-SAN.
I WONDER HOW THEY'RE GOING TO DO THE INTERMEDIARY REVIEWS.
ONE-ON-ONE MEETINGS.
...THAT'S WHAT IT SAID IN THE INFO FROM THE MAILING LIST.
VRRR
HUH?
NO WAY. GUESS I MISSED TH—
GCHAK
NO FREAKIN' WAY!
THAT'S CHEATING!
COME ON, DON'T BLAME ME 'CAUSE *YOU'RE* BAD AT THIS.
AAAAAUGH!
SHAKE
SHAKE
SHAKE
UH, WHAT ABOUT THE INTERMEDIARY REVIEWS?

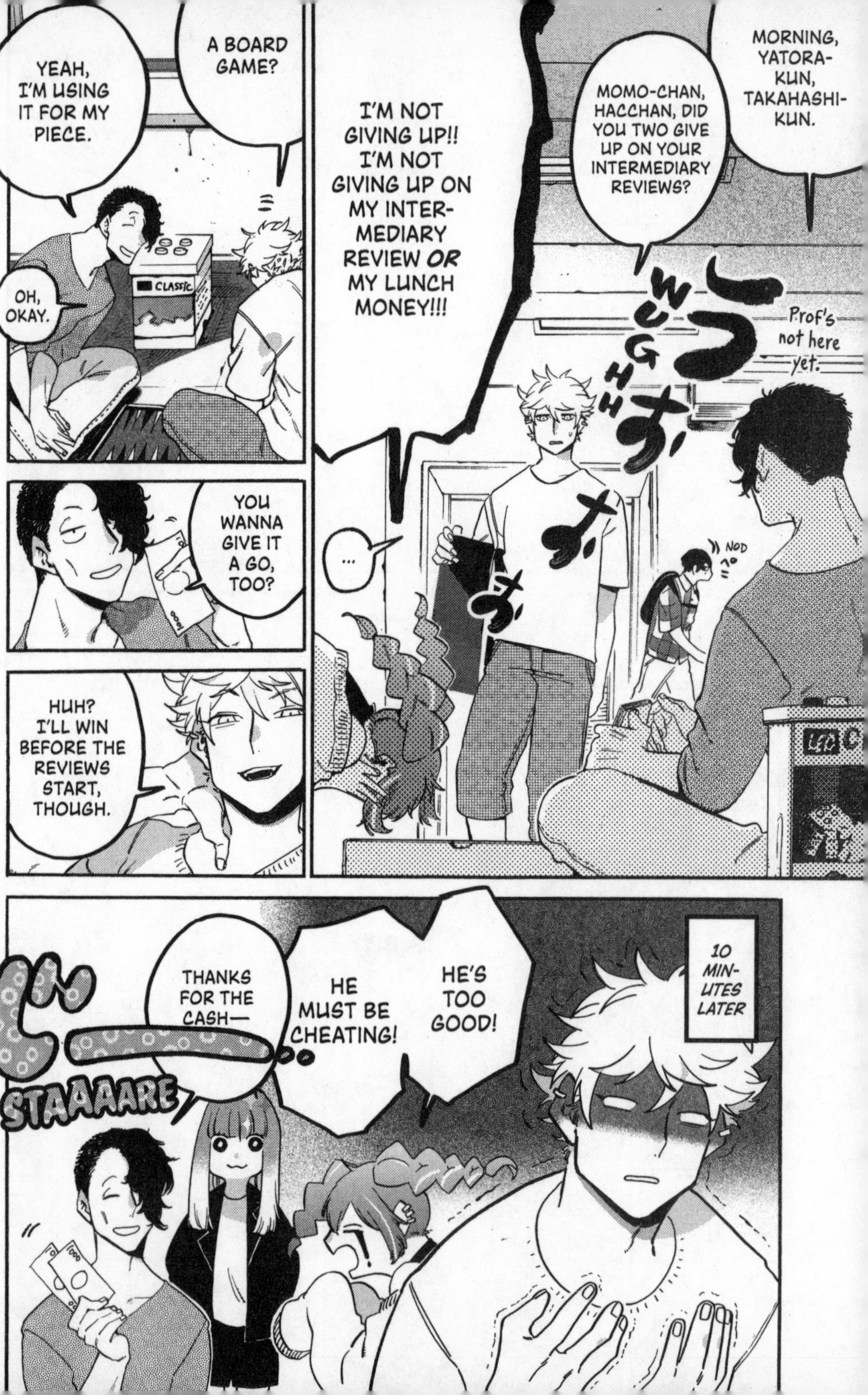
MORNING, YATORA-KUN, TAKAHASHI-KUN.
MOMO-CHAN, HACCHAN, DID YOU TWO GIVE UP ON YOUR INTERMEDIARY REVIEWS?
I'M NOT GIVING UP!! I'M NOT GIVING UP ON MY INTER-MEDIARY REVIEW *OR* MY LUNCH MONEY!!!
WUGHHH
Prof's not here yet.
NOD
...
A BOARD GAME?
YEAH, I'M USING IT FOR MY PIECE.
CLASSIC
OH, OKAY.
YOU WANNA GIVE IT A GO, TOO?
HUH? I'LL WIN BEFORE THE REVIEWS START, THOUGH.
10 MIN-UTES LATER
HE'S TOO GOOD!
HE MUST BE CHEATING!
THANKS FOR THE CASH—
STAAAARE

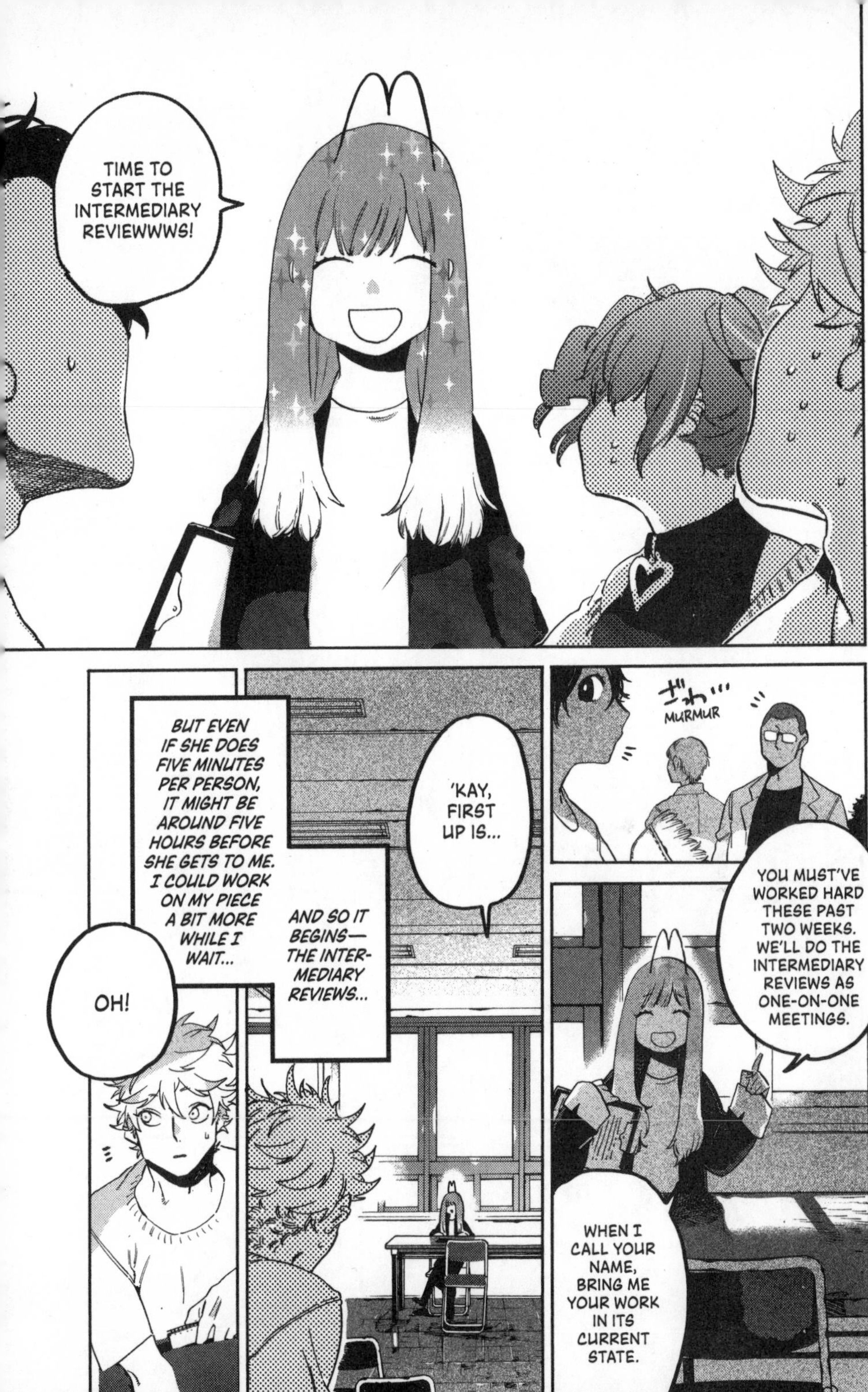
TIME TO START THE INTERMEDIARY REVIEWWWS!
ざわ…
MURMUR
YOU MUST'VE WORKED HARD THESE PAST TWO WEEKS. WE'LL DO THE INTERMEDIARY REVIEWS AS ONE-ON-ONE MEETINGS.
WHEN I CALL YOUR NAME, BRING ME YOUR WORK IN ITS CURRENT STATE.
'KAY, FIRST UP IS...
AND SO IT BEGINS—THE INTER-MEDIARY REVIEWS...
BUT EVEN IF SHE DOES FIVE MINUTES PER PERSON, IT MIGHT BE AROUND FIVE HOURS BEFORE SHE GETS TO ME. I COULD WORK ON MY PIECE A BIT MORE WHILE I WAIT...
OH!

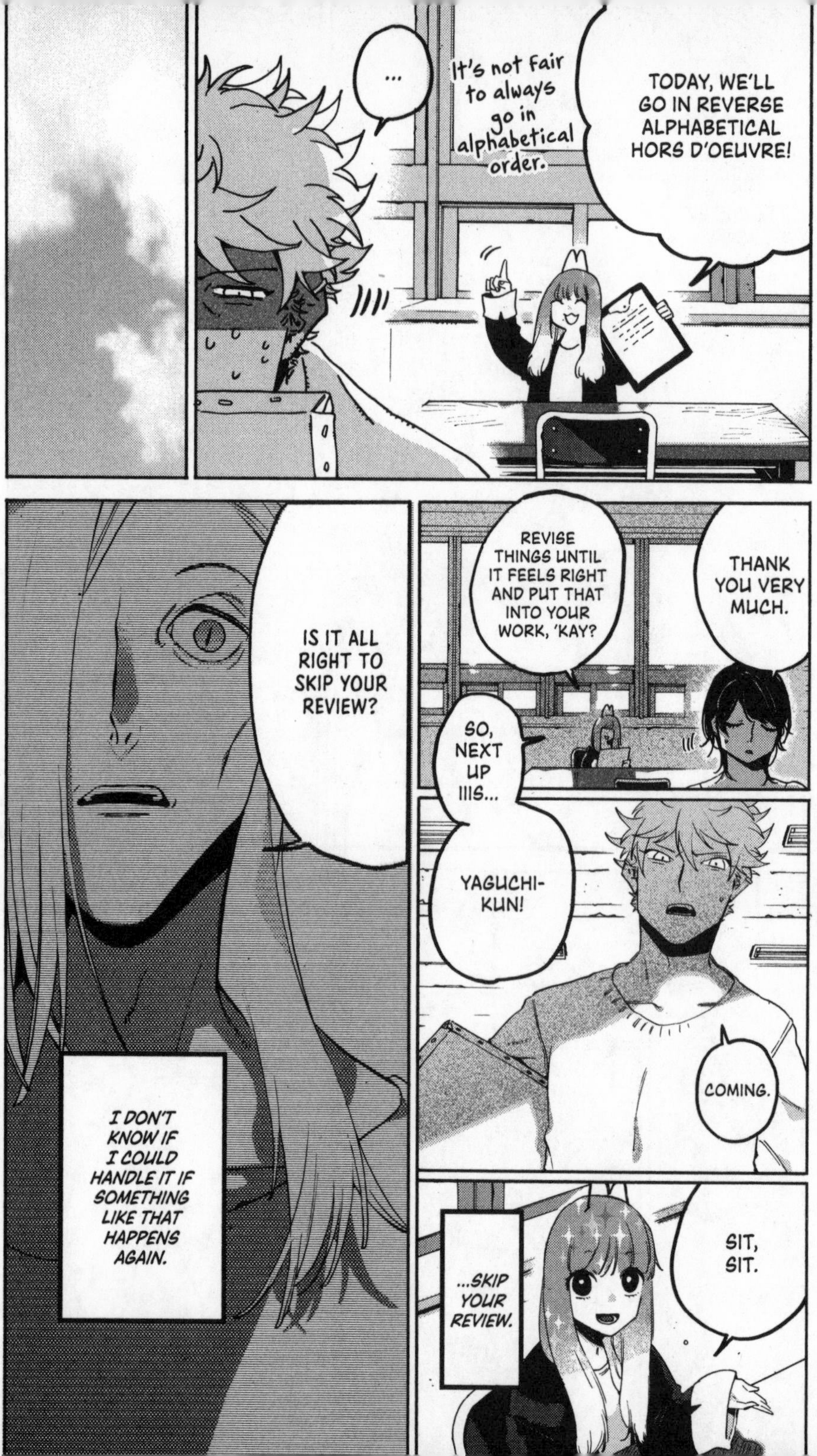
TODAY, WE'LL GO IN REVERSE ALPHABETICAL HORS D'OEUVRE!
It's not fair to always go in alphabetical order.
...
THANK YOU VERY MUCH.
REVISE THINGS UNTIL IT FEELS RIGHT AND PUT THAT INTO YOUR WORK, 'KAY?
SO, NEXT UP IIIS...
YAGUCHI-KUN!
COMING.
SIT, SIT.
...SKIP YOUR REVIEW.
IS IT ALL RIGHT TO SKIP YOUR REVIEW?
I DON'T KNOW IF I COULD HANDLE IT IF SOMETHING LIKE THAT HAPPENS AGAIN.

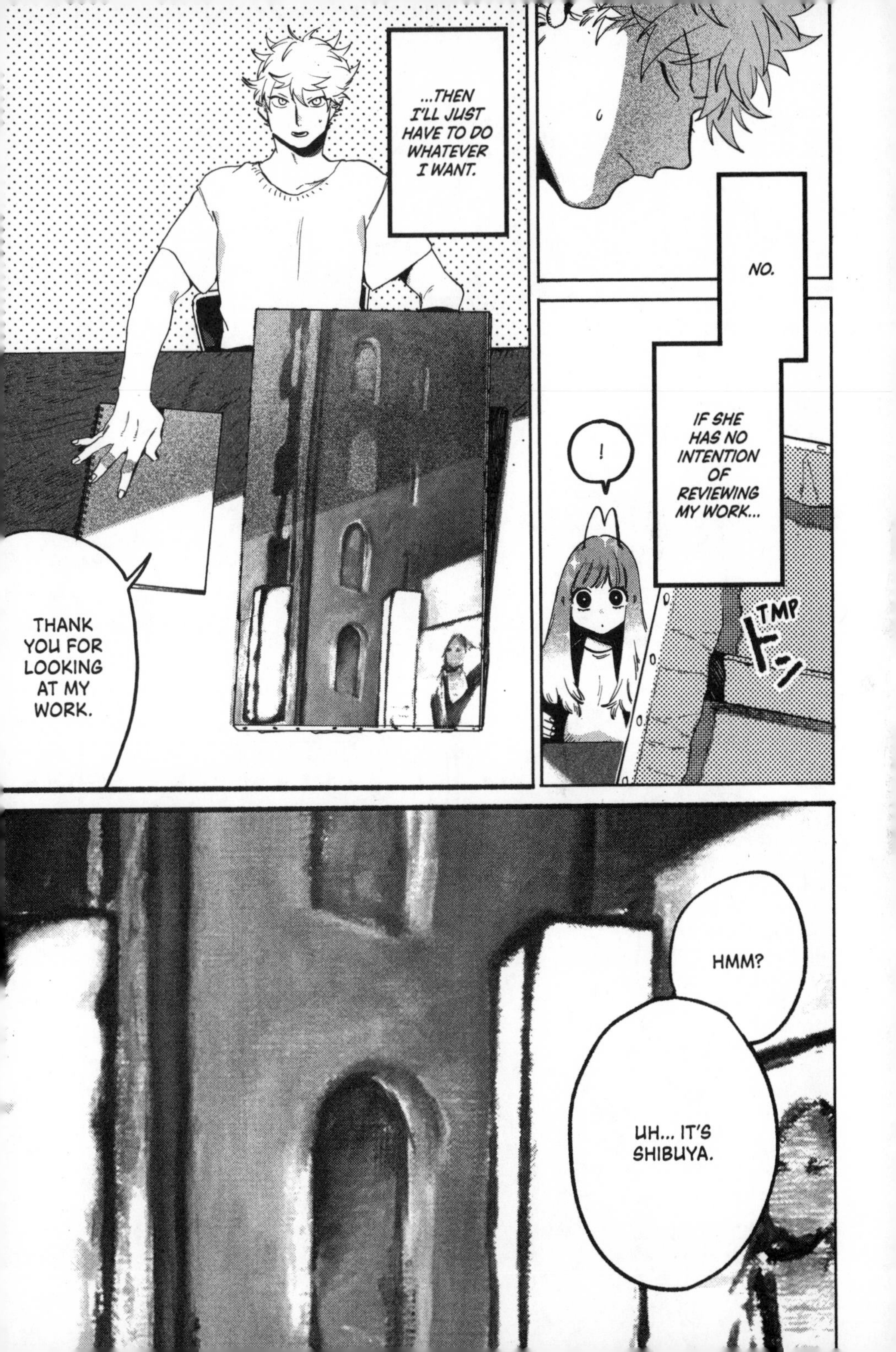
NO.
IF SHE HAS NO INTENTION OF REVIEWING MY WORK...
!
TMP
トン
...THEN I'LL JUST HAVE TO DO WHATEVER I WANT.
THANK YOU FOR LOOKING AT MY WORK.
HMM?
UH... IT'S SHIBUYA.

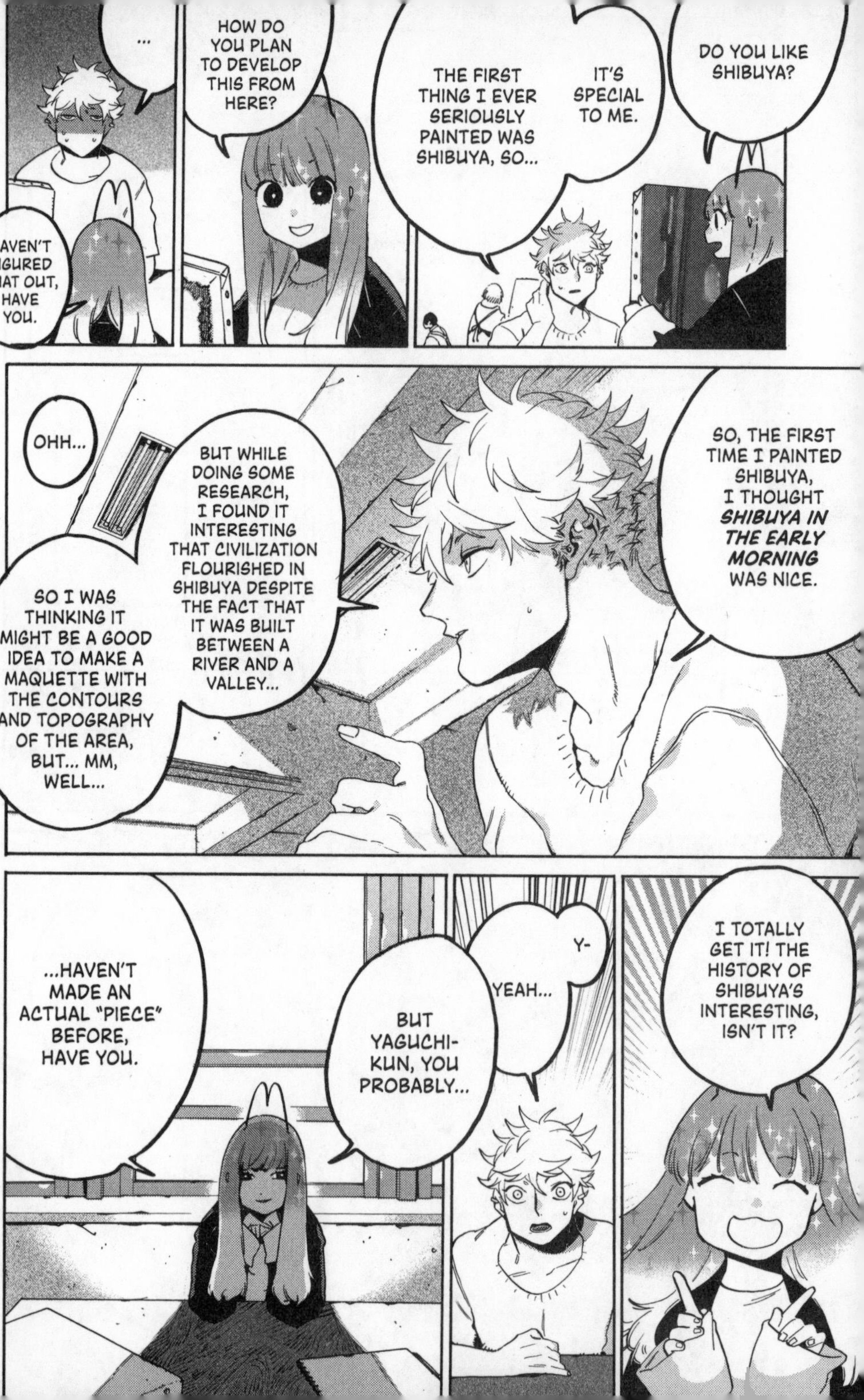
DO YOU LIKE SHIBUYA?
THE FIRST THING I EVER SERIOUSLY PAINTED WAS SHIBUYA, SO...
IT'S SPECIAL TO ME.
HOW DO YOU PLAN TO DEVELOP THIS FROM HERE?
...
HAVEN'T FIGURED THAT OUT, HAVE YOU.
SO, THE FIRST TIME I PAINTED SHIBUYA, I THOUGHT ***SHIBUYA IN THE EARLY MORNING*** WAS NICE.
BUT WHILE DOING SOME RESEARCH, I FOUND IT INTERESTING THAT CIVILIZATION FLOURISHED IN SHIBUYA DESPITE THE FACT THAT IT WAS BUILT BETWEEN A RIVER AND A VALLEY...
SO I WAS THINKING IT MIGHT BE A GOOD IDEA TO MAKE A MAQUETTE WITH THE CONTOURS AND TOPOGRAPHY OF THE AREA, BUT... MM, WELL...
OHH...
I TOTALLY GET IT! THE HISTORY OF SHIBUYA'S INTERESTING, ISN'T IT?
Y-
YEAH...
BUT YAGUCHI-KUN, YOU PROBABLY...
...HAVEN'T MADE AN ACTUAL "PIECE" BEFORE, HAVE YOU.

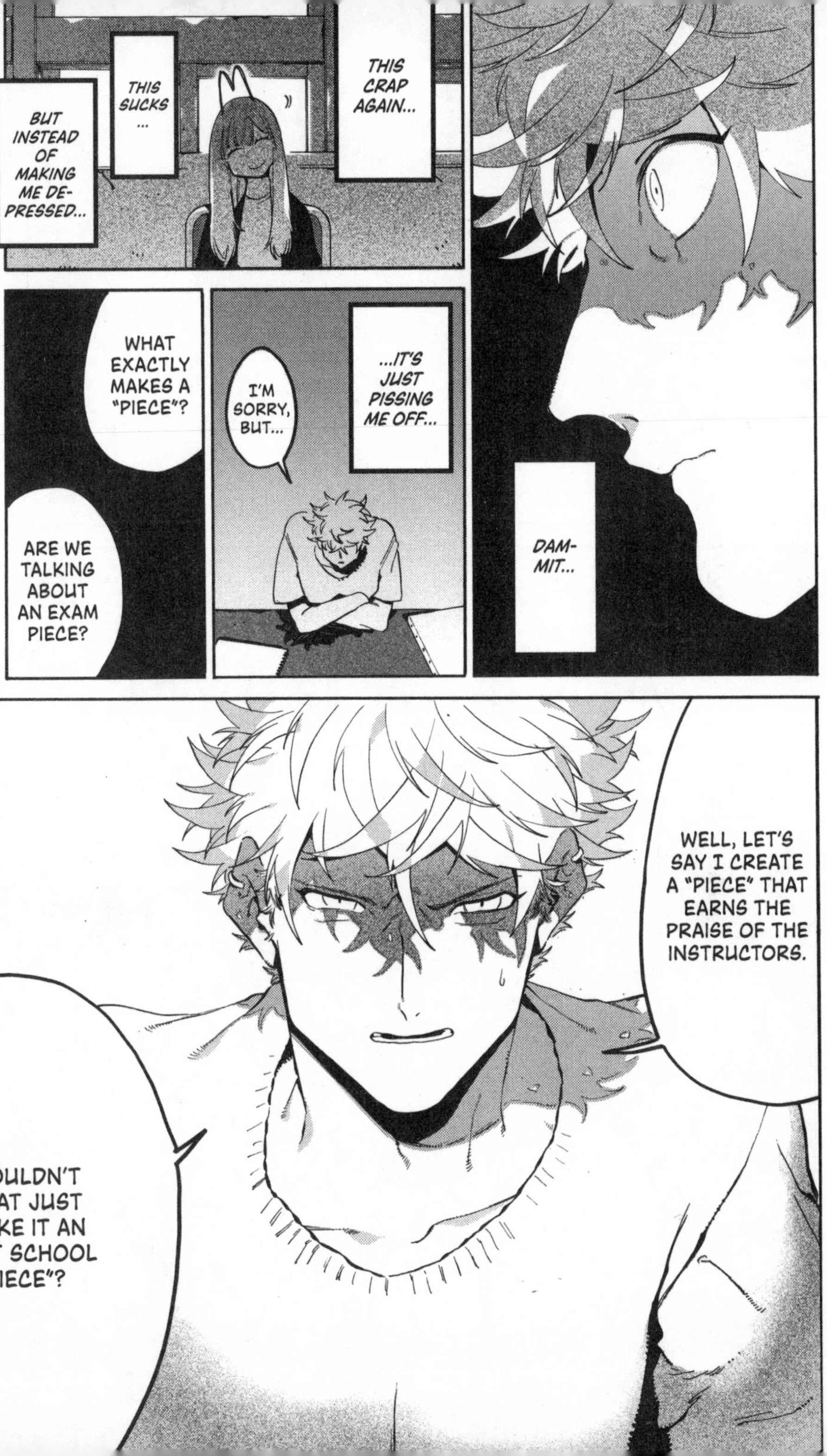
DAM-MIT...
THIS CRAP AGAIN...
THIS SUCKS...
BUT INSTEAD OF MAKING ME DE-PRESSED...
...IT'S JUST PISSING ME OFF...
I'M SORRY, BUT...
WHAT EXACTLY MAKES A "PIECE"?
ARE WE TALKING ABOUT AN EXAM PIECE?
WELL, LET'S SAY I CREATE A "PIECE" THAT EARNS THE PRAISE OF THE INSTRUCTORS.
WOULDN'T THAT JUST MAKE IT AN "ART SCHOOL PIECE"?

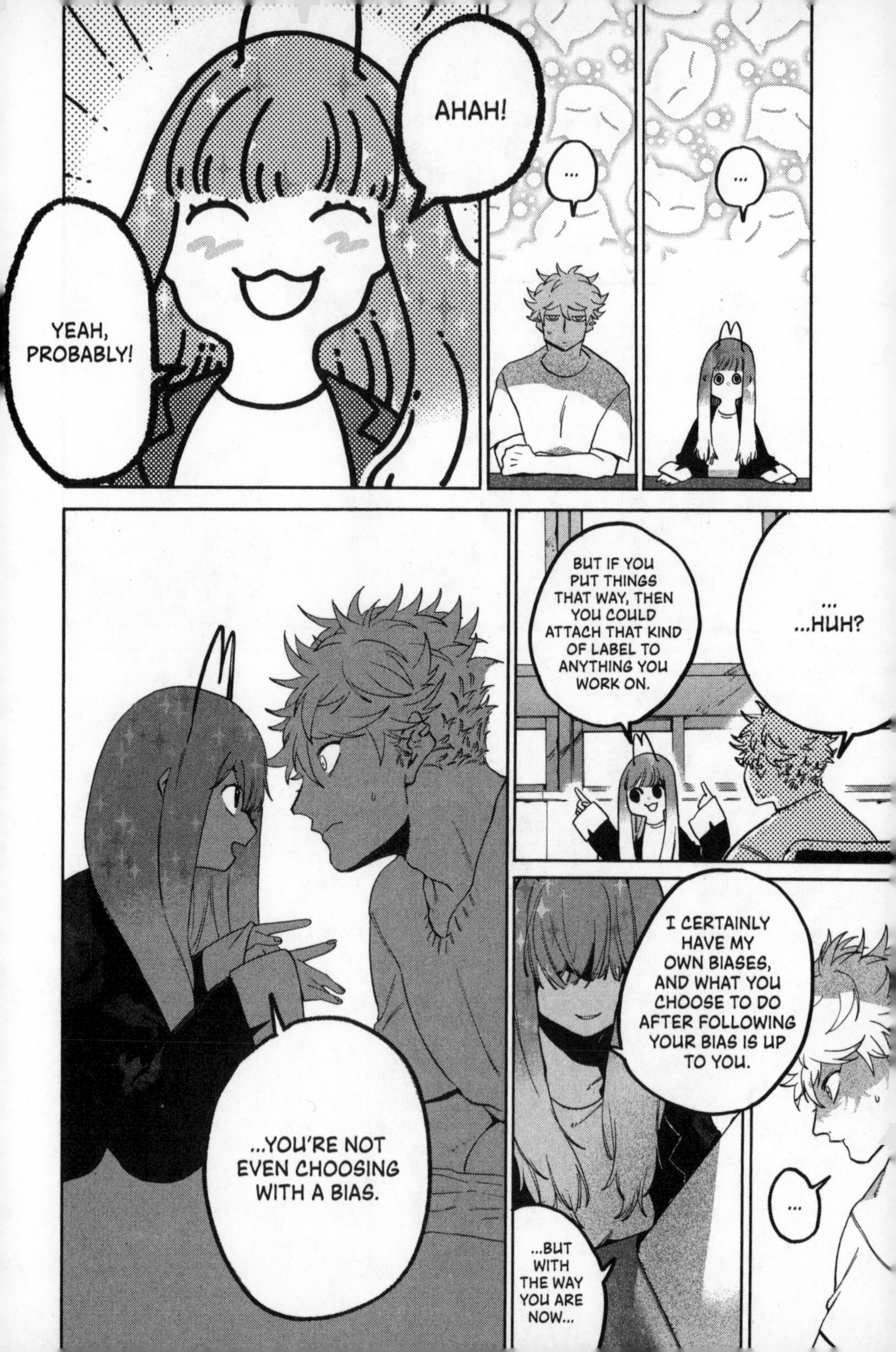
...
...
AHAH!
YEAH, PROBABLY!
... ...HUH?
BUT IF YOU PUT THINGS THAT WAY, THEN YOU COULD ATTACH THAT KIND OF LABEL TO ANYTHING YOU WORK ON.
I CERTAINLY HAVE MY OWN BIASES, AND WHAT YOU CHOOSE TO DO AFTER FOLLOWING YOUR BIAS IS UP TO YOU.
...
...BUT WITH THE WAY YOU ARE NOW...
...YOU'RE NOT EVEN CHOOSING WITH A BIAS.

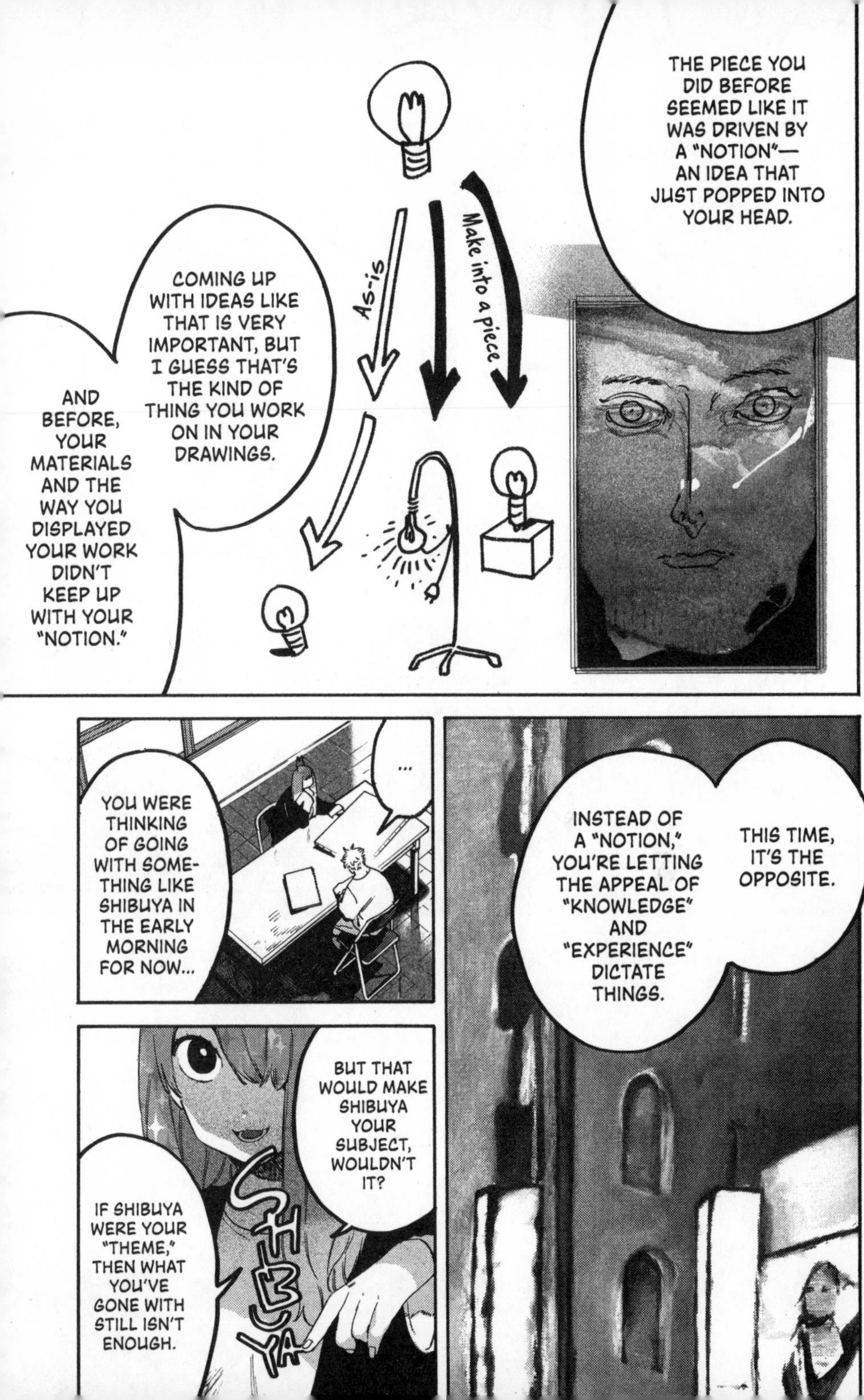
THE PIECE YOU DID BEFORE SEEMED LIKE IT WAS DRIVEN BY A "NOTION"— AN IDEA THAT JUST POPPED INTO YOUR HEAD.
Make into a piece
As-is
COMING UP WITH IDEAS LIKE THAT IS VERY IMPORTANT, BUT I GUESS THAT'S THE KIND OF THING YOU WORK ON IN YOUR DRAWINGS.
AND BEFORE, YOUR MATERIALS AND THE WAY YOU DISPLAYED YOUR WORK DIDN'T KEEP UP WITH YOUR "NOTION."
THIS TIME, IT'S THE OPPOSITE.
INSTEAD OF A "NOTION," YOU'RE LETTING THE APPEAL OF "KNOWLEDGE" AND "EXPERIENCE" DICTATE THINGS.
...
YOU WERE THINKING OF GOING WITH SOME-THING LIKE SHIBUYA IN THE EARLY MORNING FOR NOW...
BUT THAT WOULD MAKE SHIBUYA YOUR SUBJECT, WOULDN'T IT?
SHIBUYA
IF SHIBUYA WERE YOUR "THEME," THEN WHAT YOU'VE GONE WITH STILL ISN'T ENOUGH.

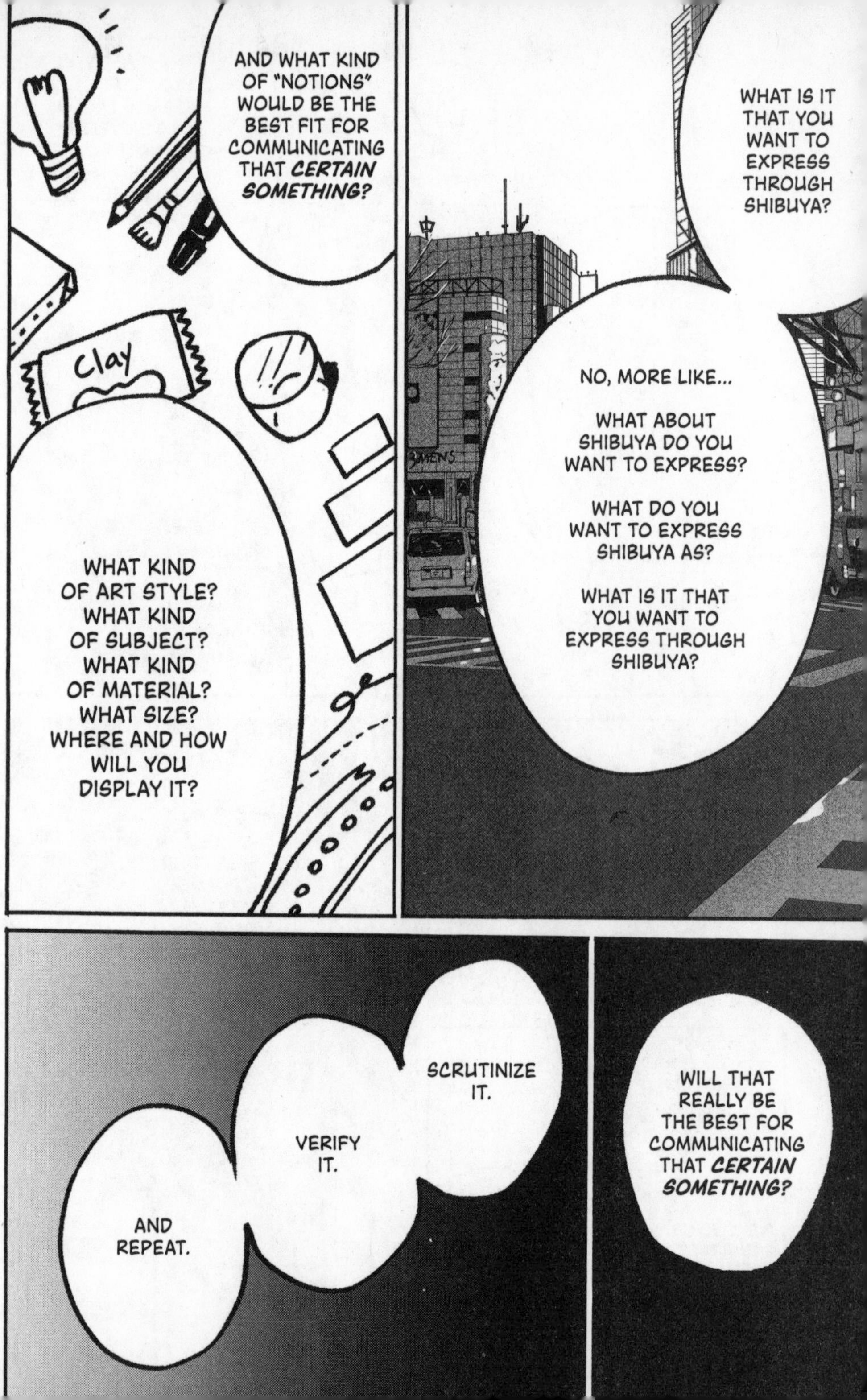
WHAT IS IT THAT YOU WANT TO EXPRESS THROUGH SHIBUYA?
NO, MORE LIKE...
WHAT ABOUT SHIBUYA DO YOU WANT TO EXPRESS?
WHAT DO YOU WANT TO EXPRESS SHIBUYA AS?
WHAT IS IT THAT YOU WANT TO EXPRESS THROUGH SHIBUYA?
AND WHAT KIND OF "NOTIONS" WOULD BE THE BEST FIT FOR COMMUNICATING THAT *CERTAIN SOMETHING?*
WHAT KIND OF ART STYLE? WHAT KIND OF SUBJECT? WHAT KIND OF MATERIAL? WHAT SIZE? WHERE AND HOW WILL YOU DISPLAY IT?
Clay
WILL THAT REALLY BE THE BEST FOR COMMUNICATING THAT *CERTAIN SOMETHING?*
SCRUTINIZE IT.
VERIFY IT.
AND REPEAT.

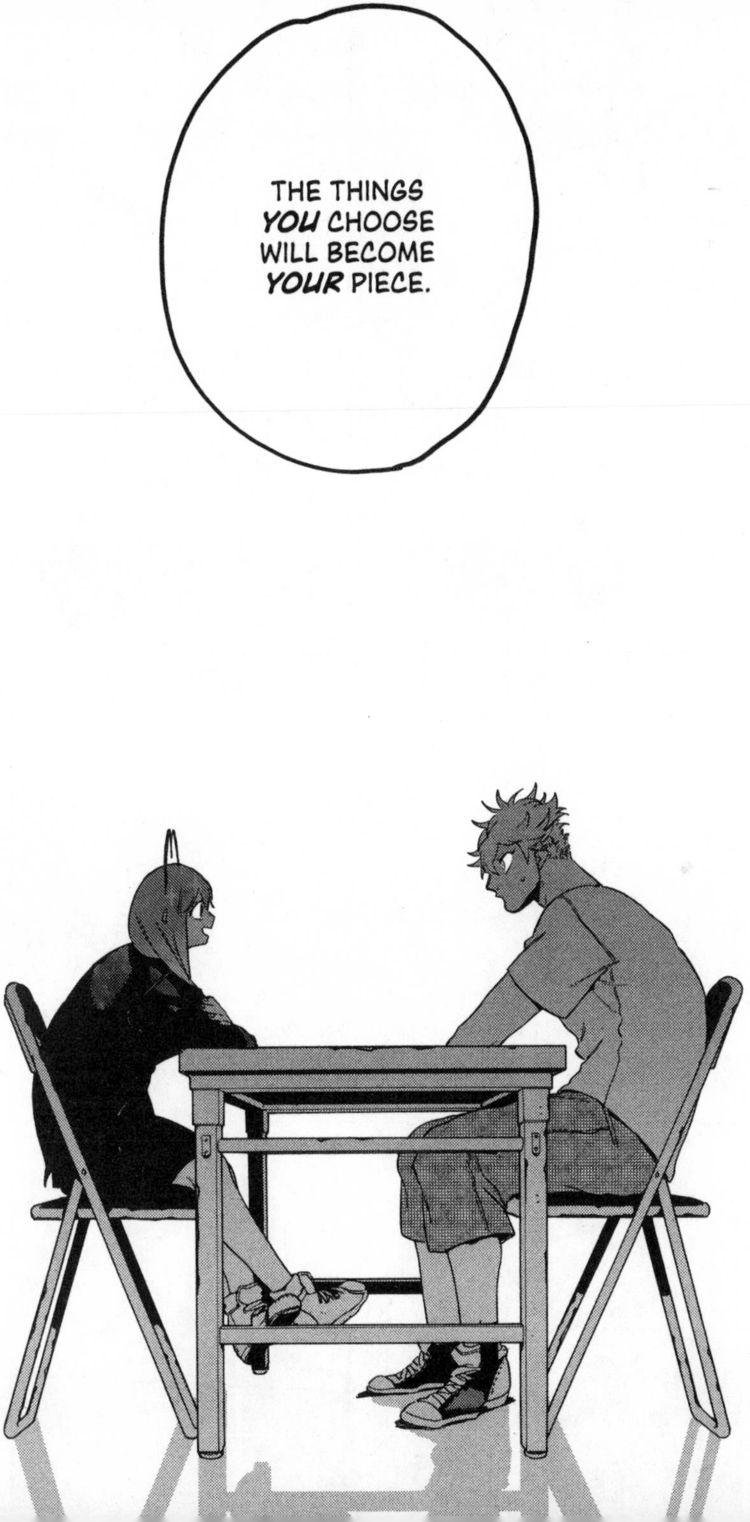
THE THINGS *YOU* CHOOSE WILL BECOME *YOUR* PIECE.

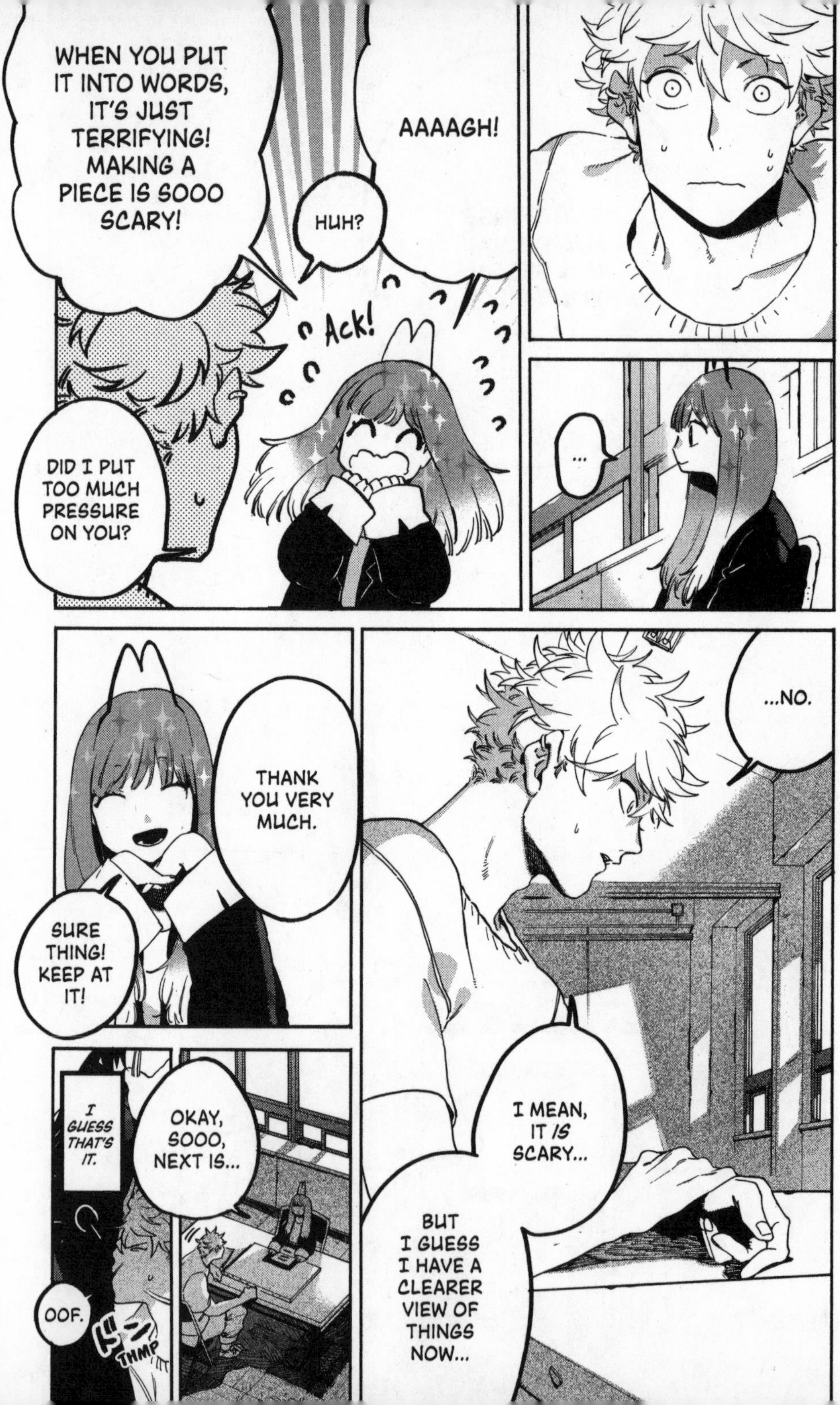
...
AAAAGH!
WHEN YOU PUT IT INTO WORDS, IT'S JUST TERRIFYING! MAKING A PIECE IS SOOO SCARY!
HUH?
Ack!
DID I PUT TOO MUCH PRESSURE ON YOU?
...NO.
I MEAN, IT *IS* SCARY...
BUT I GUESS I HAVE A CLEARER VIEW OF THINGS NOW...
THANK YOU VERY MUCH.
SURE THING! KEEP AT IT!
OKAY, SOOO, NEXT IS...
I GUESS THAT'S IT.
OOF.
THMP

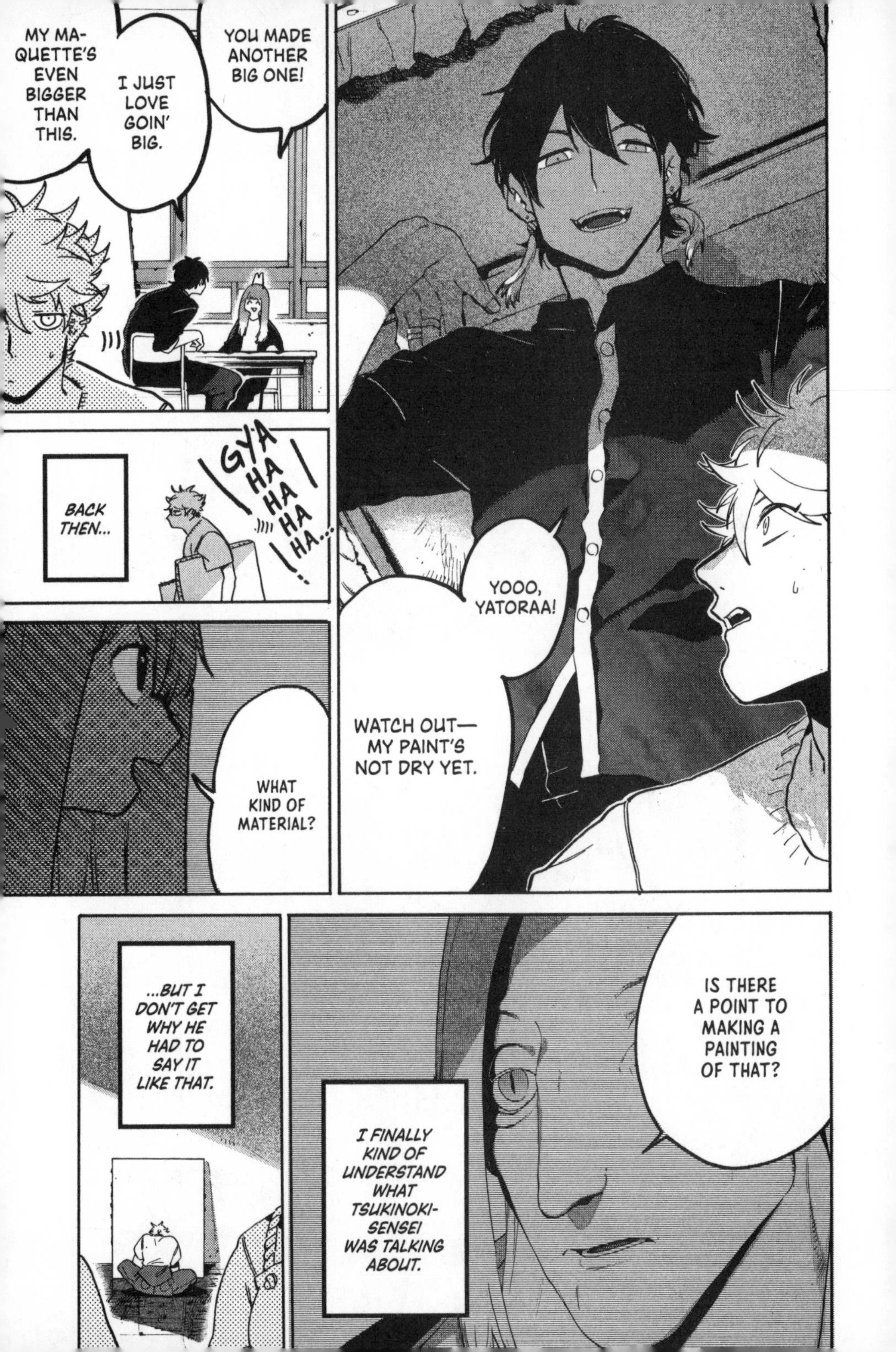
YOOO, YATORAA!
WATCH OUT—MY PAINT'S NOT DRY YET.
YOU MADE ANOTHER BIG ONE!
I JUST LOVE GOIN' BIG.
MY MA-QUETTE'S EVEN BIGGER THAN THIS.
GYA HA HA HA HA...
BACK THEN...
WHAT KIND OF MATERIAL?
IS THERE A POINT TO MAKING A PAINTING OF THAT?
I FINALLY KIND OF UNDERSTAND WHAT TSUKINOKI-SENSEI WAS TALKING ABOUT.
...BUT I DON'T GET WHY HE HAD TO SAY IT LIKE THAT.

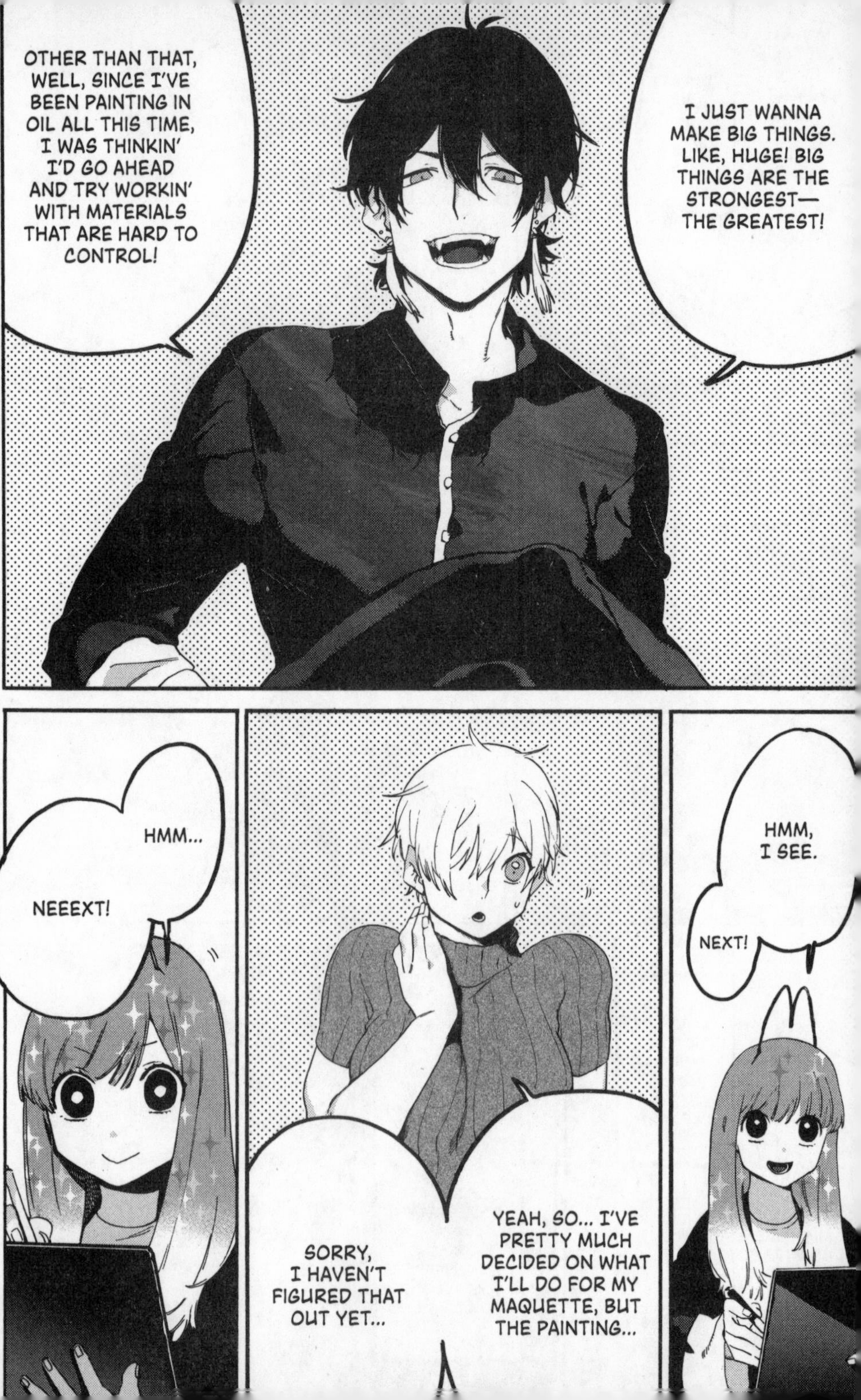
I JUST WANNA MAKE BIG THINGS. LIKE, HUGE! BIG THINGS ARE THE STRONGEST—THE GREATEST!
OTHER THAN THAT, WELL, SINCE I'VE BEEN PAINTING IN OIL ALL THIS TIME, I WAS THINKIN' I'D GO AHEAD AND TRY WORKIN' WITH MATERIALS THAT ARE HARD TO CONTROL!
HMM, I SEE.
NEXT!
YEAH, SO... I'VE PRETTY MUCH DECIDED ON WHAT I'LL DO FOR MY MAQUETTE, BUT THE PAINTING...
SORRY, I HAVEN'T FIGURED THAT OUT YET...
HMM...
NEEEXT!

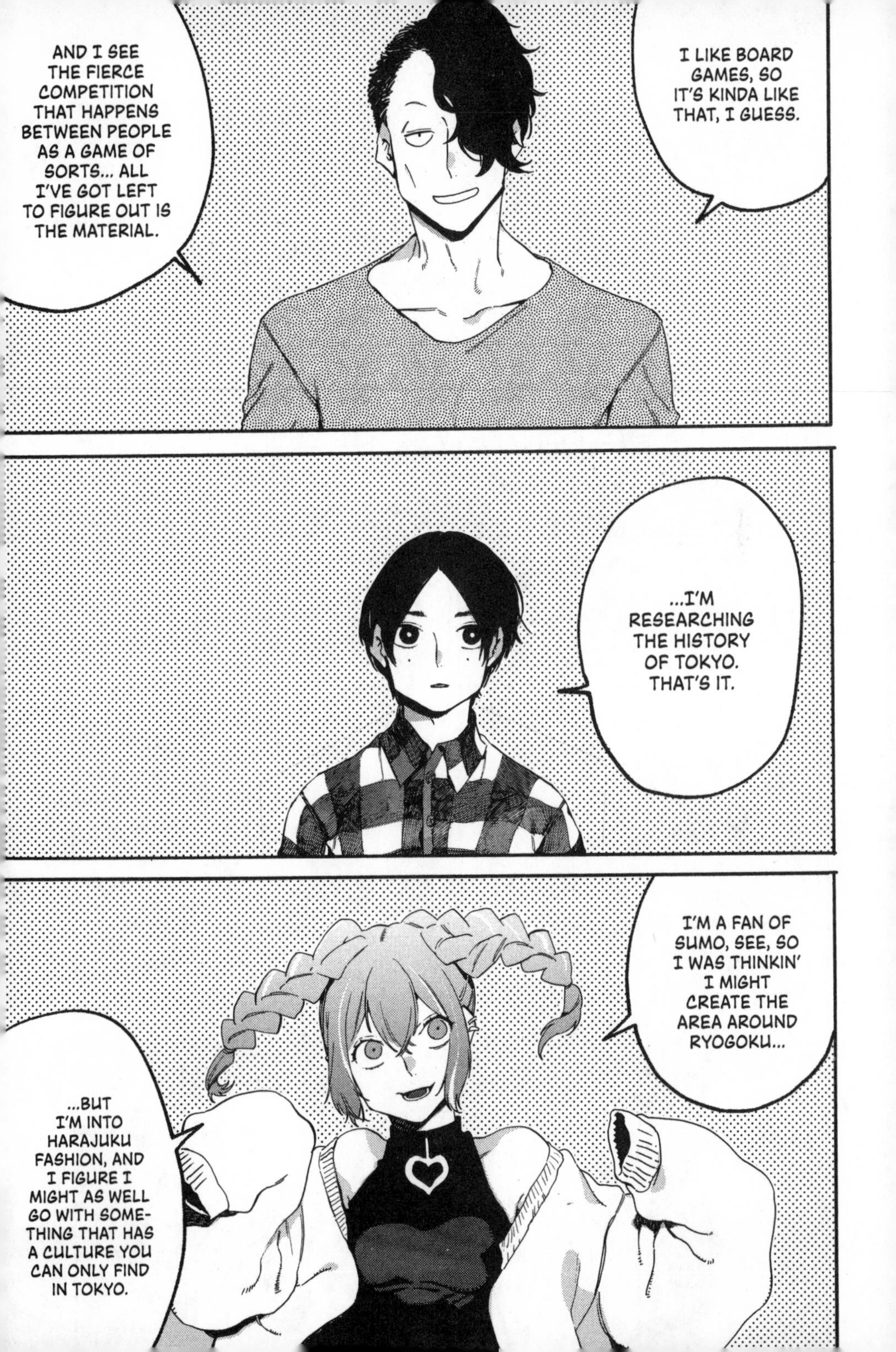
I LIKE BOARD GAMES, SO IT'S KINDA LIKE THAT, I GUESS.
AND I SEE THE FIERCE COMPETITION THAT HAPPENS BETWEEN PEOPLE AS A GAME OF SORTS... ALL I'VE GOT LEFT TO FIGURE OUT IS THE MATERIAL.
...I'M RESEARCHING THE HISTORY OF TOKYO. THAT'S IT.
I'M A FAN OF SUMO, SEE, SO I WAS THINKIN' I MIGHT CREATE THE AREA AROUND RYOGOKU...
...BUT I'M INTO HARAJUKU FASHION, AND I FIGURE I MIGHT AS WELL GO WITH SOME-THING THAT HAS A CULTURE YOU CAN ONLY FIND IN TOKYO.

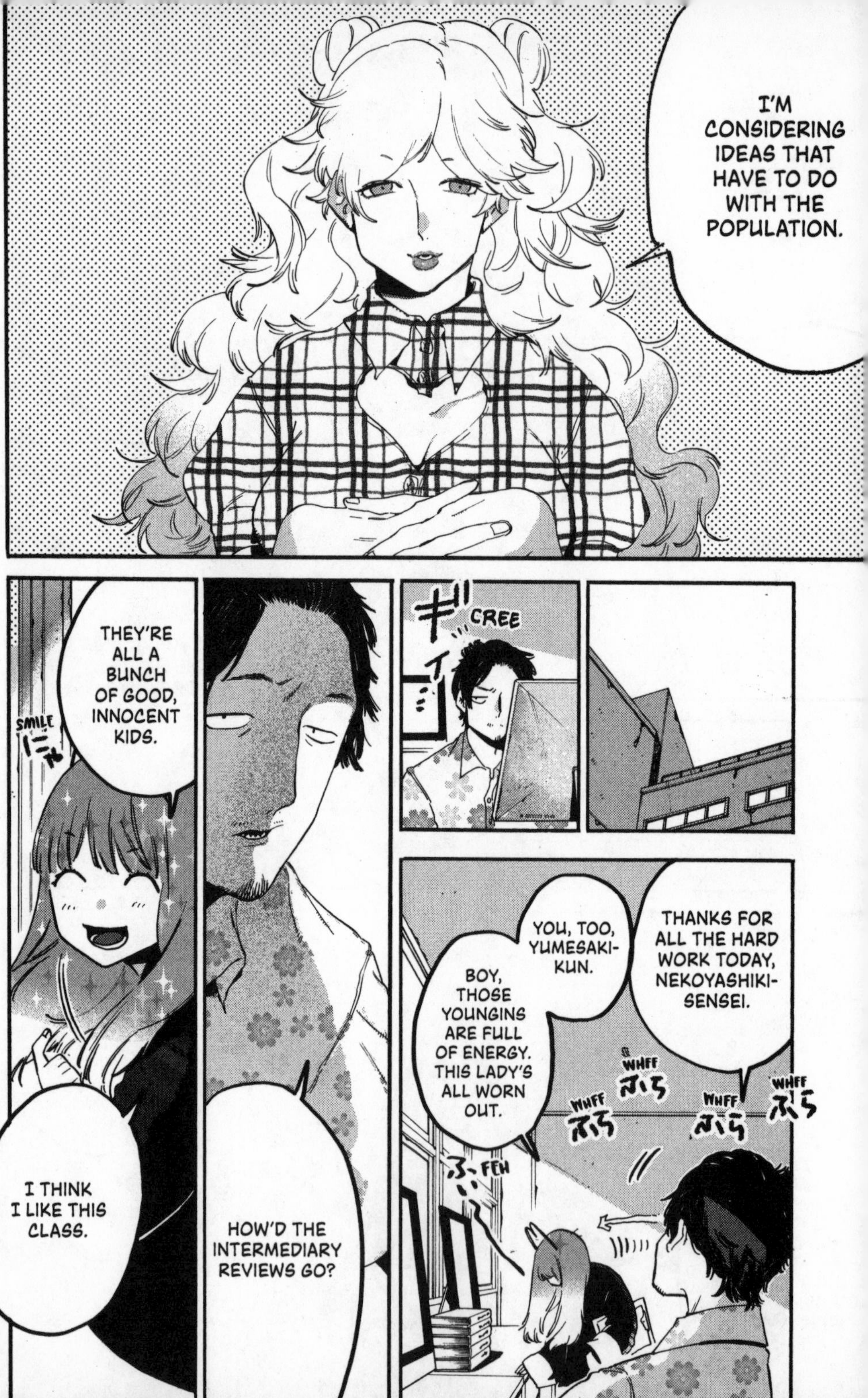
I'M CONSIDERING IDEAS THAT HAVE TO DO WITH THE POPULATION.
ギ CREE
THANKS FOR ALL THE HARD WORK TODAY, NEKOYASHIKI-SENSEI.
WHFF ふら
WHFF ふら
YOU, TOO, YUMESAKI-KUN.
WHFF ふら
WHFF ふら
BOY, THOSE YOUNGINS ARE FULL OF ENERGY. THIS LADY'S ALL WORN OUT.
FEH
HOW'D THE INTERMEDIARY REVIEWS GO?
THEY'RE ALL A BUNCH OF GOOD, INNOCENT KIDS.
SMILE
I THINK I LIKE THIS CLASS.

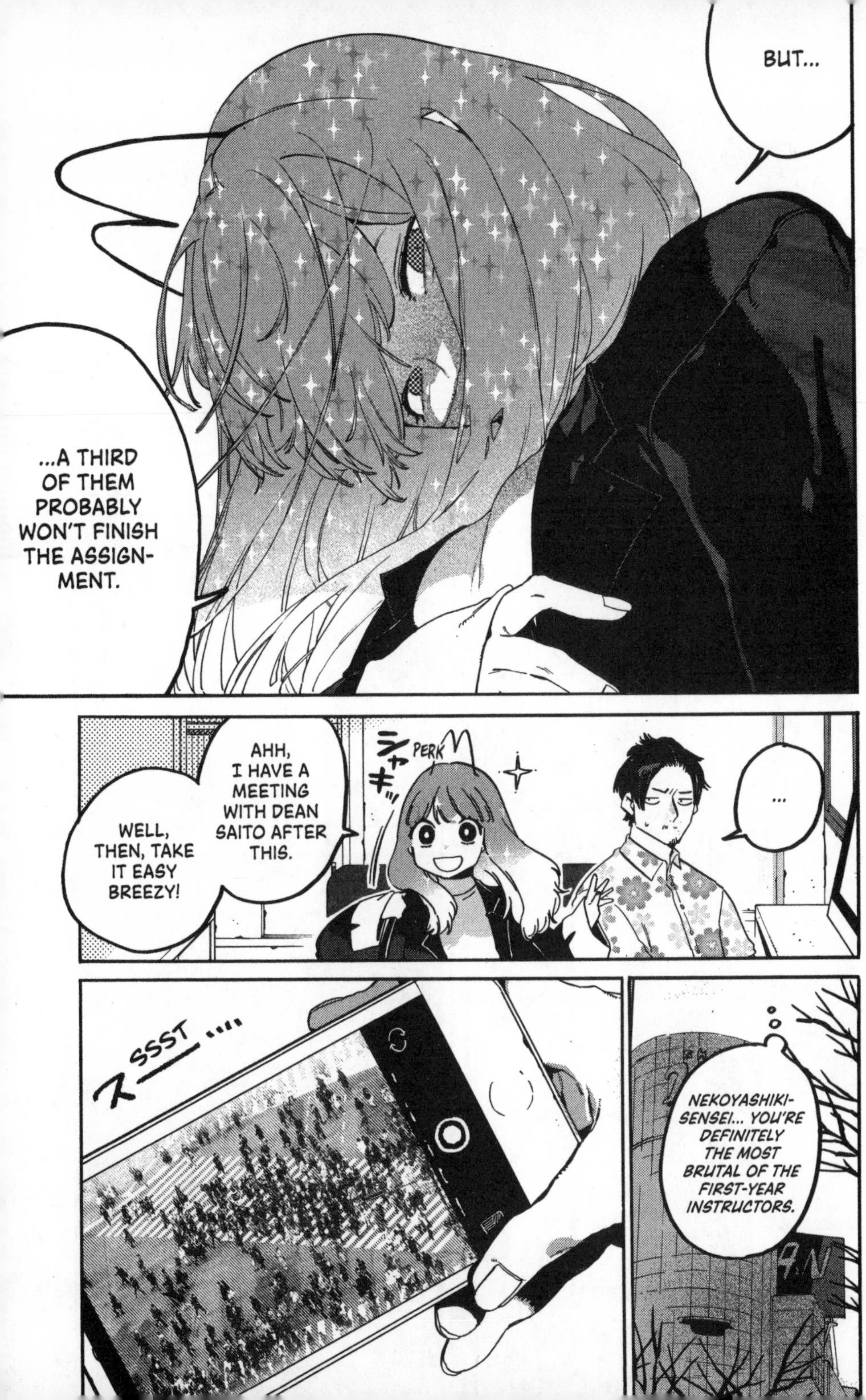
BUT...
...A THIRD OF THEM PROBABLY WON'T FINISH THE ASSIGNMENT.
...
PERK
AHH, I HAVE A MEETING WITH DEAN SAITO AFTER THIS.
WELL, THEN, TAKE IT EASY BREEZY!
NEKOYASHIKI-SENSEI... YOU'RE DEFINITELY THE MOST BRUTAL OF THE FIRST-YEAR INSTRUCTORS.
SSST....

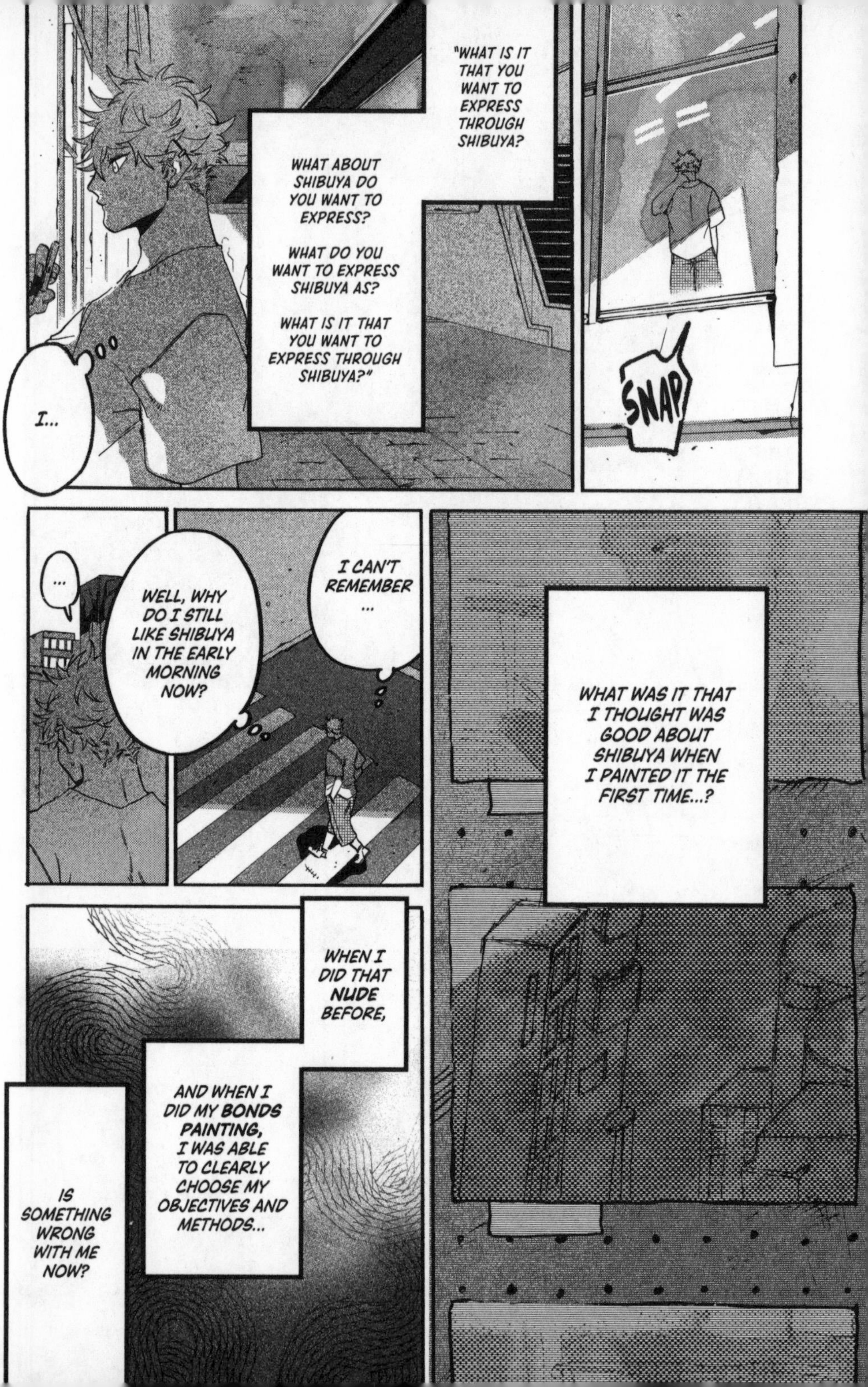
SNAP
"WHAT IS IT THAT YOU WANT TO EXPRESS THROUGH SHIBUYA?
WHAT ABOUT SHIBUYA DO YOU WANT TO EXPRESS?
WHAT DO YOU WANT TO EXPRESS SHIBUYA AS?
WHAT IS IT THAT YOU WANT TO EXPRESS THROUGH SHIBUYA?"
I...
WHAT WAS IT THAT I THOUGHT WAS GOOD ABOUT SHIBUYA WHEN I PAINTED IT THE FIRST TIME...?
I CAN'T REMEMBER...
WELL, WHY DO I STILL LIKE SHIBUYA IN THE EARLY MORNING NOW?
...
WHEN I DID THAT NUDE BEFORE,
AND WHEN I DID MY BONDS PAINTING, I WAS ABLE TO CLEARLY CHOOSE MY OBJECTIVES AND METHODS...
IS SOMETHING WRONG WITH ME NOW?

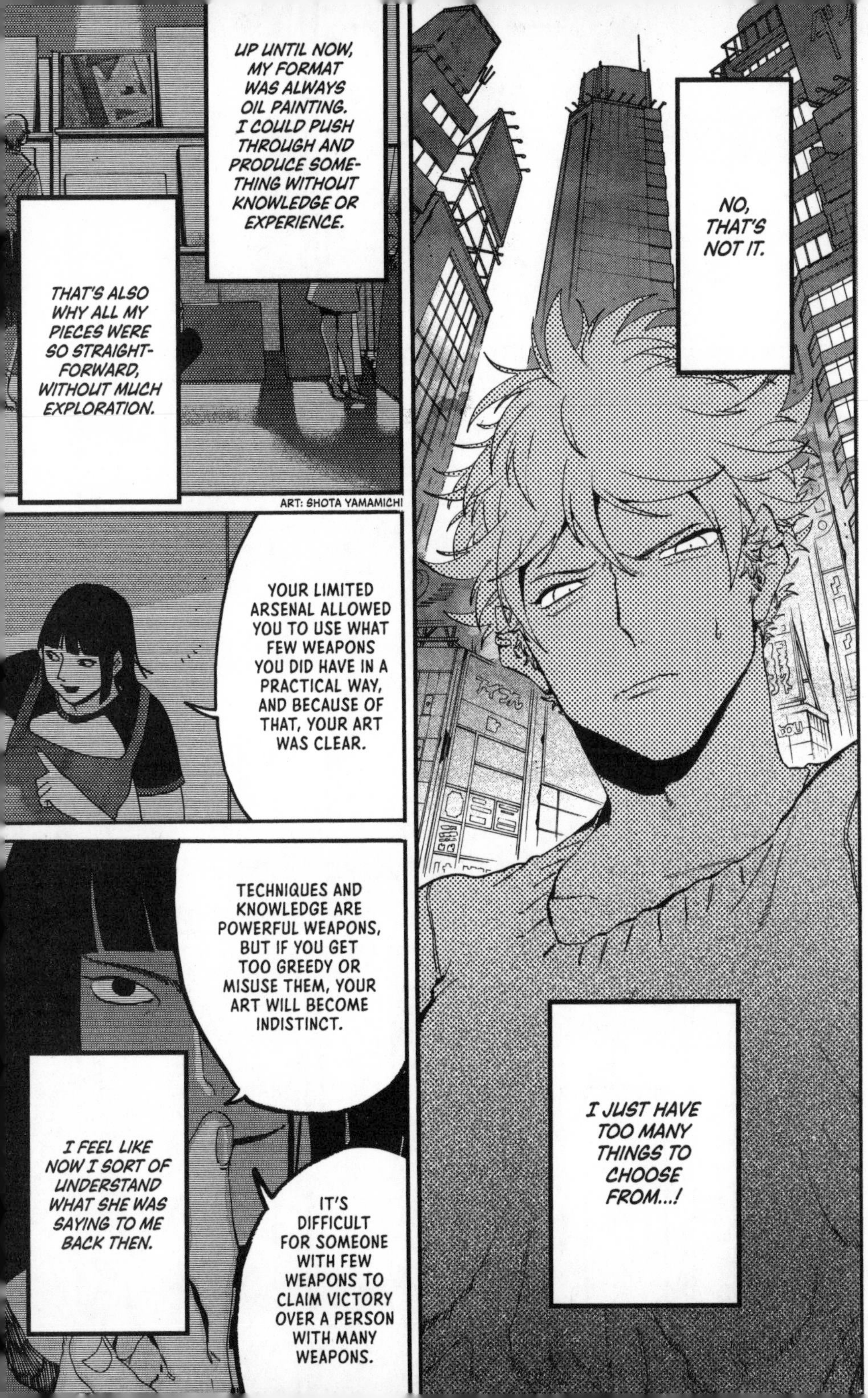
NO, THAT'S NOT IT.
I JUST HAVE TOO MANY THINGS TO CHOOSE FROM...!
UP UNTIL NOW, MY FORMAT WAS ALWAYS OIL PAINTING. I COULD PUSH THROUGH AND PRODUCE SOME-THING WITHOUT KNOWLEDGE OR EXPERIENCE.
THAT'S ALSO WHY ALL MY PIECES WERE SO STRAIGHT-FORWARD, WITHOUT MUCH EXPLORATION.
ART: SHOTA YAMAMICHI
YOUR LIMITED ARSENAL ALLOWED YOU TO USE WHAT FEW WEAPONS YOU DID HAVE IN A PRACTICAL WAY, AND BECAUSE OF THAT, YOUR ART WAS CLEAR.
TECHNIQUES AND KNOWLEDGE ARE POWERFUL WEAPONS, BUT IF YOU GET TOO GREEDY OR MISUSE THEM, YOUR ART WILL BECOME INDISTINCT.
IT'S DIFFICULT FOR SOMEONE WITH FEW WEAPONS TO CLAIM VICTORY OVER A PERSON WITH MANY WEAPONS.
I FEEL LIKE NOW I SORT OF UNDERSTAND WHAT SHE WAS SAYING TO ME BACK THEN.

IN THAT CASE...

WOLFGANG LAIB EXHIBITION

ラブ展 ヴォルフガング

5/15~ 8/20

IT FELT LIKE I WAS BEING THOUGHTFUL, BUT I MUST HAVE BEEN PAINTING A LOT ON IMPULSE.

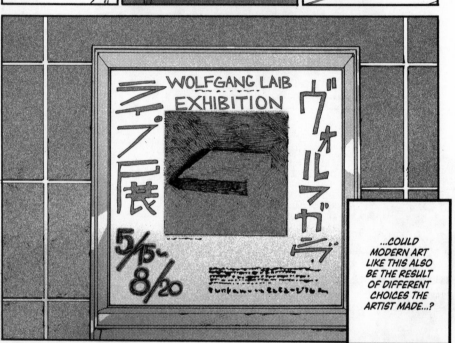

WOLFGANG LAIB EXHIBITION

ラブ展 ヴォルフガング

5/15~ 8/20

...COULD MODERN ART LIKE THIS ALSO BE THE RESULT OF DIFFERENT CHOICES THE ARTIST MADE...?

BUT...

...DON'T GET IT.

I STILL...

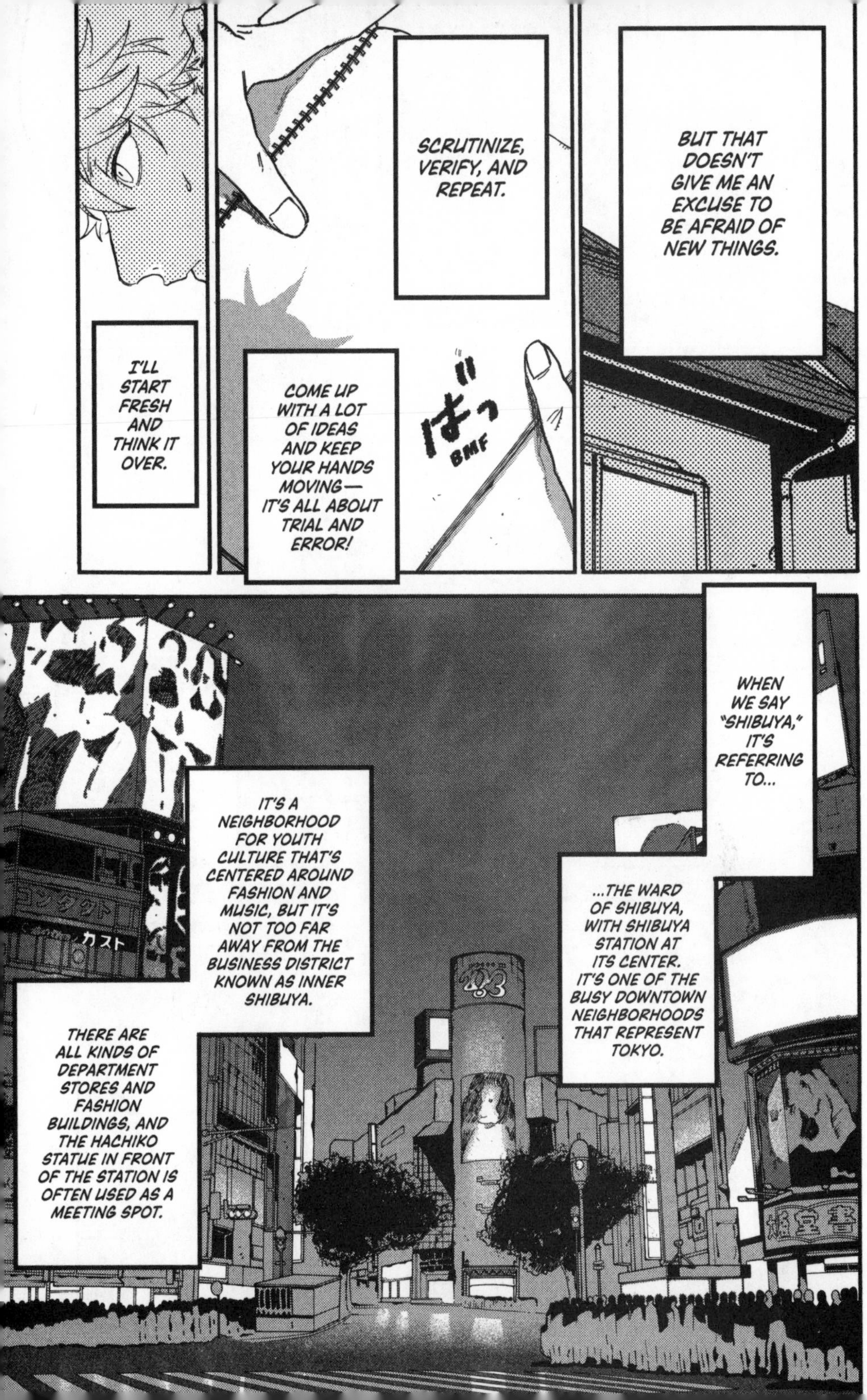
BUT THAT DOESN'T GIVE ME AN EXCUSE TO BE AFRAID OF NEW THINGS.
SCRUTINIZE, VERIFY, AND REPEAT.
ばっ
BMF
COME UP WITH A LOT OF IDEAS AND KEEP YOUR HANDS MOVING— IT'S ALL ABOUT TRIAL AND ERROR!
I'LL START FRESH AND THINK IT OVER.
WHEN WE SAY "SHIBUYA," IT'S REFERRING TO...
...THE WARD OF SHIBUYA, WITH SHIBUYA STATION AT ITS CENTER. IT'S ONE OF THE BUSY DOWNTOWN NEIGHBORHOODS THAT REPRESENT TOKYO.
IT'S A NEIGHBORHOOD FOR YOUTH CULTURE THAT'S CENTERED AROUND FASHION AND MUSIC, BUT IT'S NOT TOO FAR AWAY FROM THE BUSINESS DISTRICT KNOWN AS INNER SHIBUYA.
THERE ARE ALL KINDS OF DEPARTMENT STORES AND FASHION BUILDINGS, AND THE HACHIKO STATUE IN FRONT OF THE STATION IS OFTEN USED AS A MEETING SPOT.

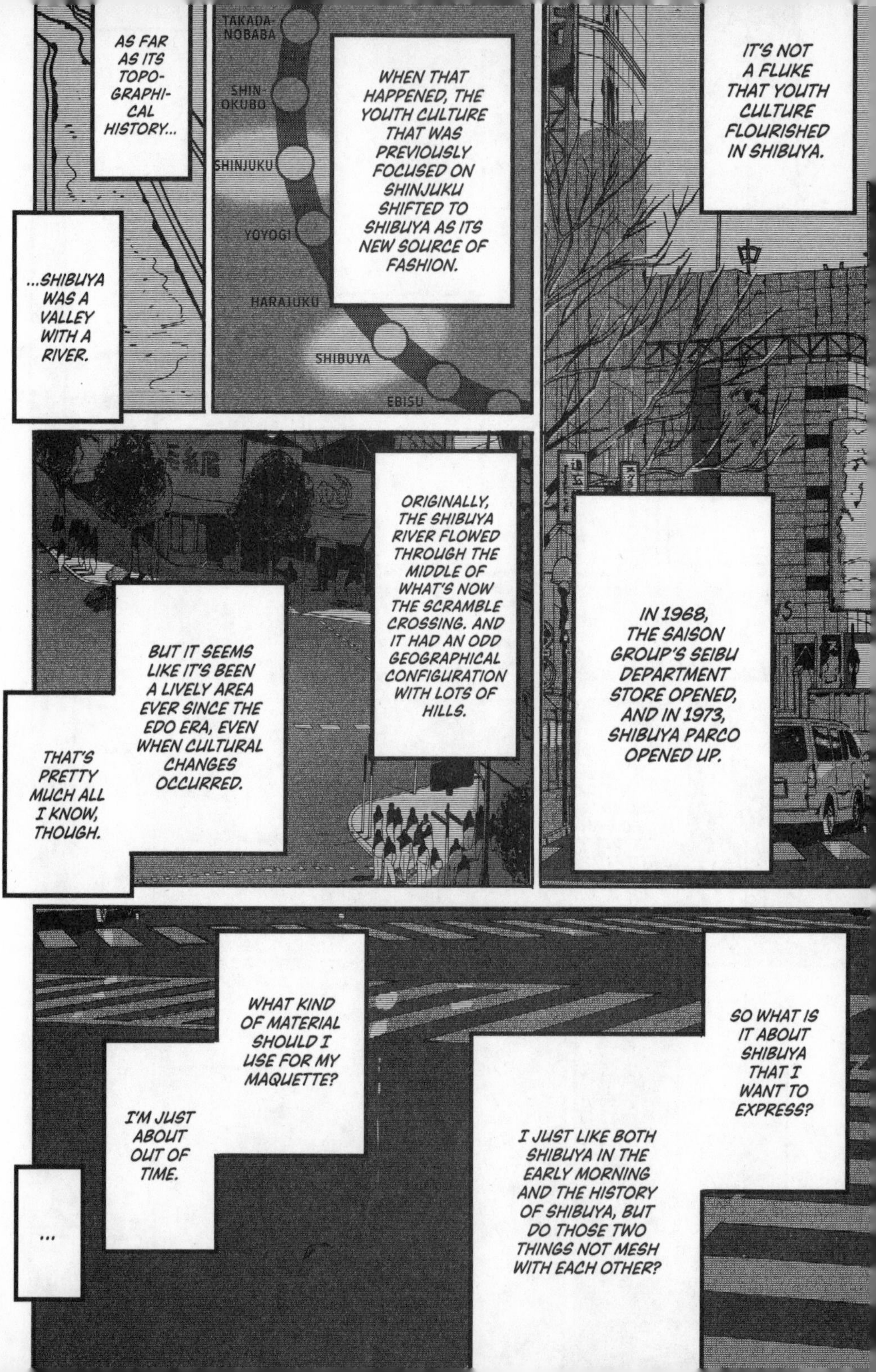
IT'S NOT A FLUKE THAT YOUTH CULTURE FLOURISHED IN SHIBUYA.
IN 1968, THE SAISON GROUP'S SEIBU DEPARTMENT STORE OPENED, AND IN 1973, SHIBUYA PARCO OPENED UP.
TAKADA-NOBABA
SHIN-OKUBO
SHINJUKU
YOYOGI
HARAJUKU
SHIBUYA
EBISU
WHEN THAT HAPPENED, THE YOUTH CULTURE THAT WAS PREVIOUSLY FOCUSED ON SHINJUKU SHIFTED TO SHIBUYA AS ITS NEW SOURCE OF FASHION.
AS FAR AS ITS TOPOGRAPHICAL HISTORY...
...SHIBUYA WAS A VALLEY WITH A RIVER.
ORIGINALLY, THE SHIBUYA RIVER FLOWED THROUGH THE MIDDLE OF WHAT'S NOW THE SCRAMBLE CROSSING. AND IT HAD AN ODD GEOGRAPHICAL CONFIGURATION WITH LOTS OF HILLS.
BUT IT SEEMS LIKE IT'S BEEN A LIVELY AREA EVER SINCE THE EDO ERA, EVEN WHEN CULTURAL CHANGES OCCURRED.
THAT'S PRETTY MUCH ALL I KNOW, THOUGH.
SO WHAT IS IT ABOUT SHIBUYA THAT I WANT TO EXPRESS?
I JUST LIKE BOTH SHIBUYA IN THE EARLY MORNING AND THE HISTORY OF SHIBUYA, BUT DO THOSE TWO THINGS NOT MESH WITH EACH OTHER?
WHAT KIND OF MATERIAL SHOULD I USE FOR MY MAQUETTE?
I'M JUST ABOUT OUT OF TIME.
...

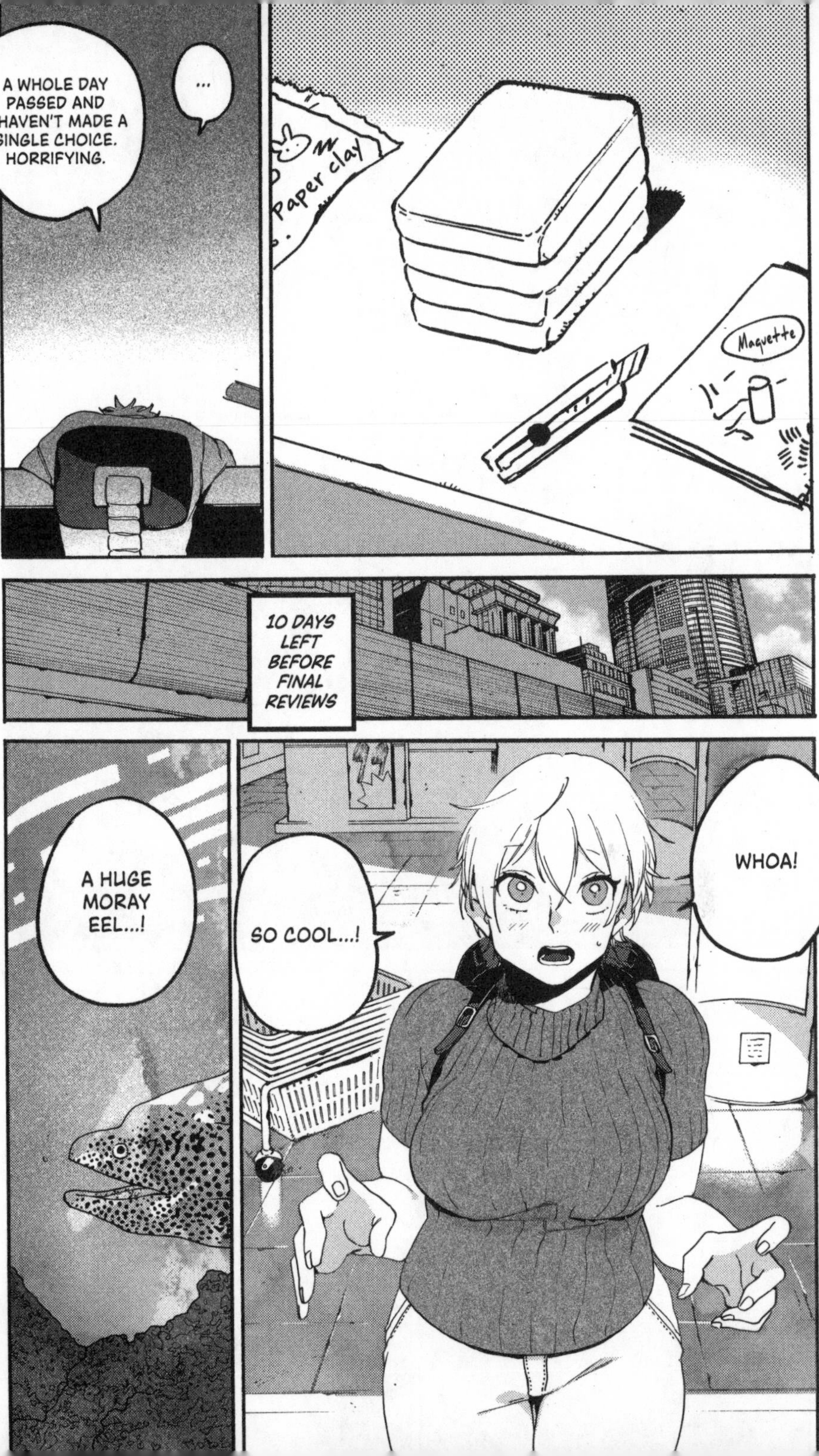
Paper clay
Maquette
...
A WHOLE DAY PASSED AND I HAVEN'T MADE A SINGLE CHOICE. HORRIFYING.
10 DAYS LEFT BEFORE FINAL REVIEWS
WHOA!
SO COOL...!
A HUGE MORAY EEL...!

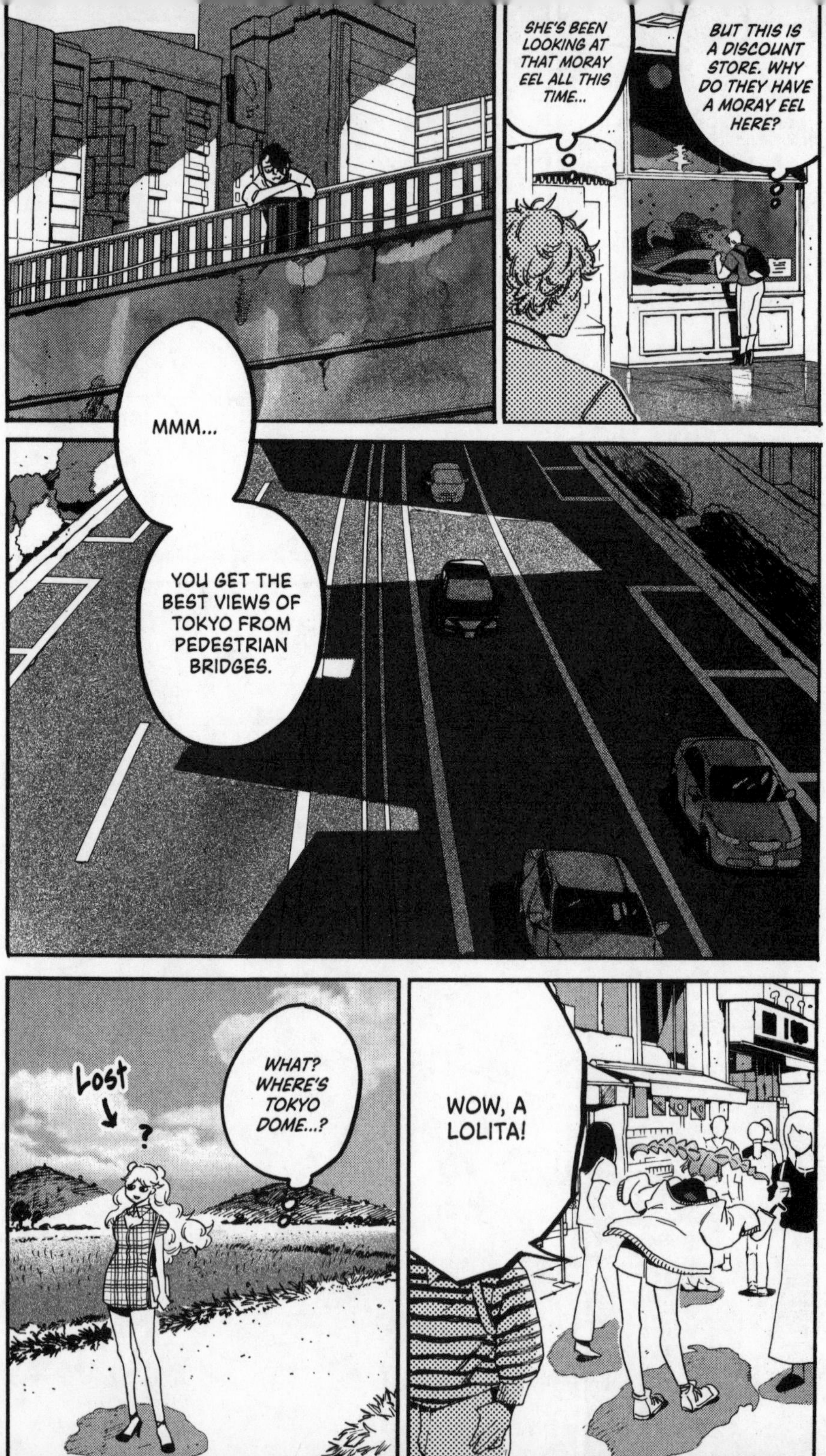
BUT THIS IS A DISCOUNT STORE. WHY DO THEY HAVE A MORAY EEL HERE?
SHE'S BEEN LOOKING AT THAT MORAY EEL ALL THIS TIME...
MMM...
YOU GET THE BEST VIEWS OF TOKYO FROM PEDESTRIAN BRIDGES.
WOW, A LOLITA!
WHAT? WHERE'S TOKYO DOME...?
Lost
?

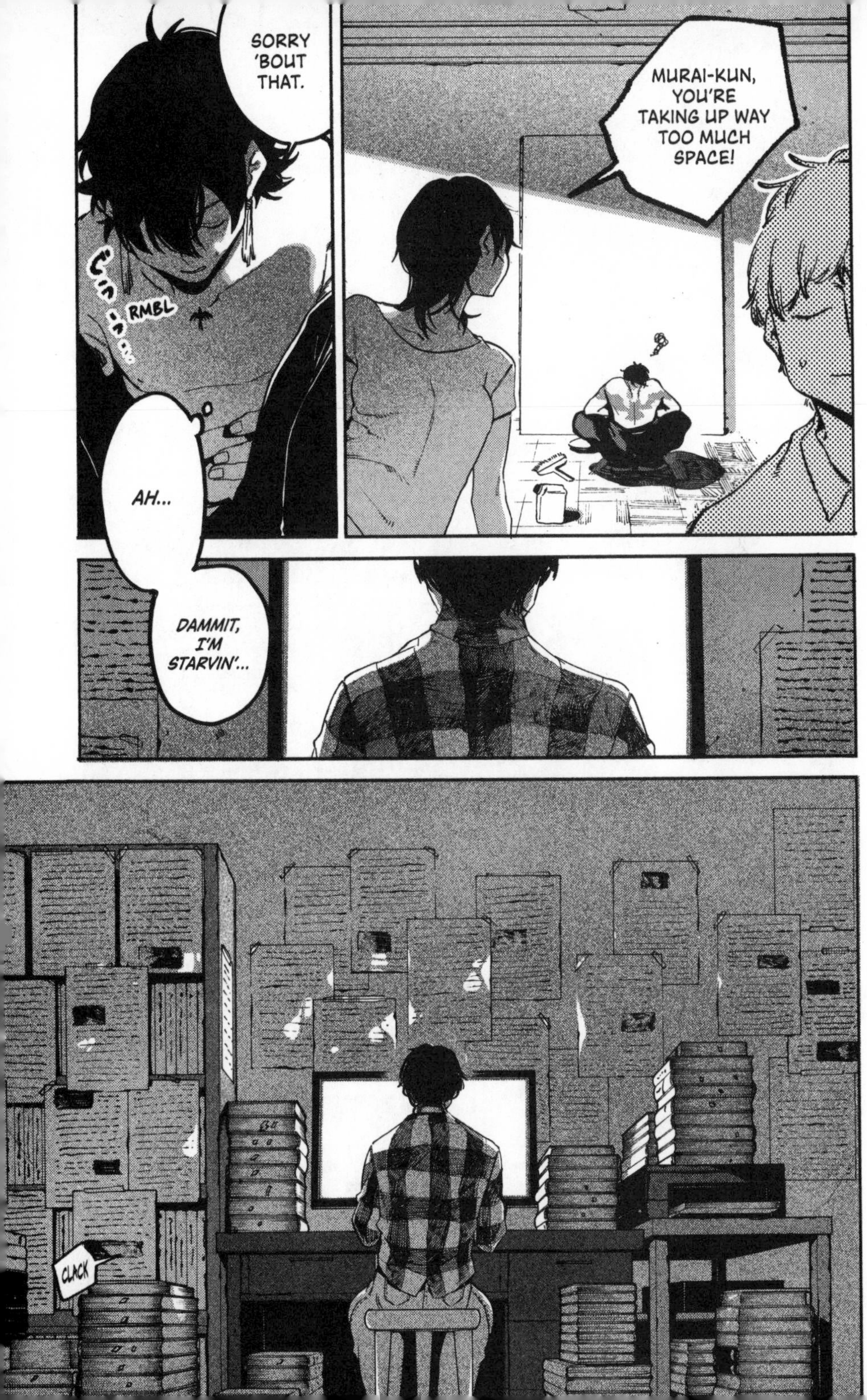
MURAI-KUN, YOU'RE TAKING UP WAY TOO MUCH SPACE!
SORRY 'BOUT THAT.
RMBL
AH...
DAMMIT, I'M STARVIN'...
CLACK

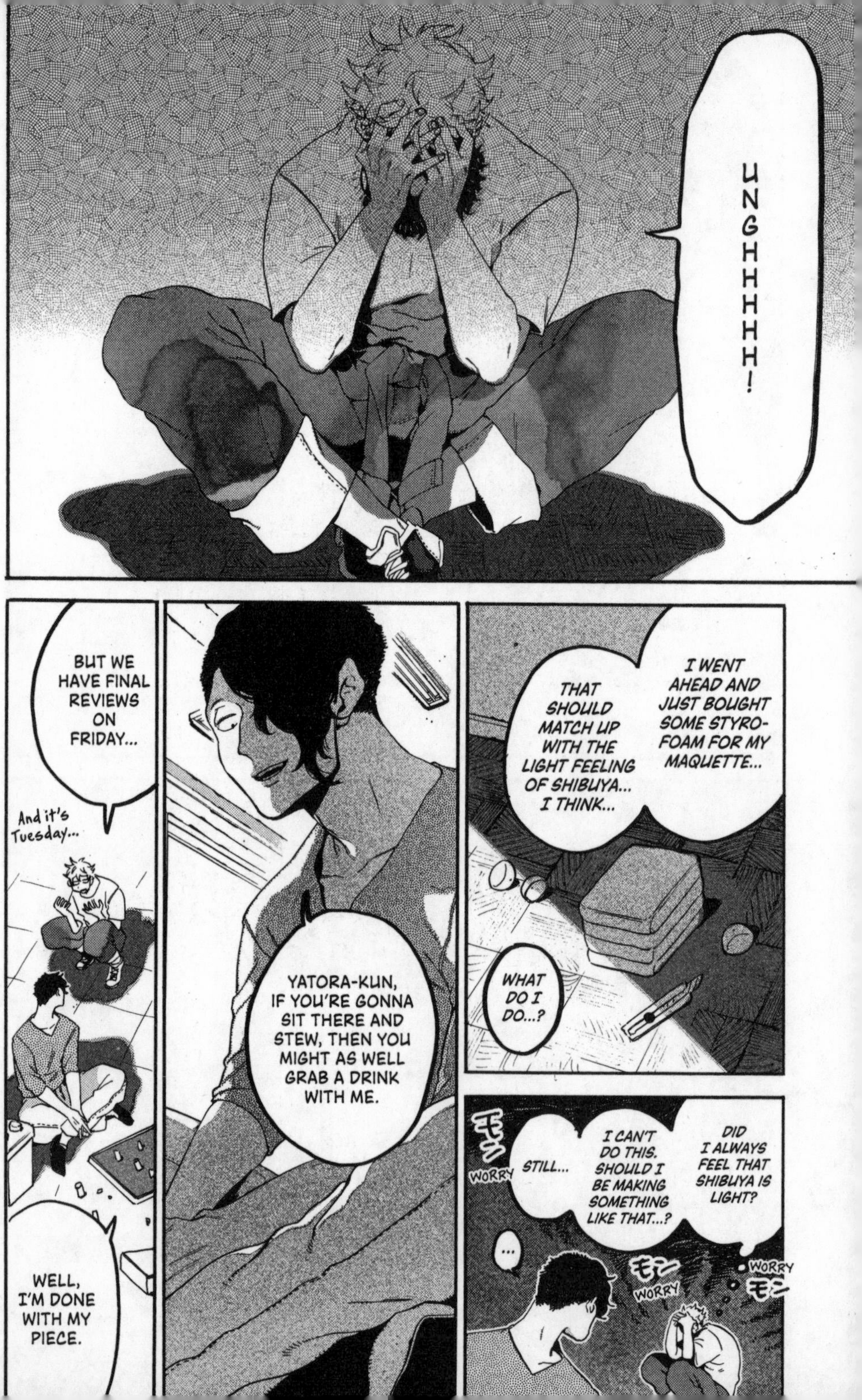
UNGHHHHHH!
I WENT AHEAD AND JUST BOUGHT SOME STYRO-FOAM FOR MY MAQUETTE...
THAT SHOULD MATCH UP WITH THE LIGHT FEELING OF SHIBUYA... I THINK...
WHAT DO I DO...?
DID I ALWAYS FEEL THAT SHIBUYA IS LIGHT?
I CAN'T DO THIS. SHOULD I BE MAKING SOMETHING LIKE THAT...?
STILL...
WORRY
...
WORRY
WORRY
YATORA-KUN, IF YOU'RE GONNA SIT THERE AND STEW, THEN YOU MIGHT AS WELL GRAB A DRINK WITH ME.
BUT WE HAVE FINAL REVIEWS ON FRIDAY...
And it's Tuesday...
WELL, I'M DONE WITH MY PIECE.

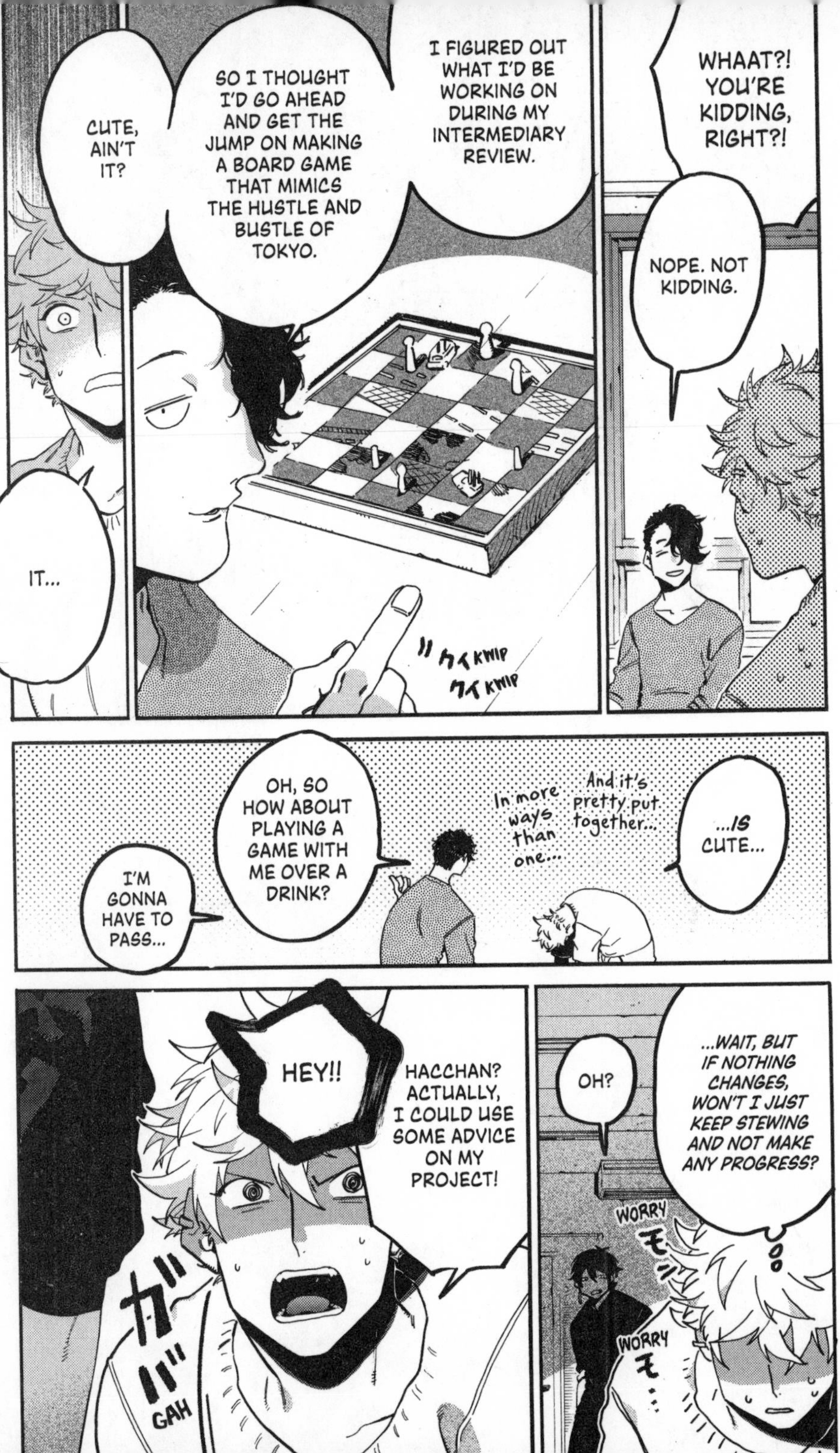
WHAAT?! YOU'RE KIDDING, RIGHT?!
NOPE. NOT KIDDING.
I FIGURED OUT WHAT I'D BE WORKING ON DURING MY INTERMEDIARY REVIEW.
SO I THOUGHT I'D GO AHEAD AND GET THE JUMP ON MAKING A BOARD GAME THAT MIMICS THE HUSTLE AND BUSTLE OF TOKYO.
CUTE, AIN'T IT?
KWIP
KWIP
IT...
...IS CUTE...
And it's pretty put together...
In more ways than one...
OH, SO HOW ABOUT PLAYING A GAME WITH ME OVER A DRINK?
I'M GONNA HAVE TO PASS...
...WAIT, BUT IF NOTHING CHANGES, WON'T I JUST KEEP STEWING AND NOT MAKE ANY PROGRESS?
OH?
WORRY
WORRY
HACCHAN? ACTUALLY, I COULD USE SOME ADVICE ON MY PROJECT!
HEY!!
GAH

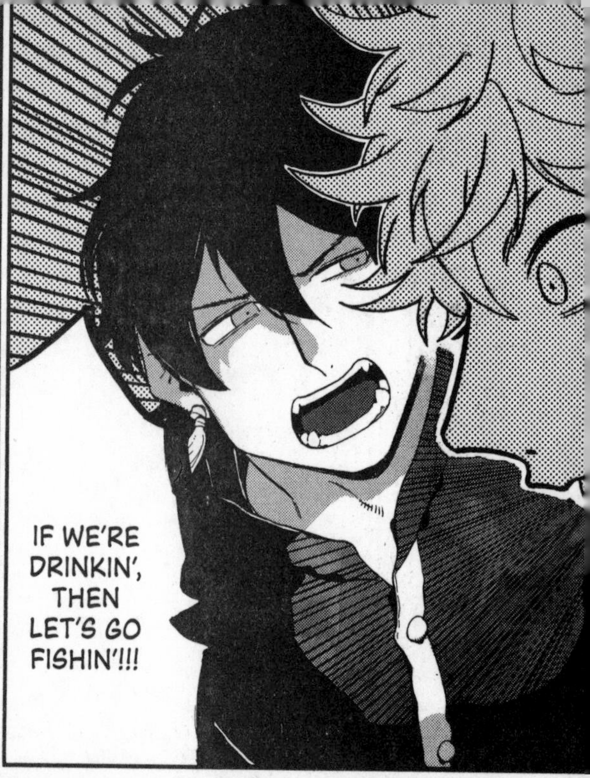
IF WE'RE DRINKIN', THEN LET'S GO FISHIN'!!!
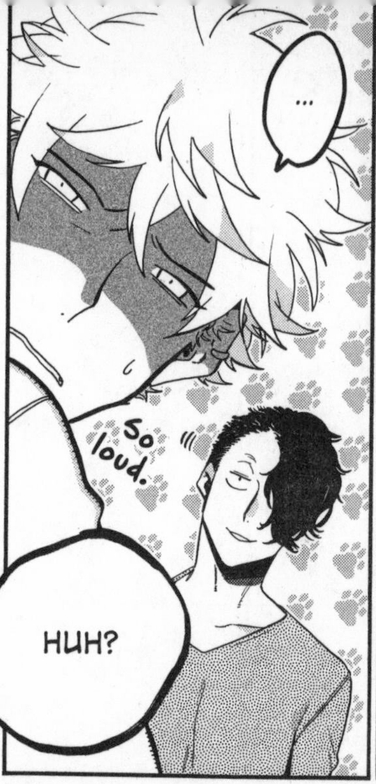
...
So loud.
HUH?
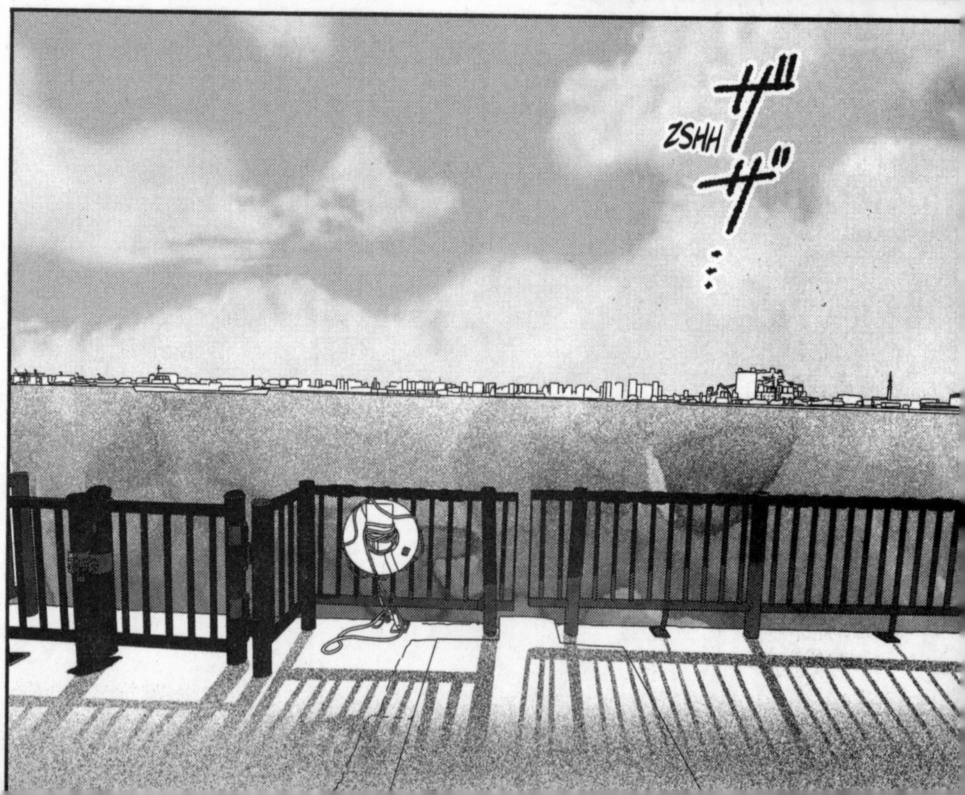
ザザ...
ZSHH

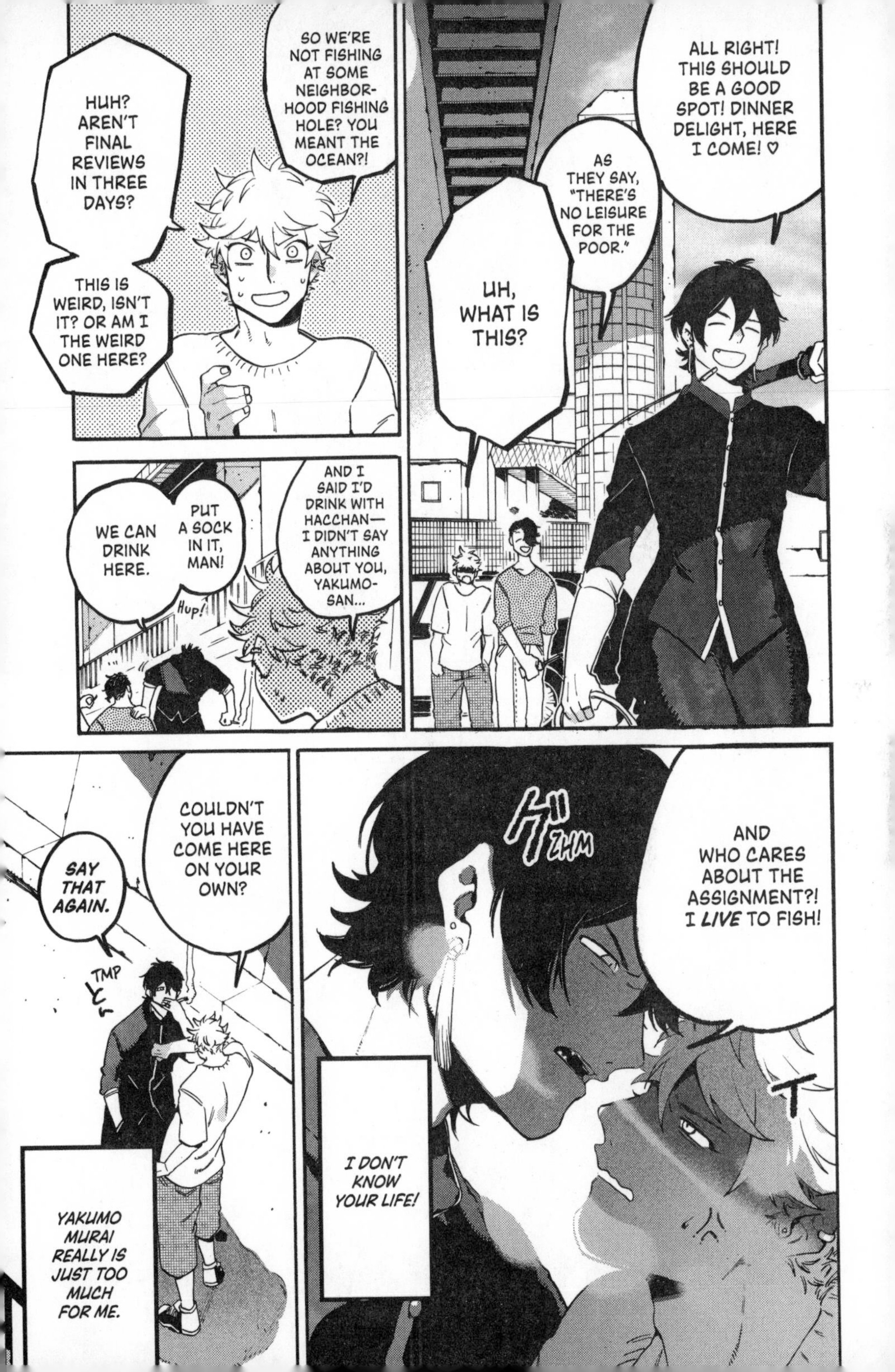
ALL RIGHT! THIS SHOULD BE A GOOD SPOT! DINNER DELIGHT, HERE I COME! ♡
AS THEY SAY, "THERE'S NO LEISURE FOR THE POOR."
UH, WHAT IS THIS?
SO WE'RE NOT FISHING AT SOME NEIGHBOR-HOOD FISHING HOLE? YOU MEANT THE OCEAN?!
HUH? AREN'T FINAL REVIEWS IN THREE DAYS?
THIS IS WEIRD, ISN'T IT? OR AM I THE WEIRD ONE HERE?
AND I SAID I'D DRINK WITH HACCHAN— I DIDN'T SAY ANYTHING ABOUT YOU, YAKUMO-SAN...
PUT A SOCK IN IT, MAN!
WE CAN DRINK HERE.
Hup!
ZHM
AND WHO CARES ABOUT THE ASSIGNMENT?! I *LIVE* TO FISH!
*I DON'T KNOW YOUR LIFE!*
COULDN'T YOU HAVE COME HERE ON YOUR OWN?
*SAY THAT AGAIN.*
TMP
*YAKUMO MURAI REALLY IS JUST TOO MUCH FOR ME.*

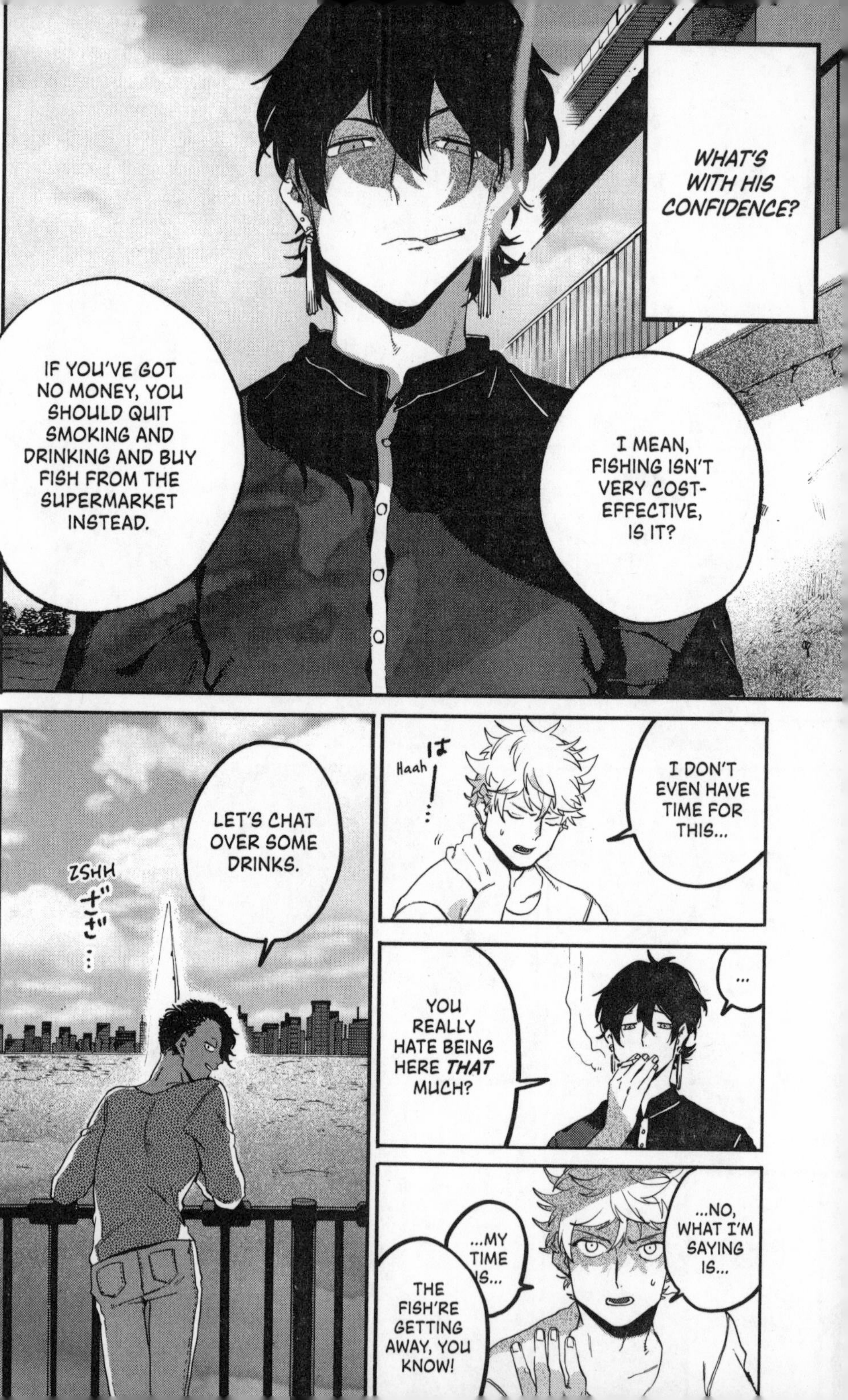
WHAT'S WITH HIS CONFIDENCE?
I MEAN, FISHING ISN'T VERY COST-EFFECTIVE, IS IT?
IF YOU'VE GOT NO MONEY, YOU SHOULD QUIT SMOKING AND DRINKING AND BUY FISH FROM THE SUPERMARKET INSTEAD.
I DON'T EVEN HAVE TIME FOR THIS...
Haah は…
...
YOU REALLY HATE BEING HERE *THAT* MUCH?
...NO, WHAT I'M SAYING IS...
...MY TIME IS...
THE FISH'RE GETTING AWAY, YOU KNOW!
LET'S CHAT OVER SOME DRINKS.
ZSHH ザざ…

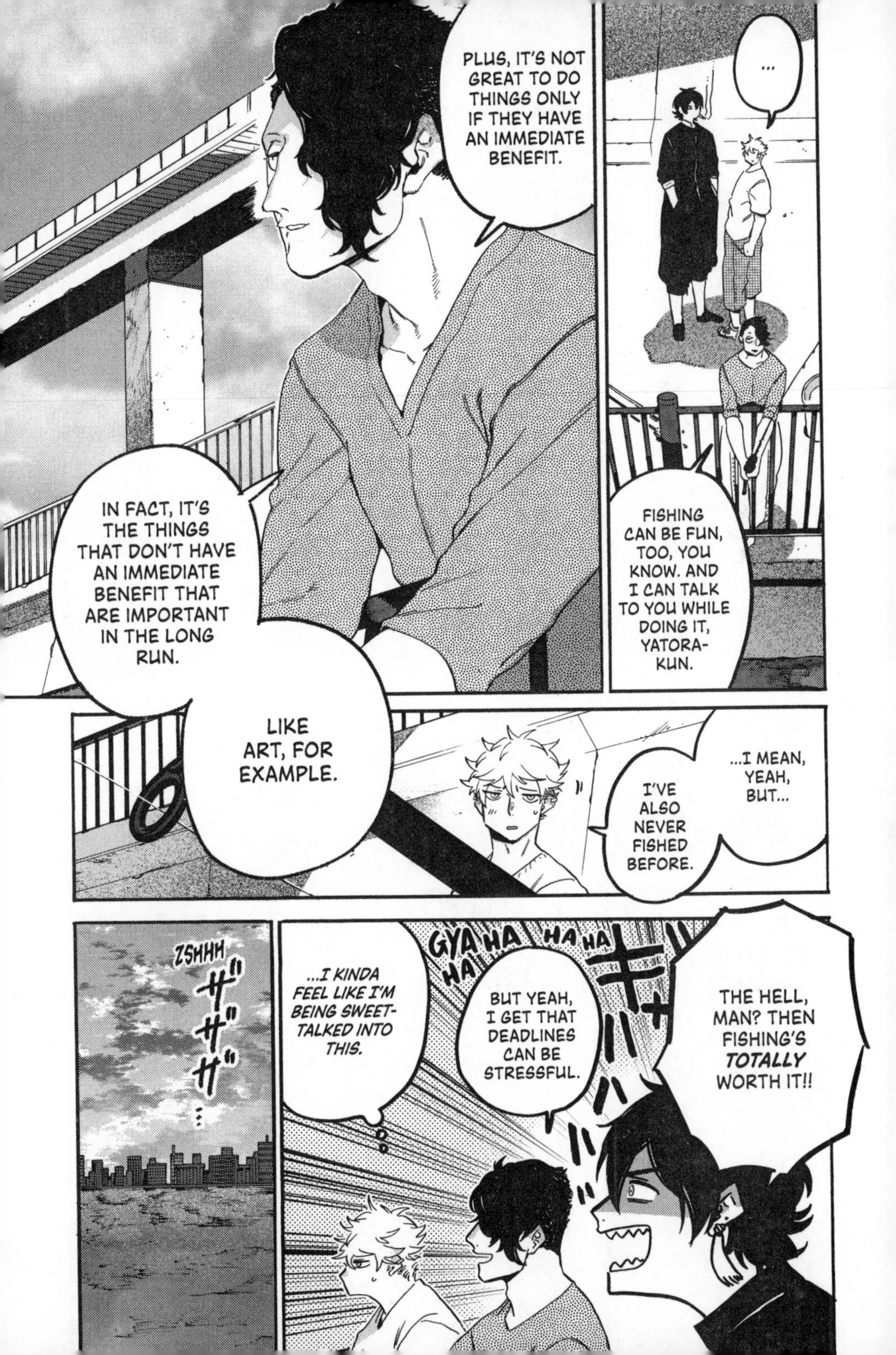
...
FISHING CAN BE FUN, TOO, YOU KNOW. AND I CAN TALK TO YOU WHILE DOING IT, YATORA-KUN.
PLUS, IT'S NOT GREAT TO DO THINGS ONLY IF THEY HAVE AN IMMEDIATE BENEFIT.
IN FACT, IT'S THE THINGS THAT DON'T HAVE AN IMMEDIATE BENEFIT THAT ARE IMPORTANT IN THE LONG RUN.
LIKE ART, FOR EXAMPLE.
...I MEAN, YEAH, BUT...
I'VE ALSO NEVER FISHED BEFORE.
THE HELL, MAN? THEN FISHING'S *TOTALLY* WORTH IT!!
GYA HA HA HA HA
BUT YEAH, I GET THAT DEADLINES CAN BE STRESSFUL.
*...I KINDA FEEL LIKE I'M BEING SWEET-TALKED INTO THIS.*
ZSHHH

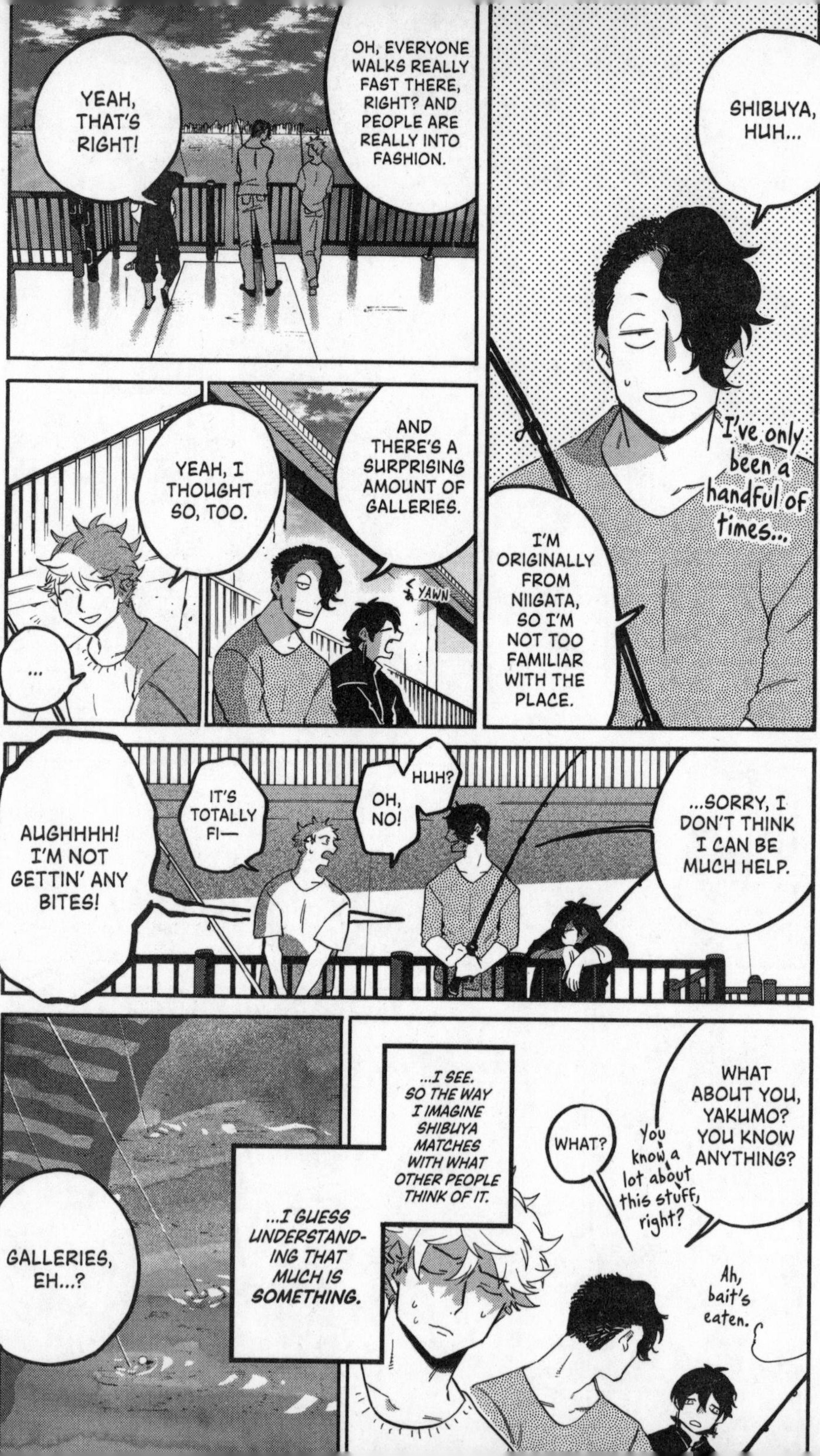
SHIBUYA, HUH...
I've only been a handful of times...
I'M ORIGINALLY FROM NIIGATA, SO I'M NOT TOO FAMILIAR WITH THE PLACE.
OH, EVERYONE WALKS REALLY FAST THERE, RIGHT? AND PEOPLE ARE REALLY INTO FASHION.
YEAH, THAT'S RIGHT!
AND THERE'S A SURPRISING AMOUNT OF GALLERIES.
YAWN
YEAH, I THOUGHT SO, TOO.
...
...SORRY, I DON'T THINK I CAN BE MUCH HELP.
HUH?
OH, NO!
IT'S TOTALLY FI—
AUGHHHH! I'M NOT GETTIN' ANY BITES!
WHAT ABOUT YOU, YAKUMO? YOU KNOW ANYTHING?
You know a lot about this stuff, right?
WHAT?
...I SEE. SO THE WAY I IMAGINE SHIBUYA MATCHES WITH WHAT OTHER PEOPLE THINK OF IT.
...I GUESS UNDERSTANDING THAT MUCH IS SOMETHING.
Ah, bait's eaten.
GALLERIES, EH...?

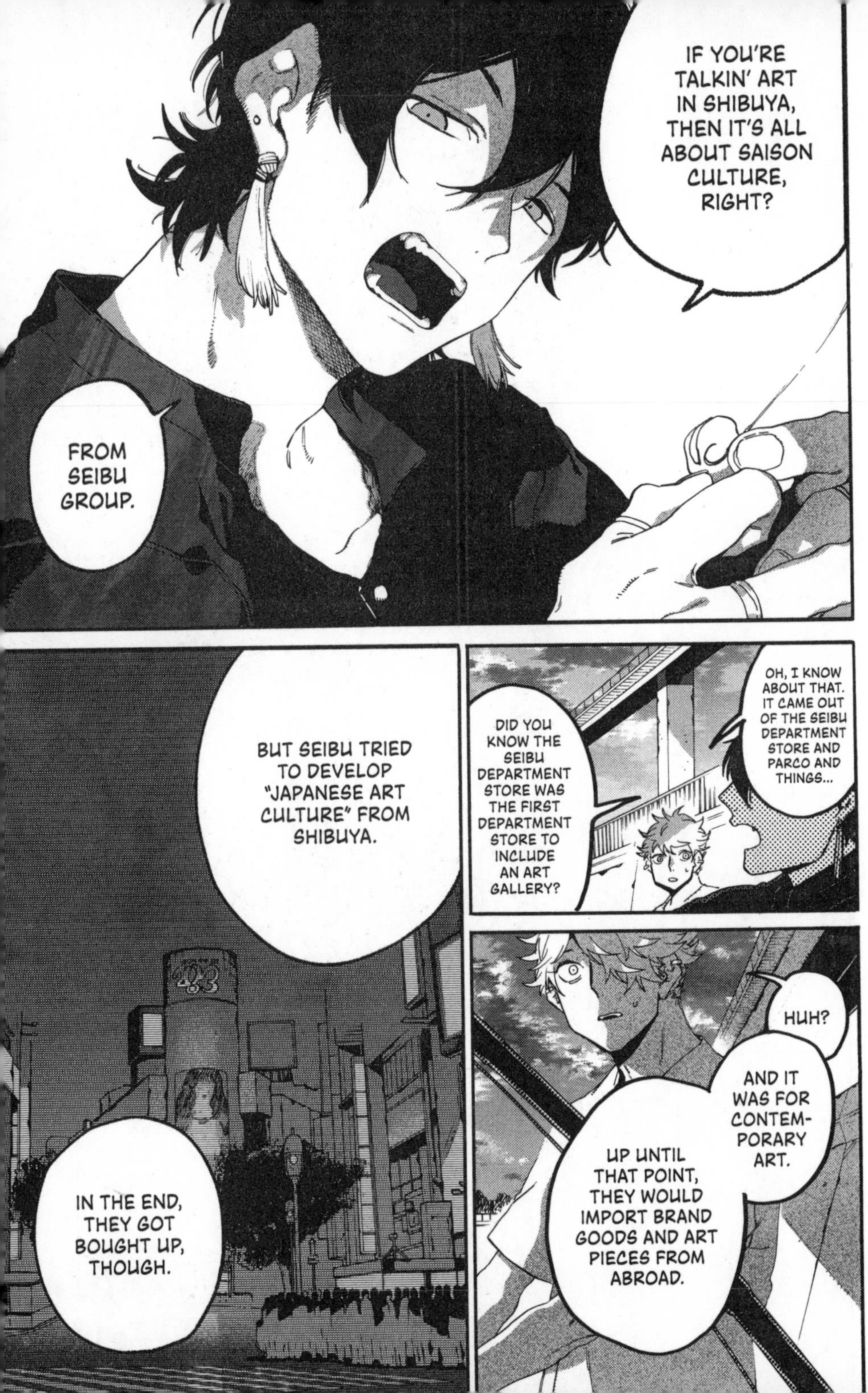
IF YOU'RE TALKIN' ART IN SHIBUYA, THEN IT'S ALL ABOUT SAISON CULTURE, RIGHT?
FROM SEIBU GROUP.
OH, I KNOW ABOUT THAT. IT CAME OUT OF THE SEIBU DEPARTMENT STORE AND PARCO AND THINGS...
DID YOU KNOW THE SEIBU DEPARTMENT STORE WAS THE FIRST DEPARTMENT STORE TO INCLUDE AN ART GALLERY?
HUH?
AND IT WAS FOR CONTEM-PORARY ART.
UP UNTIL THAT POINT, THEY WOULD IMPORT BRAND GOODS AND ART PIECES FROM ABROAD.
BUT SEIBU TRIED TO DEVELOP "JAPANESE ART CULTURE" FROM SHIBUYA.
IN THE END, THEY GOT BOUGHT UP, THOUGH.

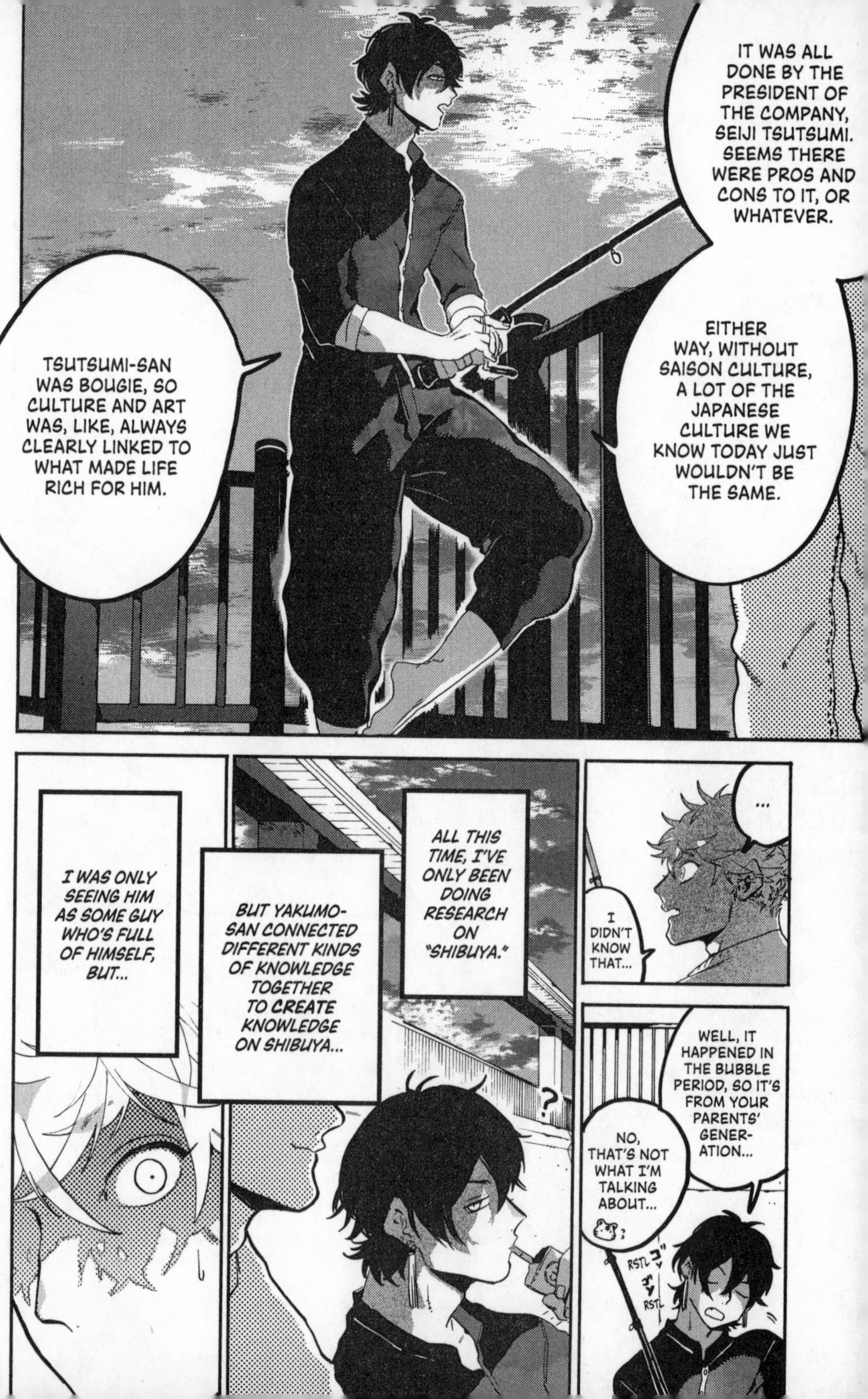

IT WAS ALL DONE BY THE PRESIDENT OF THE COMPANY, SEIJI TSUTSUMI. SEEMS THERE WERE PROS AND CONS TO IT, OR WHATEVER.
EITHER WAY, WITHOUT SAISON CULTURE, A LOT OF THE JAPANESE CULTURE WE KNOW TODAY JUST WOULDN'T BE THE SAME.
TSUTSUMI-SAN WAS BOUGIE, SO CULTURE AND ART WAS, LIKE, ALWAYS CLEARLY LINKED TO WHAT MADE LIFE RICH FOR HIM.
...
I DIDN'T KNOW THAT...
WELL, IT HAPPENED IN THE BUBBLE PERIOD, SO IT'S FROM YOUR PARENTS' GENERATION...
NO, THAT'S NOT WHAT I'M TALKING ABOUT...
RSTL
RSTL
ALL THIS TIME, I'VE ONLY BEEN DOING RESEARCH ON "SHIBUYA."
BUT YAKUMO-SAN CONNECTED DIFFERENT KINDS OF KNOWLEDGE TOGETHER TO CREATE KNOWLEDGE ON SHIBUYA...
I WAS ONLY SEEING HIM AS SOME GUY WHO'S FULL OF HIMSELF, BUT...
?

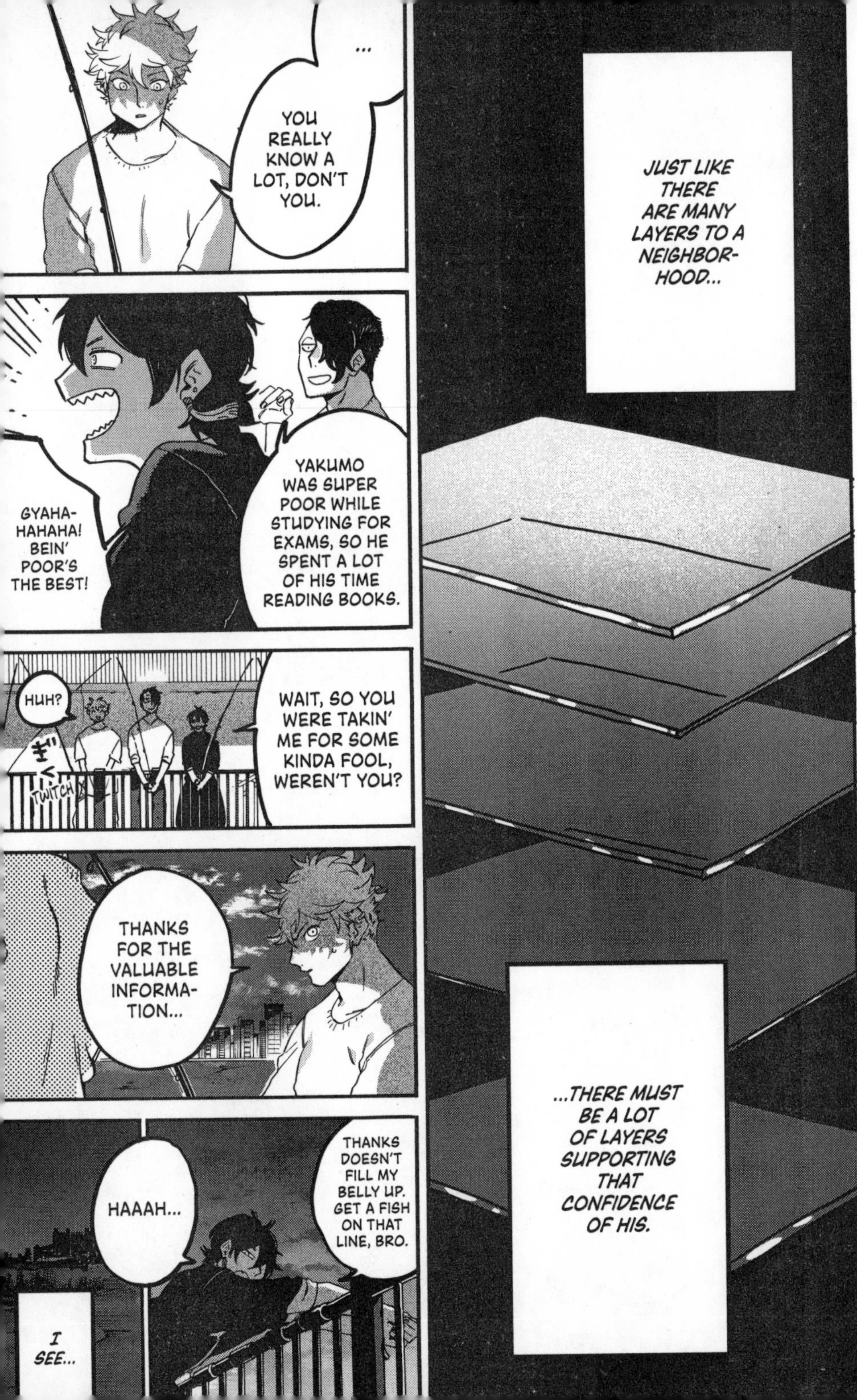

JUST LIKE THERE ARE MANY LAYERS TO A NEIGHBOR-HOOD...
...THERE MUST BE A LOT OF LAYERS SUPPORTING THAT CONFIDENCE OF HIS.
...
YOU REALLY KNOW A LOT, DON'T YOU.
YAKUMO WAS SUPER POOR WHILE STUDYING FOR EXAMS, SO HE SPENT A LOT OF HIS TIME READING BOOKS.
GYAHA-HAHAHA! BEIN' POOR'S THE BEST!
WAIT, SO YOU WERE TAKIN' ME FOR SOME KINDA FOOL, WEREN'T YOU?
HUH?
TWITCH
THANKS FOR THE VALUABLE INFORMA-TION...
THANKS DOESN'T FILL MY BELLY UP. GET A FISH ON THAT LINE, BRO.
HAAAH...
I SEE...

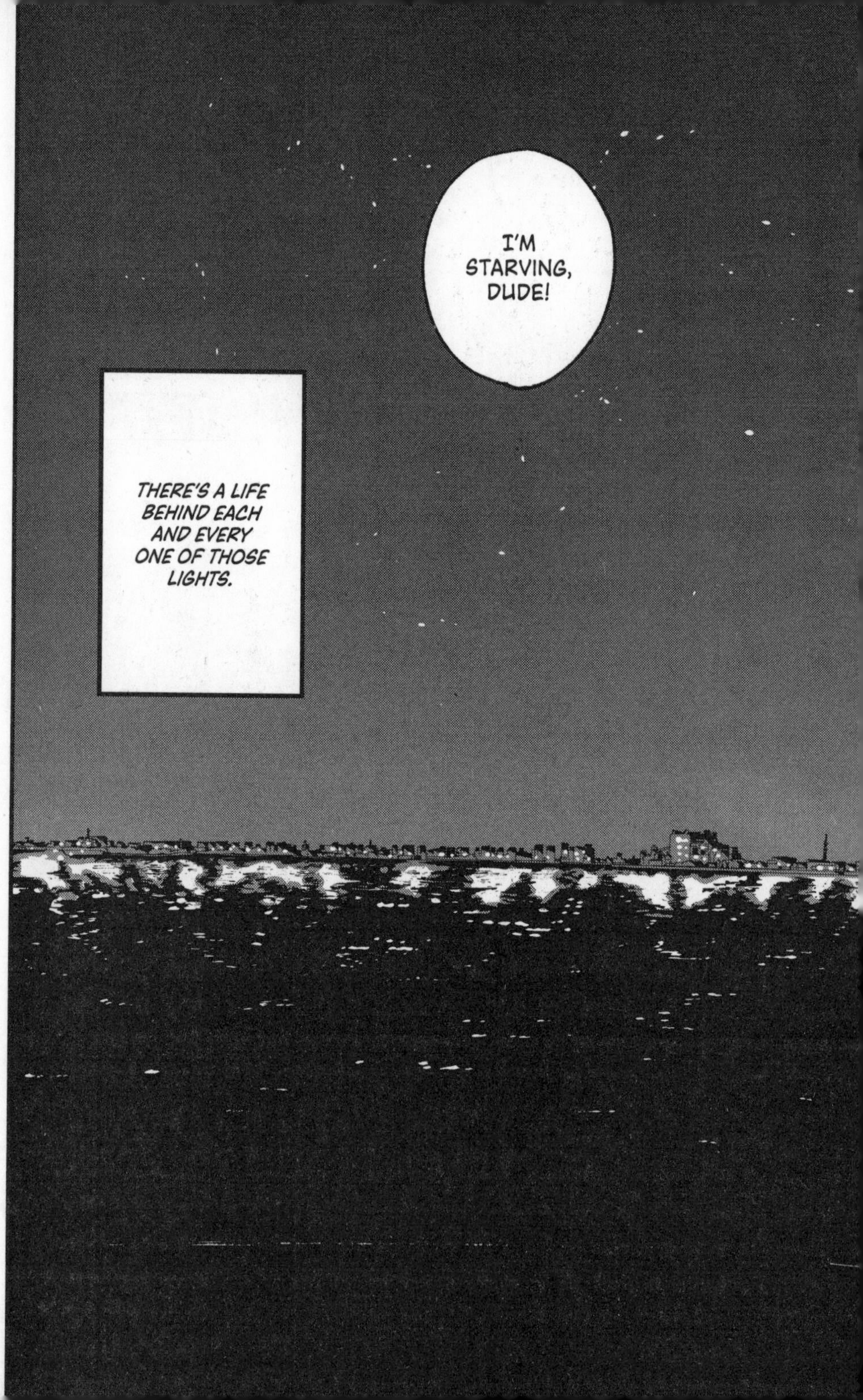
I'M STARVING, DUDE!
THERE'S A LIFE BEHIND EACH AND EVERY ONE OF THOSE LIGHTS.

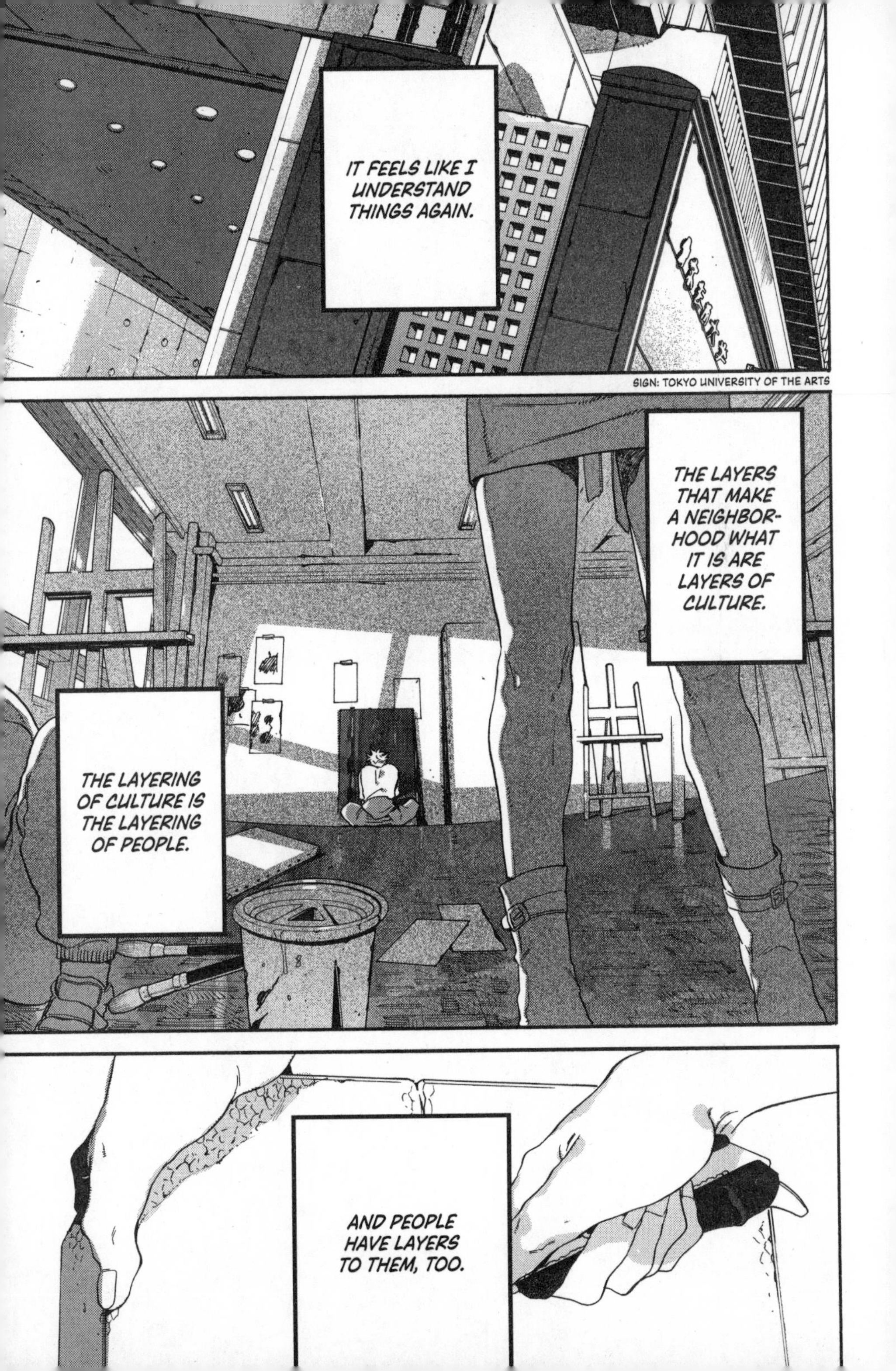
IT FEELS LIKE I UNDERSTAND THINGS AGAIN.
SIGN: TOKYO UNIVERSITY OF THE ARTS
THE LAYERS THAT MAKE A NEIGHBOR-HOOD WHAT IT IS ARE LAYERS OF CULTURE.
THE LAYERING OF CULTURE IS THE LAYERING OF PEOPLE.
AND PEOPLE HAVE LAYERS TO THEM, TOO.

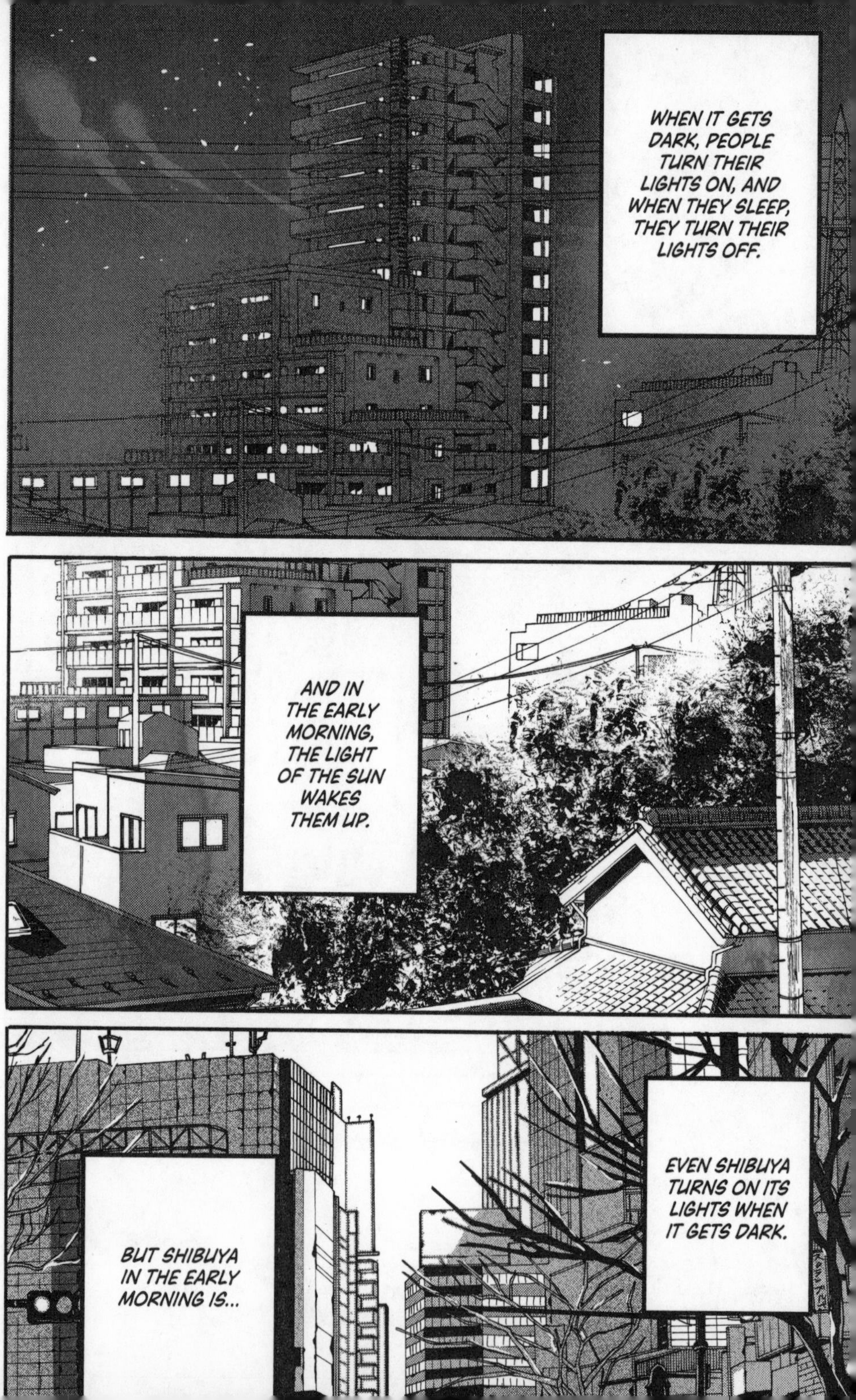
WHEN IT GETS DARK, PEOPLE TURN THEIR LIGHTS ON, AND WHEN THEY SLEEP, THEY TURN THEIR LIGHTS OFF.
AND IN THE EARLY MORNING, THE LIGHT OF THE SUN WAKES THEM UP.
EVEN SHIBUYA TURNS ON ITS LIGHTS WHEN IT GETS DARK.
BUT SHIBUYA IN THE EARLY MORNING IS...

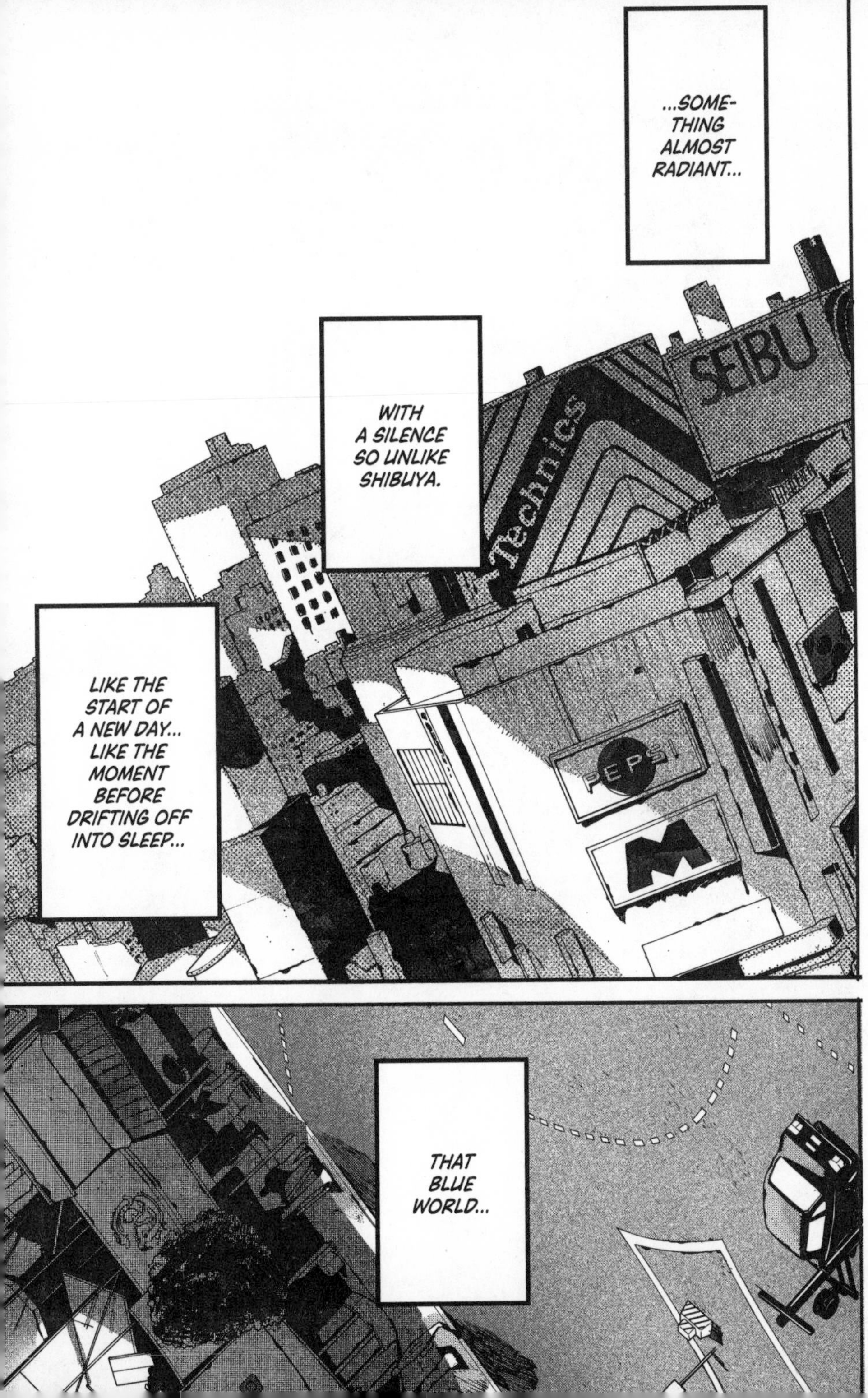
...SOME-THING ALMOST RADIANT...
SEIBU
WITH A SILENCE SO UNLIKE SHIBUYA.
Technics
PEPSI
LIKE THE START OF A NEW DAY... LIKE THE MOMENT BEFORE DRIFTING OFF INTO SLEEP...
THAT BLUE WORLD...

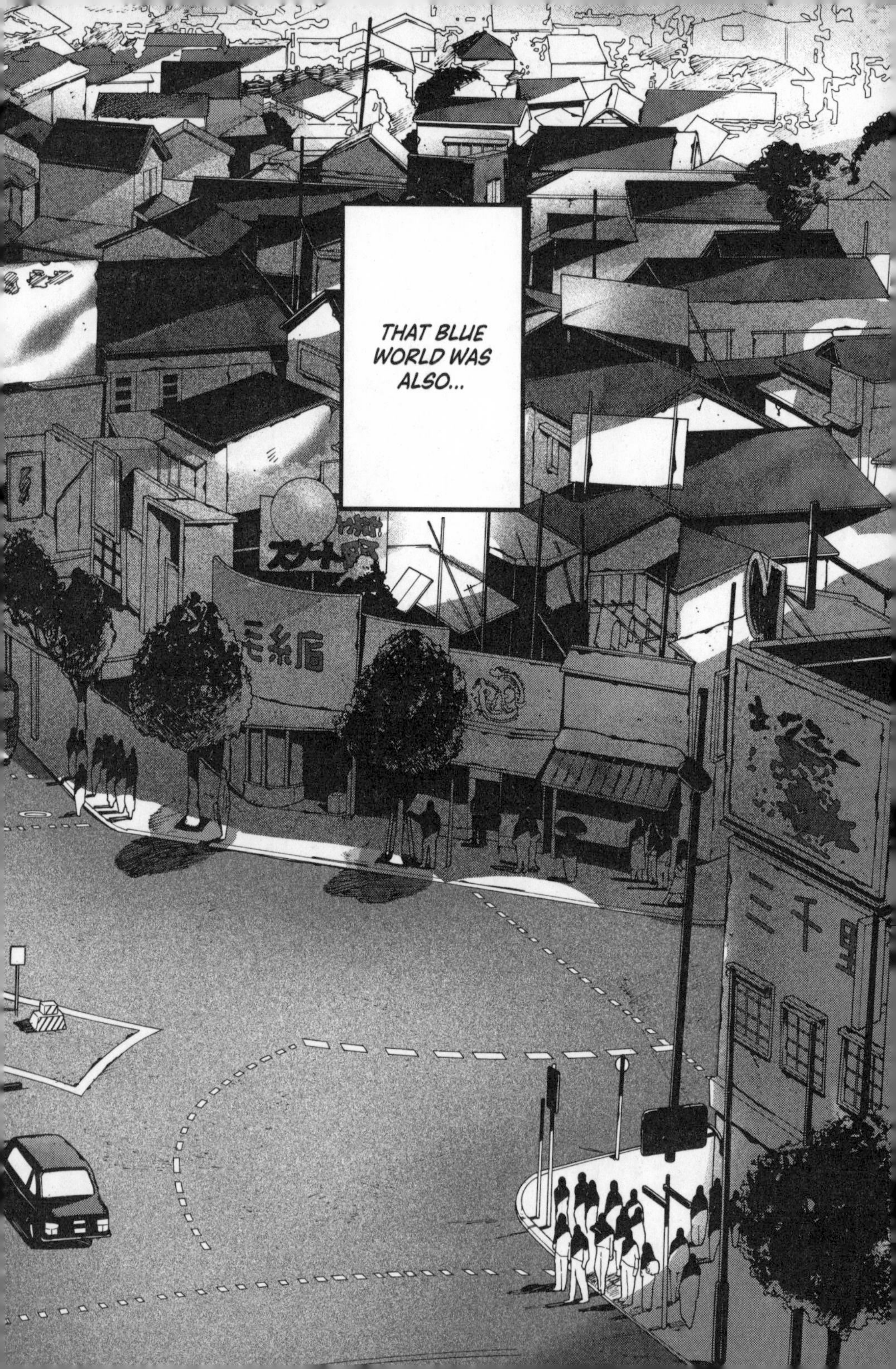
THAT BLUE WORLD WAS ALSO...

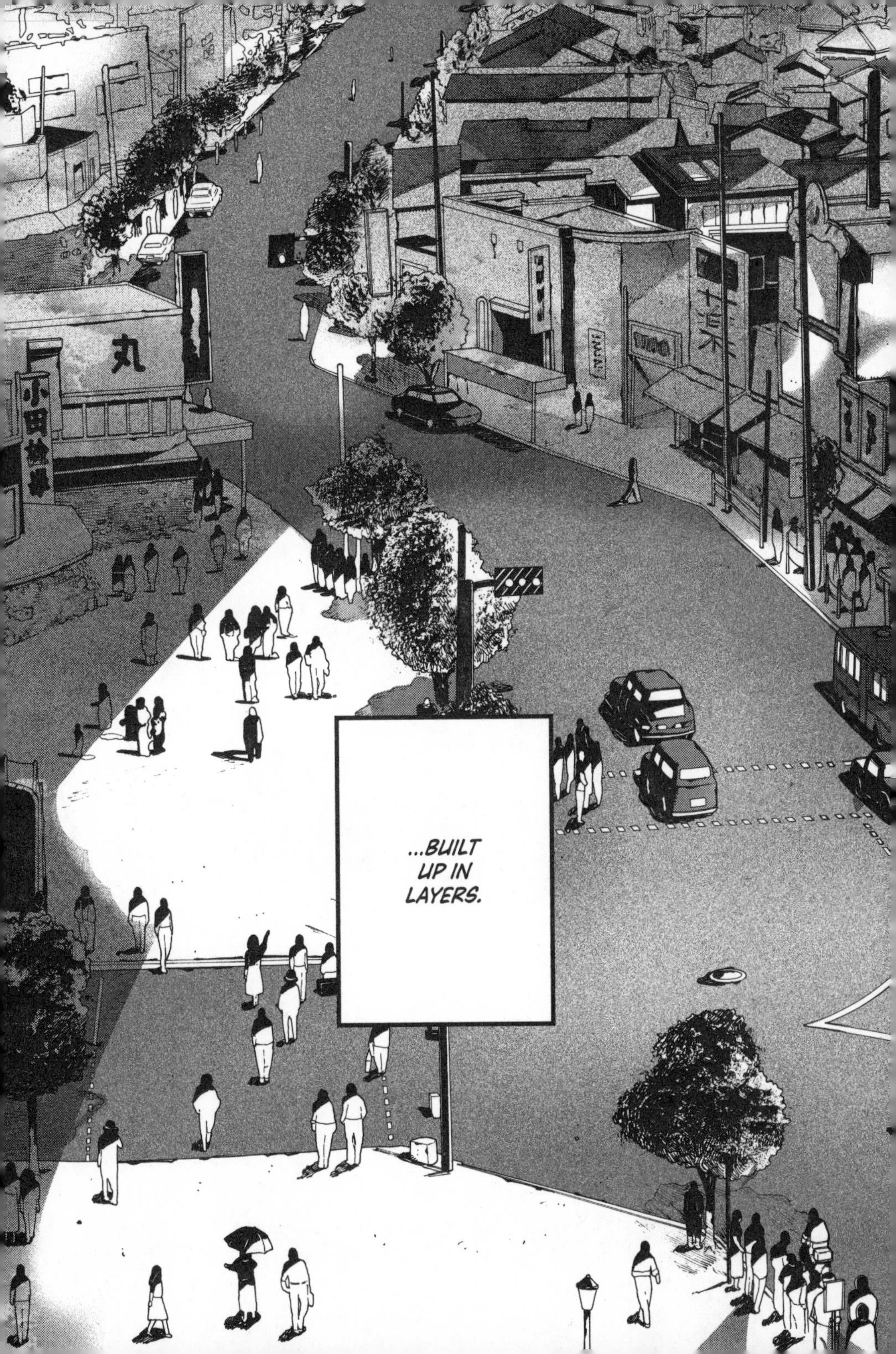
...BUILT UP IN LAYERS.

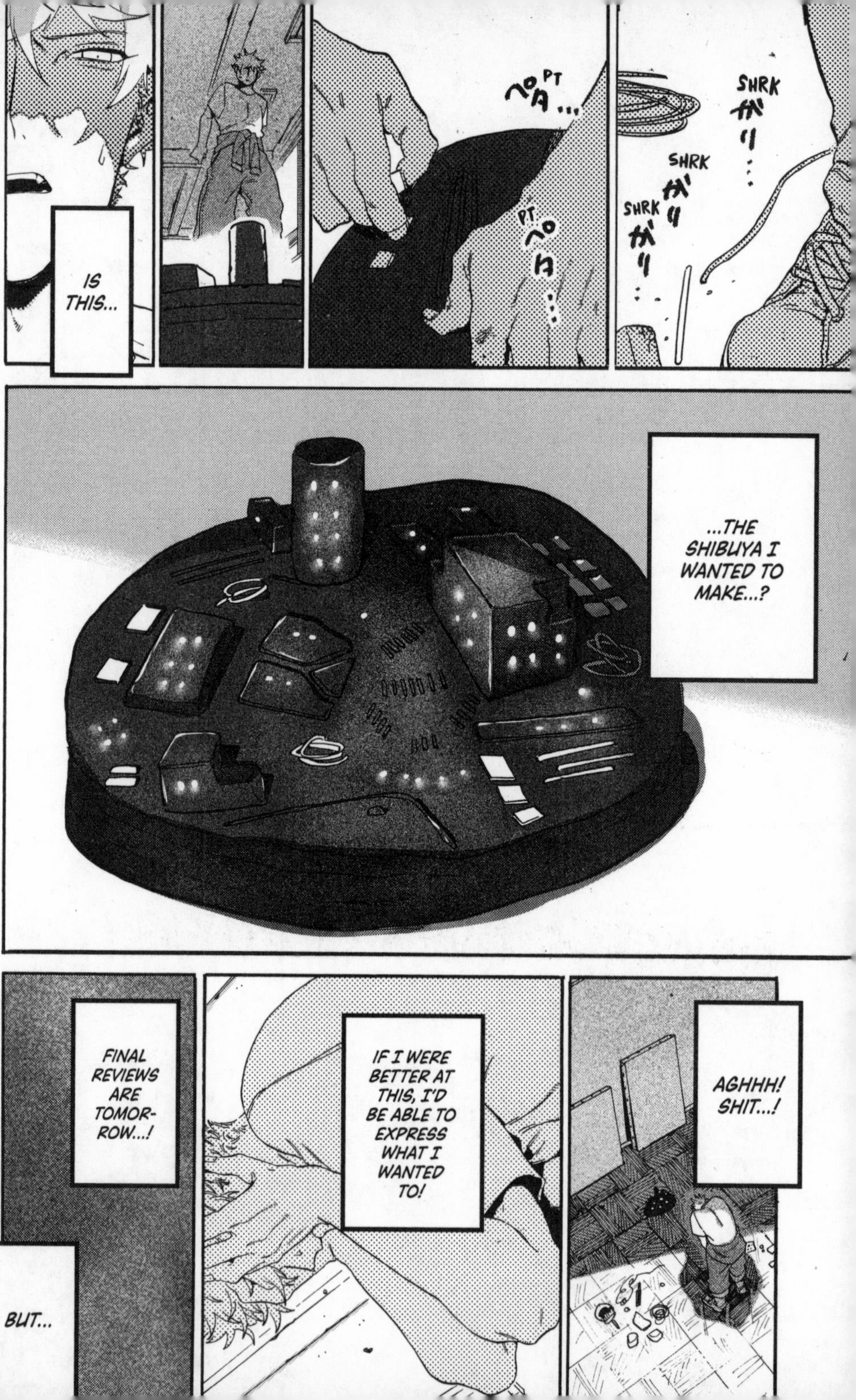
SHRK
がり…
SHRK
がり
SHRK
がり…
PT
ぺた…
PT
ぺた…
IS THIS...
...THE SHIBUYA I WANTED TO MAKE...?
AGHHH! SHIT...!
IF I WERE BETTER AT THIS, I'D BE ABLE TO EXPRESS WHAT I WANTED TO!
FINAL REVIEWS ARE TOMOR-ROW...!
BUT...

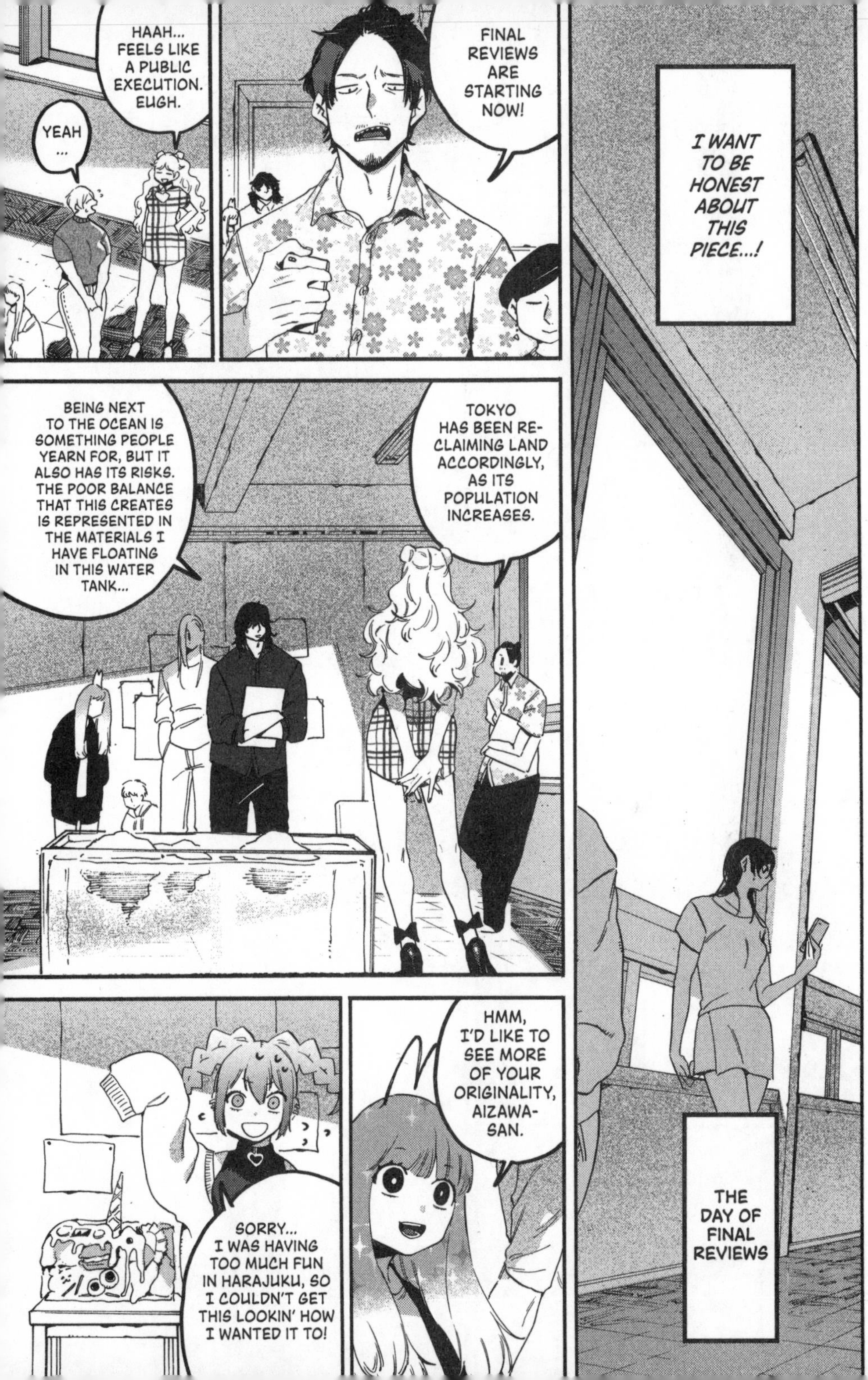
I WANT TO BE HONEST ABOUT THIS PIECE...!
THE DAY OF FINAL REVIEWS
FINAL REVIEWS ARE STARTING NOW!
HAAH... FEELS LIKE A PUBLIC EXECUTION. EUGH.
YEAH ...
BEING NEXT TO THE OCEAN IS SOMETHING PEOPLE YEARN FOR, BUT IT ALSO HAS ITS RISKS. THE POOR BALANCE THAT THIS CREATES IS REPRESENTED IN THE MATERIALS I HAVE FLOATING IN THIS WATER TANK...
TOKYO HAS BEEN RE-CLAIMING LAND ACCORDINGLY, AS ITS POPULATION INCREASES.
HMM, I'D LIKE TO SEE MORE OF YOUR ORIGINALITY, AIZAWA-SAN.
SORRY... I WAS HAVING TOO MUCH FUN IN HARAJUKU, SO I COULDN'T GET THIS LOOKIN' HOW I WANTED IT TO!

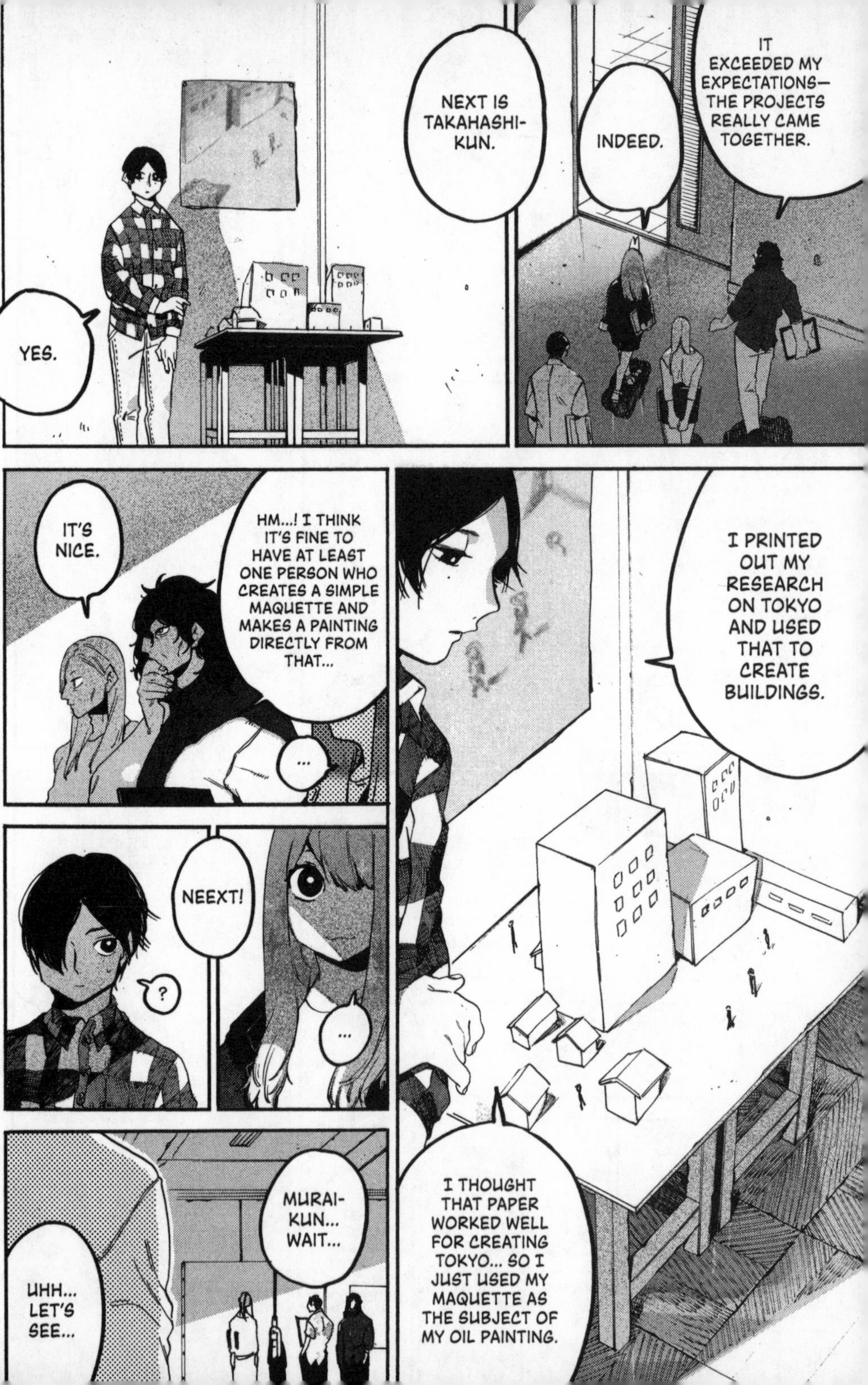
IT EXCEEDED MY EXPECTATIONS—THE PROJECTS REALLY CAME TOGETHER.
INDEED.
NEXT IS TAKAHASHI-KUN.
YES.
I PRINTED OUT MY RESEARCH ON TOKYO AND USED THAT TO CREATE BUILDINGS.
I THOUGHT THAT PAPER WORKED WELL FOR CREATING TOKYO... SO I JUST USED MY MAQUETTE AS THE SUBJECT OF MY OIL PAINTING.
HM...! I THINK IT'S FINE TO HAVE AT LEAST ONE PERSON WHO CREATES A SIMPLE MAQUETTE AND MAKES A PAINTING DIRECTLY FROM THAT...
IT'S NICE.
...
NEEXT!
...
?
MURAI-KUN... WAIT...
UHH... LET'S SEE...

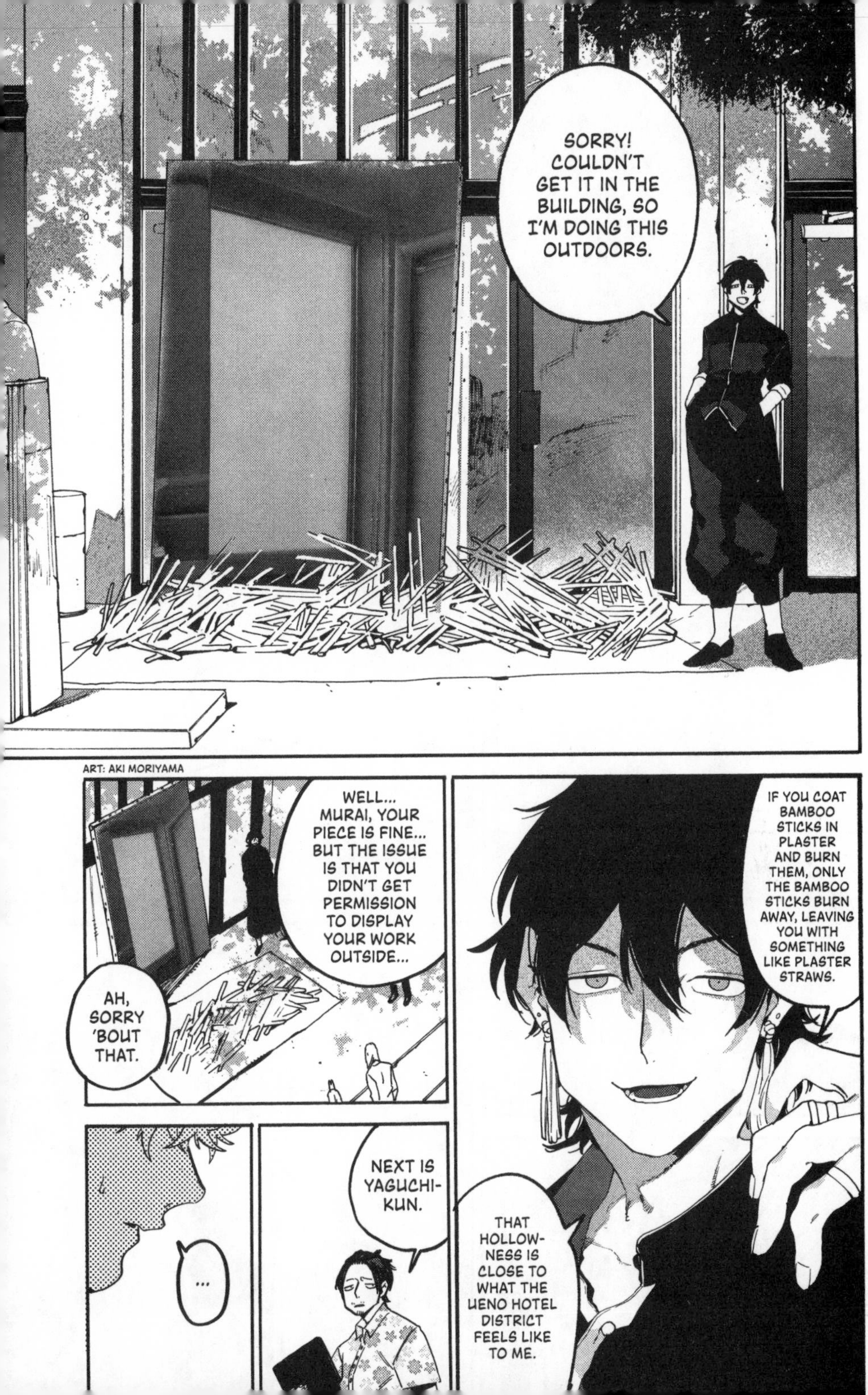
SORRY! COULDN'T GET IT IN THE BUILDING, SO I'M DOING THIS OUTDOORS.
ART: AKI MORIYAMA
IF YOU COAT BAMBOO STICKS IN PLASTER AND BURN THEM, ONLY THE BAMBOO STICKS BURN AWAY, LEAVING YOU WITH SOMETHING LIKE PLASTER STRAWS.
THAT HOLLOWNESS IS CLOSE TO WHAT THE UENO HOTEL DISTRICT FEELS LIKE TO ME.
WELL... MURAI, YOUR PIECE IS FINE... BUT THE ISSUE IS THAT YOU DIDN'T GET PERMISSION TO DISPLAY YOUR WORK OUTSIDE...
AH, SORRY 'BOUT THAT.
NEXT IS YAGUCHI-KUN.
...

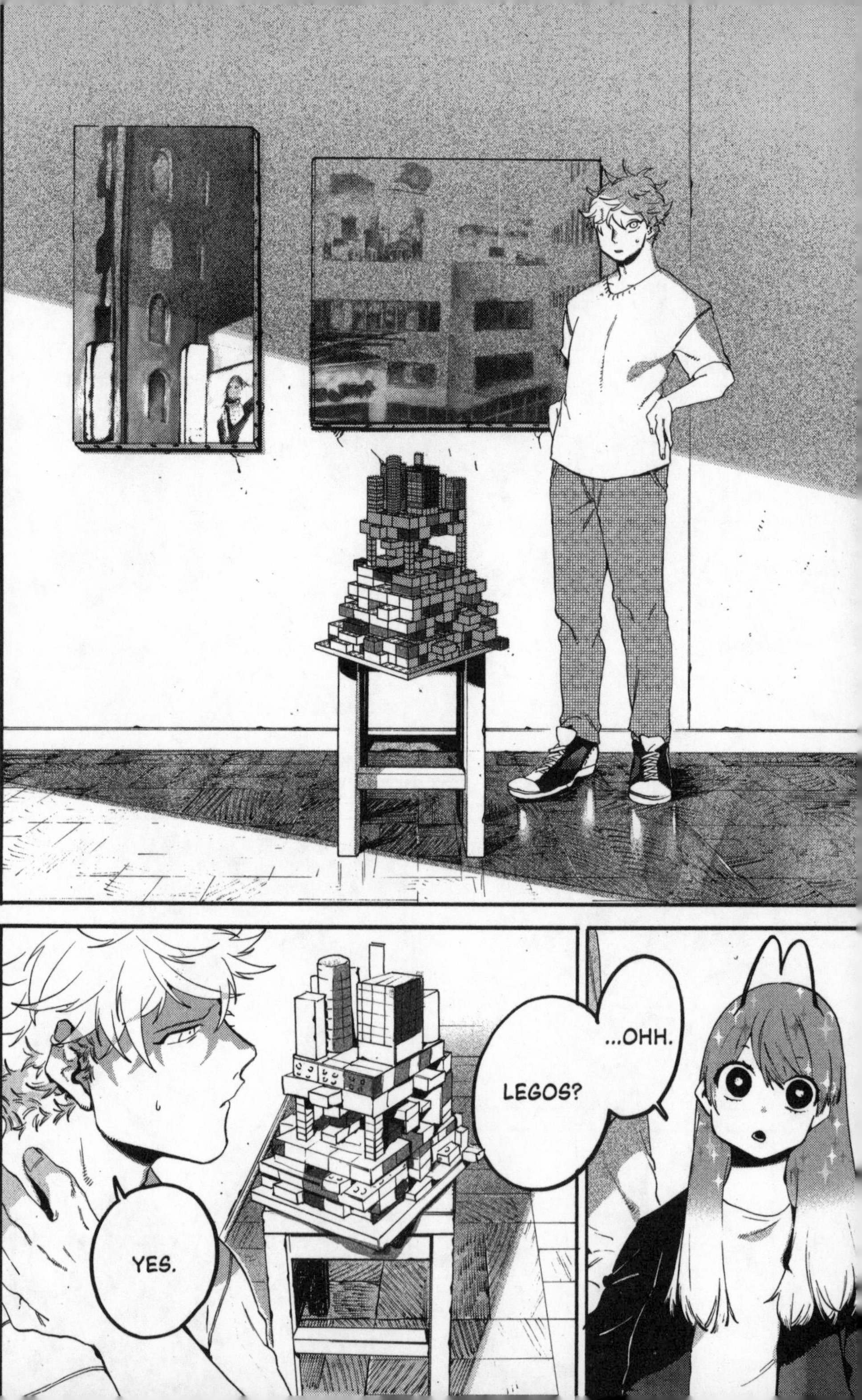
...OHH.
LEGOS?
YES.

ART: TAMANA MOTEKI

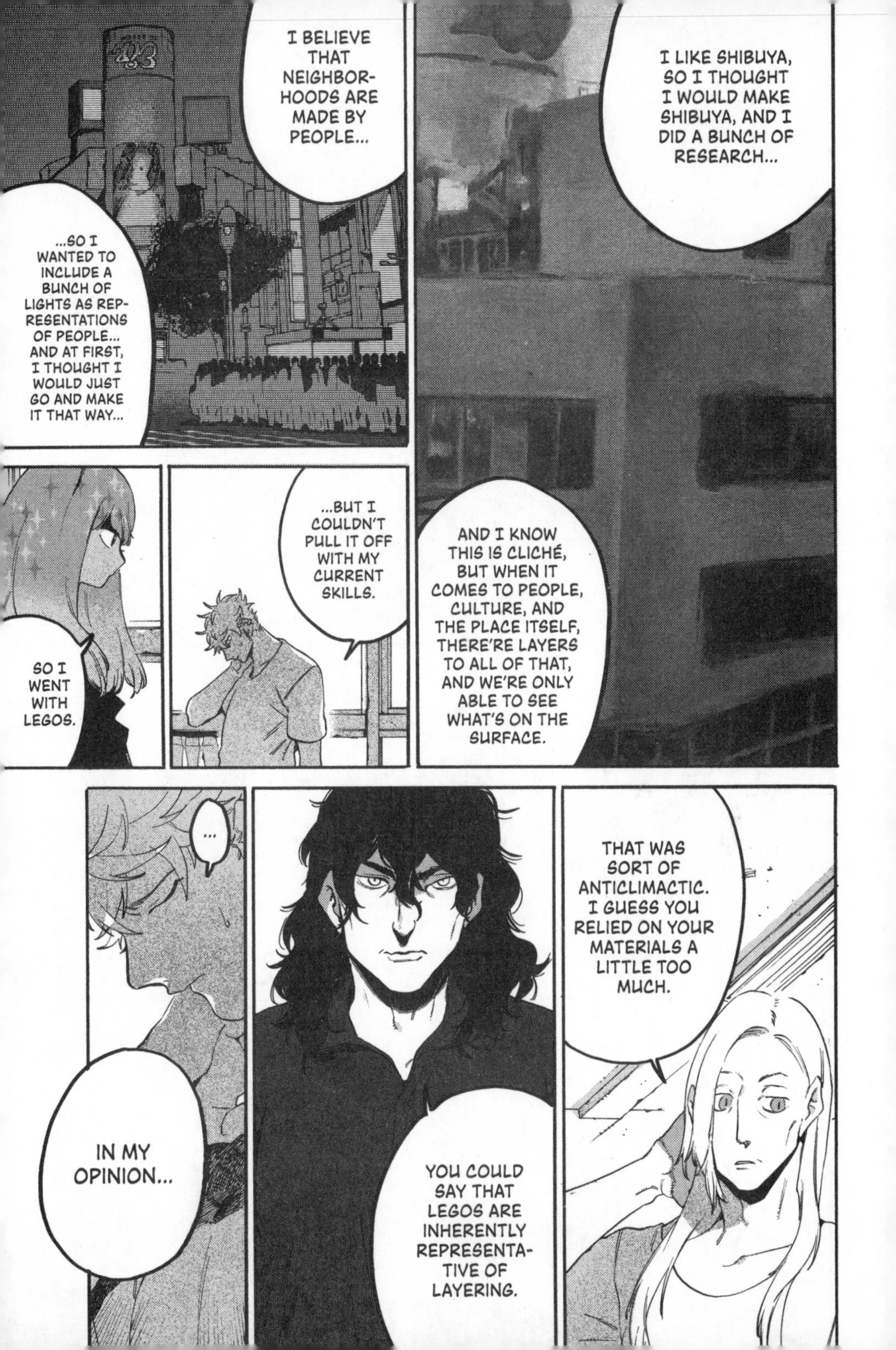
I LIKE SHIBUYA, SO I THOUGHT I WOULD MAKE SHIBUYA, AND I DID A BUNCH OF RESEARCH...
AND I KNOW THIS IS CLICHÉ, BUT WHEN IT COMES TO PEOPLE, CULTURE, AND THE PLACE ITSELF, THERE'RE LAYERS TO ALL OF THAT, AND WE'RE ONLY ABLE TO SEE WHAT'S ON THE SURFACE.
I BELIEVE THAT NEIGHBOR-HOODS ARE MADE BY PEOPLE...
...SO I WANTED TO INCLUDE A BUNCH OF LIGHTS AS REP-RESENTATIONS OF PEOPLE... AND AT FIRST, I THOUGHT I WOULD JUST GO AND MAKE IT THAT WAY...
...BUT I COULDN'T PULL IT OFF WITH MY CURRENT SKILLS.
SO I WENT WITH LEGOS.
THAT WAS SORT OF ANTICLIMACTIC. I GUESS YOU RELIED ON YOUR MATERIALS A LITTLE TOO MUCH.
YOU COULD SAY THAT LEGOS ARE INHERENTLY REPRESENTA-TIVE OF LAYERING.
...
IN MY OPINION...

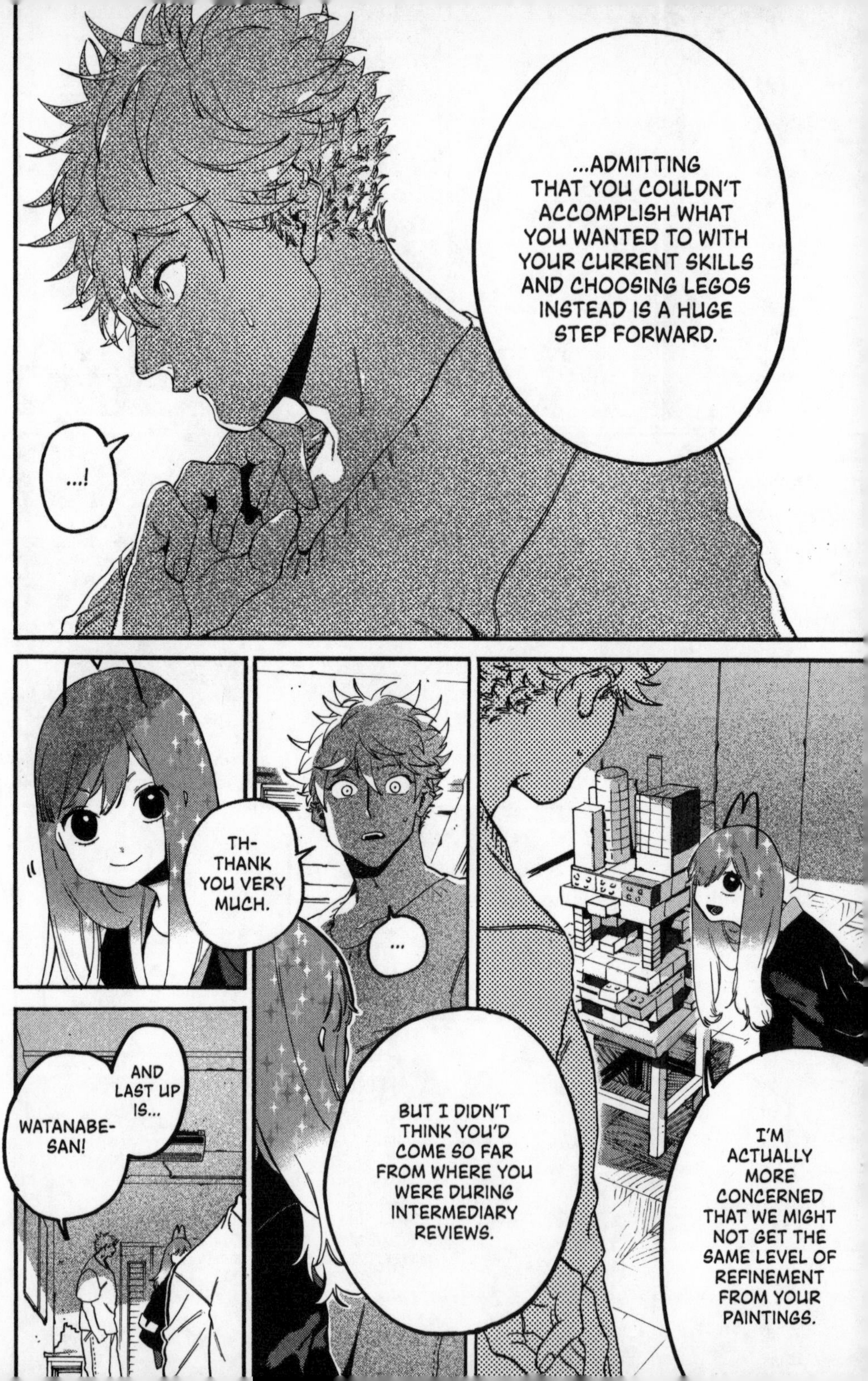
...ADMITTING THAT YOU COULDN'T ACCOMPLISH WHAT YOU WANTED TO WITH YOUR CURRENT SKILLS AND CHOOSING LEGOS INSTEAD IS A HUGE STEP FORWARD.
...!
I'M ACTUALLY MORE CONCERNED THAT WE MIGHT NOT GET THE SAME LEVEL OF REFINEMENT FROM YOUR PAINTINGS.
BUT I DIDN'T THINK YOU'D COME SO FAR FROM WHERE YOU WERE DURING INTERMEDIARY REVIEWS.
...
TH-THANK YOU VERY MUCH.
AND LAST UP IS... WATANABE-SAN!

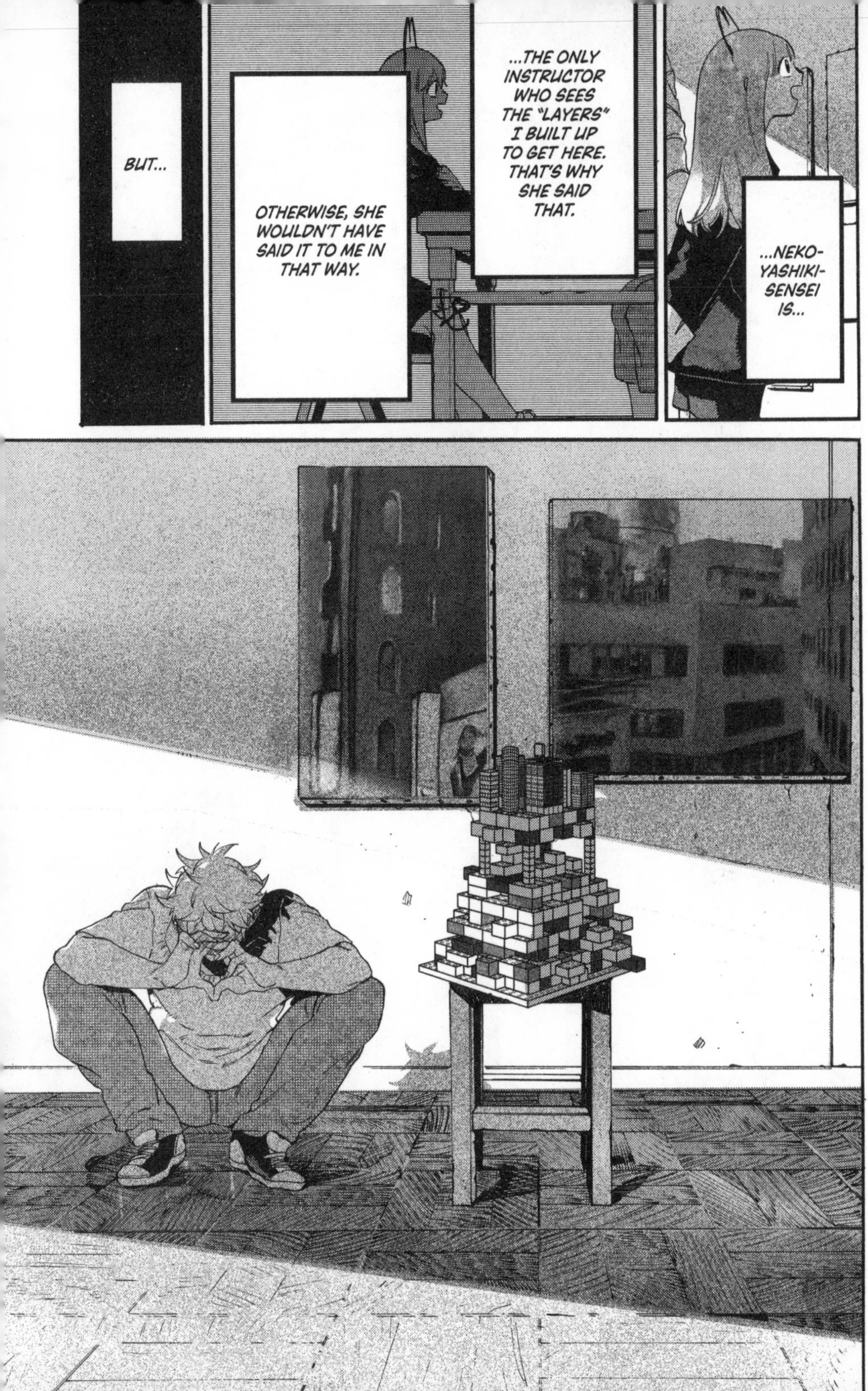
...NEKO-YASHIKI-SENSEI IS...
...THE ONLY INSTRUCTOR WHO SEES THE "LAYERS" I BUILT UP TO GET HERE. THAT'S WHY SHE SAID THAT.
OTHERWISE, SHE WOULDN'T HAVE SAID IT TO ME IN THAT WAY.
BUT...

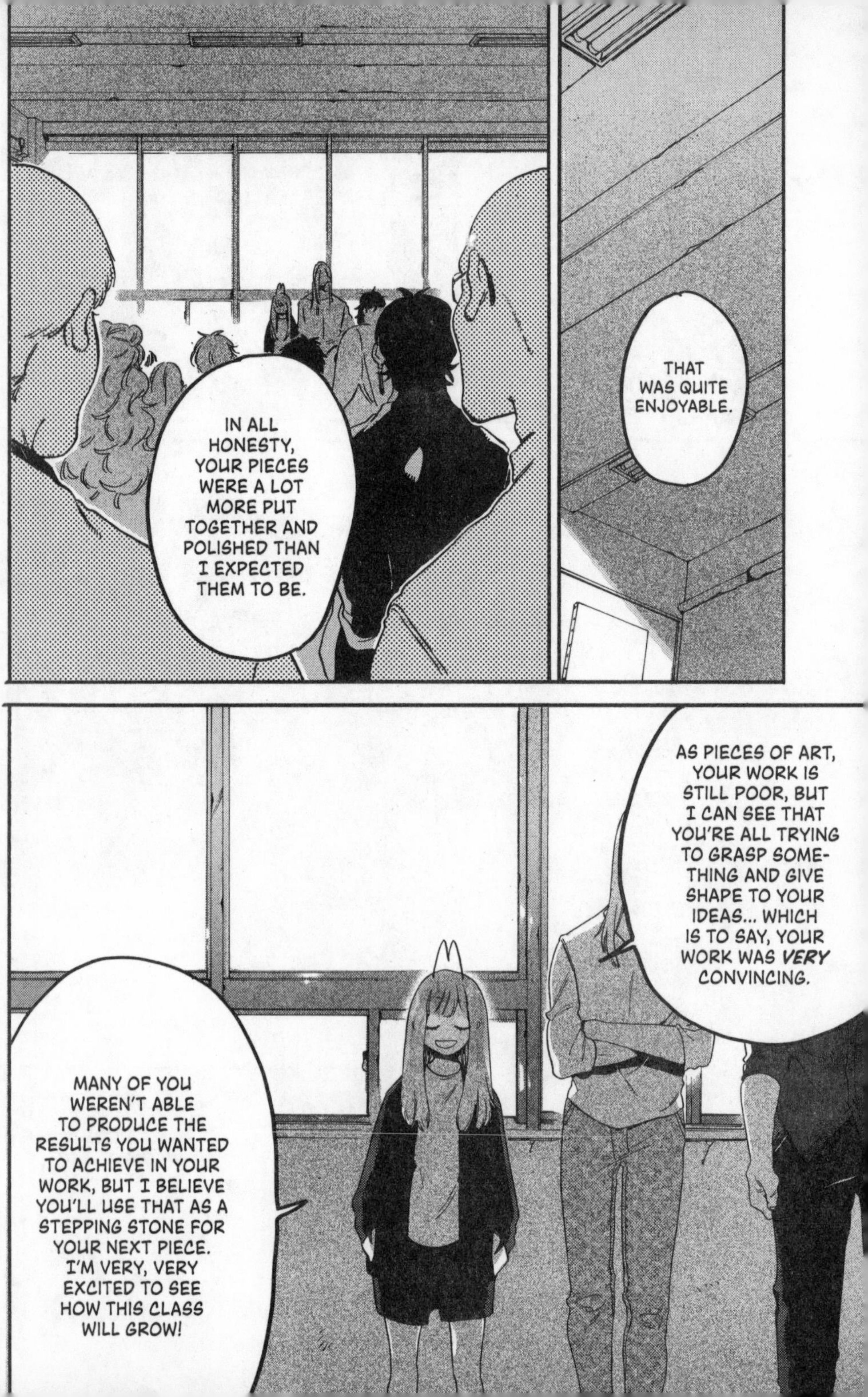
THAT WAS QUITE ENJOYABLE.
IN ALL HONESTY, YOUR PIECES WERE A LOT MORE PUT TOGETHER AND POLISHED THAN I EXPECTED THEM TO BE.
AS PIECES OF ART, YOUR WORK IS STILL POOR, BUT I CAN SEE THAT YOU'RE ALL TRYING TO GRASP SOME-THING AND GIVE SHAPE TO YOUR IDEAS... WHICH IS TO SAY, YOUR WORK WAS *VERY* CONVINCING.
MANY OF YOU WEREN'T ABLE TO PRODUCE THE RESULTS YOU WANTED TO ACHIEVE IN YOUR WORK, BUT I BELIEVE YOU'LL USE THAT AS A STEPPING STONE FOR YOUR NEXT PIECE. I'M VERY, VERY EXCITED TO SEE HOW THIS CLASS WILL GROW!

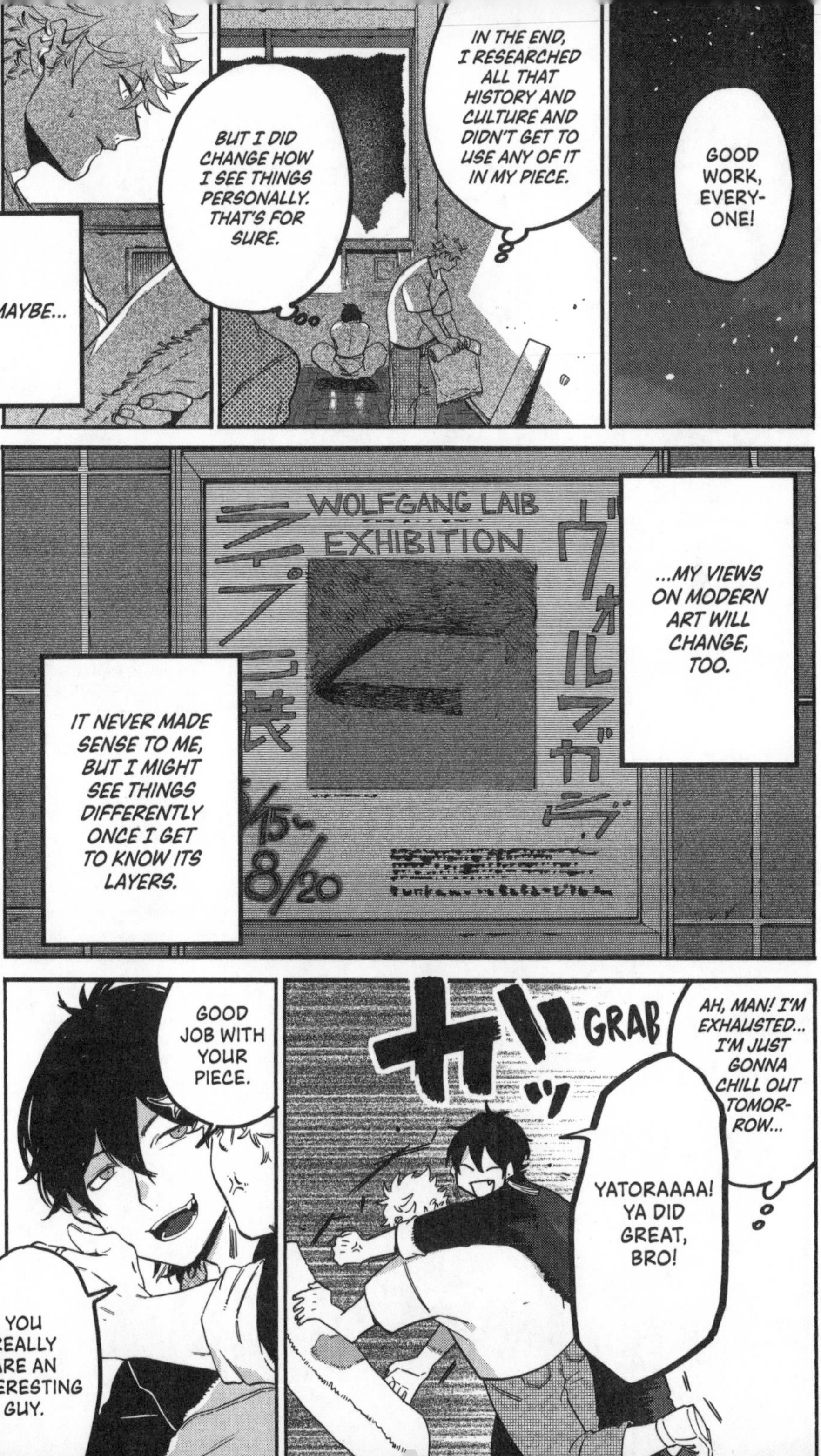
GOOD WORK, EVERY-ONE!
IN THE END, I RESEARCHED ALL THAT HISTORY AND CULTURE AND DIDN'T GET TO USE ANY OF IT IN MY PIECE.
BUT I DID CHANGE HOW I SEE THINGS PERSONALLY. THAT'S FOR SURE.
MAYBE...
WOLFGANG LAIB EXHIBITION
8/20
...MY VIEWS ON MODERN ART WILL CHANGE, TOO.
IT NEVER MADE SENSE TO ME, BUT I MIGHT SEE THINGS DIFFERENTLY ONCE I GET TO KNOW ITS LAYERS.
AH, MAN! I'M EXHAUSTED... I'M JUST GONNA CHILL OUT TOMOR-ROW...
GRAB
YATORAAAA! YA DID GREAT, BRO!
GOOD JOB WITH YOUR PIECE.
YOU REALLY ARE AN INTERESTING GUY.

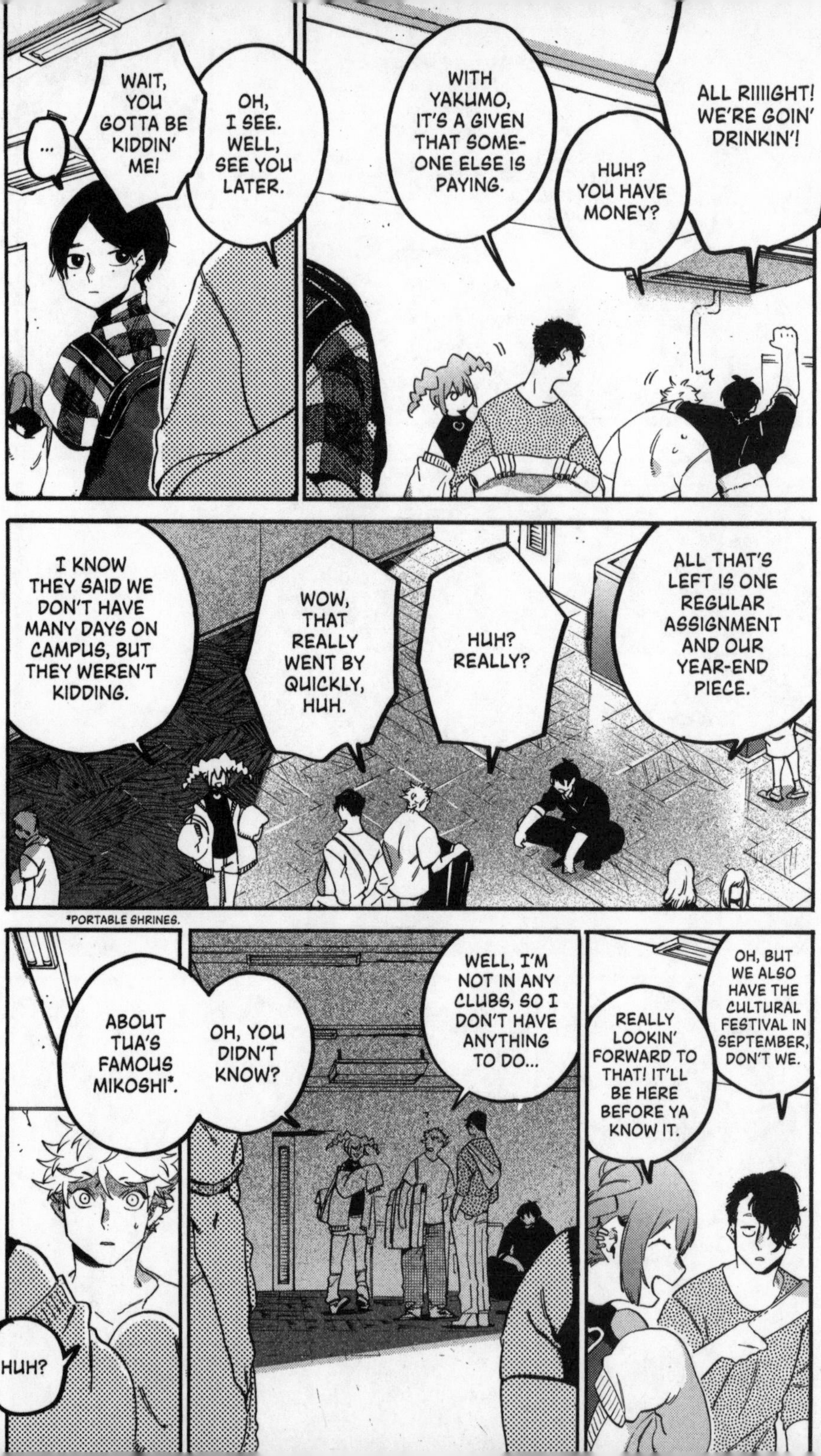
ALL RIIIGHT! WE'RE GOIN' DRINKIN'!
HUH? YOU HAVE MONEY?
WITH YAKUMO, IT'S A GIVEN THAT SOME-ONE ELSE IS PAYING.
OH, I SEE. WELL, SEE YOU LATER.
WAIT, YOU GOTTA BE KIDDIN' ME!
...
ALL THAT'S LEFT IS ONE REGULAR ASSIGNMENT AND OUR YEAR-END PIECE.
HUH? REALLY?
WOW, THAT REALLY WENT BY QUICKLY, HUH.
I KNOW THEY SAID WE DON'T HAVE MANY DAYS ON CAMPUS, BUT THEY WEREN'T KIDDING.
OH, BUT WE ALSO HAVE THE CULTURAL FESTIVAL IN SEPTEMBER, DON'T WE.
REALLY LOOKIN' FORWARD TO THAT! IT'LL BE HERE BEFORE YA KNOW IT.
WELL, I'M NOT IN ANY CLUBS, SO I DON'T HAVE ANYTHING TO DO...
OH, YOU DIDN'T KNOW?
ABOUT TUA'S FAMOUS MIKOSHI*.
HUH?

*PORTABLE SHRINES.

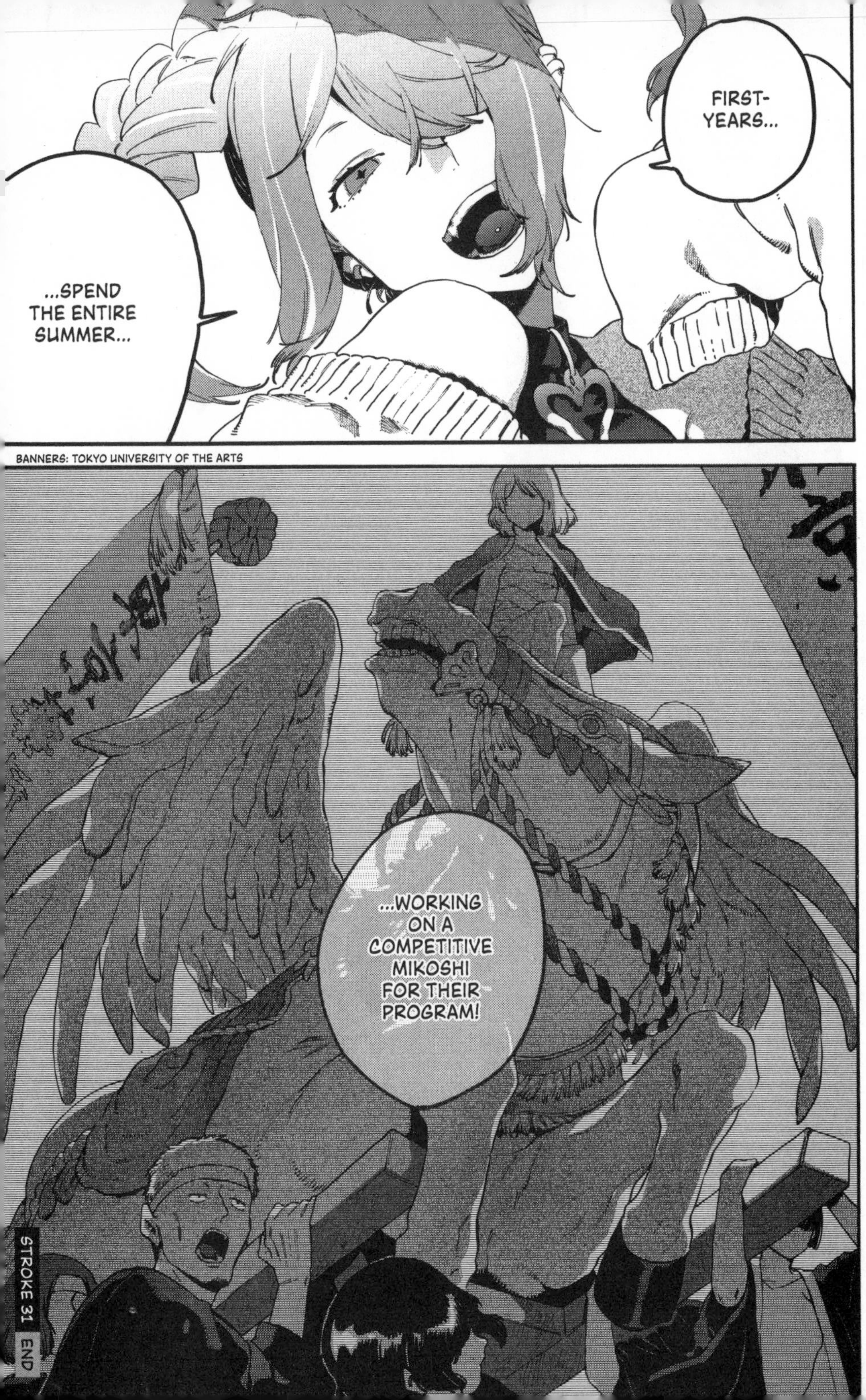
FIRST-YEARS...
...SPEND THE ENTIRE SUMMER...
BANNERS: TOKYO UNIVERSITY OF THE ARTS
...WORKING ON A COMPETITIVE MIKOSHI FOR THEIR PROGRAM!
STROKE 31 END

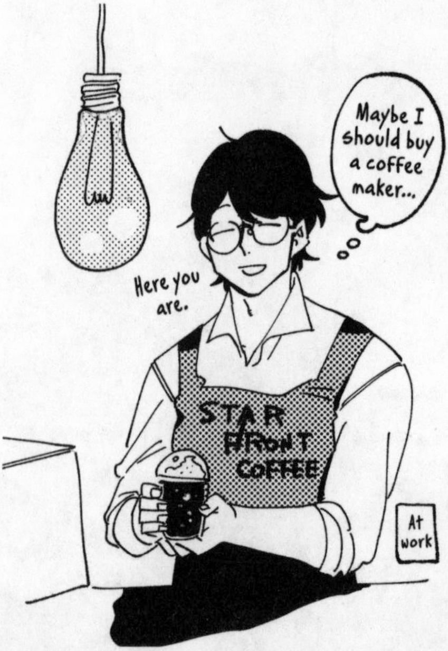
Maybe I should buy a coffee maker...
Here you are.
STAR FRONT COFFEE
At work

## STROKE 32

## FESTIVAL PREP BEGINS

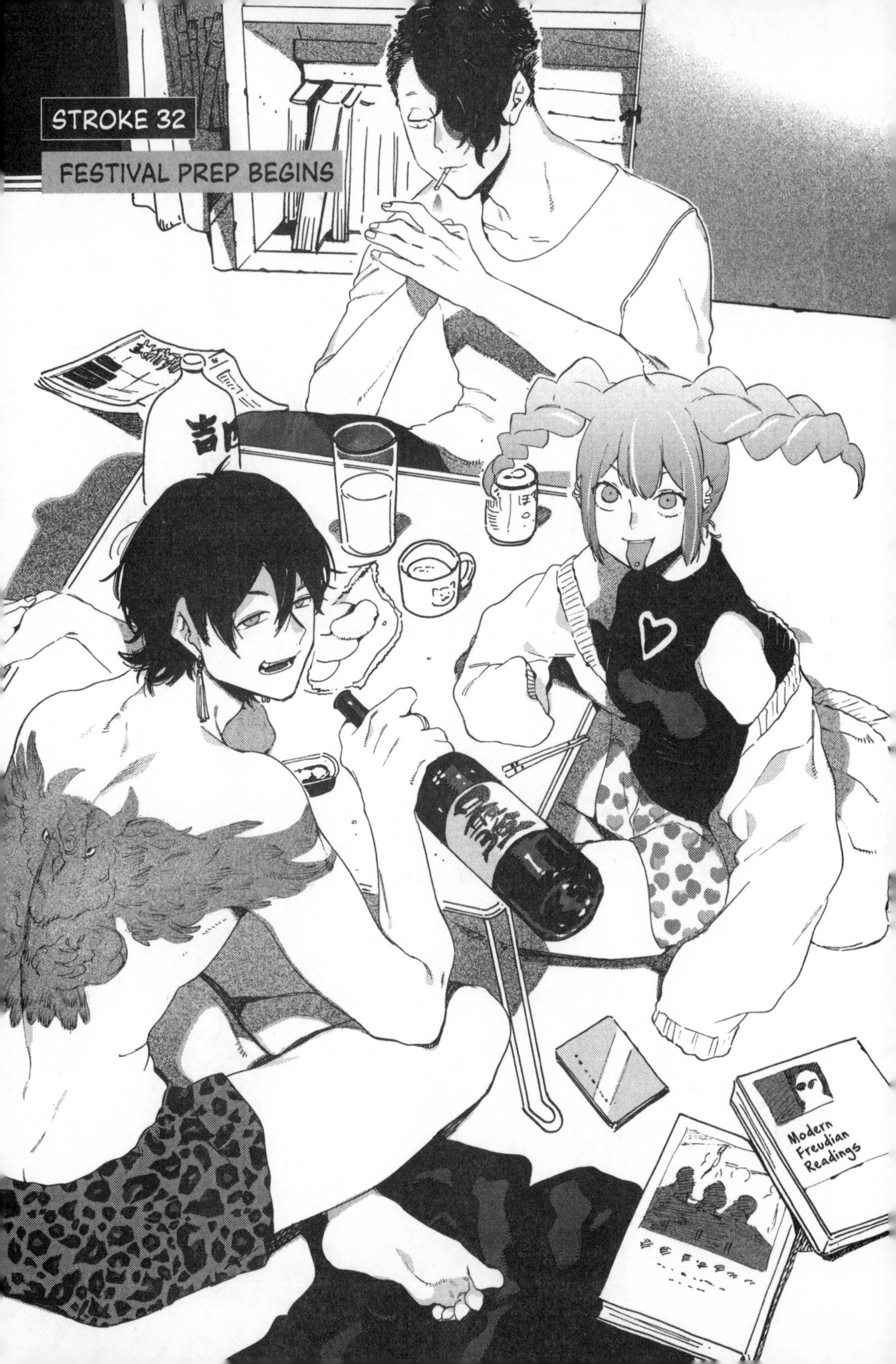
Modern Freudian Readings

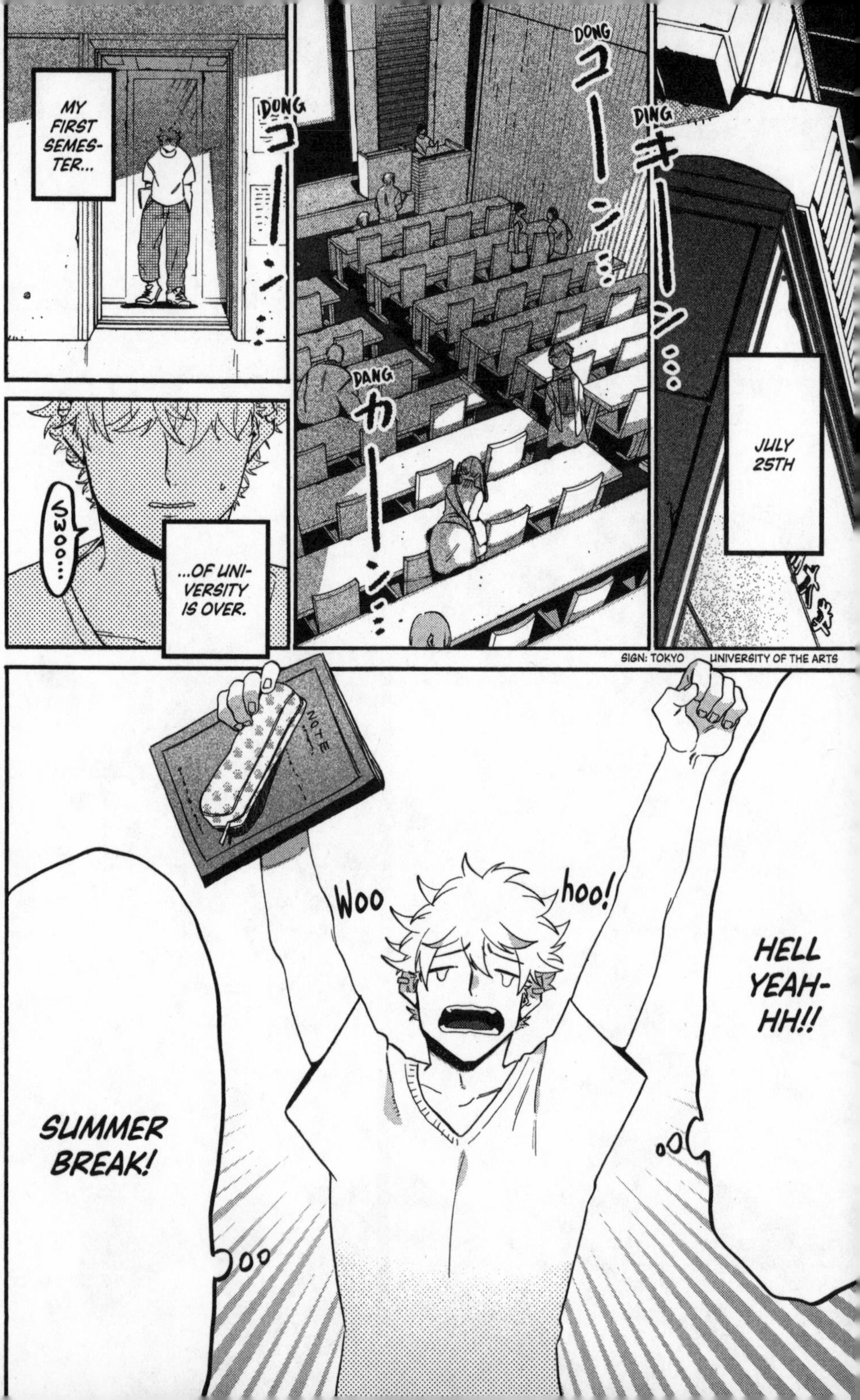

JULY 25TH
DONG
コーーン…
DING
キーーン…
DONG
コーーン…
DANG
カーーン…
MY FIRST SEMESTER...
SWOO...
...OF UNIVERSITY IS OVER.
SIGN: TOKYO UNIVERSITY OF THE ARTS
NOTE
Woo hoo!
HELL YEAH-HH!!
SUMMER BREAK!

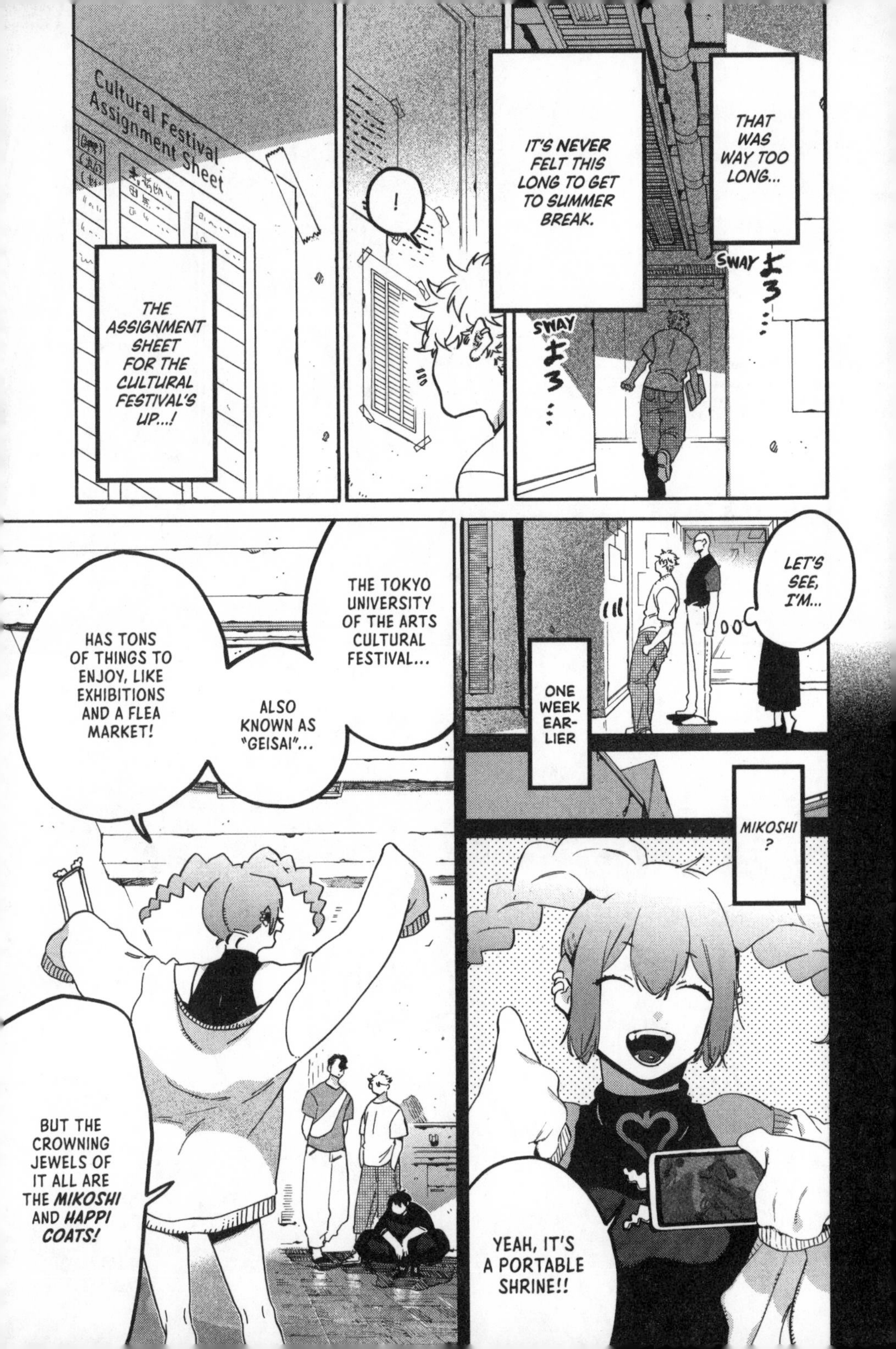
THAT WAS WAY TOO LONG...
IT'S NEVER FELT THIS LONG TO GET TO SUMMER BREAK.
SWAY よろ...
SWAY よろ...
!
Cultural Festival Assignment Sheet
THE ASSIGNMENT SHEET FOR THE CULTURAL FESTIVAL'S UP...!
LET'S SEE, I'M...
ONE WEEK EARLIER
MIKOSHI?
YEAH, IT'S A PORTABLE SHRINE!!
THE TOKYO UNIVERSITY OF THE ARTS CULTURAL FESTIVAL...
ALSO KNOWN AS "GEISAI"...
HAS TONS OF THINGS TO ENJOY, LIKE EXHIBITIONS AND A FLEA MARKET!
BUT THE CROWNING JEWELS OF IT ALL ARE THE *MIKOSHI* AND *HAPPI COATS!*

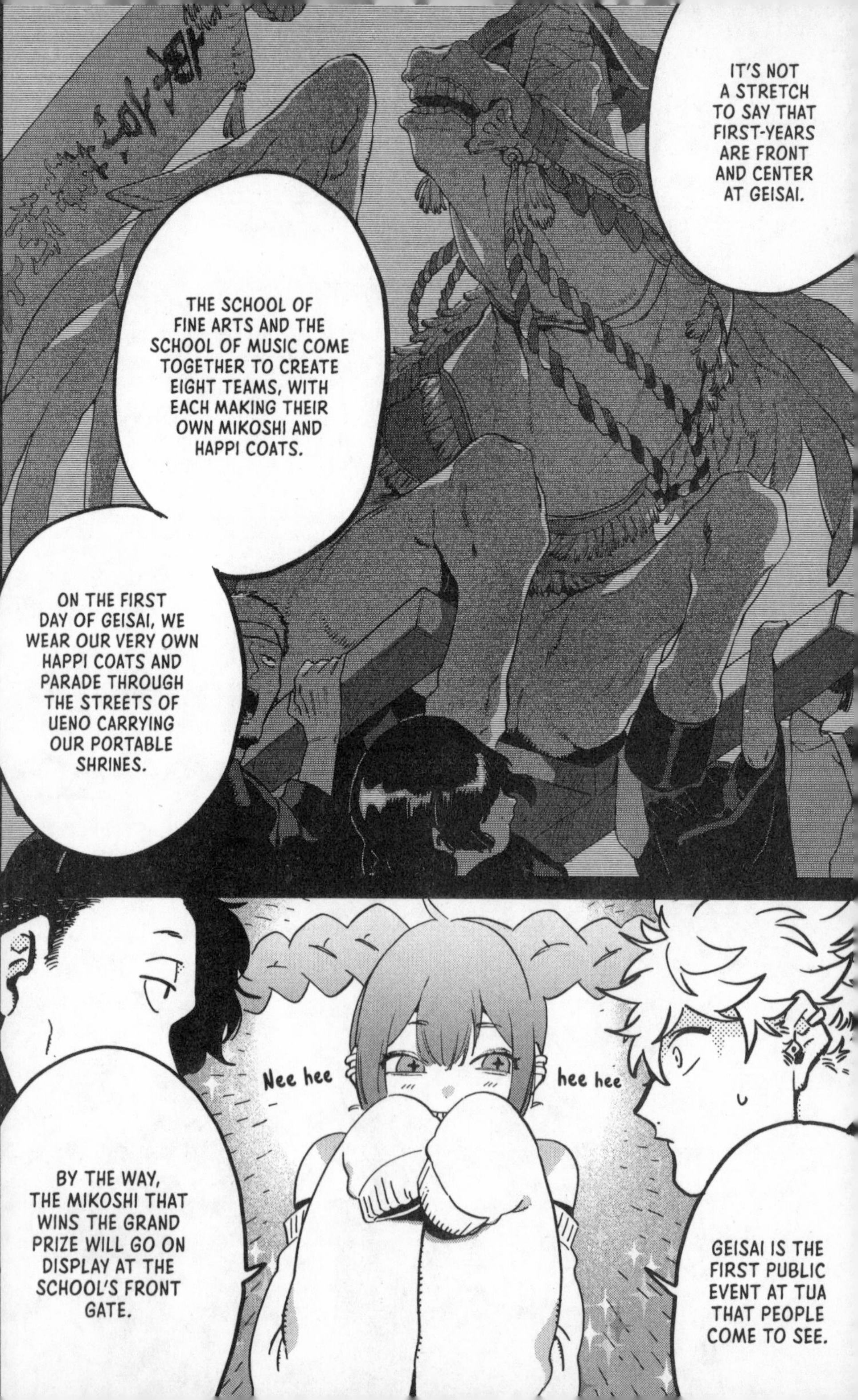
IT'S NOT A STRETCH TO SAY THAT FIRST-YEARS ARE FRONT AND CENTER AT GEISAI.
THE SCHOOL OF FINE ARTS AND THE SCHOOL OF MUSIC COME TOGETHER TO CREATE EIGHT TEAMS, WITH EACH MAKING THEIR OWN MIKOSHI AND HAPPI COATS.
ON THE FIRST DAY OF GEISAI, WE WEAR OUR VERY OWN HAPPI COATS AND PARADE THROUGH THE STREETS OF UENO CARRYING OUR PORTABLE SHRINES.
GEISAI IS THE FIRST PUBLIC EVENT AT TUA THAT PEOPLE COME TO SEE.
hee hee
Nee hee
BY THE WAY, THE MIKOSHI THAT WINS THE GRAND PRIZE WILL GO ON DISPLAY AT THE SCHOOL'S FRONT GATE.

BANNER: TOKYO UNIVERSITY OF THE ARTS

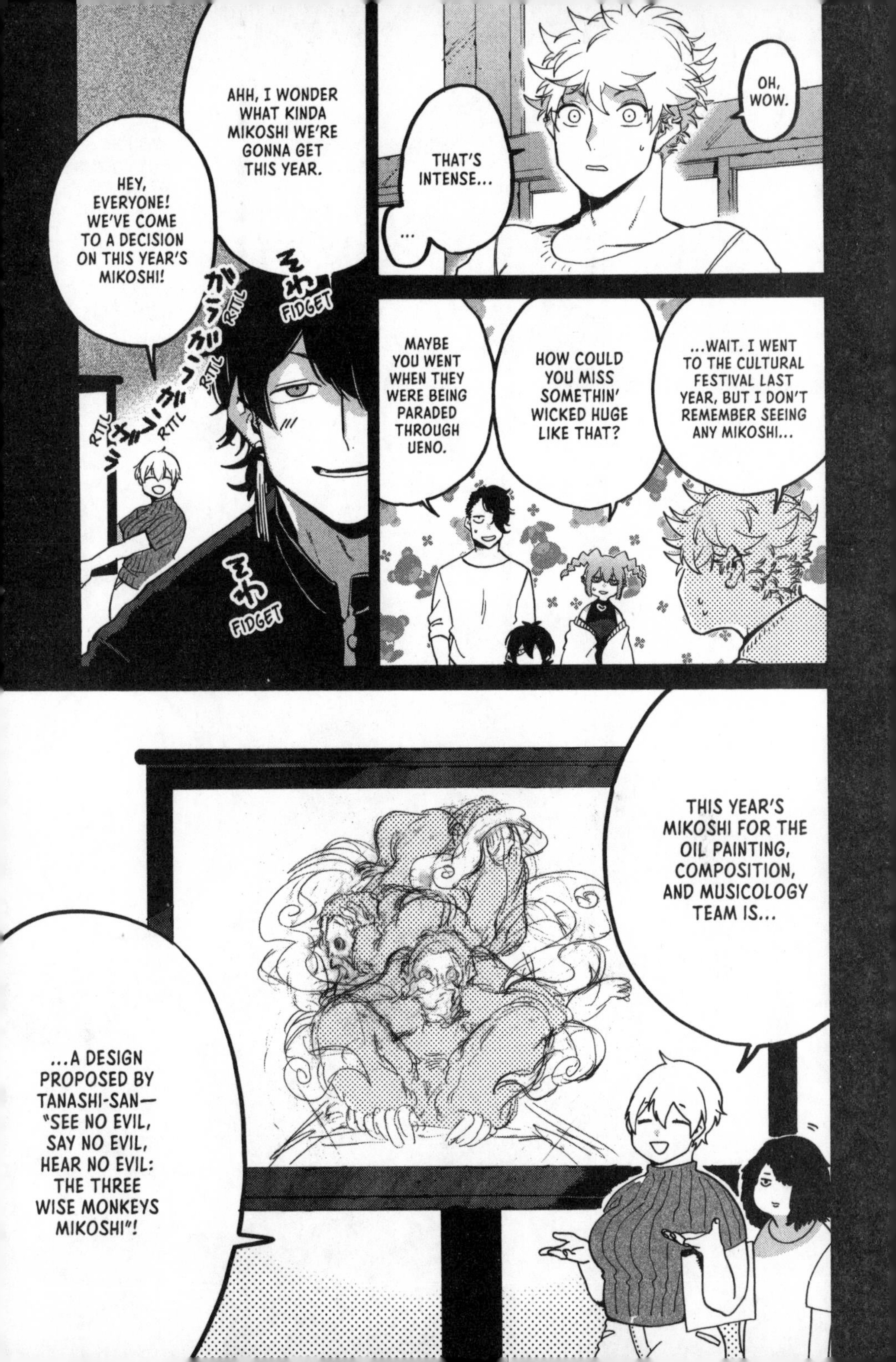

OH, WOW.
THAT'S INTENSE...
...
...WAIT. I WENT TO THE CULTURAL FESTIVAL LAST YEAR, BUT I DON'T REMEMBER SEEING ANY MIKOSHI...
HOW COULD YOU MISS SOMETHIN' WICKED HUGE LIKE THAT?
MAYBE YOU WENT WHEN THEY WERE BEING PARADED THROUGH UENO.
AHH, I WONDER WHAT KINDA MIKOSHI WE'RE GONNA GET THIS YEAR.
そわ FIDGET
HEY, EVERYONE! WE'VE COME TO A DECISION ON THIS YEAR'S MIKOSHI!
RTL RTL RTL RTL
そわ FIDGET
THIS YEAR'S MIKOSHI FOR THE OIL PAINTING, COMPOSITION, AND MUSICOLOGY TEAM IS...
...A DESIGN PROPOSED BY TANASHI-SAN— "SEE NO EVIL, SAY NO EVIL, HEAR NO EVIL: THE THREE WISE MONKEYS MIKOSHI"!

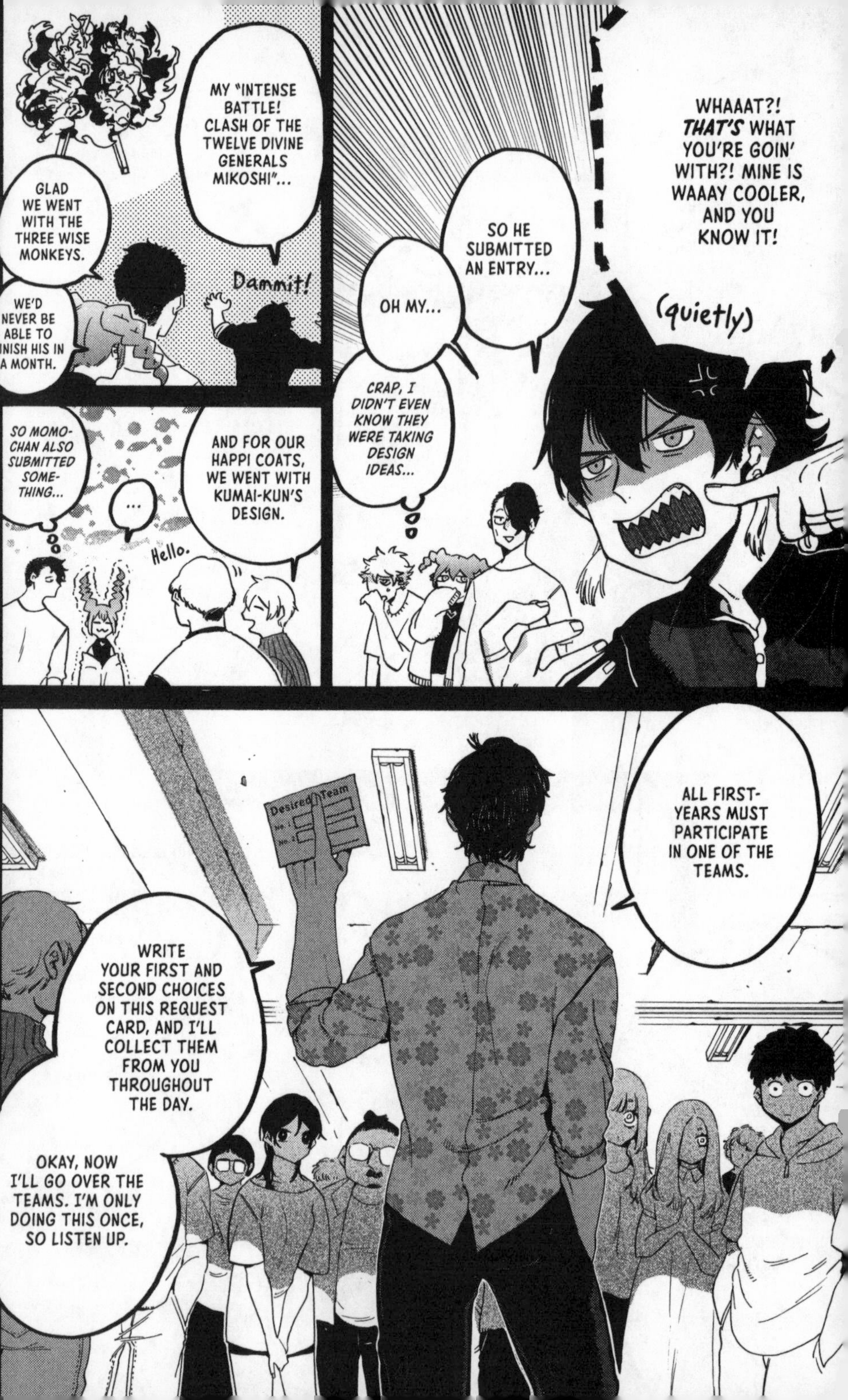
WHAAAT?! ***THAT'S*** WHAT YOU'RE GOIN' WITH?! MINE IS WAAAY COOLER, AND YOU KNOW IT!
(quietly)
SO HE SUBMITTED AN ENTRY...
OH MY...
*CRAP, I DIDN'T EVEN KNOW THEY WERE TAKING DESIGN IDEAS...*
MY "INTENSE BATTLE! CLASH OF THE TWELVE DIVINE GENERALS MIKOSHI"...
Dammit!
GLAD WE WENT WITH THE THREE WISE MONKEYS.
WE'D NEVER BE ABLE TO FINISH HIS IN A MONTH.
AND FOR OUR HAPPI COATS, WE WENT WITH KUMAI-KUN'S DESIGN.
Hello.
...
*SO MOMO-CHAN ALSO SUBMITTED SOME-THING...*
ALL FIRST-YEARS MUST PARTICIPATE IN ONE OF THE TEAMS.
Desired Team
WRITE YOUR FIRST AND SECOND CHOICES ON THIS REQUEST CARD, AND I'LL COLLECT THEM FROM YOU THROUGHOUT THE DAY.
OKAY, NOW I'LL GO OVER THE TEAMS. I'M ONLY DOING THIS ONCE, SO LISTEN UP.

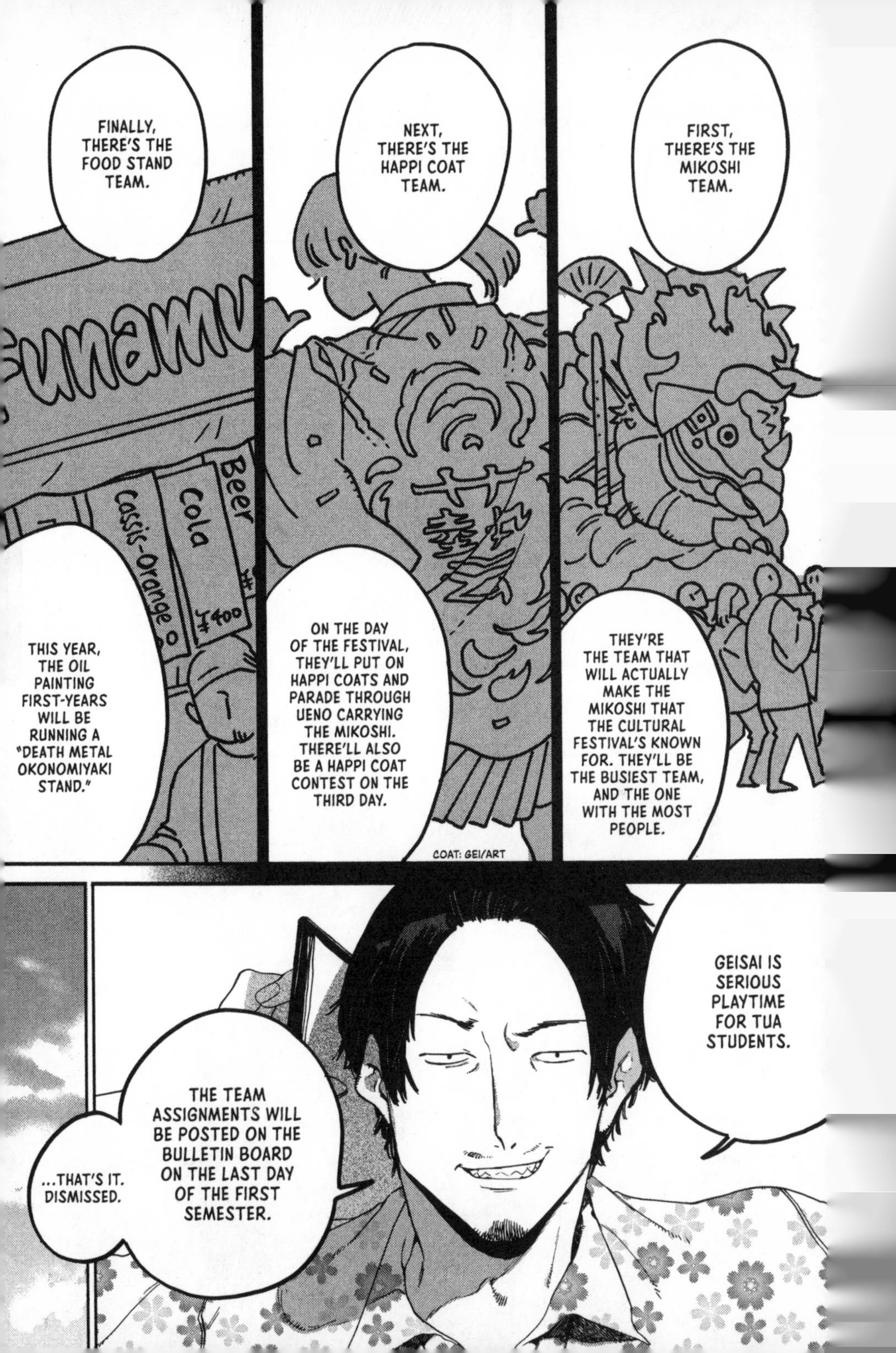
FIRST, THERE'S THE MIKOSHI TEAM.
THEY'RE THE TEAM THAT WILL ACTUALLY MAKE THE MIKOSHI THAT THE CULTURAL FESTIVAL'S KNOWN FOR. THEY'LL BE THE BUSIEST TEAM, AND THE ONE WITH THE MOST PEOPLE.
NEXT, THERE'S THE HAPPI COAT TEAM.
ON THE DAY OF THE FESTIVAL, THEY'LL PUT ON HAPPI COATS AND PARADE THROUGH UENO CARRYING THE MIKOSHI. THERE'LL ALSO BE A HAPPI COAT CONTEST ON THE THIRD DAY.
COAT: GEI/ART
FINALLY, THERE'S THE FOOD STAND TEAM.
Beer
Cola
Cassis-Orange
THIS YEAR, THE OIL PAINTING FIRST-YEARS WILL BE RUNNING A "DEATH METAL OKONOMIYAKI STAND."
GEISAI IS SERIOUS PLAYTIME FOR TUA STUDENTS.
THE TEAM ASSIGNMENTS WILL BE POSTED ON THE BULLETIN BOARD ON THE LAST DAY OF THE FIRST SEMESTER.
...THAT'S IT. DISMISSED.

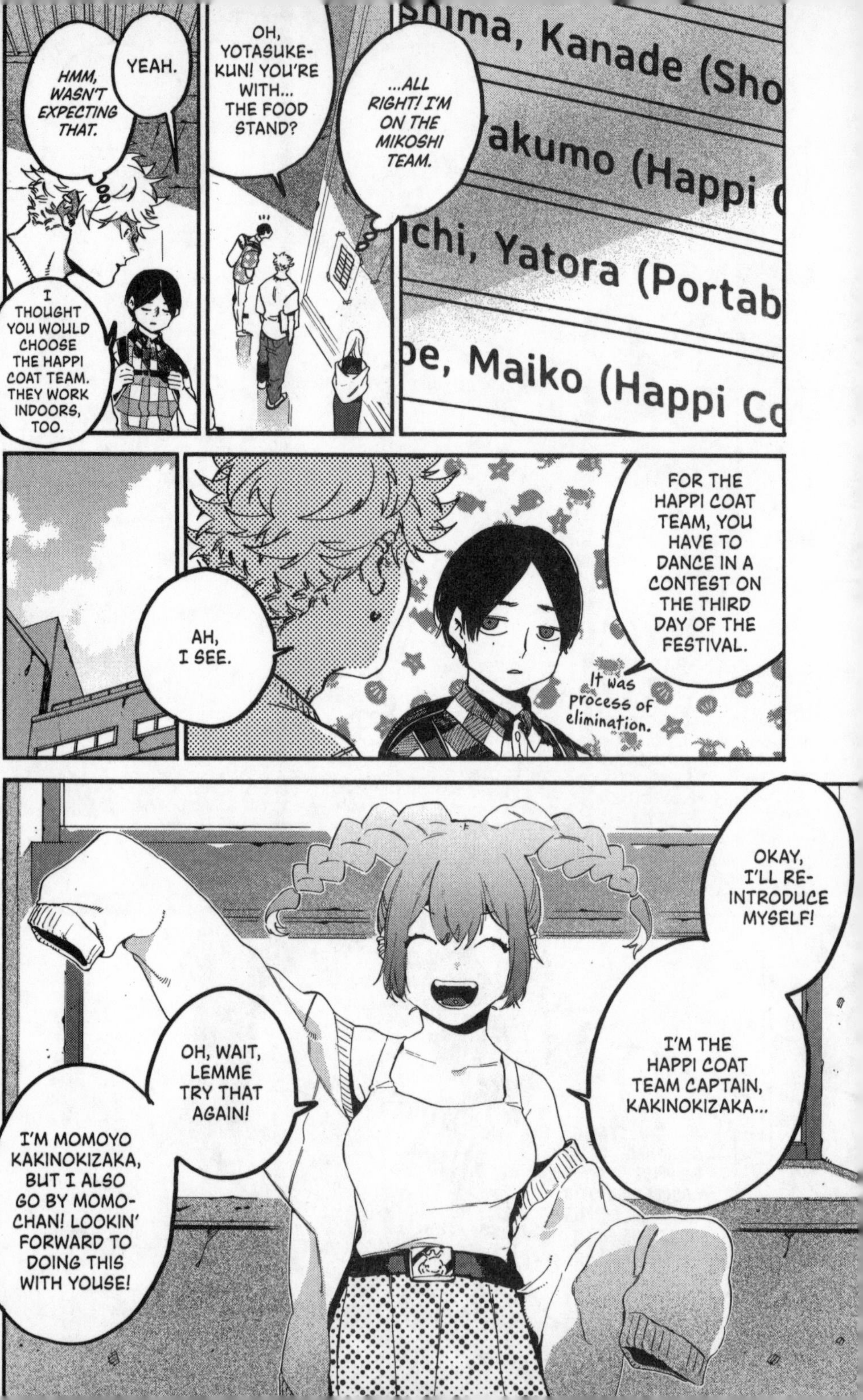

Shima, Kanade (Sho
akumo (Happi
ichi, Yatora (Portab
be, Maiko (Happi Co
OH, YOTASUKE-KUN! YOU'RE WITH... THE FOOD STAND?
...ALL RIGHT! I'M ON THE MIKOSHI TEAM.
YEAH.
HMM, WASN'T EXPECTING THAT.
I THOUGHT YOU WOULD CHOOSE THE HAPPI COAT TEAM. THEY WORK INDOORS, TOO.
FOR THE HAPPI COAT TEAM, YOU HAVE TO DANCE IN A CONTEST ON THE THIRD DAY OF THE FESTIVAL.
It was process of elimination.
AH, I SEE.
OKAY, I'LL RE-INTRODUCE MYSELF!
I'M THE HAPPI COAT TEAM CAPTAIN, KAKINOKIZAKA...
OH, WAIT, LEMME TRY THAT AGAIN!
I'M MOMOYO KAKINOKIZAKA, BUT I ALSO GO BY MOMO-CHAN! LOOKIN' FORWARD TO DOING THIS WITH YOUSE!

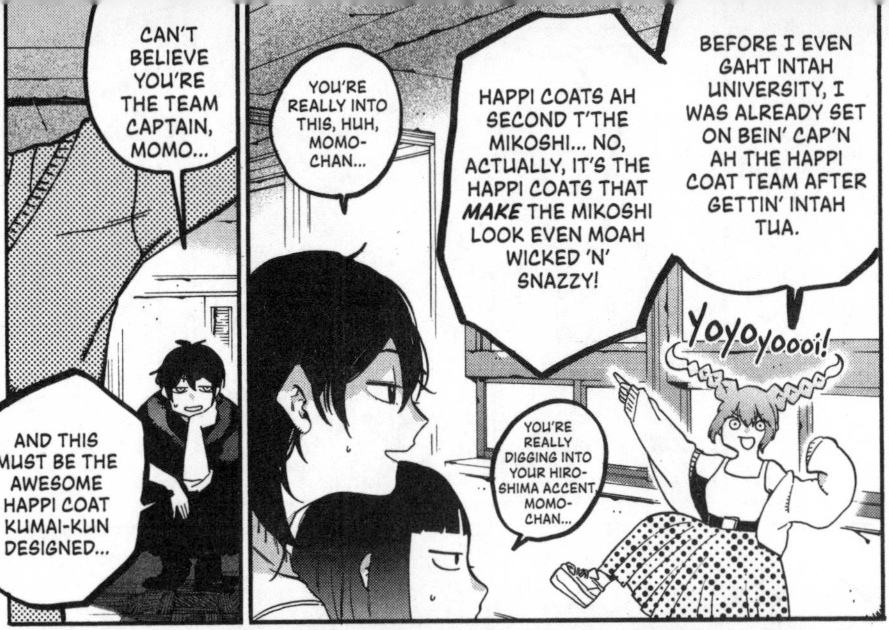
BEFORE I EVEN GAHT INTAH UNIVERSITY, I WAS ALREADY SET ON BEIN' CAP'N AH THE HAPPI COAT TEAM AFTER GETTIN' INTAH TUA.
HAPPI COATS AH SECOND T'THE MIKOSHI... NO, ACTUALLY, IT'S THE HAPPI COATS THAT ***MAKE*** THE MIKOSHI LOOK EVEN MOAH WICKED 'N' SNAZZY!
YOU'RE REALLY INTO THIS, HUH, MOMO-CHAN...
Yoyoyoooi!
YOU'RE REALLY DIGGING INTO YOUR HIROSHIMA ACCENT, MOMO-CHAN...
CAN'T BELIEVE YOU'RE THE TEAM CAPTAIN, MOMO...
AND THIS MUST BE THE AWESOME HAPPI COAT KUMAI-KUN DESIGNED...

*SYMBOL ON COAT: "ART"; ALSO THE FIRST PART OF TUA'S NAME IN JAPANESE (THE "GEI" IN GEIDAI).

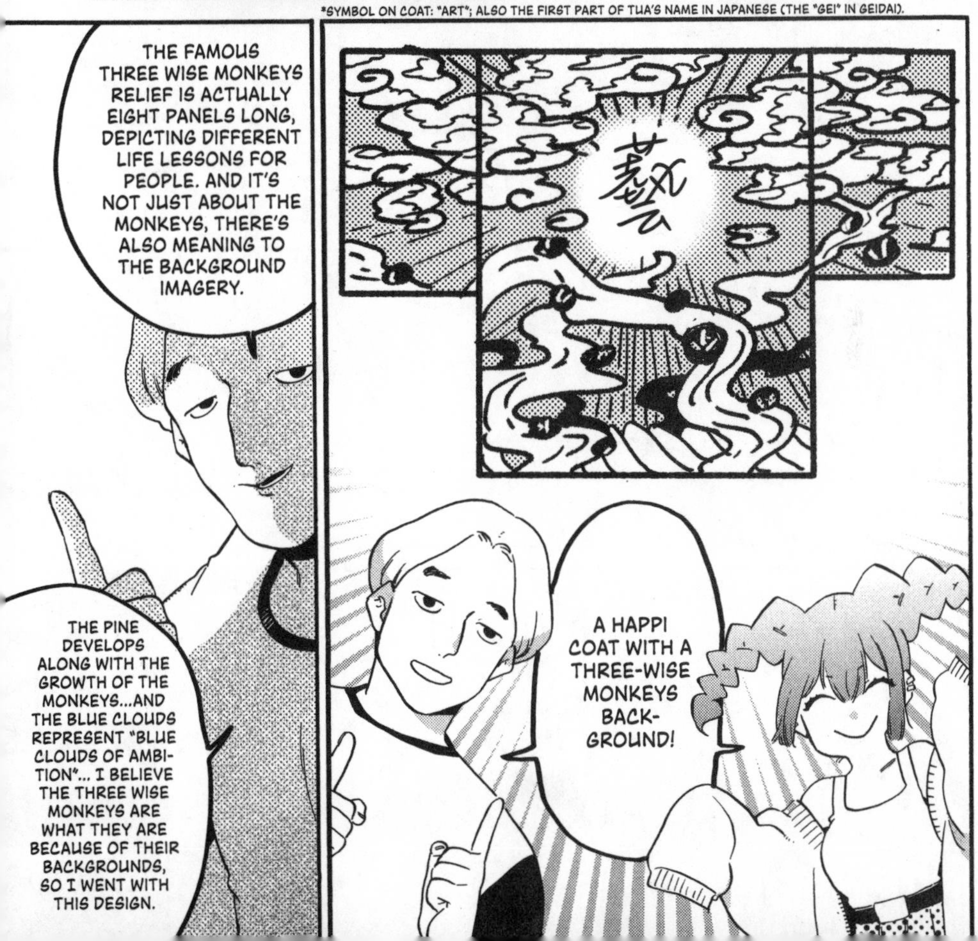
A HAPPI COAT WITH A THREE-WISE MONKEYS BACK-GROUND!
THE FAMOUS THREE WISE MONKEYS RELIEF IS ACTUALLY EIGHT PANELS LONG, DEPICTING DIFFERENT LIFE LESSONS FOR PEOPLE. AND IT'S NOT JUST ABOUT THE MONKEYS, THERE'S ALSO MEANING TO THE BACKGROUND IMAGERY.
THE PINE DEVELOPS ALONG WITH THE GROWTH OF THE MONKEYS...AND THE BLUE CLOUDS REPRESENT "BLUE CLOUDS OF AMBI-TION"... I BELIEVE THE THREE WISE MONKEYS ARE WHAT THEY ARE BECAUSE OF THEIR BACKGROUNDS, SO I WENT WITH THIS DESIGN.

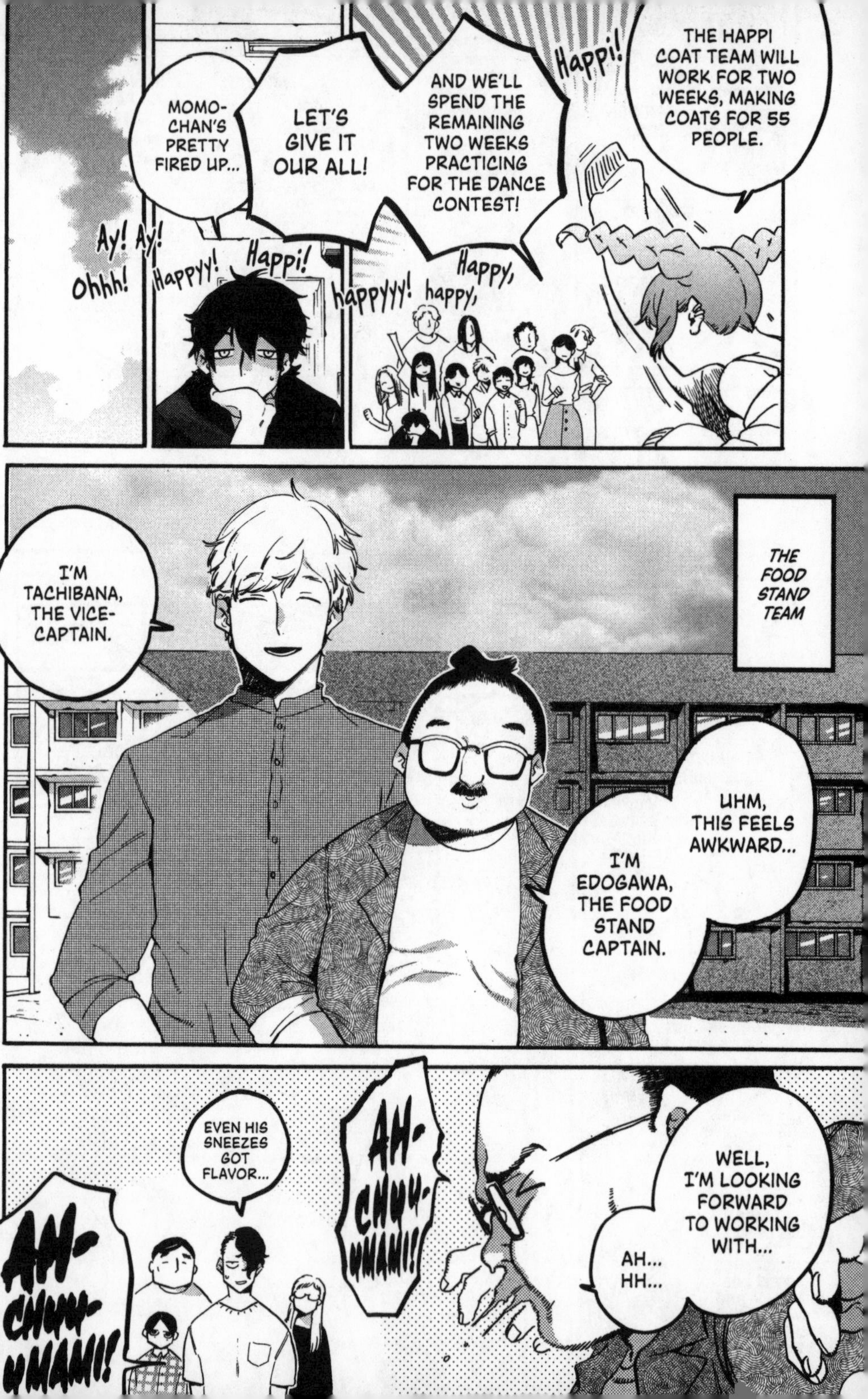
THE HAPPI COAT TEAM WILL WORK FOR TWO WEEKS, MAKING COATS FOR 55 PEOPLE.
Happi!
AND WE'LL SPEND THE REMAINING TWO WEEKS PRACTICING FOR THE DANCE CONTEST!
LET'S GIVE IT OUR ALL!
Happy, happy, happyyy!
Happi!
Happyy!
Ay! Ay! Ohhh!
MOMO-CHAN'S PRETTY FIRED UP...
THE FOOD STAND TEAM
UHM, THIS FEELS AWKWARD...
I'M EDOGAWA, THE FOOD STAND CAPTAIN.
I'M TACHIBANA, THE VICE-CAPTAIN.
WELL, I'M LOOKING FORWARD TO WORKING WITH...
AH... HH...
AH-CHUU-UMAMI!!
EVEN HIS SNEEZES GOT FLAVOR...
AH-CHUU-UMAMI!

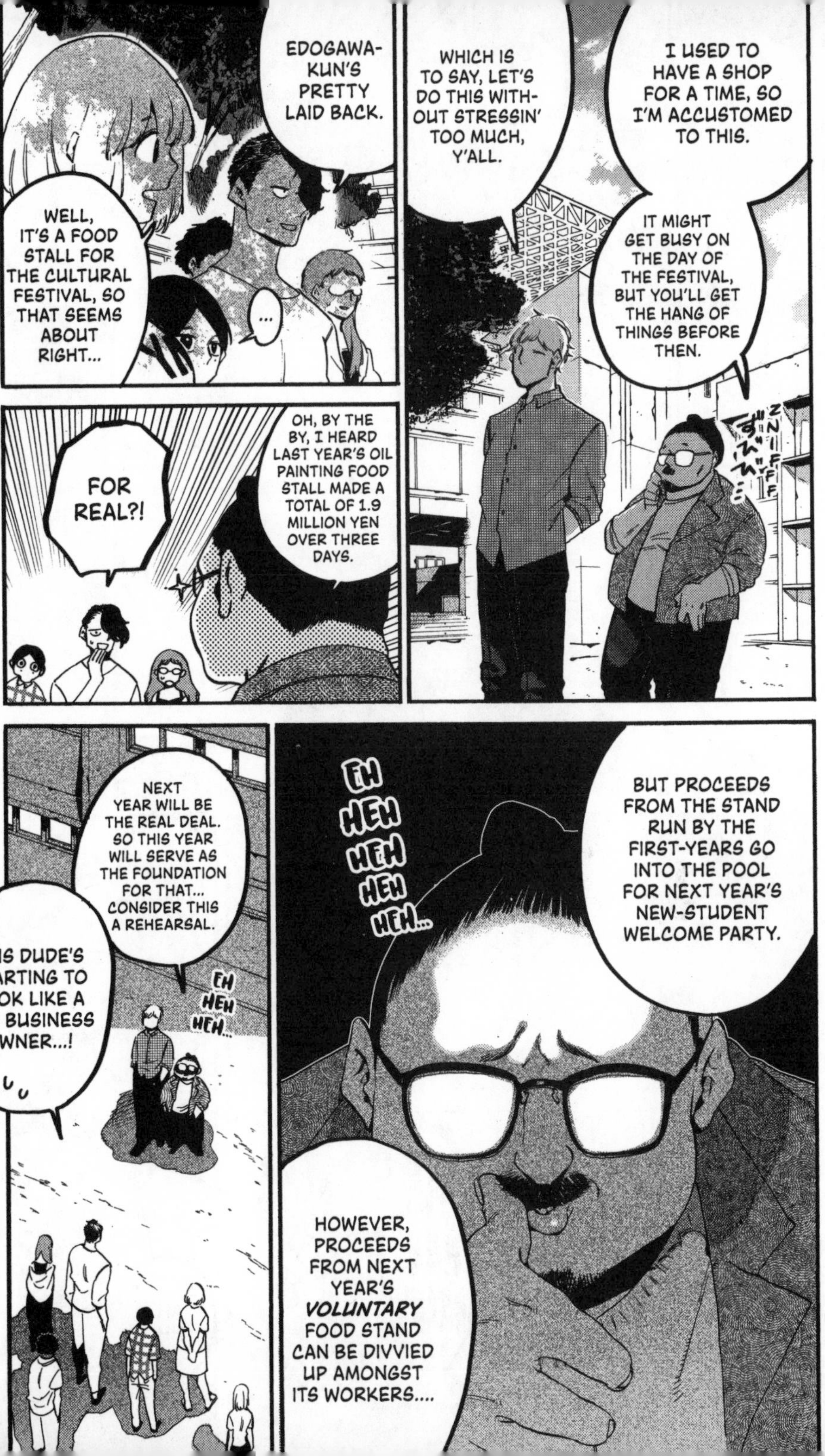
I USED TO HAVE A SHOP FOR A TIME, SO I'M ACCUSTOMED TO THIS.
IT MIGHT GET BUSY ON THE DAY OF THE FESTIVAL, BUT YOU'LL GET THE HANG OF THINGS BEFORE THEN.
WHICH IS TO SAY, LET'S DO THIS WITH-OUT STRESSIN' TOO MUCH, Y'ALL.
ZNIFF
EDOGAWA-KUN'S PRETTY LAID BACK.
...
WELL, IT'S A FOOD STALL FOR THE CULTURAL FESTIVAL, SO THAT SEEMS ABOUT RIGHT...
OH, BY THE BY, I HEARD LAST YEAR'S OIL PAINTING FOOD STALL MADE A TOTAL OF 1.9 MILLION YEN OVER THREE DAYS.
FOR REAL?!
BUT PROCEEDS FROM THE STAND RUN BY THE FIRST-YEARS GO INTO THE POOL FOR NEXT YEAR'S NEW-STUDENT WELCOME PARTY.
EH HEH HEH HEH HEH...
HOWEVER, PROCEEDS FROM NEXT YEAR'S ***VOLUNTARY*** FOOD STAND CAN BE DIVVIED UP AMONGST ITS WORKERS....
NEXT YEAR WILL BE THE REAL DEAL. SO THIS YEAR WILL SERVE AS THE FOUNDATION FOR THAT... CONSIDER THIS A REHEARSAL.
EH HEH HEH...
THIS DUDE'S STARTING TO LOOK LIKE A BAD BUSINESS OWNER...!

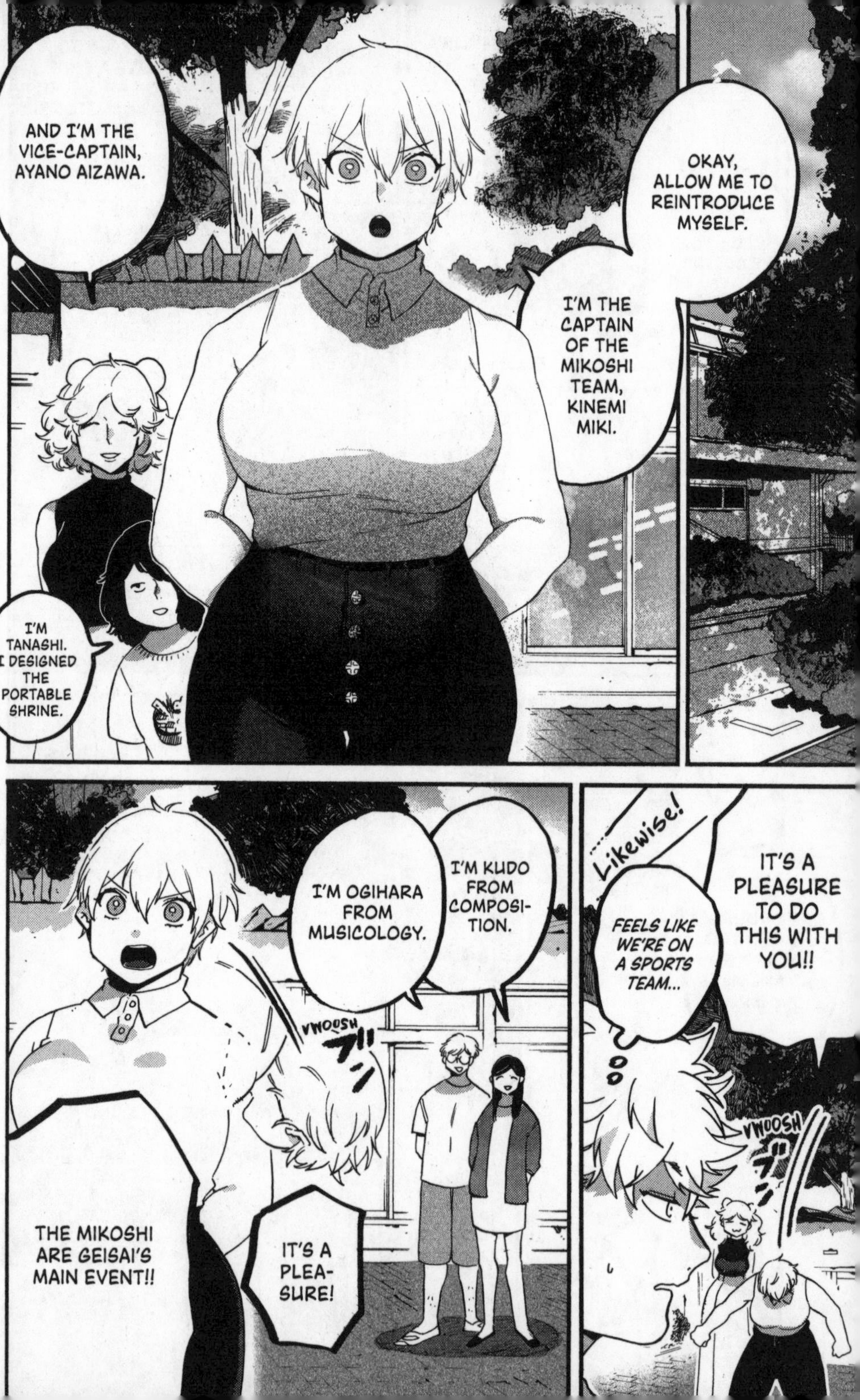
OKAY, ALLOW ME TO REINTRODUCE MYSELF.
I'M THE CAPTAIN OF THE MIKOSHI TEAM, KINEMI MIKI.
AND I'M THE VICE-CAPTAIN, AYANO AIZAWA.
I'M TANASHI. I DESIGNED THE PORTABLE SHRINE.
IT'S A PLEASURE TO DO THIS WITH YOU!!
...Likewise!
FEELS LIKE WE'RE ON A SPORTS TEAM...
VWOOSH
I'M KUDO FROM COMPOSITION.
I'M OGIHARA FROM MUSICOLOGY.
VWOOSH
IT'S A PLEASURE!
THE MIKOSHI ARE GEISAI'S MAIN EVENT!!

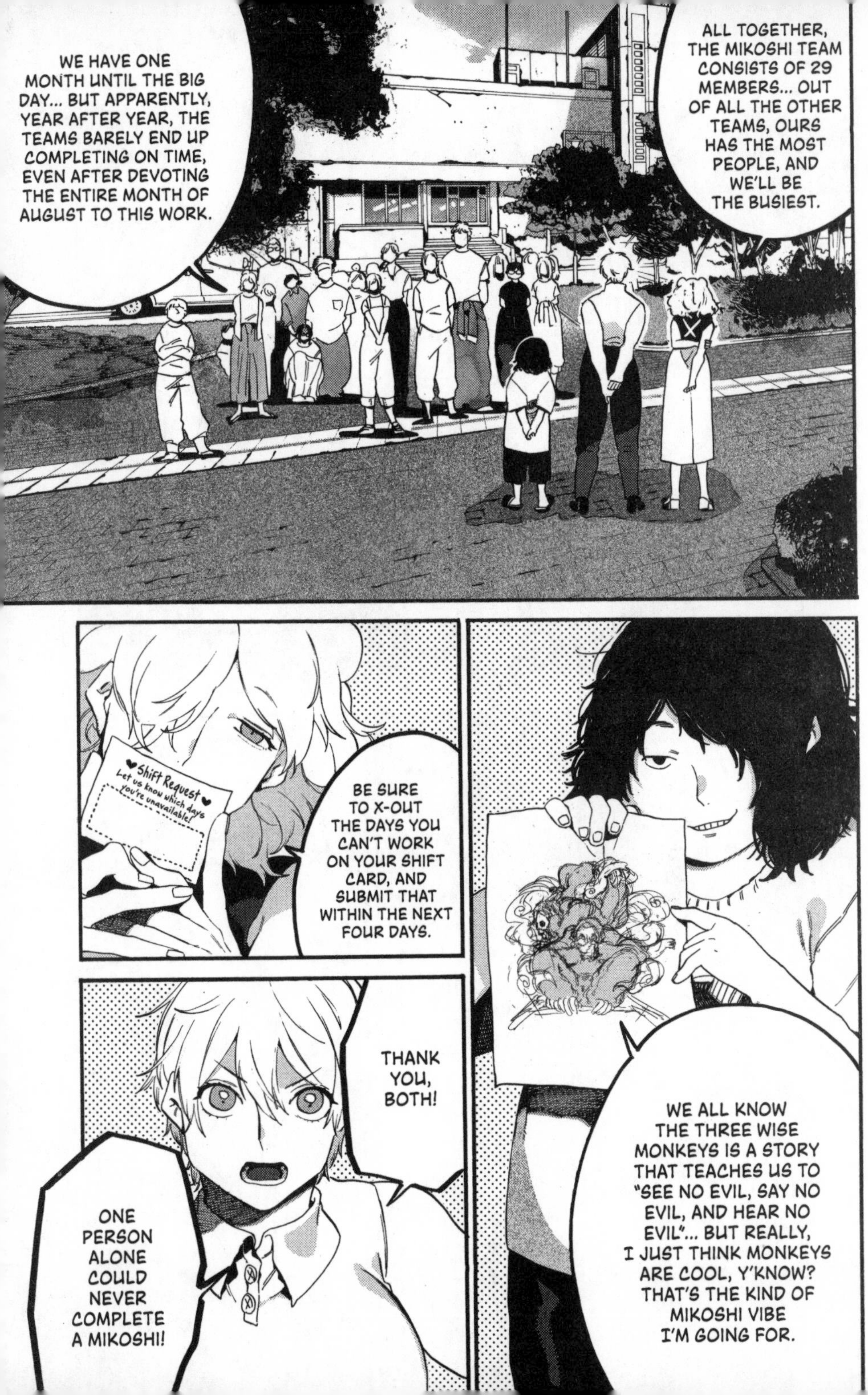
ALL TOGETHER, THE MIKOSHI TEAM CONSISTS OF 29 MEMBERS... OUT OF ALL THE OTHER TEAMS, OURS HAS THE MOST PEOPLE, AND WE'LL BE THE BUSIEST.
WE HAVE ONE MONTH UNTIL THE BIG DAY... BUT APPARENTLY, YEAR AFTER YEAR, THE TEAMS BARELY END UP COMPLETING ON TIME, EVEN AFTER DEVOTING THE ENTIRE MONTH OF AUGUST TO THIS WORK.
WE ALL KNOW THE THREE WISE MONKEYS IS A STORY THAT TEACHES US TO "SEE NO EVIL, SAY NO EVIL, AND HEAR NO EVIL"... BUT REALLY, I JUST THINK MONKEYS ARE COOL, Y'KNOW? THAT'S THE KIND OF MIKOSHI VIBE I'M GOING FOR.
Shift Request
Let us know which days you're unavailable!
BE SURE TO X-OUT THE DAYS YOU CAN'T WORK ON YOUR SHIFT CARD, AND SUBMIT THAT WITHIN THE NEXT FOUR DAYS.
THANK YOU, BOTH!
ONE PERSON ALONE COULD NEVER COMPLETE A MIKOSHI!

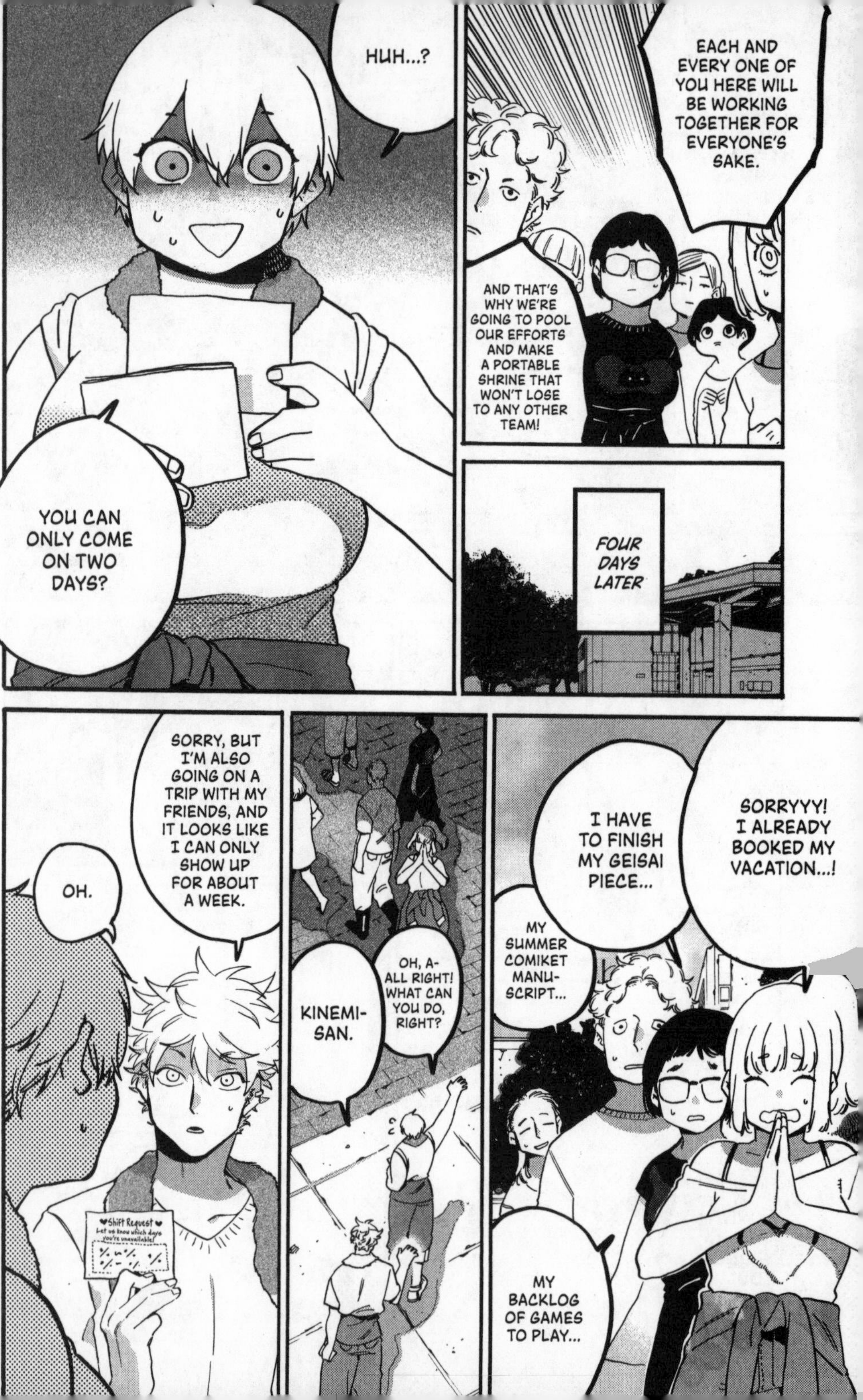
EACH AND EVERY ONE OF YOU HERE WILL BE WORKING TOGETHER FOR EVERYONE'S SAKE.
AND THAT'S WHY WE'RE GOING TO POOL OUR EFFORTS AND MAKE A PORTABLE SHRINE THAT WON'T LOSE TO ANY OTHER TEAM!
FOUR DAYS LATER
HUH...?
YOU CAN ONLY COME ON TWO DAYS?
SORRYYY! I ALREADY BOOKED MY VACATION...!
I HAVE TO FINISH MY GEISAI PIECE...
MY SUMMER COMIKET MANU-SCRIPT...
MY BACKLOG OF GAMES TO PLAY...
OH, A-ALL RIGHT! WHAT CAN YOU DO, RIGHT?
KINEMI-SAN.
SORRY, BUT I'M ALSO GOING ON A TRIP WITH MY FRIENDS, AND IT LOOKS LIKE I CAN ONLY SHOW UP FOR ABOUT A WEEK.
OH.
Shift Request
Let us know which days you're unavailable!

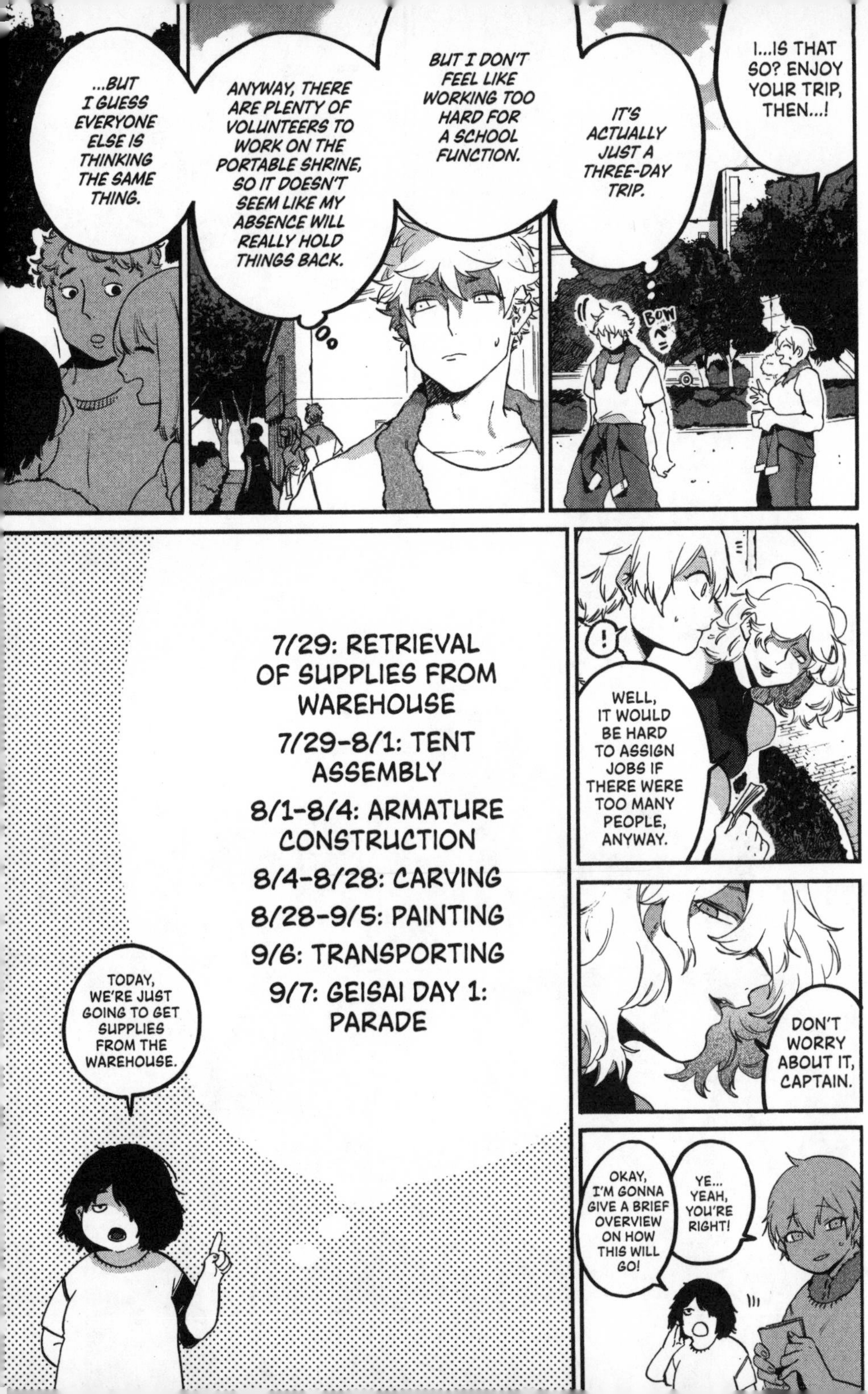
I...IS THAT SO? ENJOY YOUR TRIP, THEN...!
IT'S ACTUALLY JUST A THREE-DAY TRIP.
BOW
BUT I DON'T FEEL LIKE WORKING TOO HARD FOR A SCHOOL FUNCTION.
ANYWAY, THERE ARE PLENTY OF VOLUNTEERS TO WORK ON THE PORTABLE SHRINE, SO IT DOESN'T SEEM LIKE MY ABSENCE WILL REALLY HOLD THINGS BACK.
...BUT I GUESS EVERYONE ELSE IS THINKING THE SAME THING.
!
WELL, IT WOULD BE HARD TO ASSIGN JOBS IF THERE WERE TOO MANY PEOPLE, ANYWAY.
DON'T WORRY ABOUT IT, CAPTAIN.
YE... YEAH, YOU'RE RIGHT!
OKAY, I'M GONNA GIVE A BRIEF OVERVIEW ON HOW THIS WILL GO!
7/29: RETRIEVAL OF SUPPLIES FROM WAREHOUSE
7/29-8/1: TENT ASSEMBLY
8/1-8/4: ARMATURE CONSTRUCTION
8/4-8/28: CARVING
8/28-9/5: PAINTING
9/6: TRANSPORTING
9/7: GEISAI DAY 1: PARADE
TODAY, WE'RE JUST GOING TO GET SUPPLIES FROM THE WAREHOUSE.

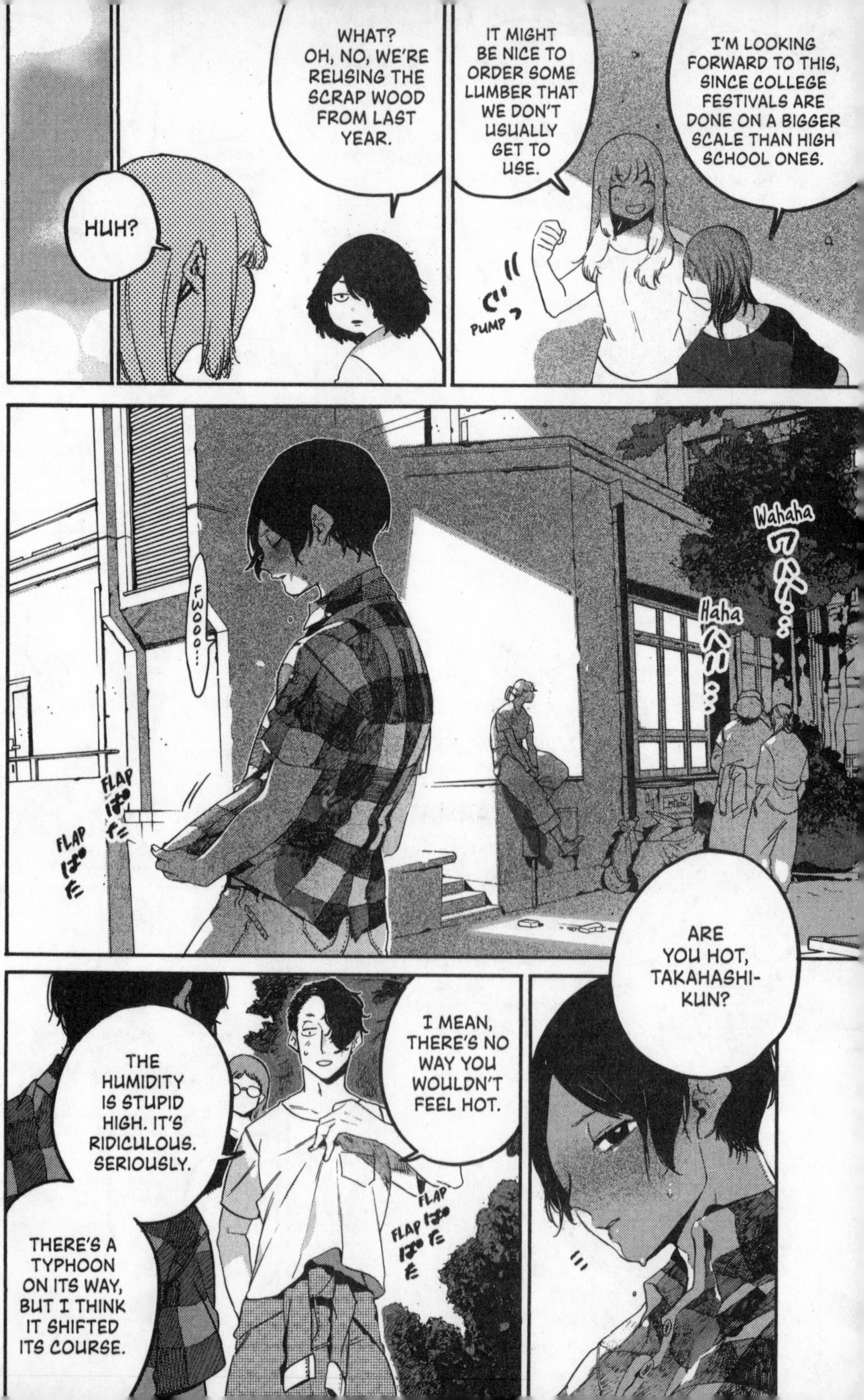
I'M LOOKING FORWARD TO THIS, SINCE COLLEGE FESTIVALS ARE DONE ON A BIGGER SCALE THAN HIGH SCHOOL ONES.
IT MIGHT BE NICE TO ORDER SOME LUMBER THAT WE DON'T USUALLY GET TO USE.
PUMP
WHAT? OH, NO, WE'RE REUSING THE SCRAP WOOD FROM LAST YEAR.
HUH?
Wahaha
Haha
FWOOO...
FLAP
FLAP
ARE YOU HOT, TAKAHASHI-KUN?
I MEAN, THERE'S NO WAY YOU WOULDN'T FEEL HOT.
THE HUMIDITY IS STUPID HIGH. IT'S RIDICULOUS. SERIOUSLY.
FLAP
FLAP
THERE'S A TYPHOON ON ITS WAY, BUT I THINK IT SHIFTED ITS COURSE.

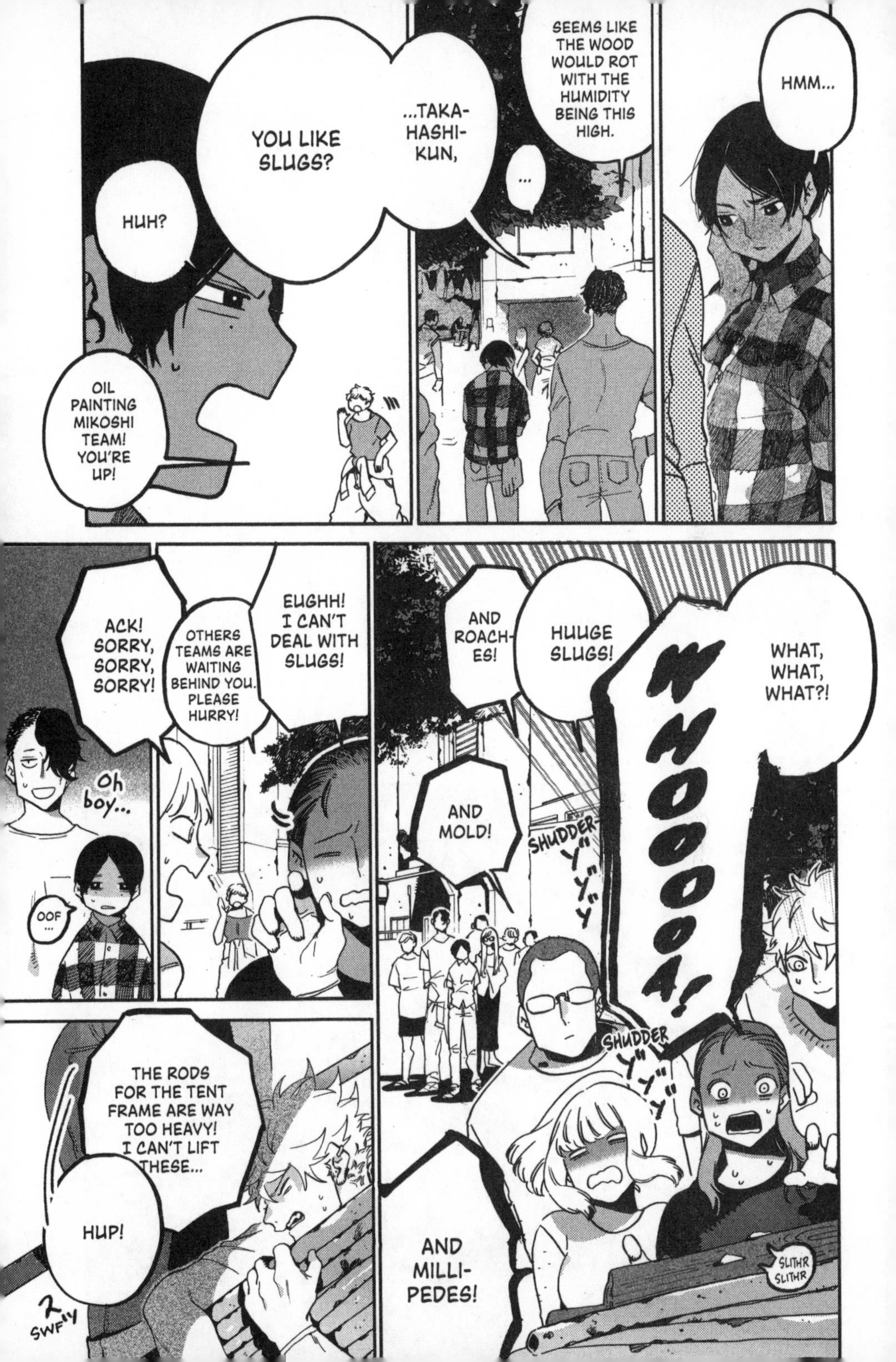
HMM...
SEEMS LIKE THE WOOD WOULD ROT WITH THE HUMIDITY BEING THIS HIGH.
...
...TAKA-HASHI-KUN,
YOU LIKE SLUGS?
HUH?
OIL PAINTING MIKOSHI TEAM! YOU'RE UP!
WHAT, WHAT, WHAT?!
WHOOOOA!
HUUGE SLUGS!
AND ROACH-ES!
AND MOLD!
SHUDDER
SHUDDER
AND MILLI-PEDES!
SLITHR SLITHR
EUGHH! I CAN'T DEAL WITH SLUGS!
OTHERS TEAMS ARE WAITING BEHIND YOU. PLEASE HURRY!
ACK! SORRY, SORRY, SORRY!
Oh boy...
OOF ...
THE RODS FOR THE TENT FRAME ARE WAY TOO HEAVY! I CAN'T LIFT THESE...
HUP!
SWF'Y

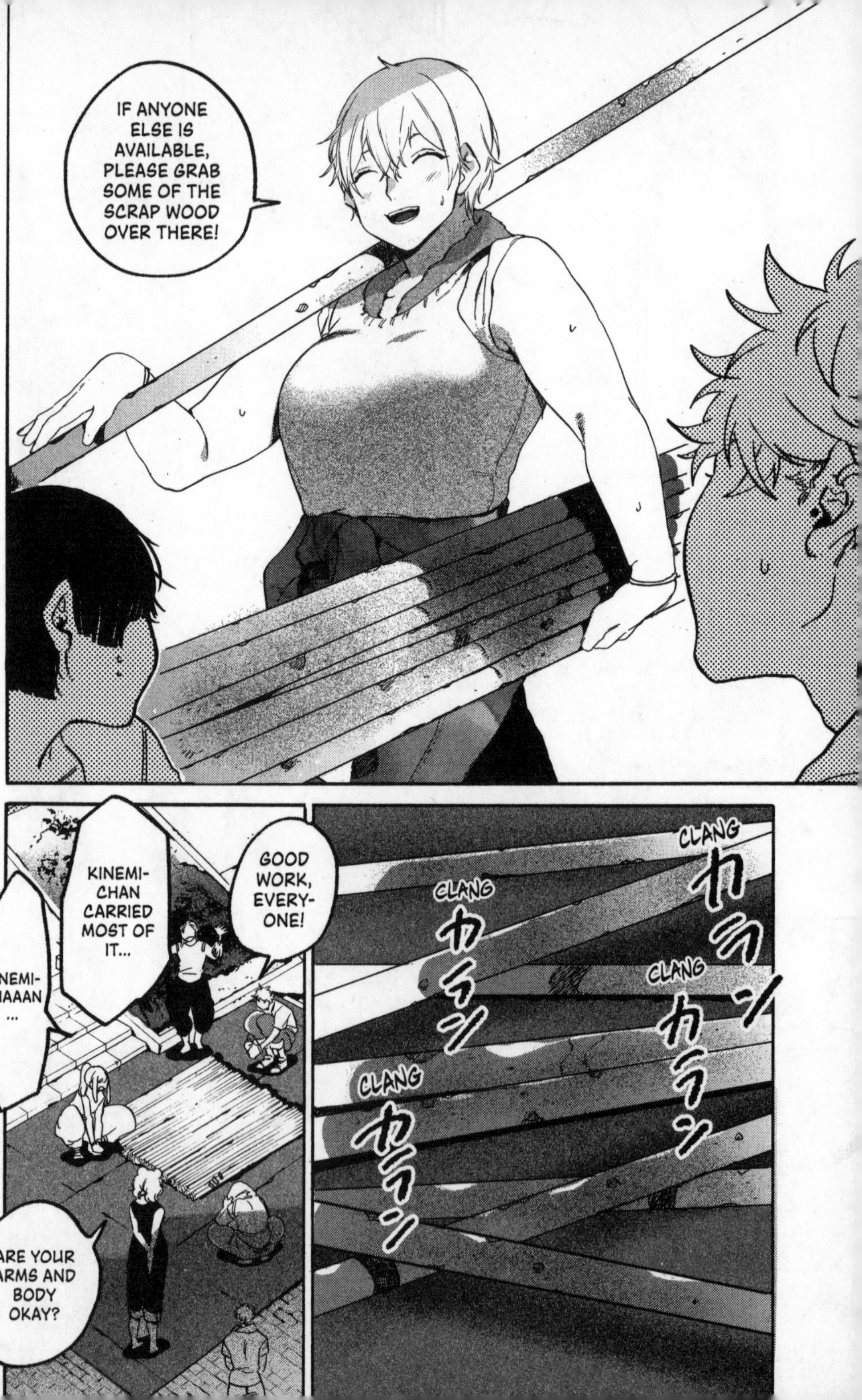
IF ANYONE ELSE IS AVAILABLE, PLEASE GRAB SOME OF THE SCRAP WOOD OVER THERE!
CLANG
カラン
CLANG
カラン
CLANG
カラン
CLANG
カラン
GOOD WORK, EVERY-ONE!
KINEMI-CHAN CARRIED MOST OF IT...
KINEMI-CHAAAN ...
ARE YOUR ARMS AND BODY OKAY?

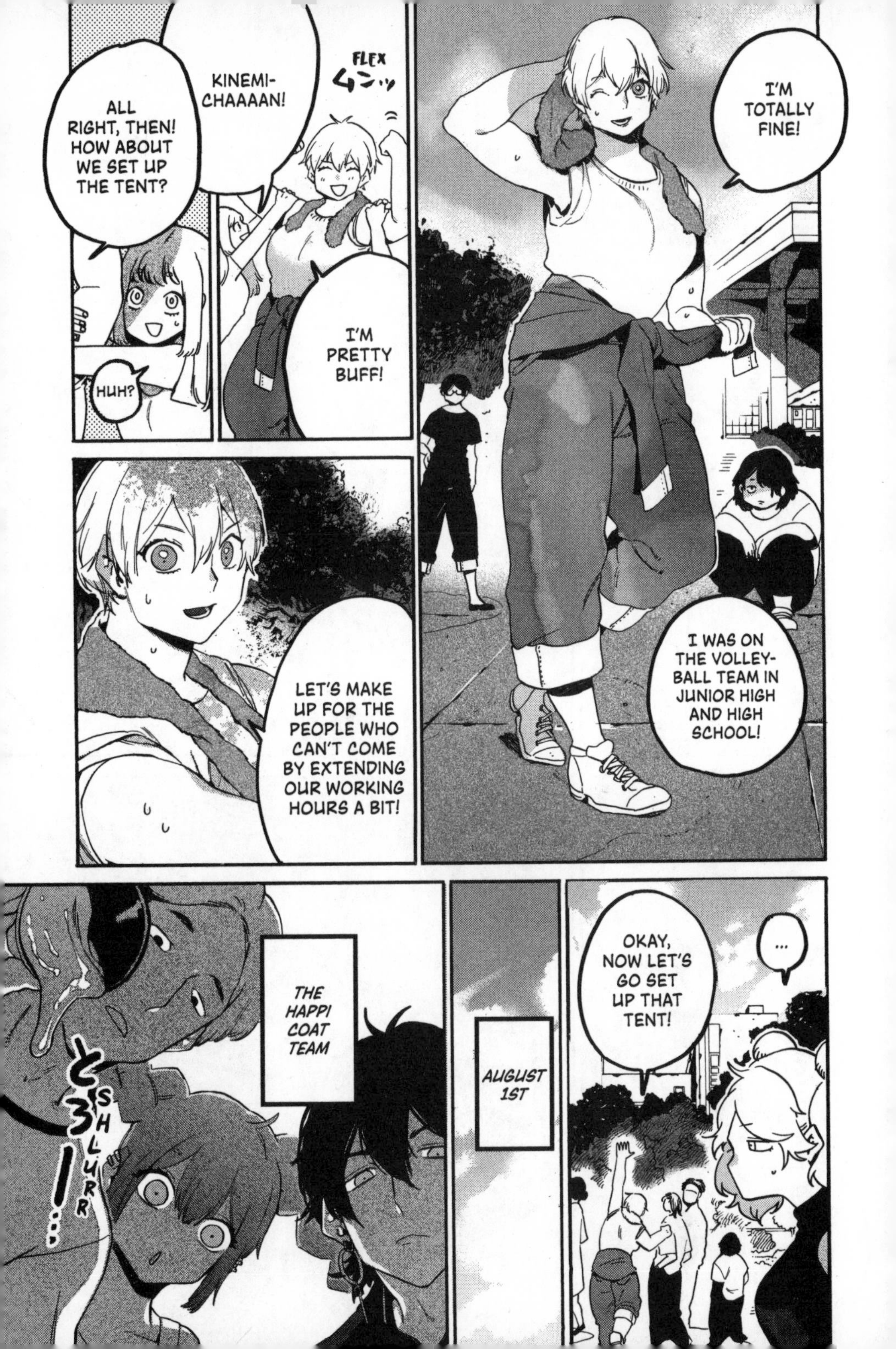
I'M TOTALLY FINE!
I WAS ON THE VOLLEY-BALL TEAM IN JUNIOR HIGH AND HIGH SCHOOL!
KINEMI-CHAAAAN!
FLEX
I'M PRETTY BUFF!
ALL RIGHT, THEN! HOW ABOUT WE SET UP THE TENT?
HUH?
LET'S MAKE UP FOR THE PEOPLE WHO CAN'T COME BY EXTENDING OUR WORKING HOURS A BIT!
...
OKAY, NOW LET'S GO SET UP THAT TENT!
AUGUST 1ST
THE HAPPI COAT TEAM
SHLURR

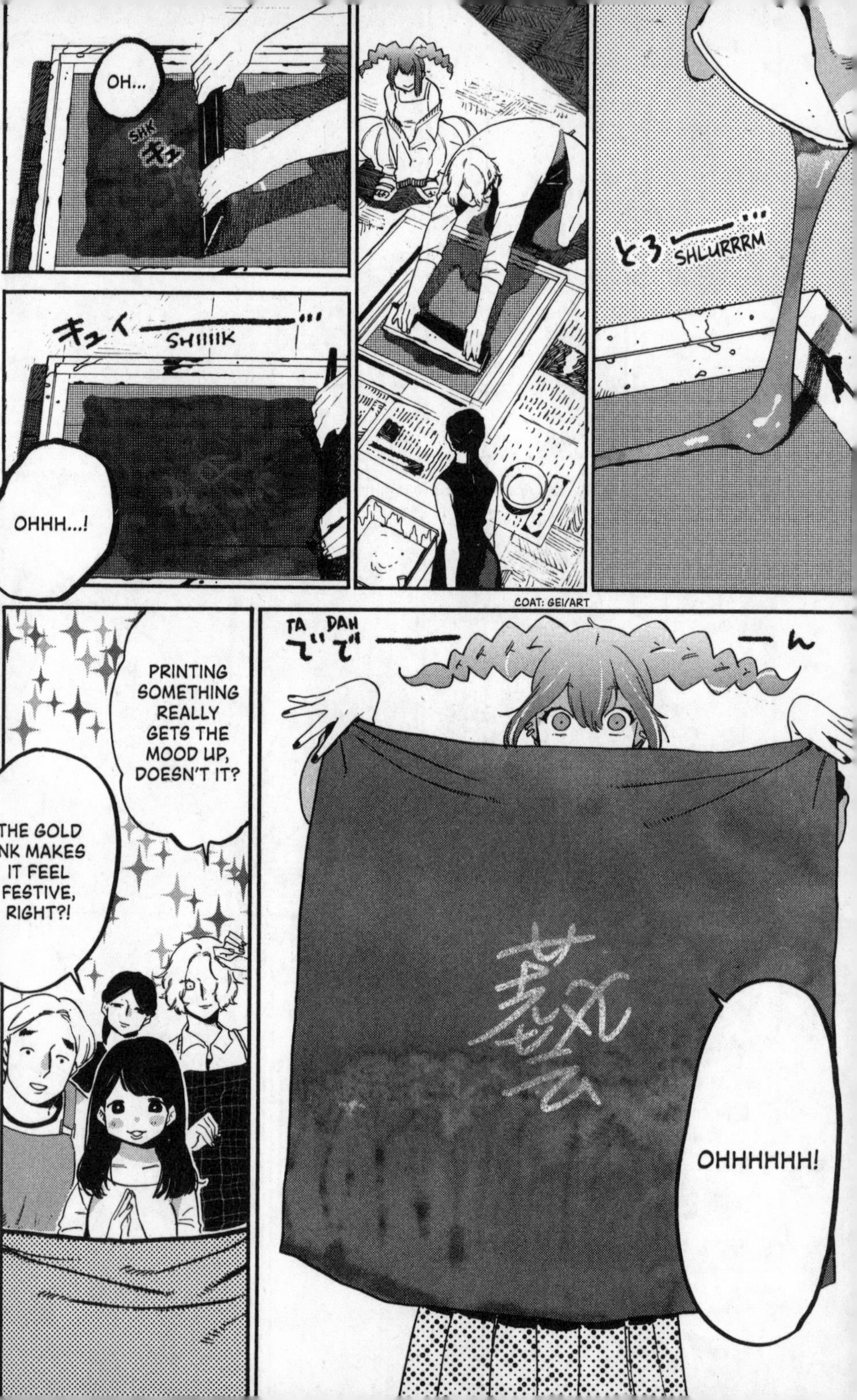

とろ SHLURRRM
COAT: GEI/ART
OH...
キュ SHK
キュイ SHIIIIK
OHHH...!
でで ん TA DAH
OHHHHHH!
PRINTING SOMETHING REALLY GETS THE MOOD UP, DOESN'T IT?
THE GOLD INK MAKES IT FEEL FESTIVE, RIGHT?!

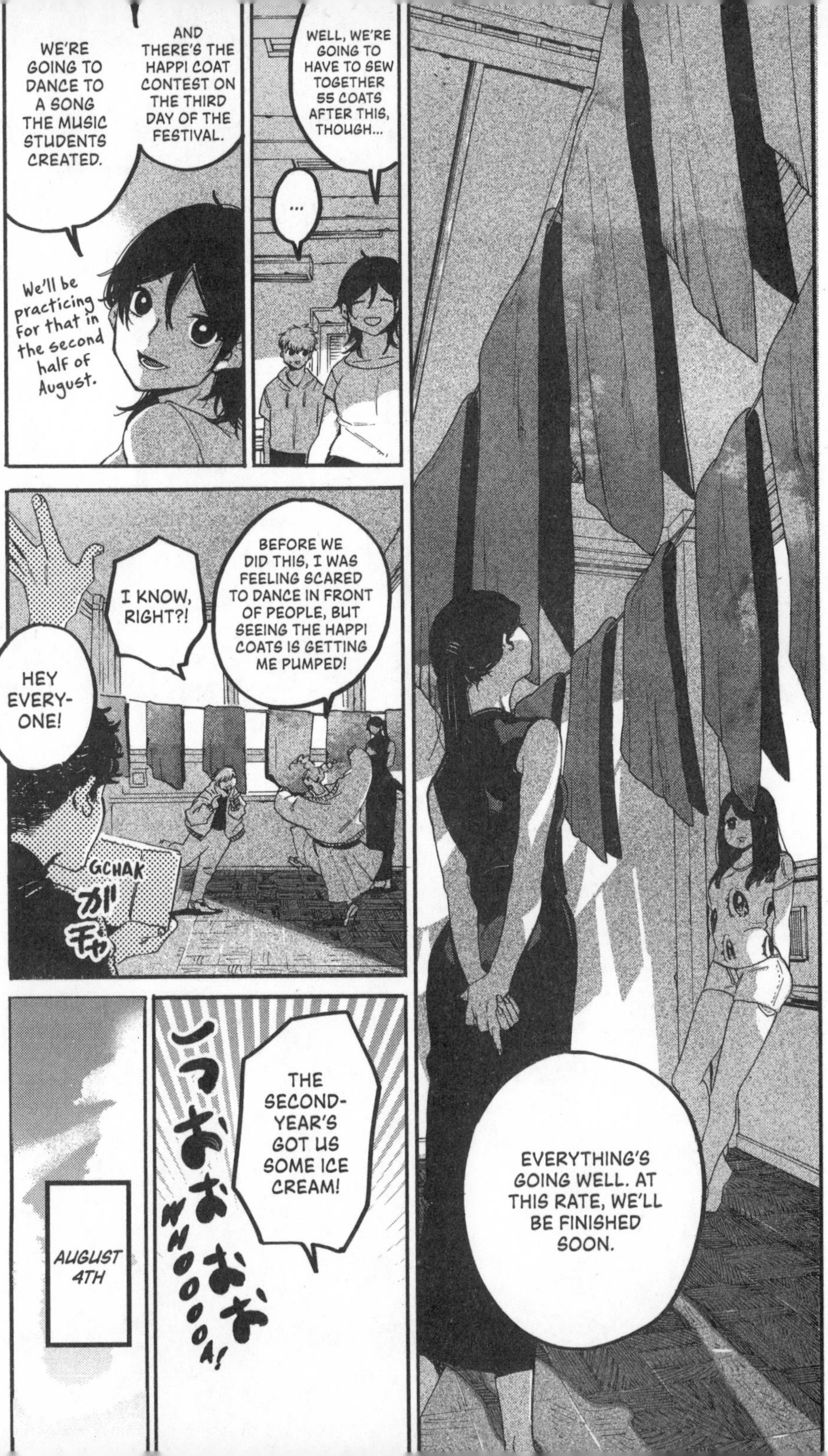
EVERYTHING'S GOING WELL. AT THIS RATE, WE'LL BE FINISHED SOON.
WELL, WE'RE GOING TO HAVE TO SEW TOGETHER 55 COATS AFTER THIS, THOUGH...
...
AND THERE'S THE HAPPI COAT CONTEST ON THE THIRD DAY OF THE FESTIVAL.
WE'RE GOING TO DANCE TO A SONG THE MUSIC STUDENTS CREATED.
We'll be practicing for that in the second half of August.
BEFORE WE DID THIS, I WAS FEELING SCARED TO DANCE IN FRONT OF PEOPLE, BUT SEEING THE HAPPI COATS IS GETTING ME PUMPED!
I KNOW, RIGHT?!
HEY EVERY-ONE!
GCHAK
ガチャ
うおおお
WHOOOOA!
THE SECOND-YEAR'S GOT US SOME ICE CREAM!
AUGUST 4TH

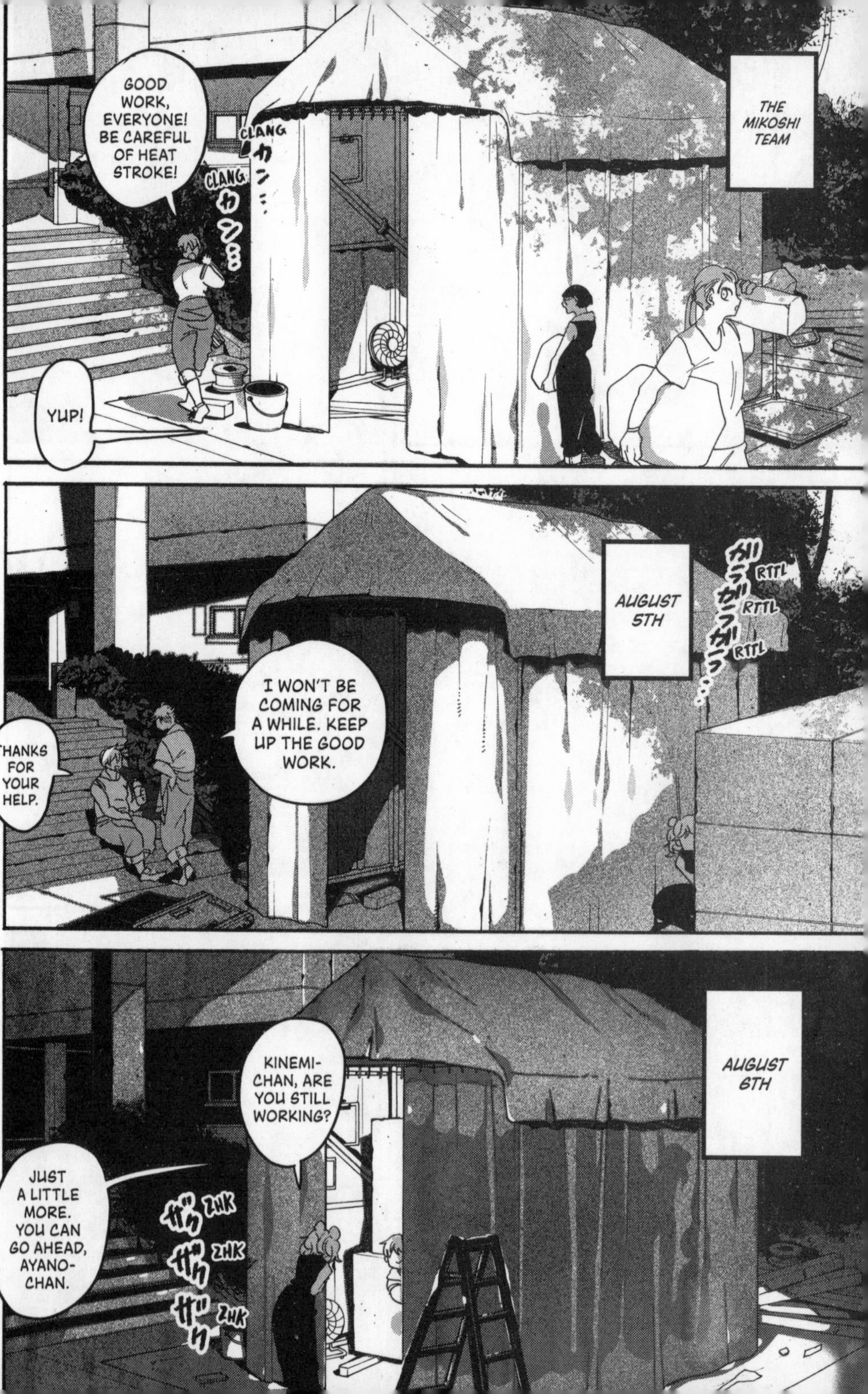
THE MIKOSHI TEAM
CLANG
CLANG
GOOD WORK, EVERYONE! BE CAREFUL OF HEAT STROKE!
YUP!
AUGUST 5TH
RTTL
RTTL
RTTL
I WON'T BE COMING FOR A WHILE. KEEP UP THE GOOD WORK.
THANKS FOR YOUR HELP.
AUGUST 6TH
KINEMI-CHAN, ARE YOU STILL WORKING?
JUST A LITTLE MORE. YOU CAN GO AHEAD, AYANO-CHAN.
ZHK
ZHK
ZHK

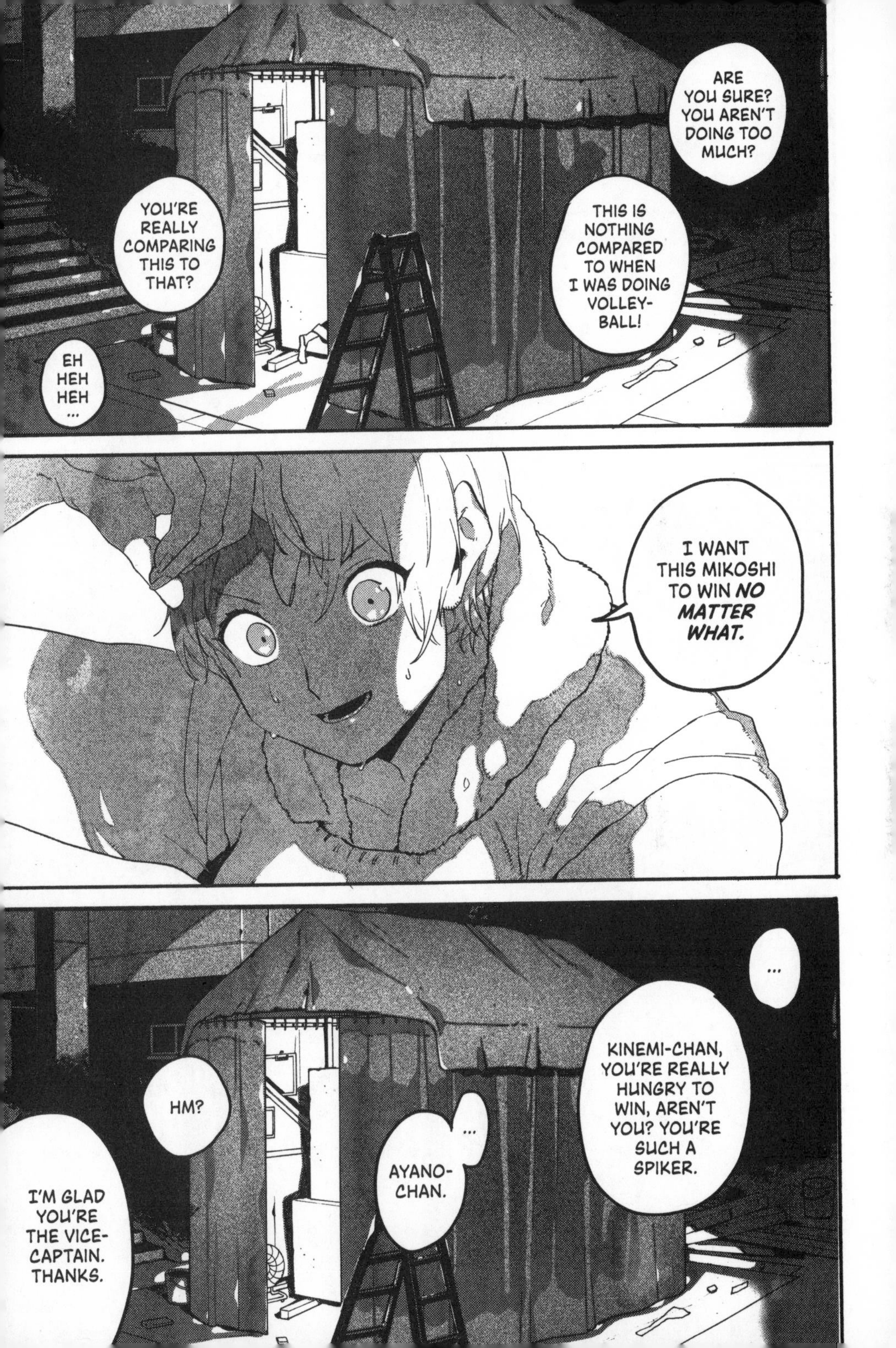
ARE YOU SURE? YOU AREN'T DOING TOO MUCH?
THIS IS NOTHING COMPARED TO WHEN I WAS DOING VOLLEY-BALL!
YOU'RE REALLY COMPARING THIS TO THAT?
EH HEH HEH ...
I WANT THIS MIKOSHI TO WIN *NO MATTER WHAT.*
...
KINEMI-CHAN, YOU'RE REALLY HUNGRY TO WIN, AREN'T YOU? YOU'RE SUCH A SPIKER.
...
AYANO-CHAN.
HM?
I'M GLAD YOU'RE THE VICE-CAPTAIN. THANKS.

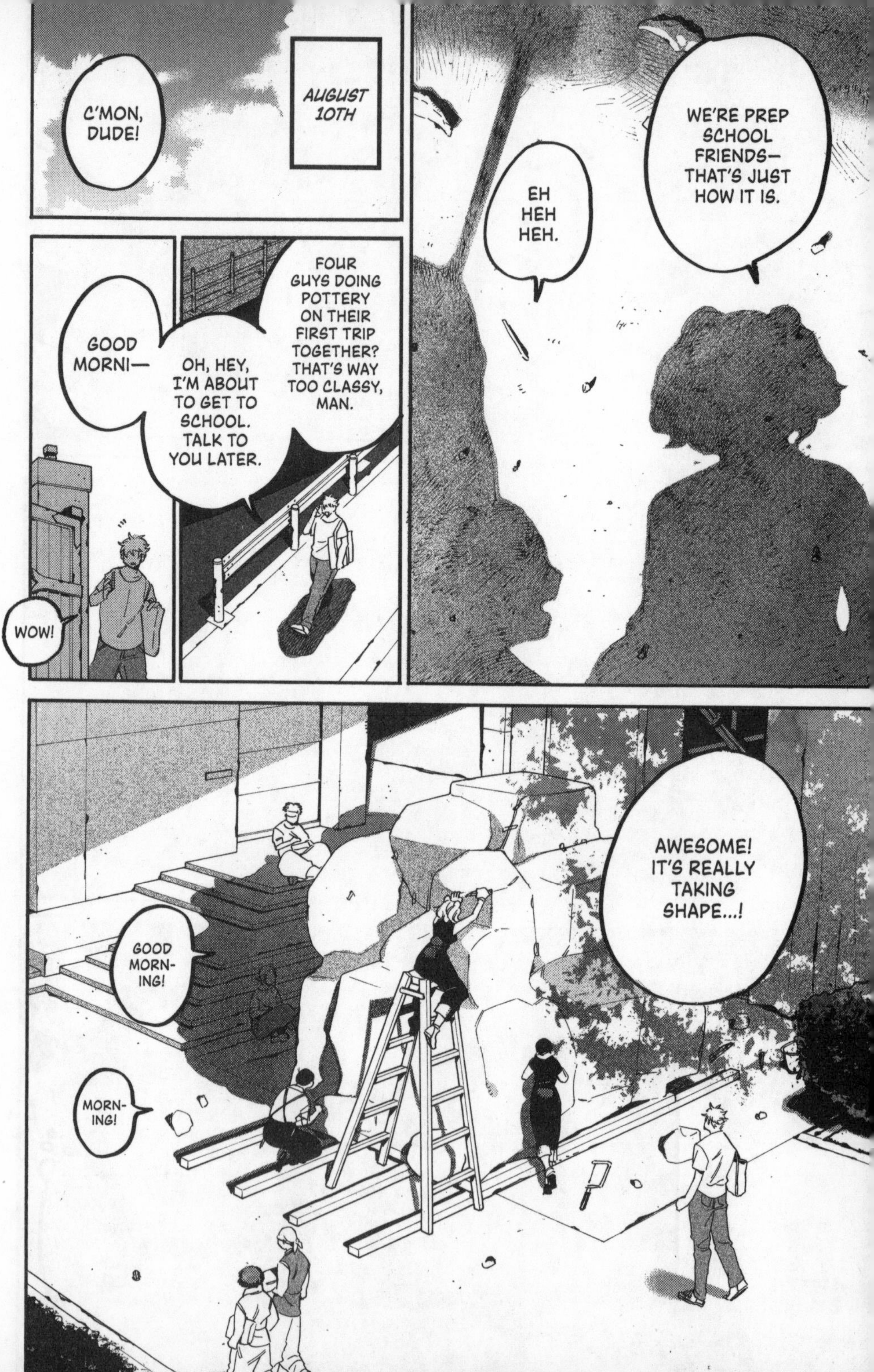
WE'RE PREP SCHOOL FRIENDS— THAT'S JUST HOW IT IS.
EH HEH HEH.
AUGUST 10TH
C'MON, DUDE!
FOUR GUYS DOING POTTERY ON THEIR FIRST TRIP TOGETHER? THAT'S WAY TOO CLASSY, MAN.
OH, HEY, I'M ABOUT TO GET TO SCHOOL. TALK TO YOU LATER.
GOOD MORNI—
WOW!
AWESOME! IT'S REALLY TAKING SHAPE...!
GOOD MORN-ING!
MORN-ING!

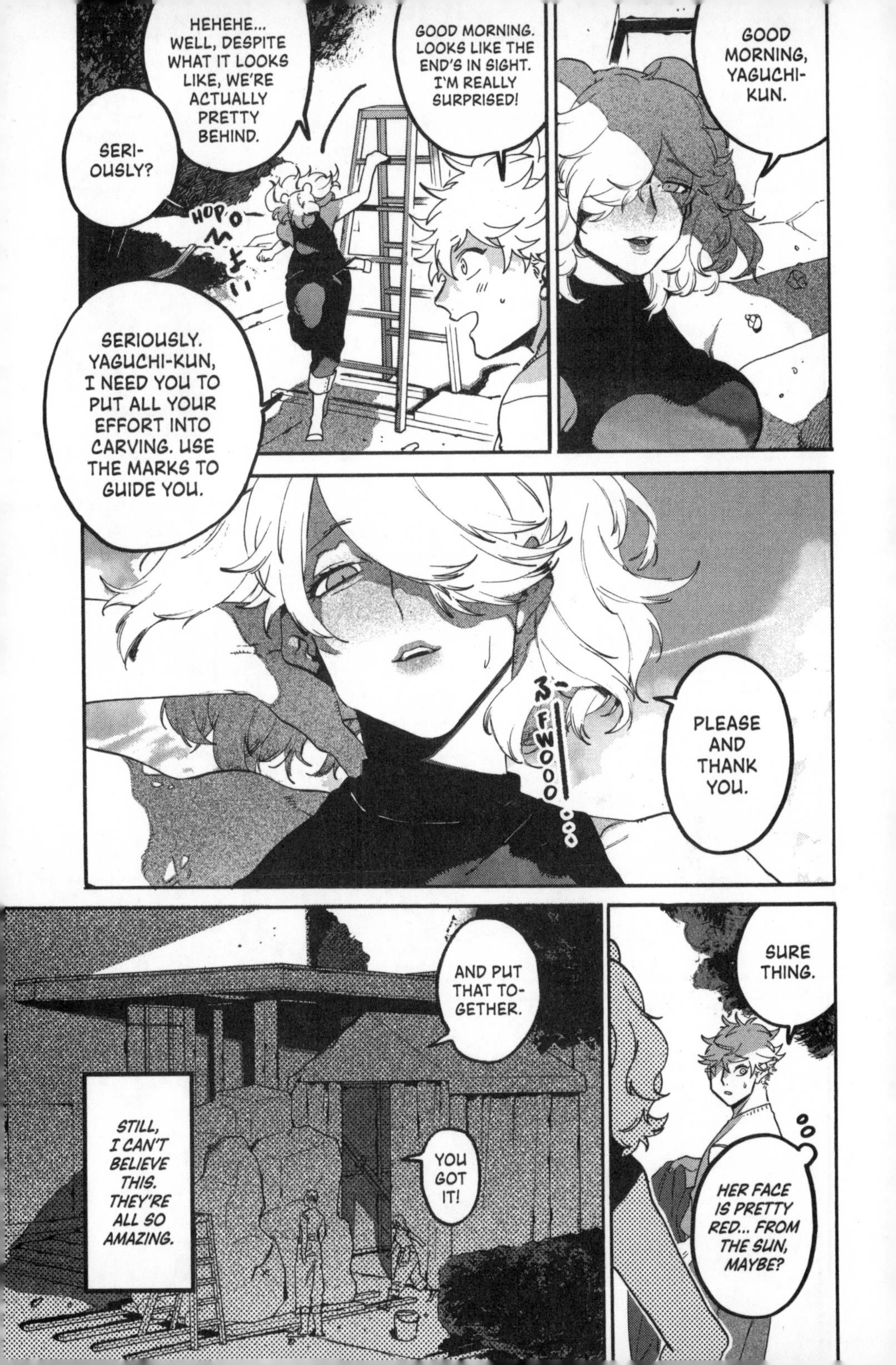
GOOD MORNING, YAGUCHI-KUN.
GOOD MORNING. LOOKS LIKE THE END'S IN SIGHT. I'M REALLY SURPRISED!
HEHEHE... WELL, DESPITE WHAT IT LOOKS LIKE, WE'RE ACTUALLY PRETTY BEHIND.
SERI-OUSLY?
HOP
SERIOUSLY. YAGUCHI-KUN, I NEED YOU TO PUT ALL YOUR EFFORT INTO CARVING. USE THE MARKS TO GUIDE YOU.
PLEASE AND THANK YOU.
ふー
FWOOOOOOO
SURE THING.
HER FACE IS PRETTY RED... FROM THE SUN, MAYBE?
AND PUT THAT TO-GETHER.
YOU GOT IT!
STILL, I CAN'T BELIEVE THIS. THEY'RE ALL SO AMAZING.

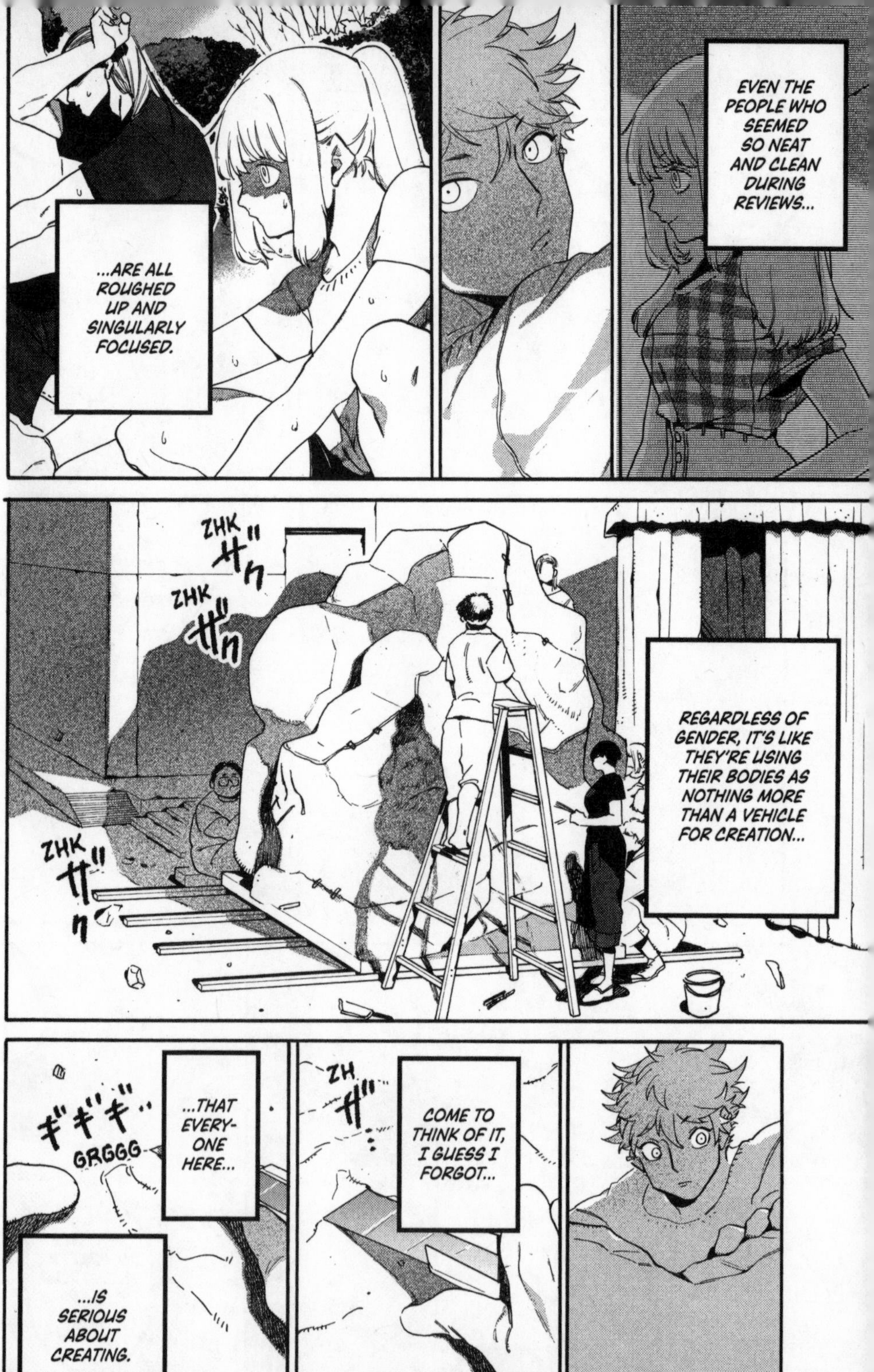
EVEN THE PEOPLE WHO SEEMED SO NEAT AND CLEAN DURING REVIEWS...
...ARE ALL ROUGHED UP AND SINGULARLY FOCUSED.
ZHK
ザク
ZHK
ザク
REGARDLESS OF GENDER, IT'S LIKE THEY'RE USING THEIR BODIES AS NOTHING MORE THAN A VEHICLE FOR CREATION...
ZHK
ザク
ZH
ザ
COME TO THINK OF IT, I GUESS I FORGOT...
...THAT EVERY-ONE HERE...
ギギギ
GRGGG
...IS SERIOUS ABOUT CREATING.

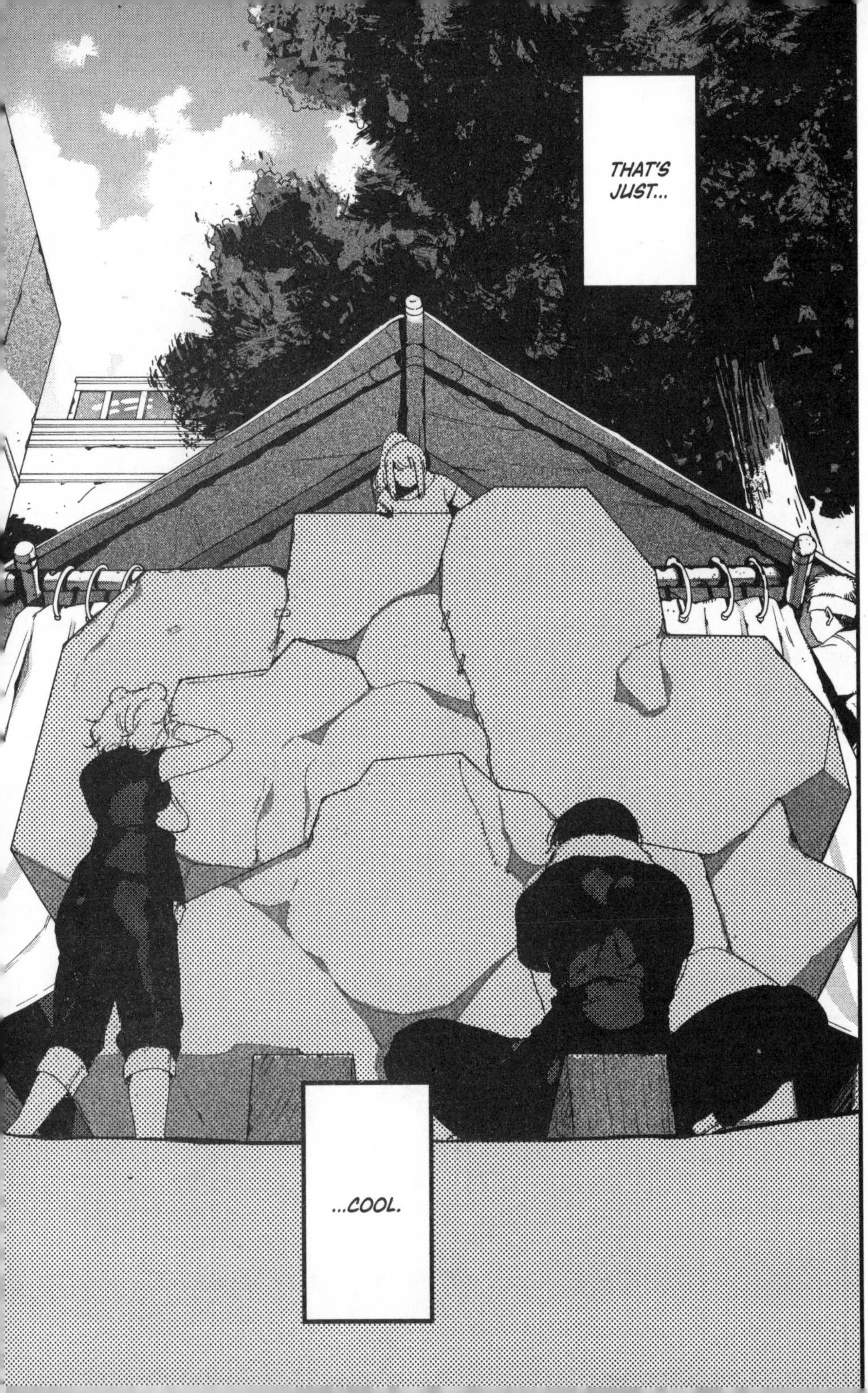
THAT'S JUST...
...COOL.

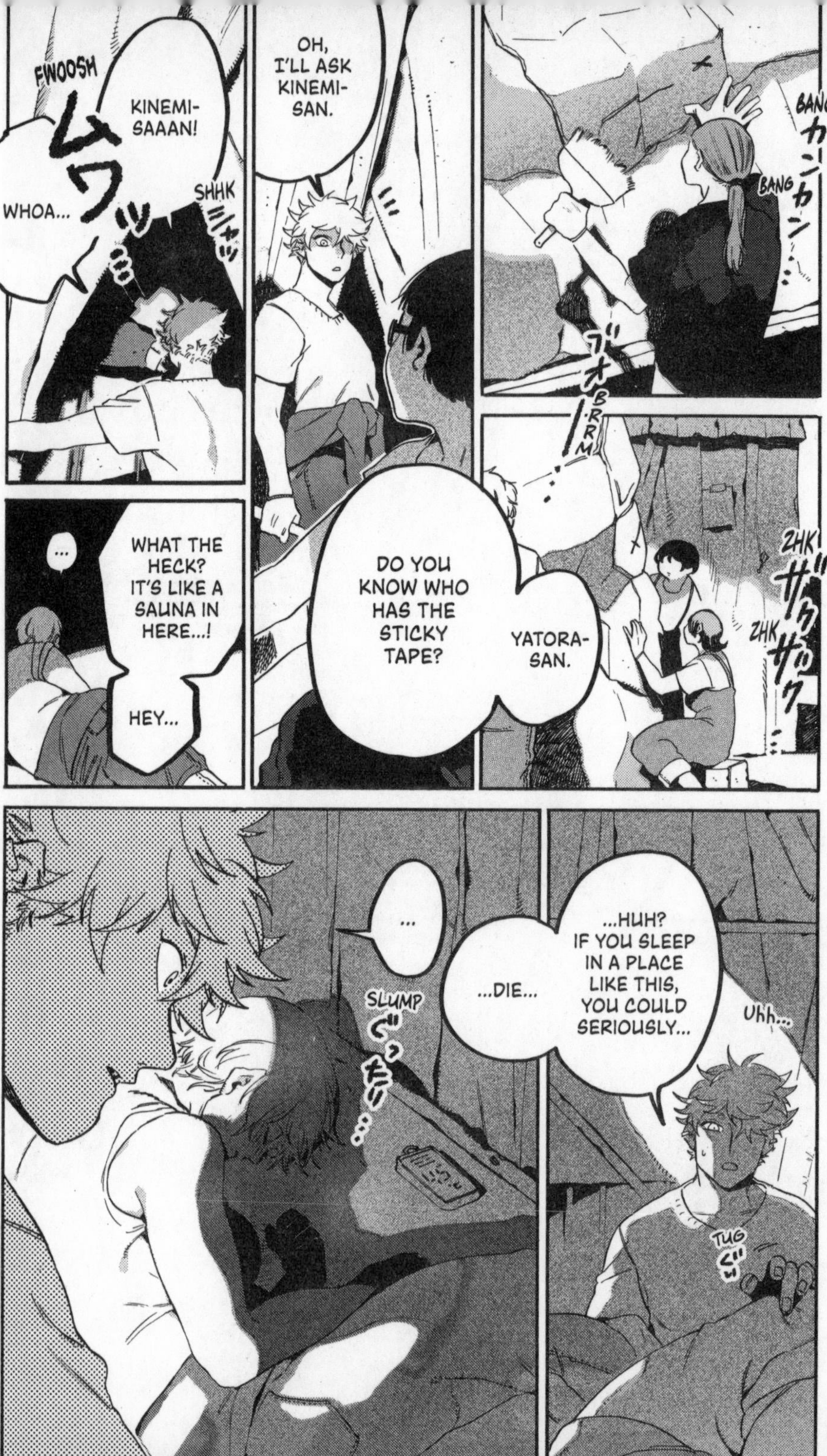
BANG
BANG
BRRM
DO YOU KNOW WHO HAS THE STICKY TAPE?
YATORA-SAN.
ZHK
ZHK
OH, I'LL ASK KINEMI-SAN.
FWOOSH
KINEMI-SAAAN!
WHOA...
SHHK
...
WHAT THE HECK? IT'S LIKE A SAUNA IN HERE...!
HEY...
...HUH? IF YOU SLEEP IN A PLACE LIKE THIS, YOU COULD SERIOUSLY...
Uhh...
...DIE...
TUG
...
SLUMP

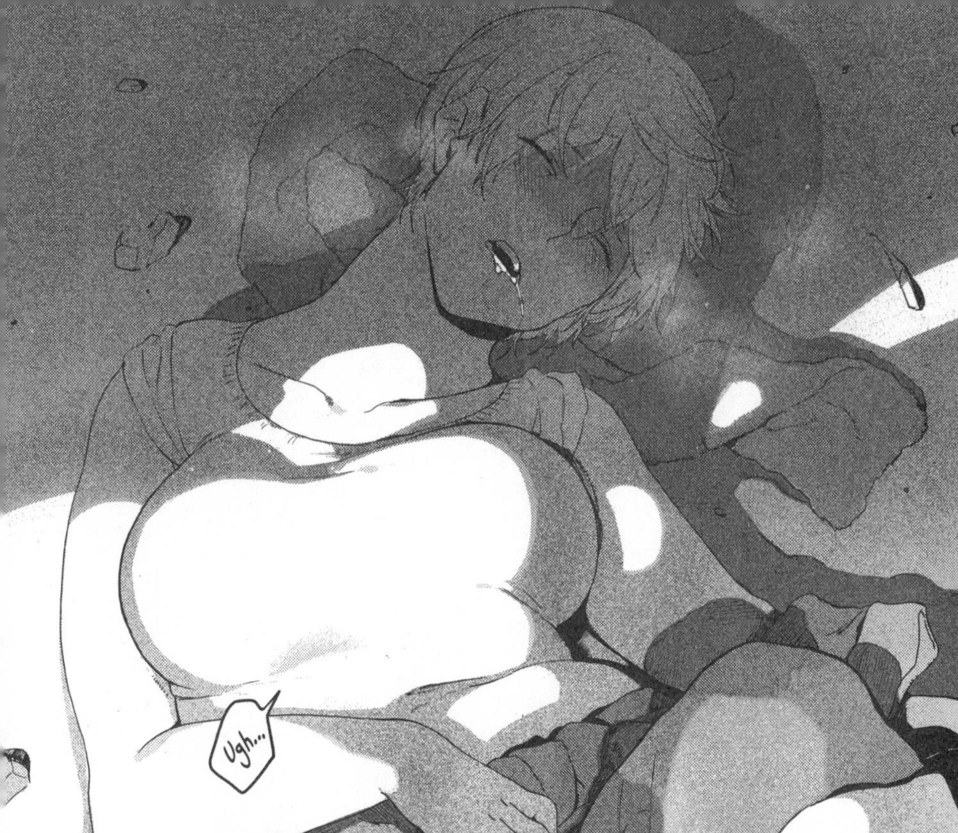
Ugh...
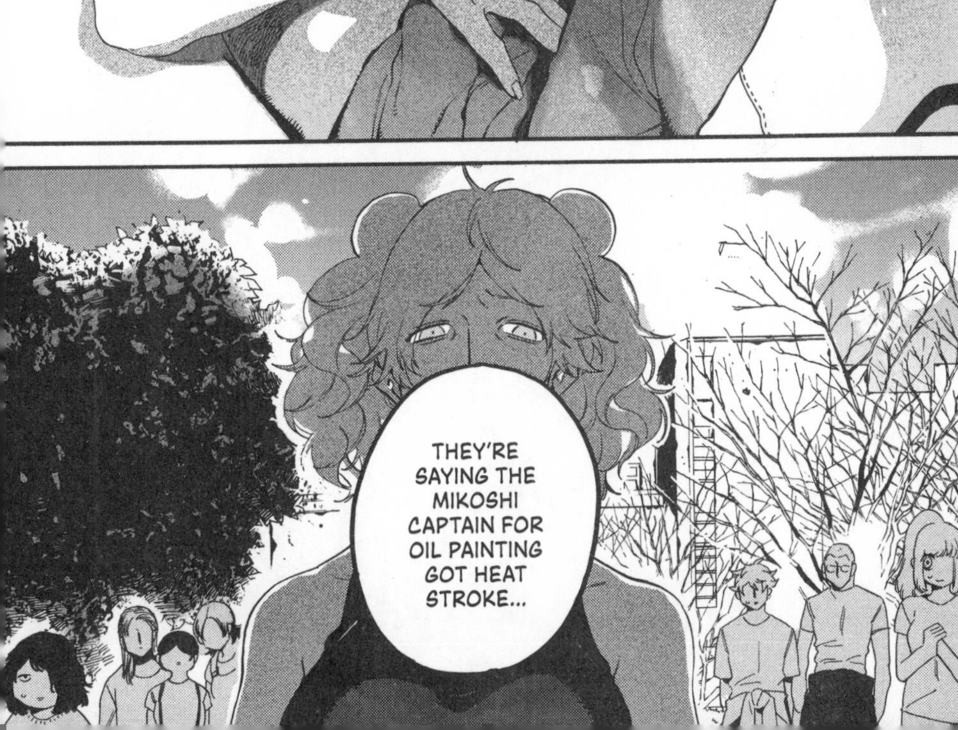
THEY'RE SAYING THE MIKOSHI CAPTAIN FOR OIL PAINTING GOT HEAT STROKE...

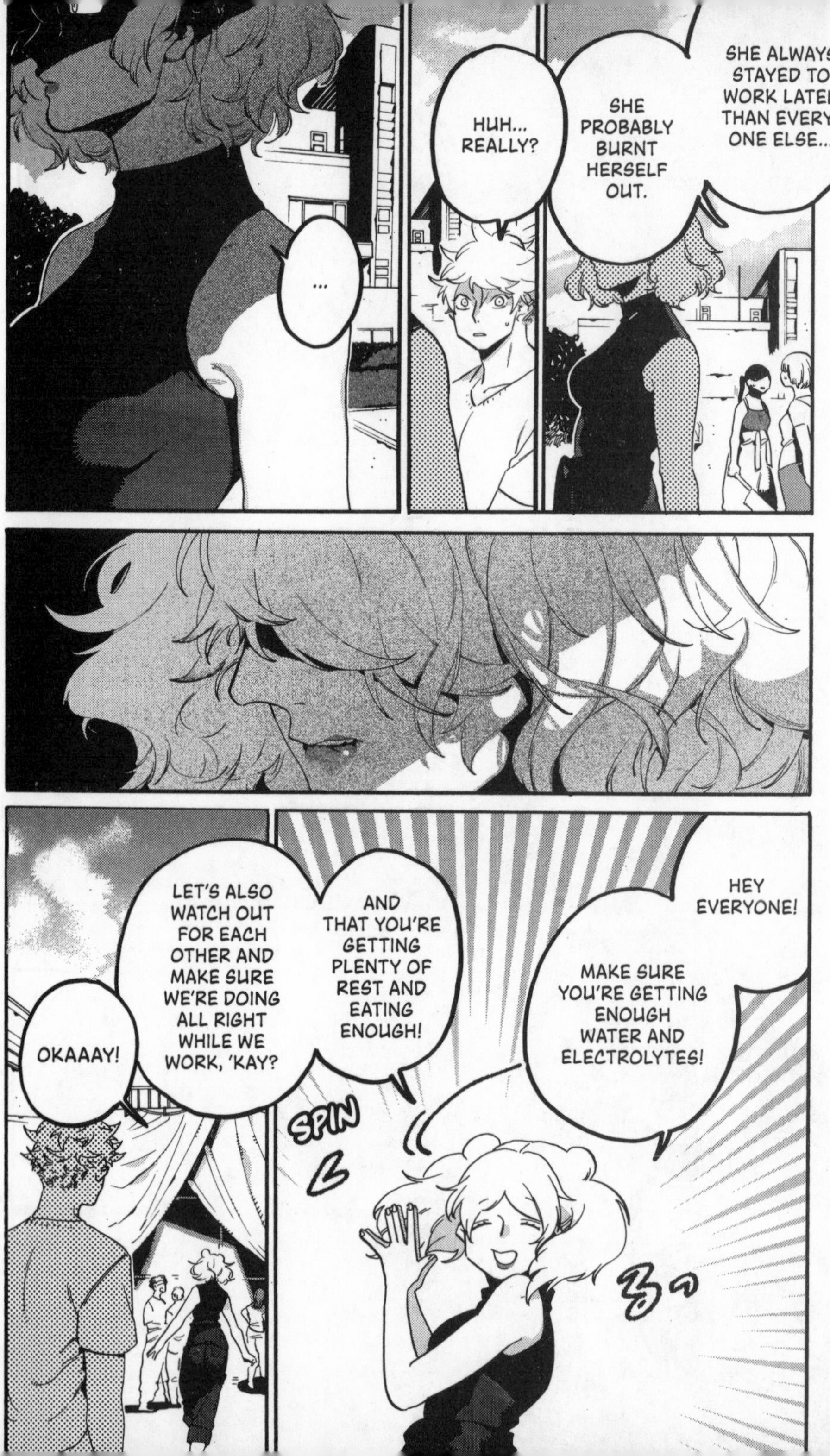
SHE ALWAYS STAYED TO WORK LATER THAN EVERY-ONE ELSE...
SHE PROBABLY BURNT HERSELF OUT.
HUH... REALLY?
...
HEY EVERYONE!
MAKE SURE YOU'RE GETTING ENOUGH WATER AND ELECTROLYTES!
AND THAT YOU'RE GETTING PLENTY OF REST AND EATING ENOUGH!
SPIN
LET'S ALSO WATCH OUT FOR EACH OTHER AND MAKE SURE WE'RE DOING ALL RIGHT WHILE WE WORK, 'KAY?
OKAAAY!

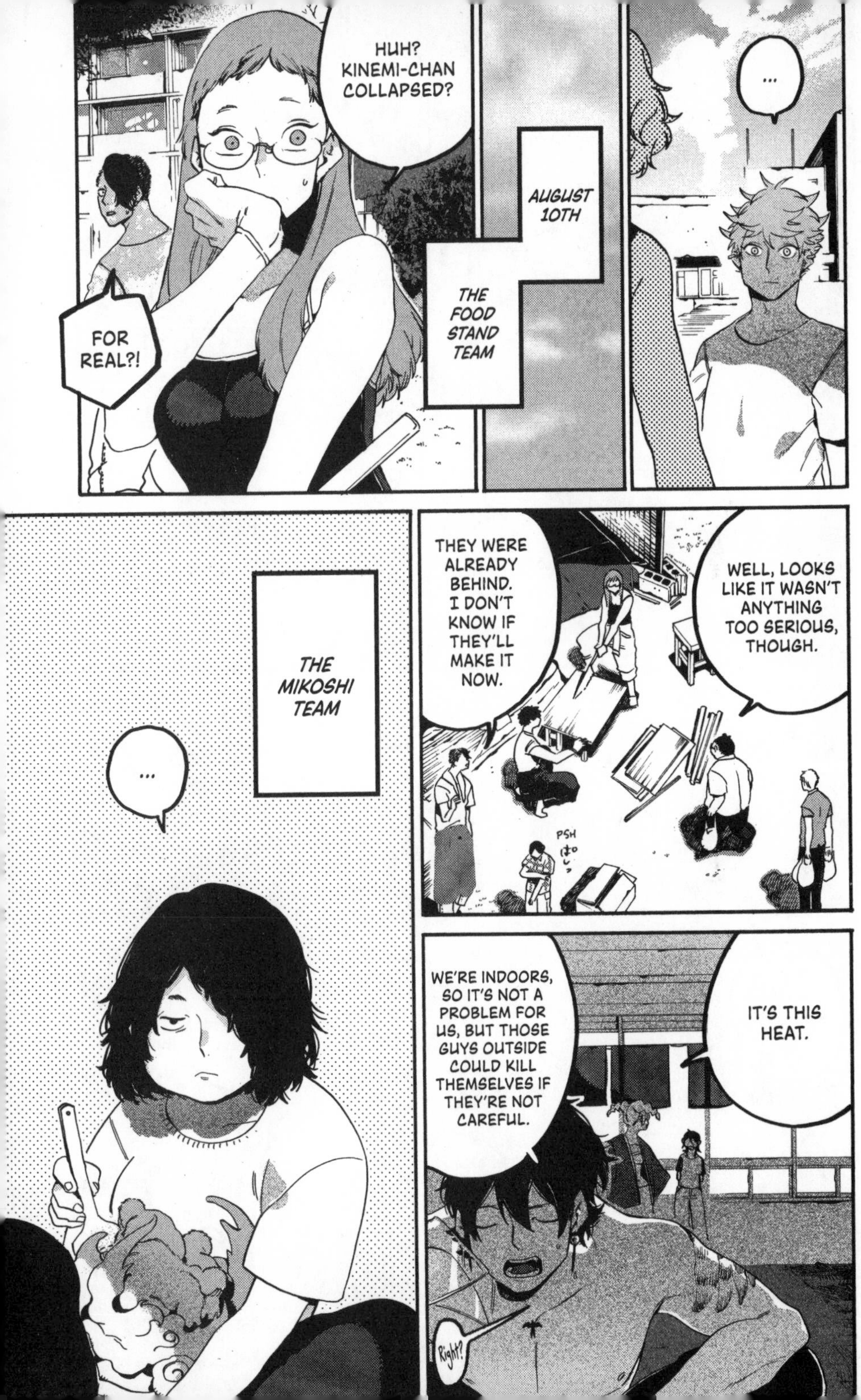
...
AUGUST 10TH
THE FOOD STAND TEAM
HUH? KINEMI-CHAN COLLAPSED?
FOR REAL?!
WELL, LOOKS LIKE IT WASN'T ANYTHING TOO SERIOUS, THOUGH.
THEY WERE ALREADY BEHIND. I DON'T KNOW IF THEY'LL MAKE IT NOW.
PSH
IT'S THIS HEAT.
WE'RE INDOORS, SO IT'S NOT A PROBLEM FOR US, BUT THOSE GUYS OUTSIDE COULD KILL THEMSELVES IF THEY'RE NOT CAREFUL.
Right?
THE MIKOSHI TEAM
...

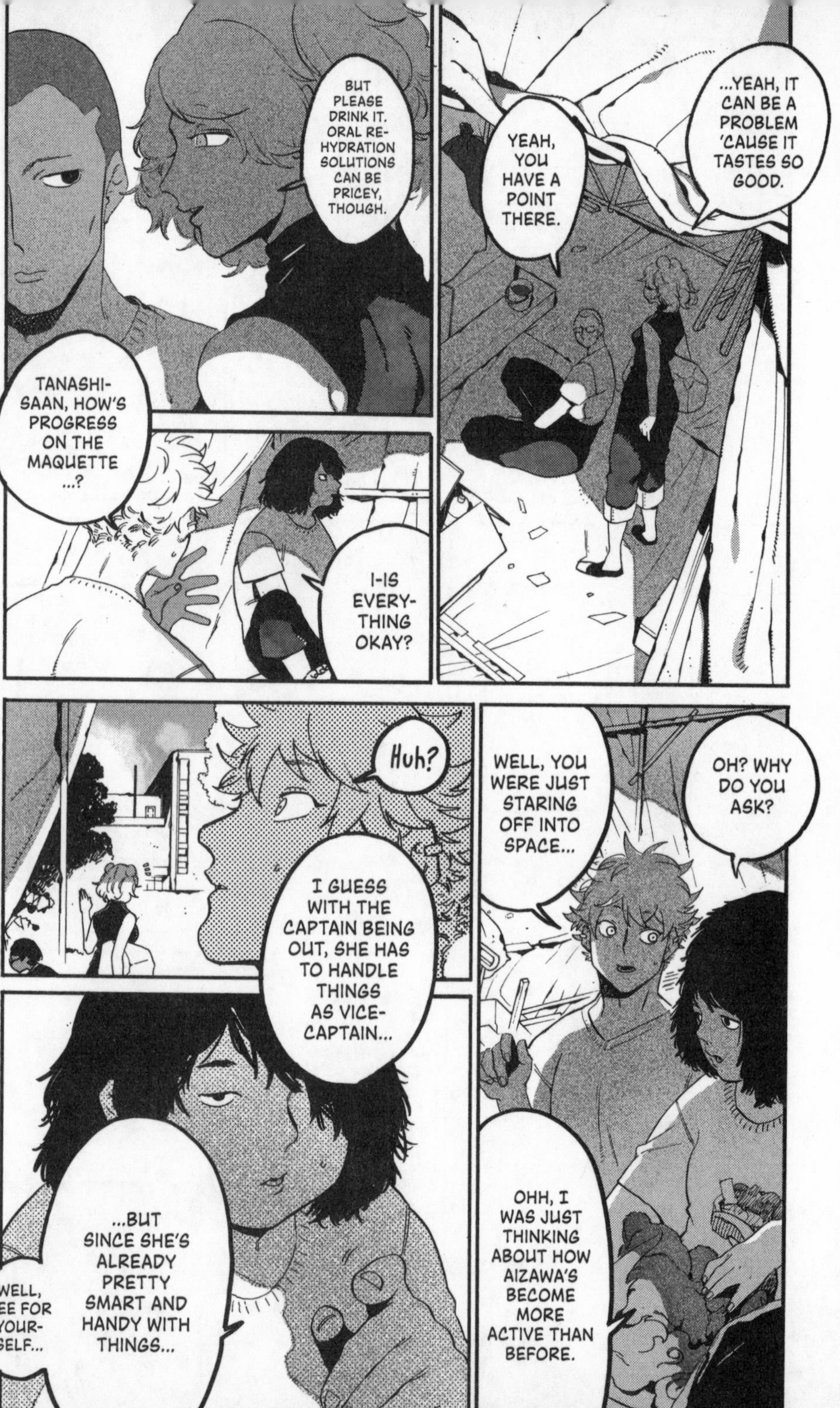
...YEAH, IT CAN BE A PROBLEM 'CAUSE IT TASTES SO GOOD.
YEAH, YOU HAVE A POINT THERE.
BUT PLEASE DRINK IT. ORAL RE-HYDRATION SOLUTIONS CAN BE PRICEY, THOUGH.
I-IS EVERY-THING OKAY?
TANASHI-SAAN, HOW'S PROGRESS ON THE MAQUETTE ...?
OH? WHY DO YOU ASK?
WELL, YOU WERE JUST STARING OFF INTO SPACE...
OHH, I WAS JUST THINKING ABOUT HOW AIZAWA'S BECOME MORE ACTIVE THAN BEFORE.
Huh?
I GUESS WITH THE CAPTAIN BEING OUT, SHE HAS TO HANDLE THINGS AS VICE-CAPTAIN...
...BUT SINCE SHE'S ALREADY PRETTY SMART AND HANDY WITH THINGS...
WELL, SEE FOR YOUR-SELF...

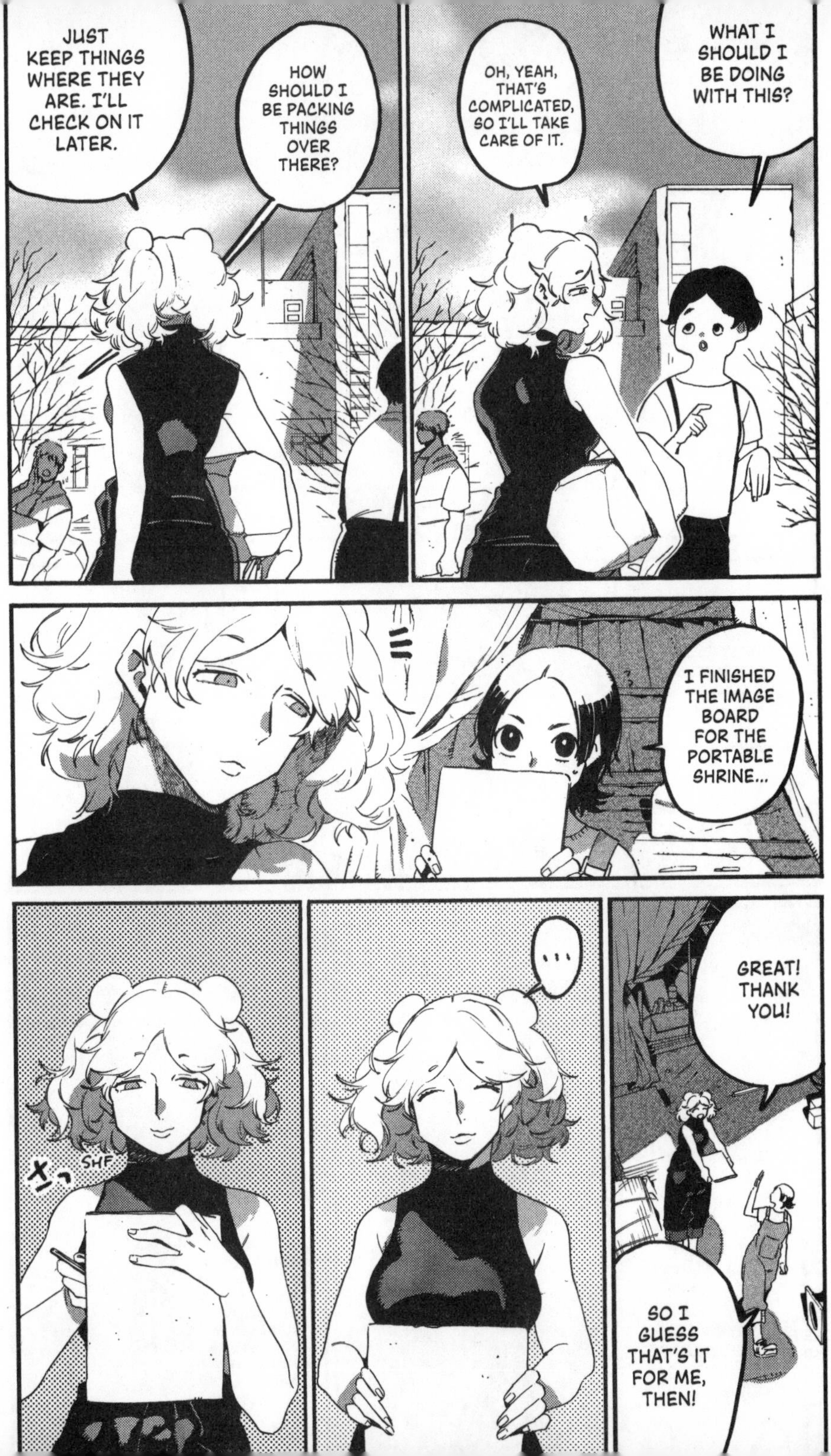
WHAT I SHOULD I BE DOING WITH THIS?
OH, YEAH, THAT'S COMPLICATED, SO I'LL TAKE CARE OF IT.
HOW SHOULD I BE PACKING THINGS OVER THERE?
JUST KEEP THINGS WHERE THEY ARE. I'LL CHECK ON IT LATER.
I FINISHED THE IMAGE BOARD FOR THE PORTABLE SHRINE...
GREAT! THANK YOU!
SO I GUESS THAT'S IT FOR ME, THEN!
...
SHF

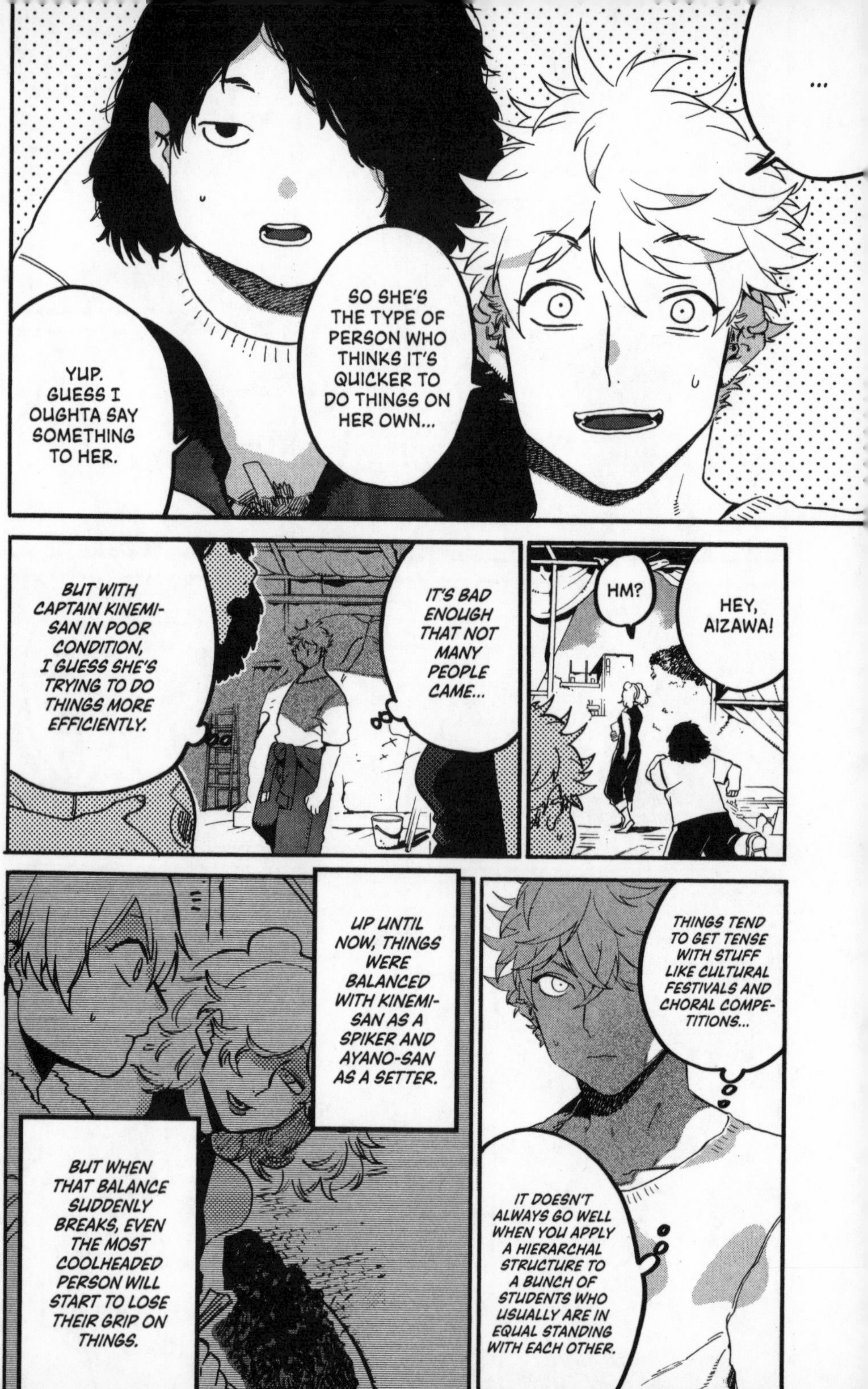
...
SO SHE'S THE TYPE OF PERSON WHO THINKS IT'S QUICKER TO DO THINGS ON HER OWN...
YUP. GUESS I OUGHTA SAY SOMETHING TO HER.
HEY, AIZAWA!
HM?
IT'S BAD ENOUGH THAT NOT MANY PEOPLE CAME...
BUT WITH CAPTAIN KINEMI-SAN IN POOR CONDITION, I GUESS SHE'S TRYING TO DO THINGS MORE EFFICIENTLY.
THINGS TEND TO GET TENSE WITH STUFF LIKE CULTURAL FESTIVALS AND CHORAL COMPE-TITIONS...
IT DOESN'T ALWAYS GO WELL WHEN YOU APPLY A HIERARCHAL STRUCTURE TO A BUNCH OF STUDENTS WHO USUALLY ARE IN EQUAL STANDING WITH EACH OTHER.
UP UNTIL NOW, THINGS WERE BALANCED WITH KINEMI-SAN AS A SPIKER AND AYANO-SAN AS A SETTER.
BUT WHEN THAT BALANCE SUDDENLY BREAKS, EVEN THE MOST COOLHEADED PERSON WILL START TO LOSE THEIR GRIP ON THINGS.

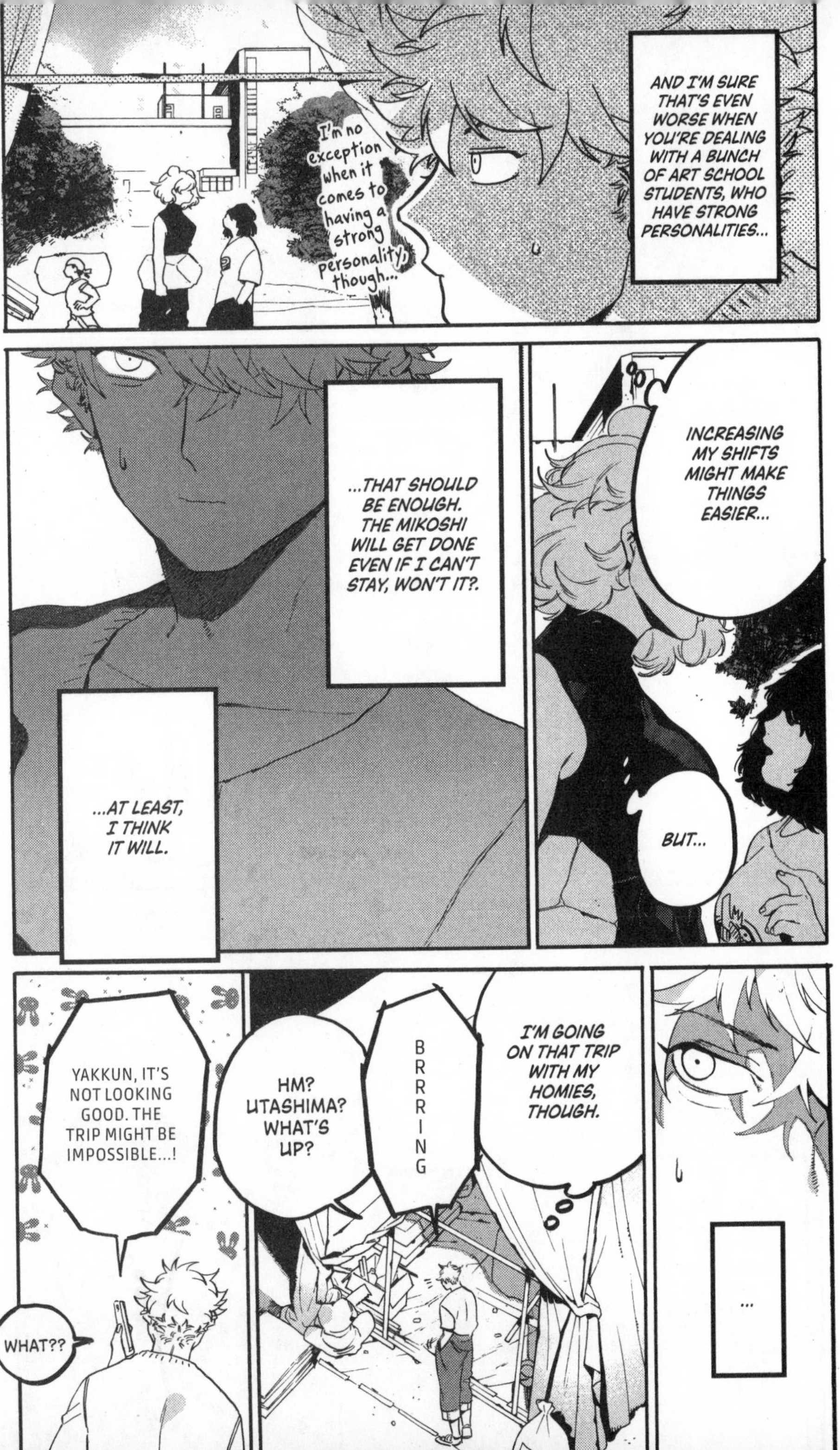
AND I'M SURE THAT'S EVEN WORSE WHEN YOU'RE DEALING WITH A BUNCH OF ART SCHOOL STUDENTS, WHO HAVE STRONG PERSONALITIES...
I'm no exception when it comes to having a strong personality, though...
INCREASING MY SHIFTS MIGHT MAKE THINGS EASIER...
BUT...
...THAT SHOULD BE ENOUGH. THE MIKOSHI WILL GET DONE EVEN IF I CAN'T STAY, WON'T IT?.
...AT LEAST, I THINK IT WILL.
...
I'M GOING ON THAT TRIP WITH MY HOMIES, THOUGH.
BRRRING
HM? UTASHIMA? WHAT'S UP?
YAKKUN, IT'S NOT LOOKING GOOD. THE TRIP MIGHT BE IMPOSSIBLE...!
WHAT??

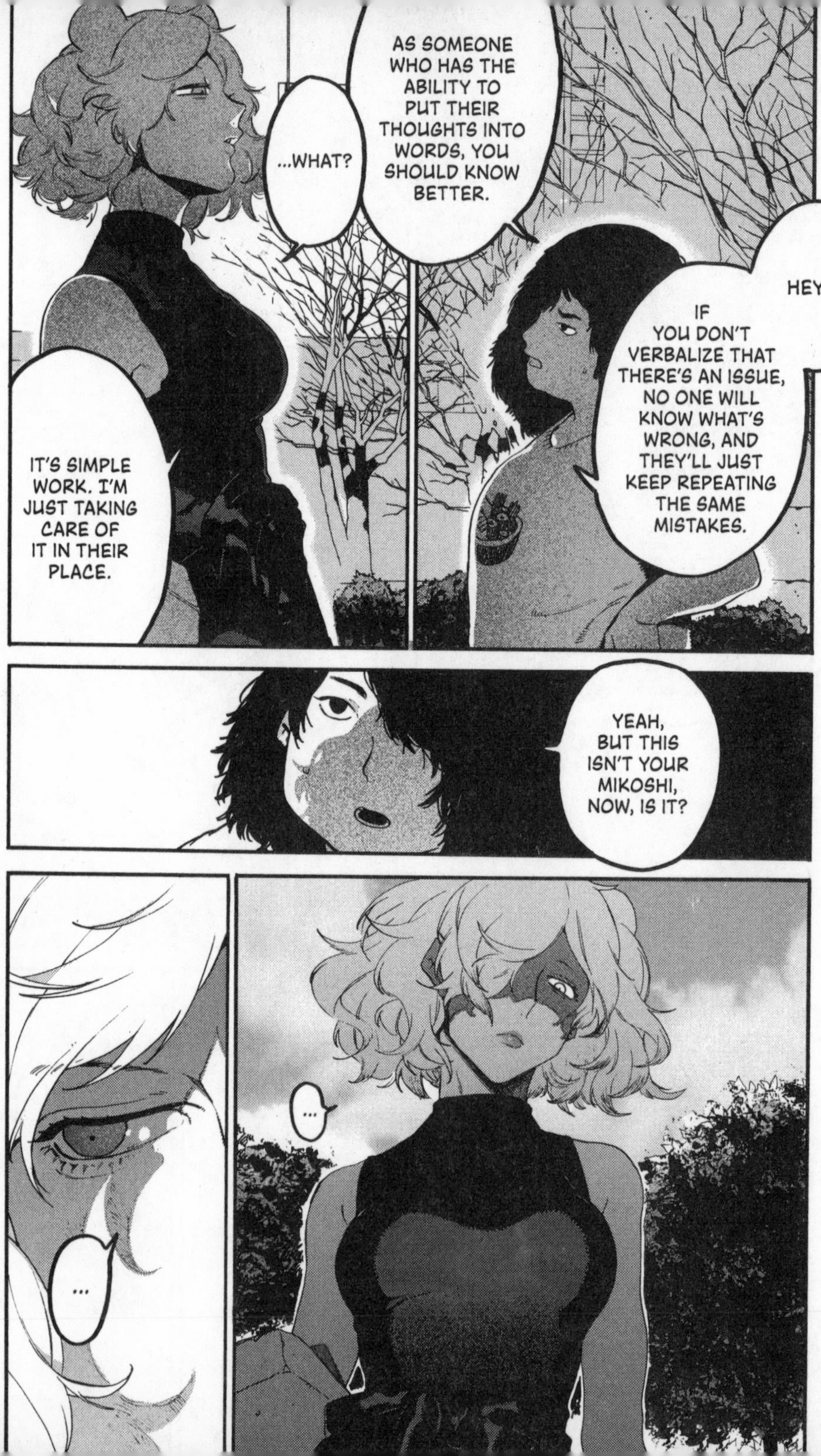
HEY...
IF YOU DON'T VERBALIZE THAT THERE'S AN ISSUE, NO ONE WILL KNOW WHAT'S WRONG, AND THEY'LL JUST KEEP REPEATING THE SAME MISTAKES.
IT'S SIMPLE WORK. I'M JUST TAKING CARE OF IT IN THEIR PLACE.
AS SOMEONE WHO HAS THE ABILITY TO PUT THEIR THOUGHTS INTO WORDS, YOU SHOULD KNOW BETTER.
...WHAT?
YEAH, BUT THIS ISN'T YOUR MIKOSHI, NOW, IS IT?
...
...

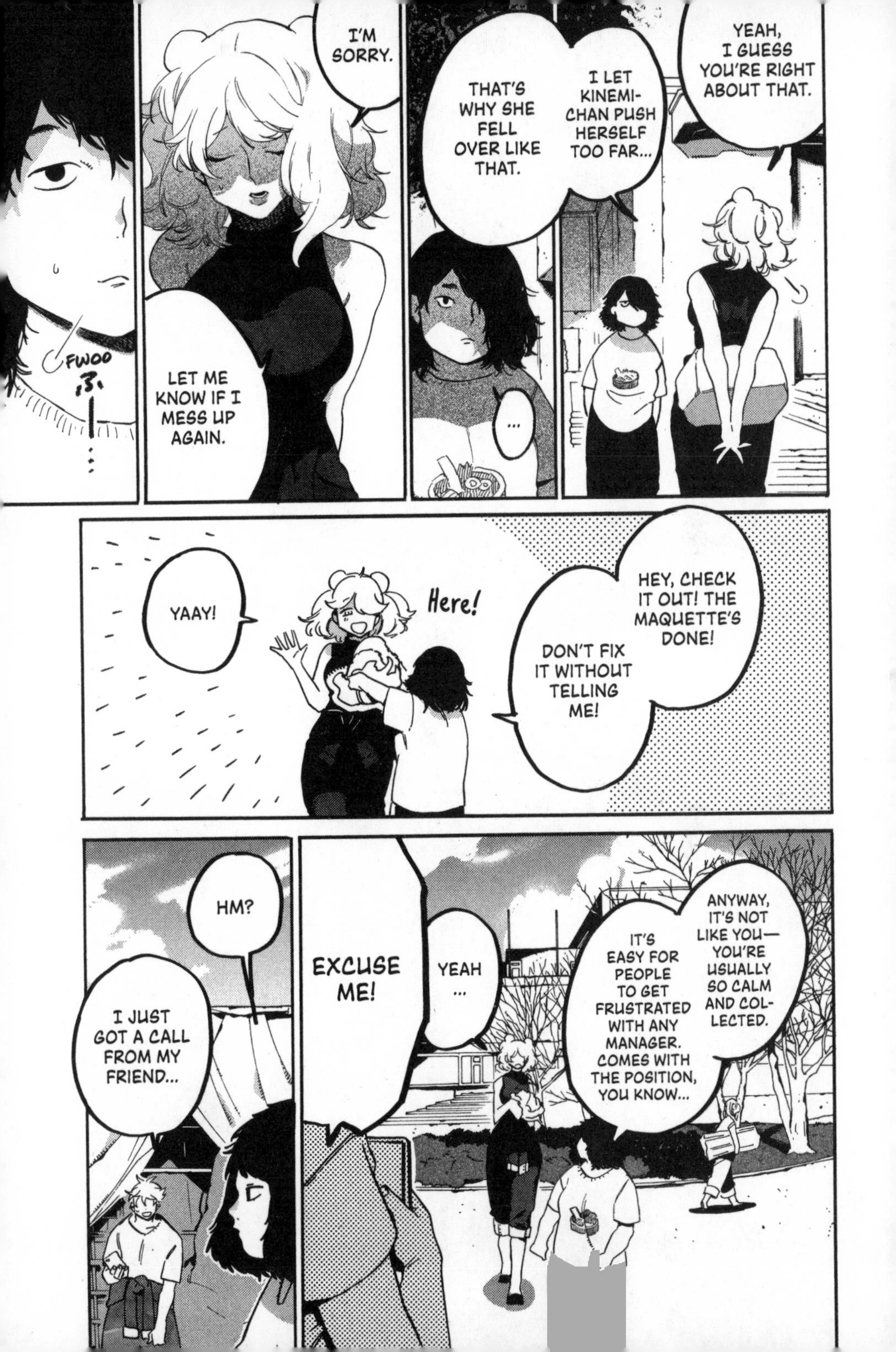
YEAH, I GUESS YOU'RE RIGHT ABOUT THAT.
I LET KINEMI-CHAN PUSH HERSELF TOO FAR...
THAT'S WHY SHE FELL OVER LIKE THAT.
...
I'M SORRY.
LET ME KNOW IF I MESS UP AGAIN.
FWOO
HEY, CHECK IT OUT! THE MAQUETTE'S DONE!
DON'T FIX IT WITHOUT TELLING ME!
Here!
YAAY!
ANYWAY, IT'S NOT LIKE YOU— YOU'RE USUALLY SO CALM AND COL-LECTED.
IT'S EASY FOR PEOPLE TO GET FRUSTRATED WITH ANY MANAGER. COMES WITH THE POSITION, YOU KNOW...
YEAH ...
EXCUSE ME!
HM?
I JUST GOT A CALL FROM MY FRIEND...

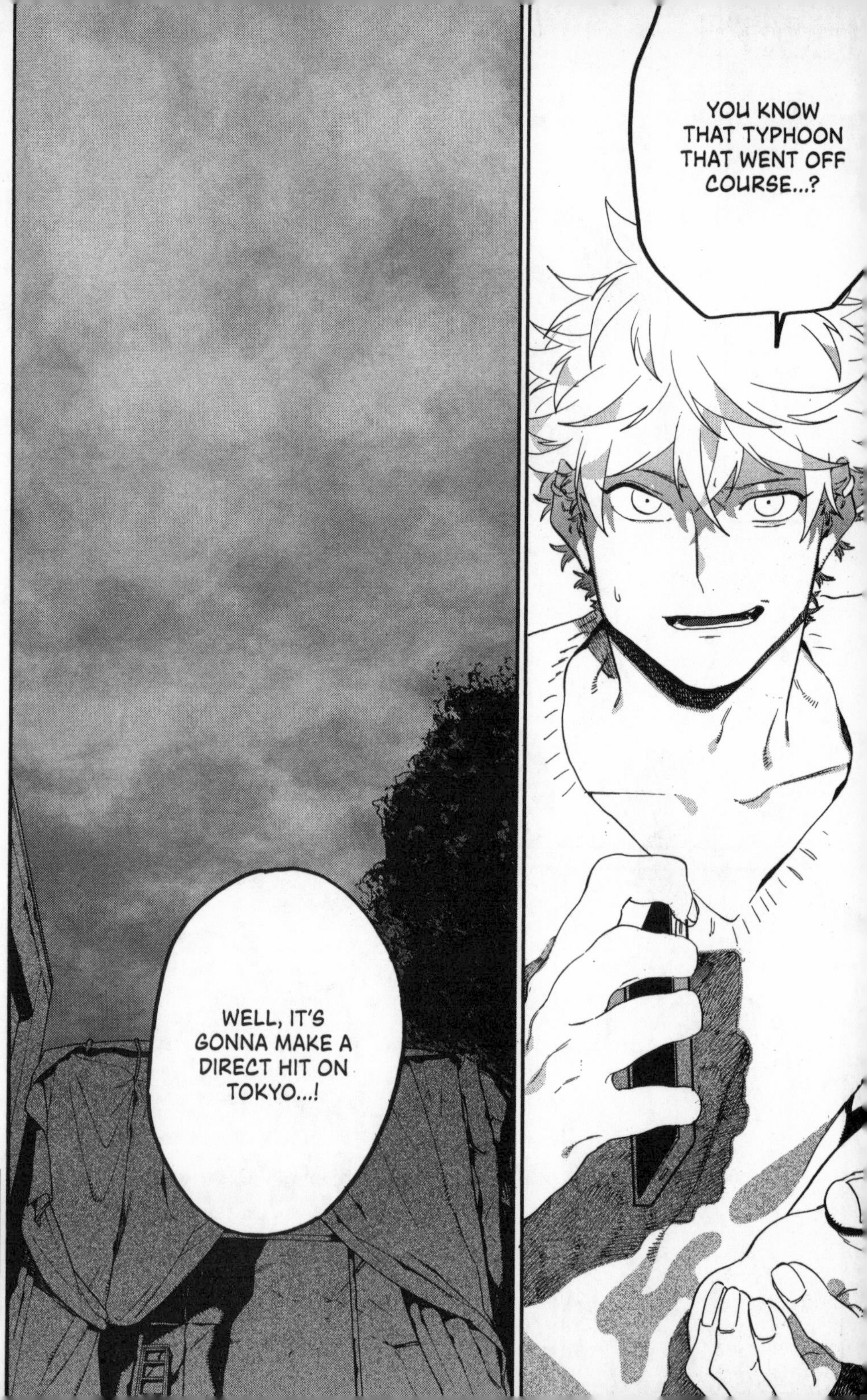
YOU KNOW THAT TYPHOON THAT WENT OFF COURSE...?
WELL, IT'S GONNA MAKE A DIRECT HIT ON TOKYO...!

STROKE 32 END

# STROKE 33

## SPIRIT OF SELF-SACRIFICE

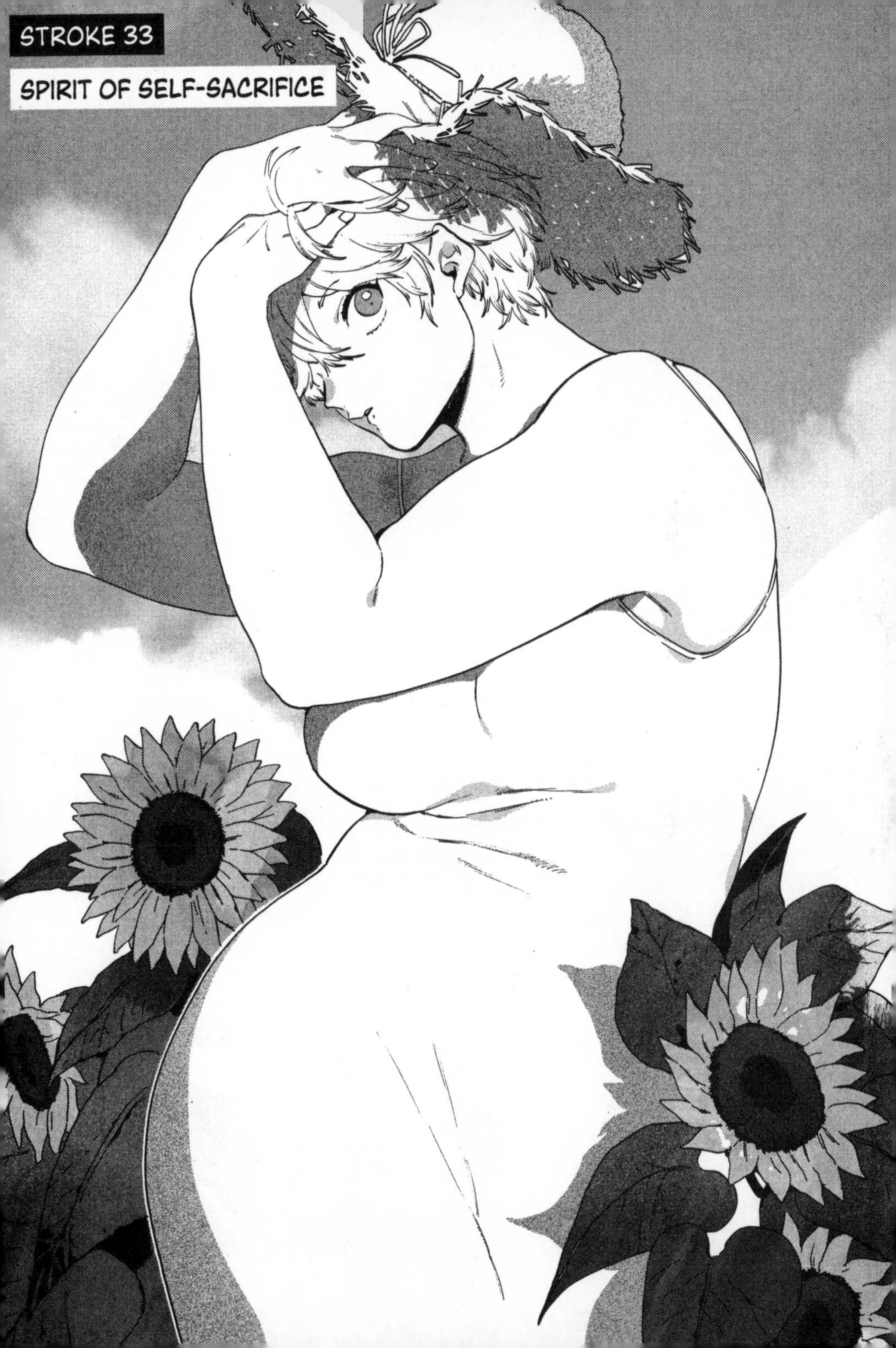

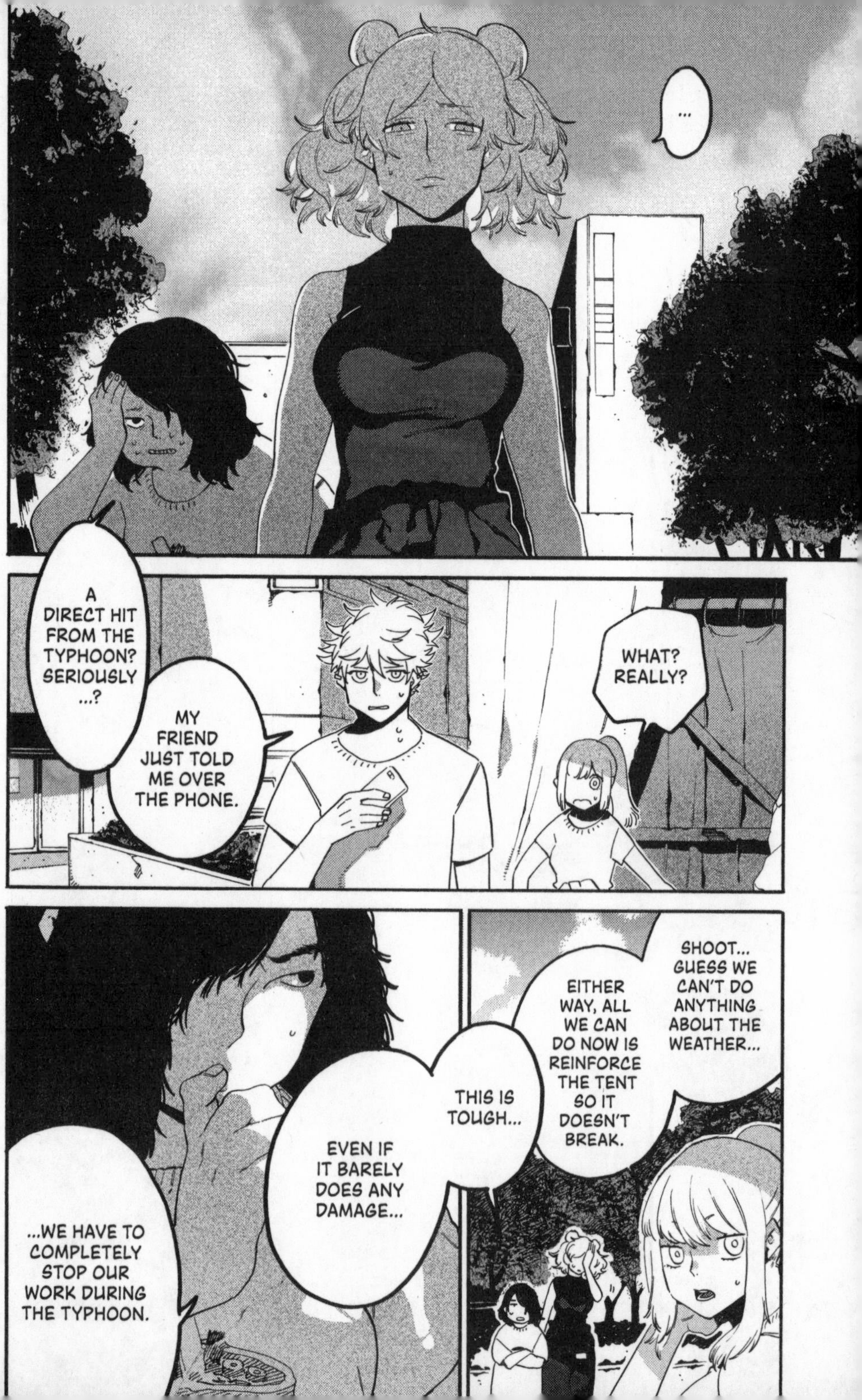

...
A DIRECT HIT FROM THE TYPHOON? SERIOUSLY ...?
WHAT? REALLY?
MY FRIEND JUST TOLD ME OVER THE PHONE.
SHOOT... GUESS WE CAN'T DO ANYTHING ABOUT THE WEATHER...
EITHER WAY, ALL WE CAN DO NOW IS REINFORCE THE TENT SO IT DOESN'T BREAK.
THIS IS TOUGH...
EVEN IF IT BARELY DOES ANY DAMAGE...
...WE HAVE TO COMPLETELY STOP OUR WORK DURING THE TYPHOON.

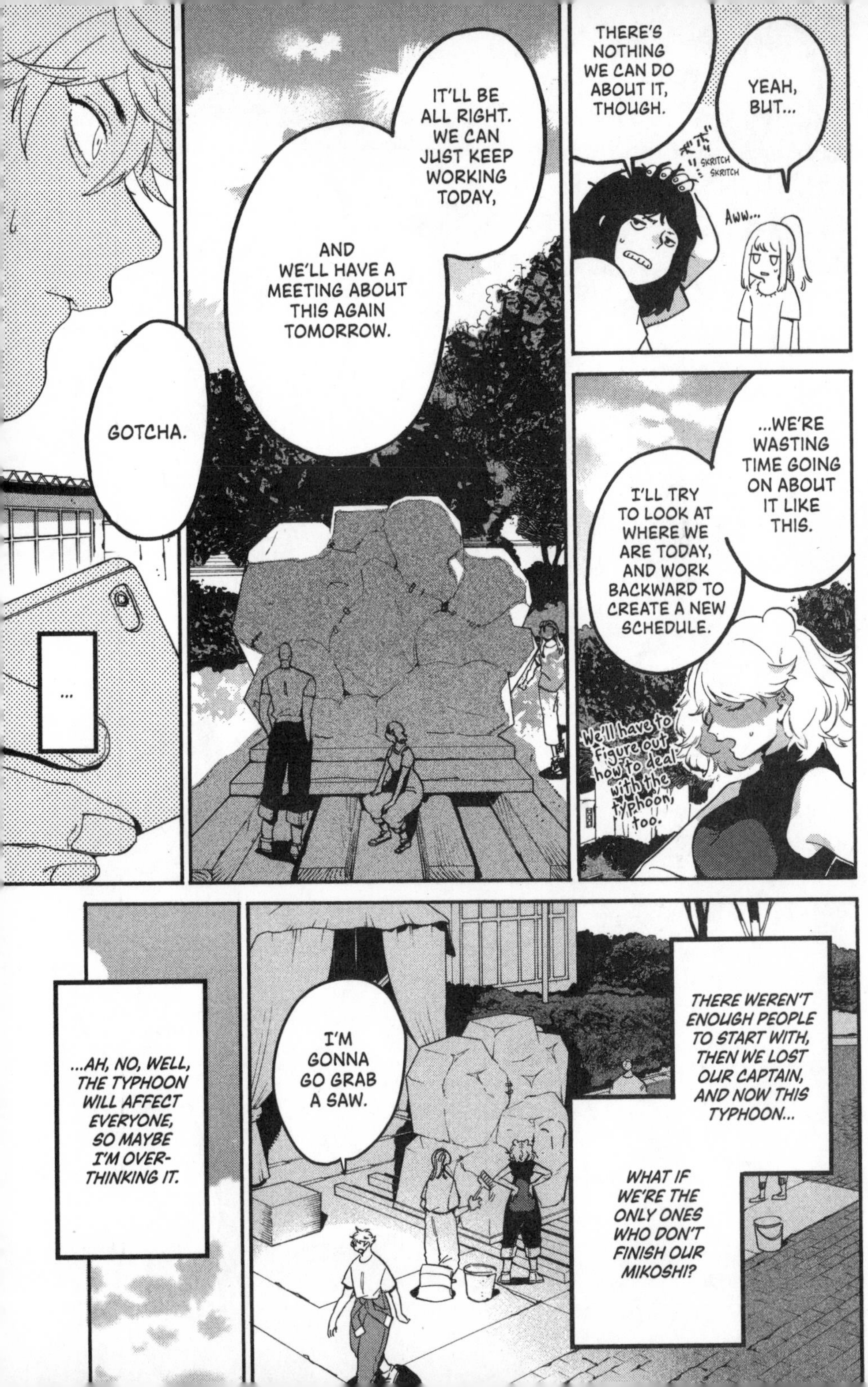
YEAH, BUT...
THERE'S NOTHING WE CAN DO ABOUT IT, THOUGH.
SKRITCH SKRITCH
Aww...
...WE'RE WASTING TIME GOING ON ABOUT IT LIKE THIS.
I'LL TRY TO LOOK AT WHERE WE ARE TODAY, AND WORK BACKWARD TO CREATE A NEW SCHEDULE.
We'll have to figure out how to deal with the typhoon, too.
IT'LL BE ALL RIGHT. WE CAN JUST KEEP WORKING TODAY,
AND WE'LL HAVE A MEETING ABOUT THIS AGAIN TOMORROW.
GOTCHA.
...
THERE WEREN'T ENOUGH PEOPLE TO START WITH, THEN WE LOST OUR CAPTAIN, AND NOW THIS TYPHOON...
WHAT IF WE'RE THE ONLY ONES WHO DON'T FINISH OUR MIKOSHI?
I'M GONNA GO GRAB A SAW.
...AH, NO, WELL, THE TYPHOON WILL AFFECT EVERYONE, SO MAYBE I'M OVER-THINKING IT.

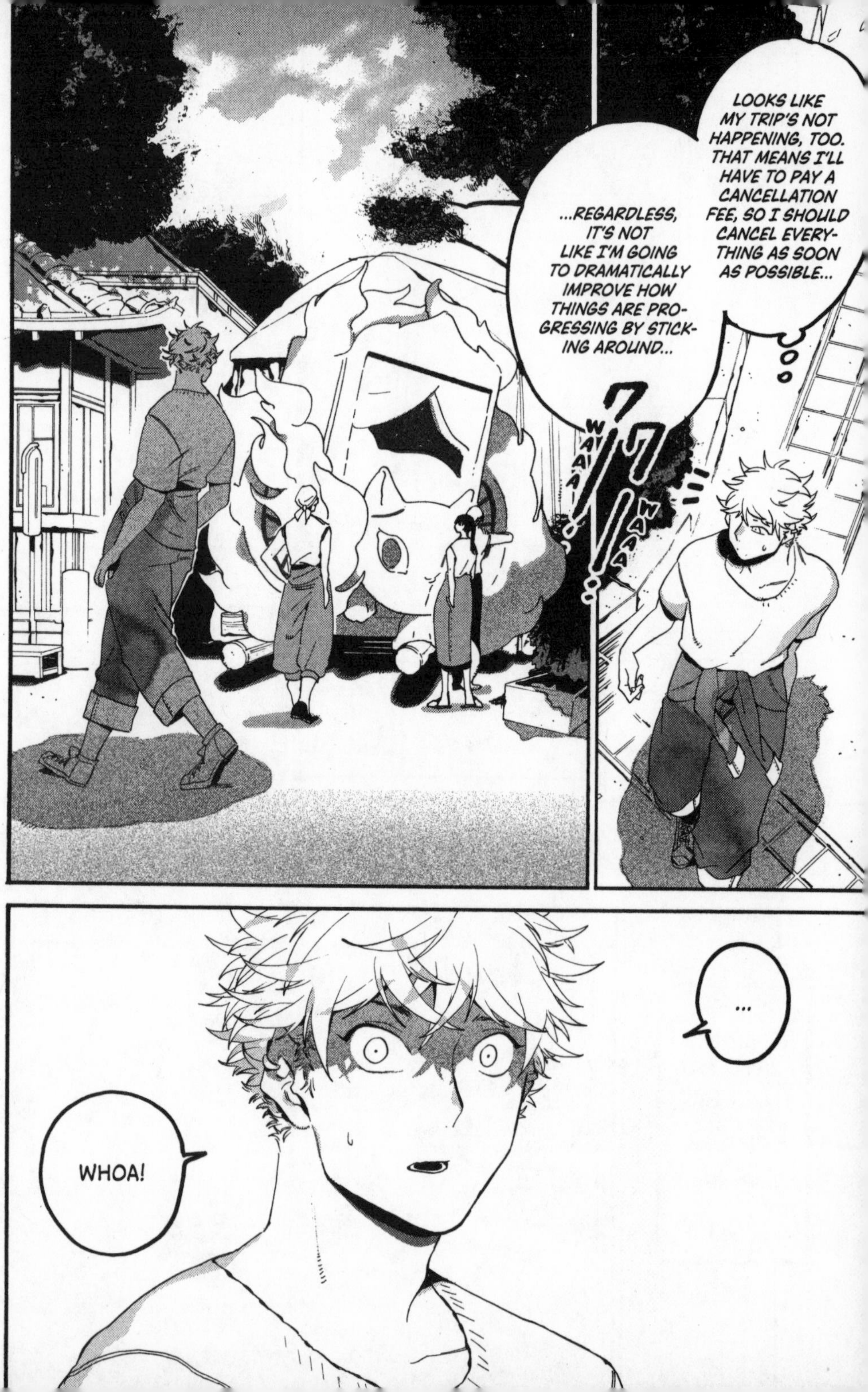
LOOKS LIKE MY TRIP'S NOT HAPPENING, TOO. THAT MEANS I'LL HAVE TO PAY A CANCELLATION FEE, SO I SHOULD CANCEL EVERY-THING AS SOON AS POSSIBLE...
...REGARDLESS, IT'S NOT LIKE I'M GOING TO DRAMATICALLY IMPROVE HOW THINGS ARE PRO-GRESSING BY STICK-ING AROUND...
WAAAA
WAAAA
...
WHOA!

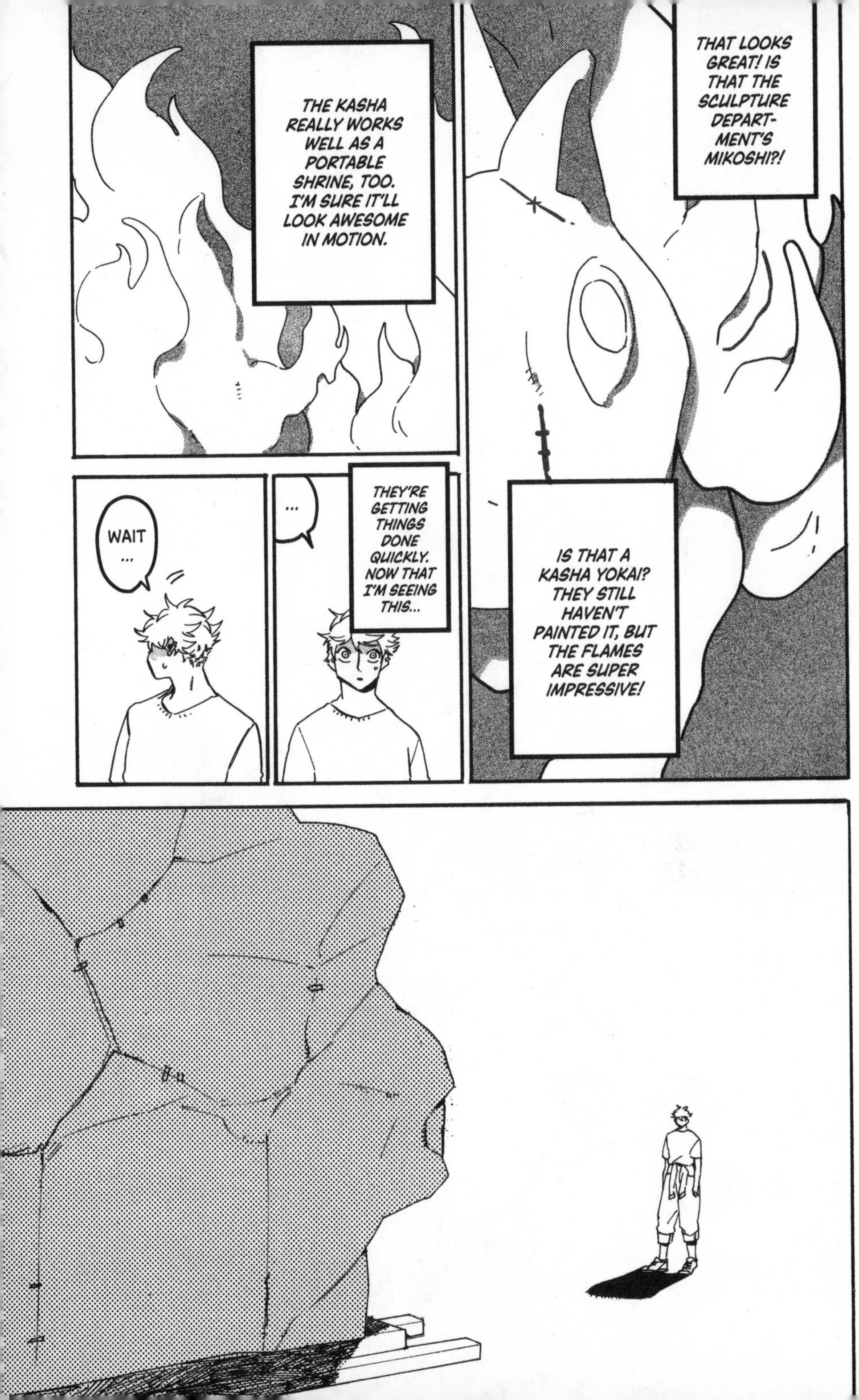
THAT LOOKS GREAT! IS THAT THE SCULPTURE DEPART-MENT'S MIKOSHI?!
IS THAT A KASHA YOKAI? THEY STILL HAVEN'T PAINTED IT, BUT THE FLAMES ARE SUPER IMPRESSIVE!
THE KASHA REALLY WORKS WELL AS A PORTABLE SHRINE, TOO. I'M SURE IT'LL LOOK AWESOME IN MOTION.
THEY'RE GETTING THINGS DONE QUICKLY. NOW THAT I'M SEEING THIS...
...
WAIT ...

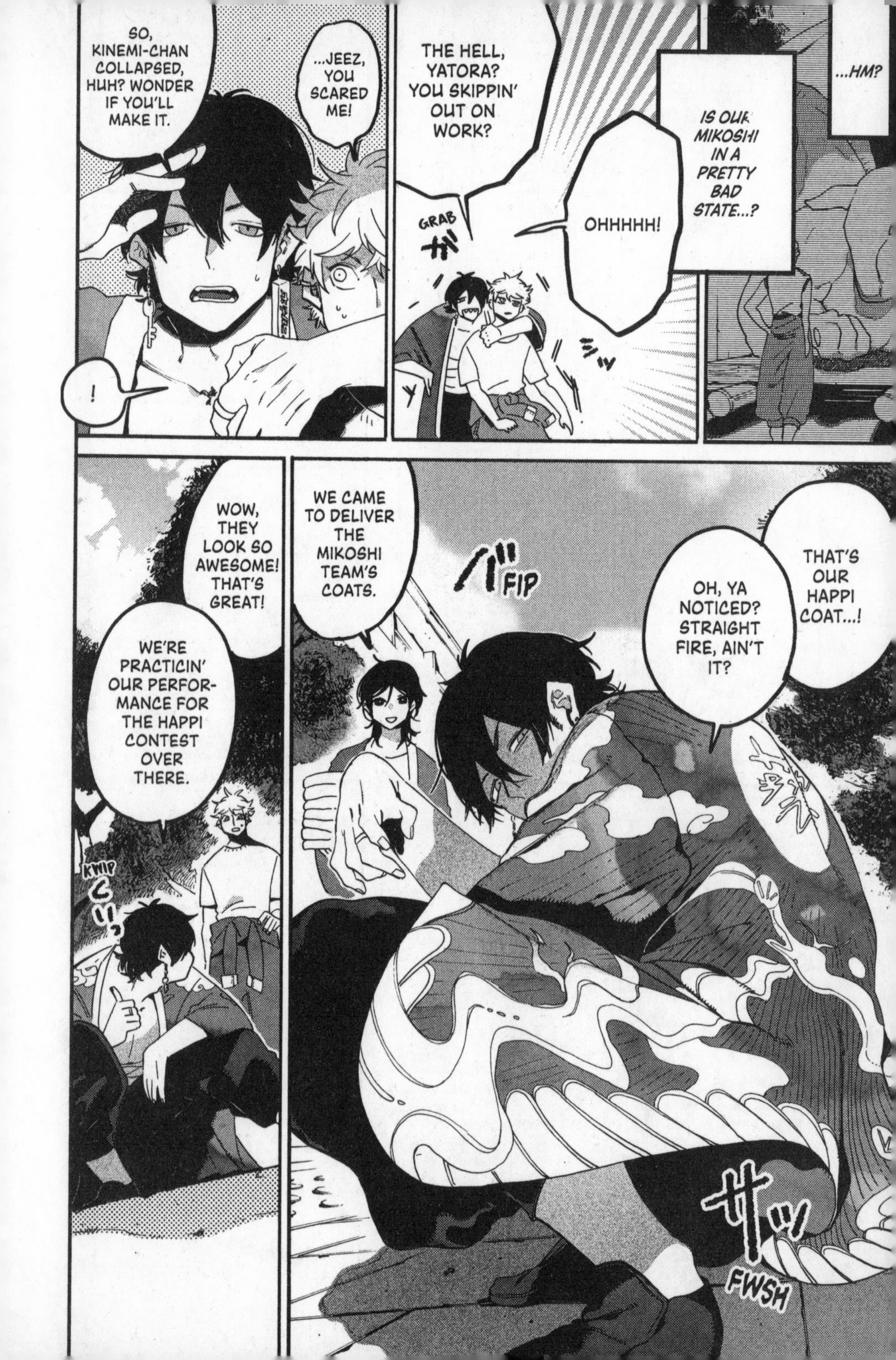
...HM?
IS OUR MIKOSHI IN A PRETTY BAD STATE...?
OHHHHH!
THE HELL, YATORA? YOU SKIPPIN' OUT ON WORK?
GRAB
...JEEZ, YOU SCARED ME!
SO, KINEMI-CHAN COLLAPSED, HUH? WONDER IF YOU'LL MAKE IT.
!
THAT'S OUR HAPPI COAT...!
OH, YA NOTICED? STRAIGHT FIRE, AIN'T IT?
FIP
WE CAME TO DELIVER THE MIKOSHI TEAM'S COATS.
FWSH
WOW, THEY LOOK SO AWESOME! THAT'S GREAT!
WE'RE PRACTICIN' OUR PERFORMANCE FOR THE HAPPI CONTEST OVER THERE.
KWIP

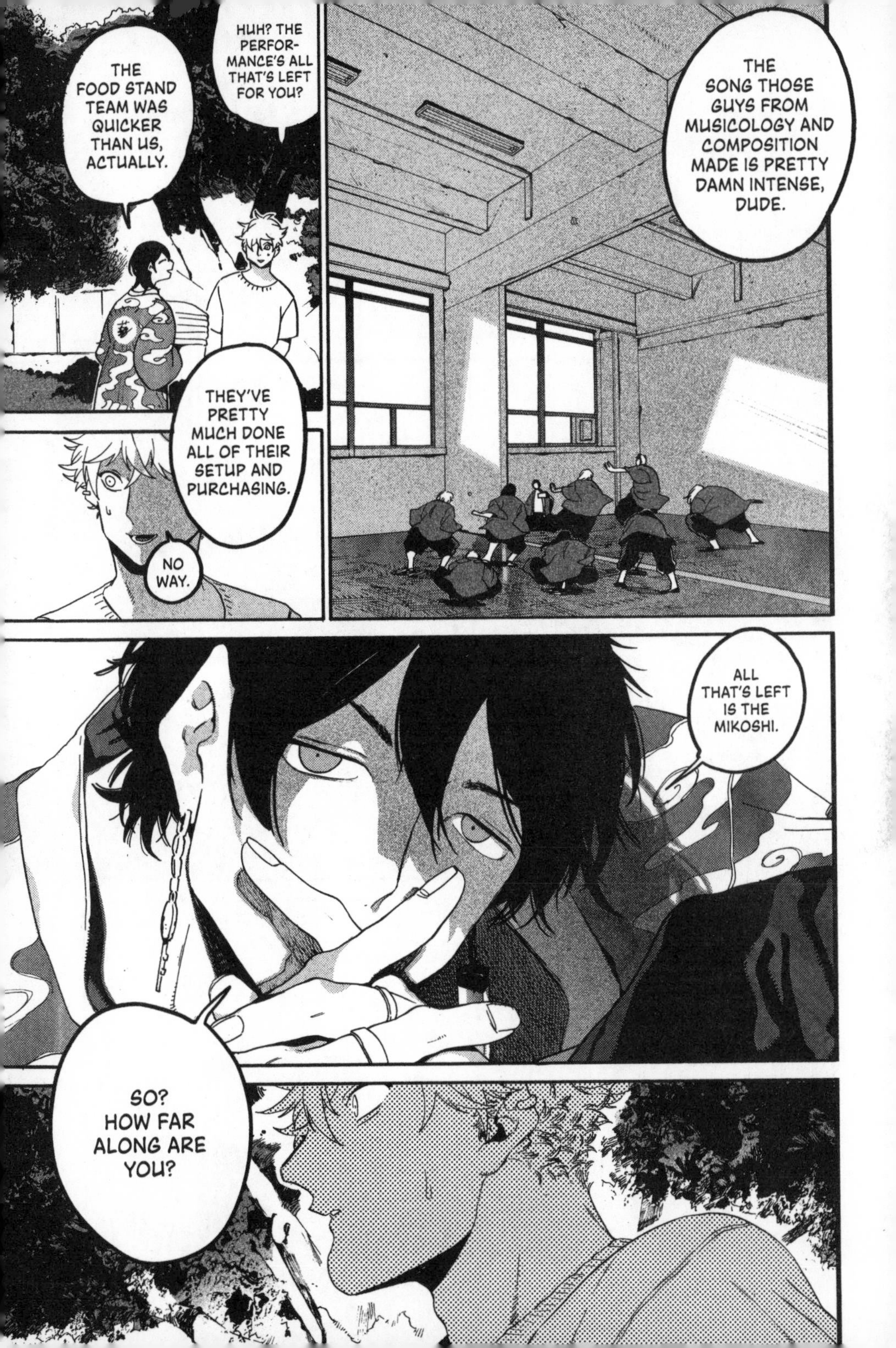
THE SONG THOSE GUYS FROM MUSICOLOGY AND COMPOSITION MADE IS PRETTY DAMN INTENSE, DUDE.
HUH? THE PERFOR-MANCE'S ALL THAT'S LEFT FOR YOU?
THE FOOD STAND TEAM WAS QUICKER THAN US, ACTUALLY.
THEY'VE PRETTY MUCH DONE ALL OF THEIR SETUP AND PURCHASING.
NO WAY.
ALL THAT'S LEFT IS THE MIKOSHI.
SO? HOW FAR ALONG ARE YOU?

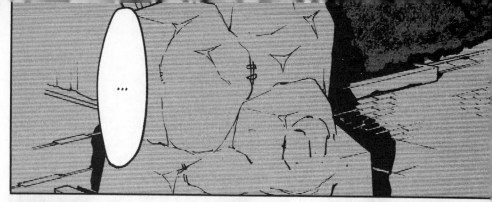

...

I WISH
I KNEW...

I LOOKED AT
OUR SCHEDULE
AFTER FACTORING
IN THE NUMBER OF
PEOPLE PER SHIFT,
THE REMAINING
NUMBER OF DAYS,
AND HOW MUCH
PROGRESS WE'VE
MADE, BUT...

...SORRY.

TO BE
HONEST, AT
THIS RATE, IT
WILL BE FAIRLY
DIFFICULT FOR
US TO FINISH
ON TIME.

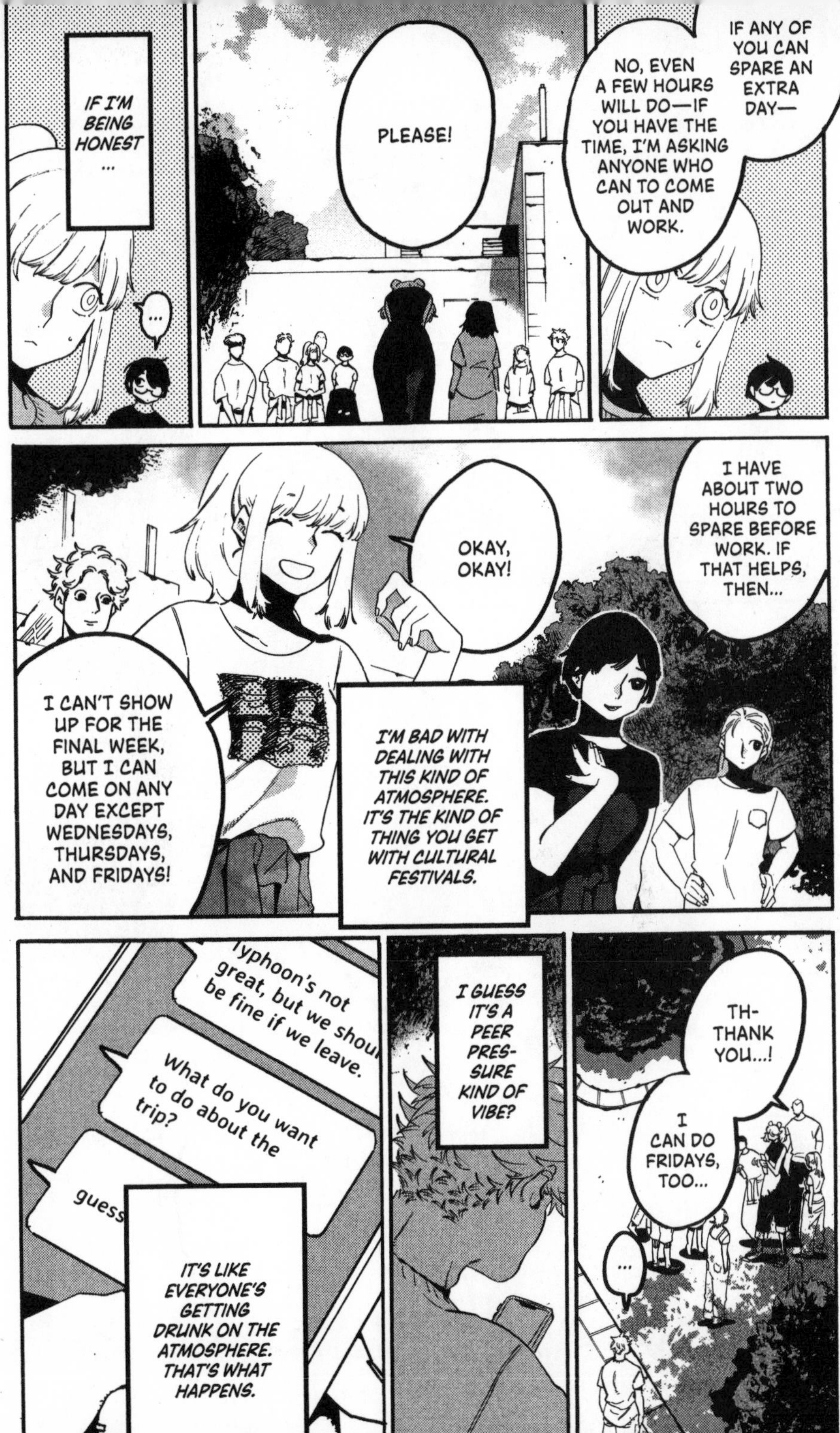
IF ANY OF YOU CAN SPARE AN EXTRA DAY—
NO, EVEN A FEW HOURS WILL DO—IF YOU HAVE THE TIME, I'M ASKING ANYONE WHO CAN TO COME OUT AND WORK.
PLEASE!
IF I'M BEING HONEST ...
...
I HAVE ABOUT TWO HOURS TO SPARE BEFORE WORK. IF THAT HELPS, THEN...
OKAY, OKAY!
I CAN'T SHOW UP FOR THE FINAL WEEK, BUT I CAN COME ON ANY DAY EXCEPT WEDNESDAYS, THURSDAYS, AND FRIDAYS!
I'M BAD WITH DEALING WITH THIS KIND OF ATMOSPHERE. IT'S THE KIND OF THING YOU GET WITH CULTURAL FESTIVALS.
TH- THANK YOU...!
I CAN DO FRIDAYS, TOO...
...
I GUESS IT'S A PEER PRES- SURE KIND OF VIBE?
yphoon's not great, but we shou be fine if we leave.
What do you want to do about the trip?
guess
IT'S LIKE EVERYONE'S GETTING DRUNK ON THE ATMOSPHERE. THAT'S WHAT HAPPENS.

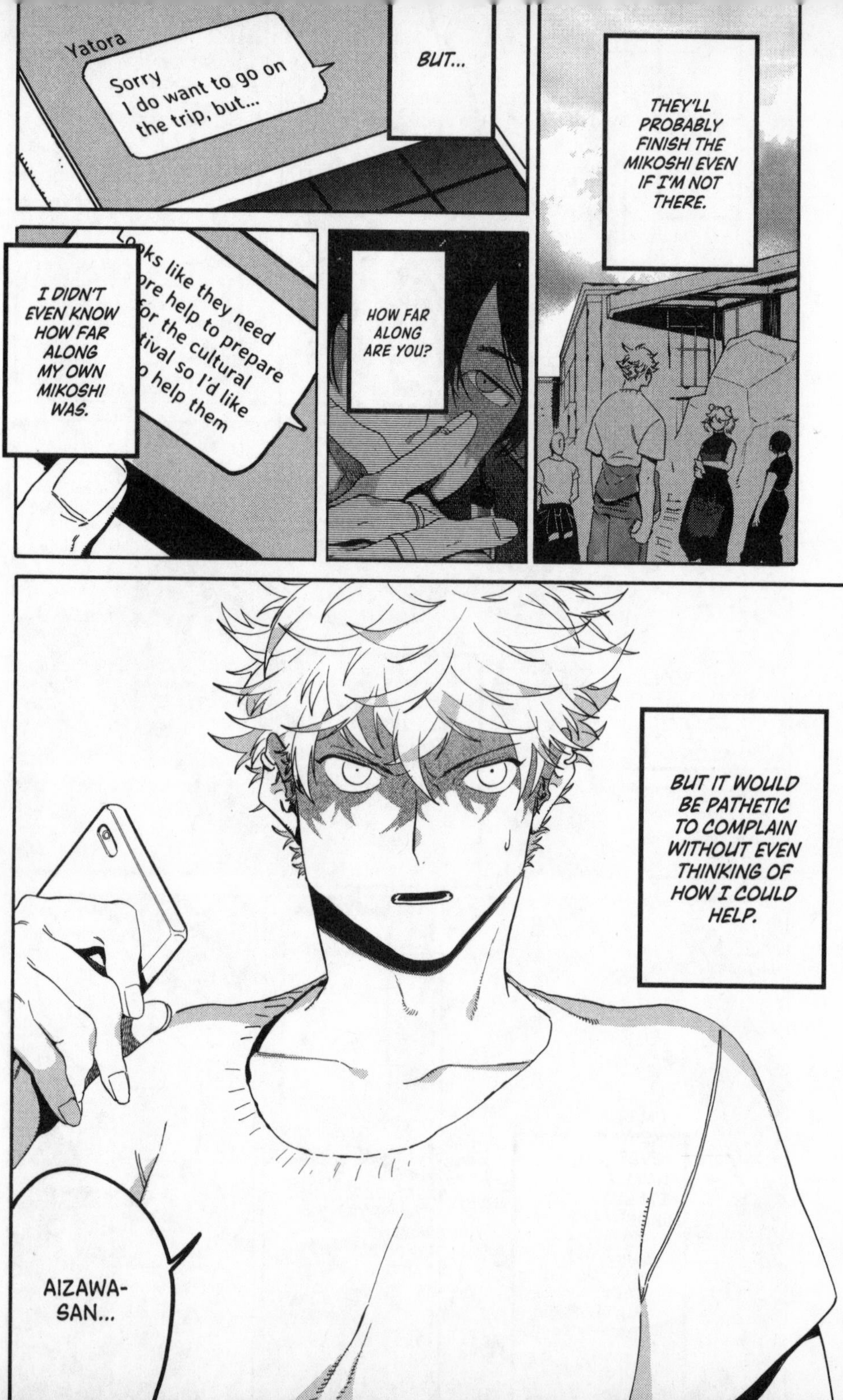

THEY'LL PROBABLY FINISH THE MIKOSHI EVEN IF I'M NOT THERE.
BUT...
Yatora
Sorry
I do want to go on the trip, but...
HOW FAR ALONG ARE YOU?
Looks like they need
ore help to prepare
for the cultural
tival so I'd like
o help them
I DIDN'T EVEN KNOW HOW FAR ALONG MY OWN MIKOSHI WAS.
BUT IT WOULD BE PATHETIC TO COMPLAIN WITHOUT EVEN THINKING OF HOW I COULD HELP.
AIZAWA-SAN...

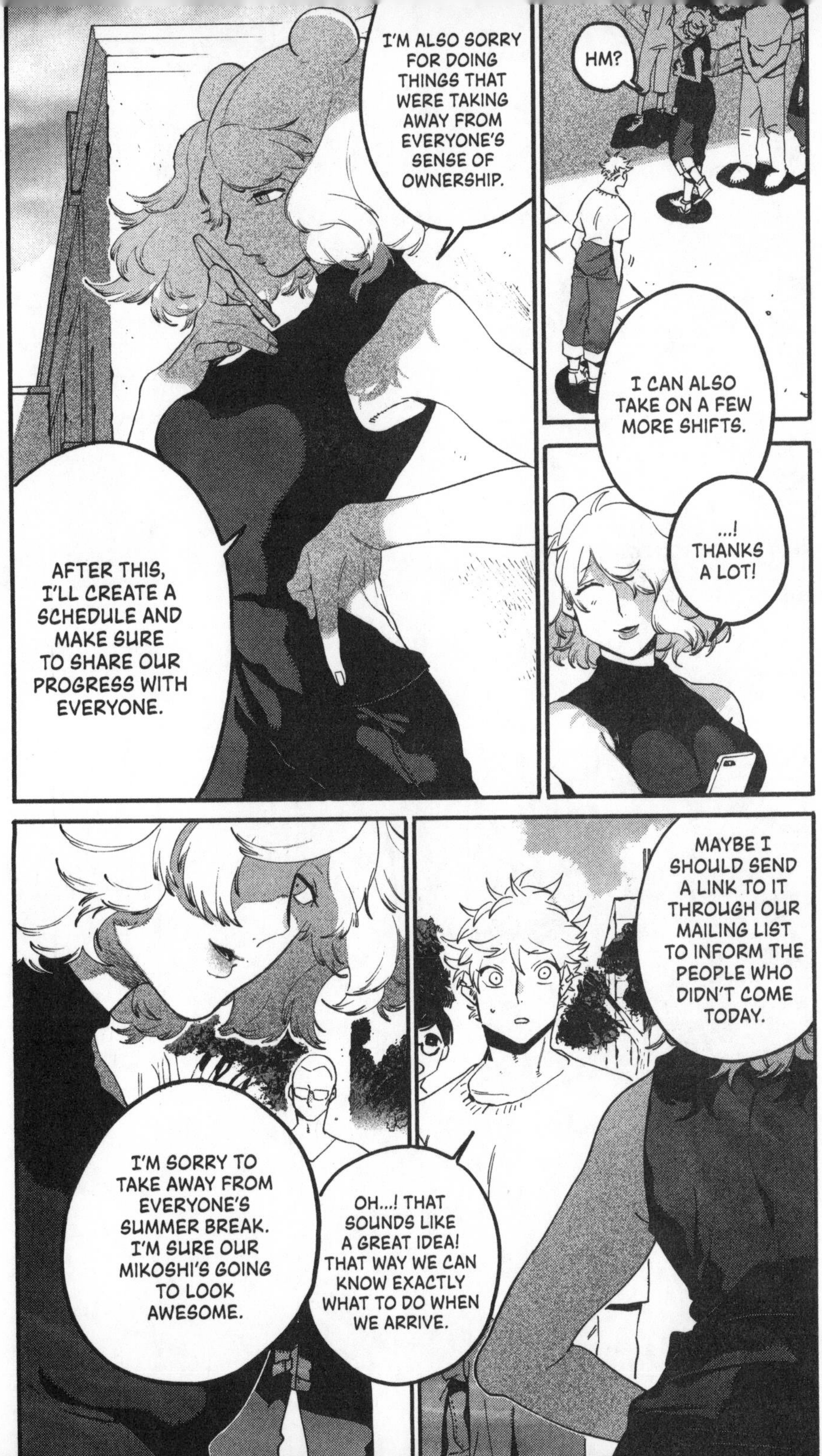
HM?
I CAN ALSO TAKE ON A FEW MORE SHIFTS.
...! THANKS A LOT!
I'M ALSO SORRY FOR DOING THINGS THAT WERE TAKING AWAY FROM EVERYONE'S SENSE OF OWNERSHIP.
AFTER THIS, I'LL CREATE A SCHEDULE AND MAKE SURE TO SHARE OUR PROGRESS WITH EVERYONE.
MAYBE I SHOULD SEND A LINK TO IT THROUGH OUR MAILING LIST TO INFORM THE PEOPLE WHO DIDN'T COME TODAY.
OH...! THAT SOUNDS LIKE A GREAT IDEA! THAT WAY WE CAN KNOW EXACTLY WHAT TO DO WHEN WE ARRIVE.
I'M SORRY TO TAKE AWAY FROM EVERYONE'S SUMMER BREAK. I'M SURE OUR MIKOSHI'S GOING TO LOOK AWESOME.

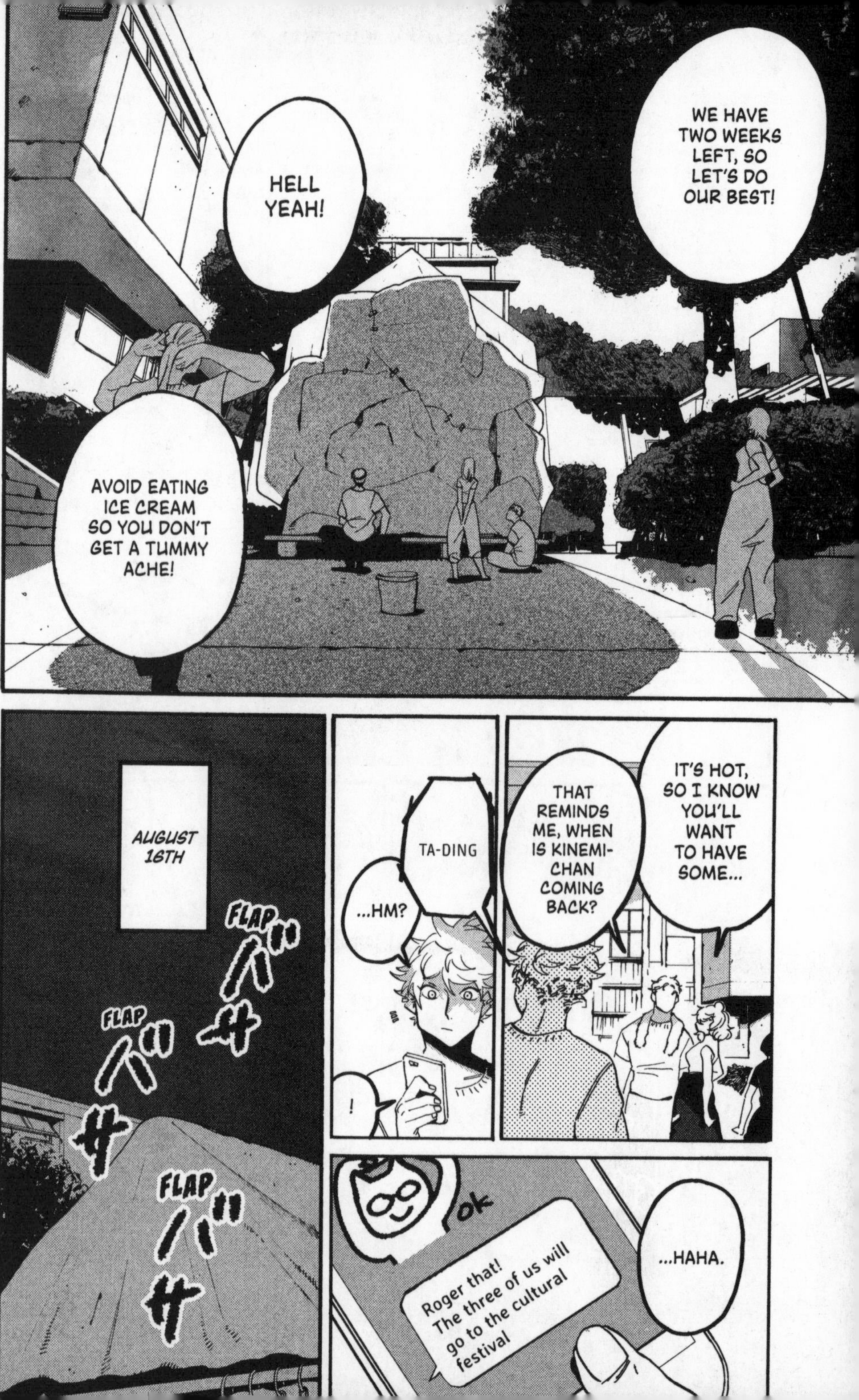

WE HAVE TWO WEEKS LEFT, SO LET'S DO OUR BEST!
HELL YEAH!
AVOID EATING ICE CREAM SO YOU DON'T GET A TUMMY ACHE!
IT'S HOT, SO I KNOW YOU'LL WANT TO HAVE SOME...
THAT REMINDS ME, WHEN IS KINEMI-CHAN COMING BACK?
TA-DING
...HM?
!
...HAHA.
ok
Roger that! The three of us will go to the cultural festival
AUGUST 16TH
FLAP
FLAP
FLAP

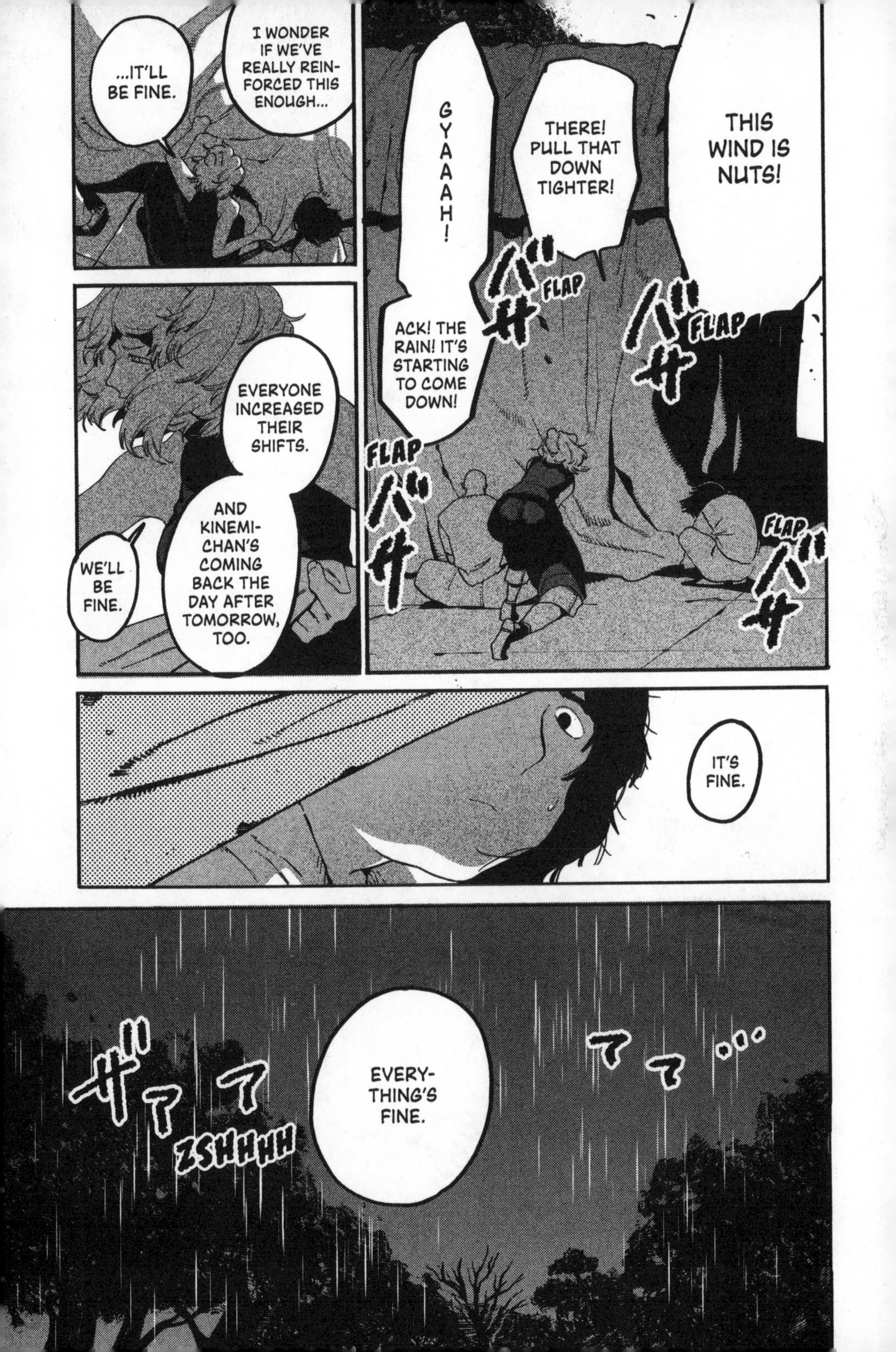
THIS WIND IS NUTS!
THERE! PULL THAT DOWN TIGHTER!
GYAAAAH!
バサ FLAP
バサ FLAP
ACK! THE RAIN! IT'S STARTING TO COME DOWN!
バサ FLAP
バサ FLAP
I WONDER IF WE'VE REALLY REIN-FORCED THIS ENOUGH...
...IT'LL BE FINE.
EVERYONE INCREASED THEIR SHIFTS.
AND KINEMI-CHAN'S COMING BACK THE DAY AFTER TOMORROW, TOO.
WE'LL BE FINE.
IT'S FINE.
ザァァァ…
EVERY-THING'S FINE.
ZSHHHH

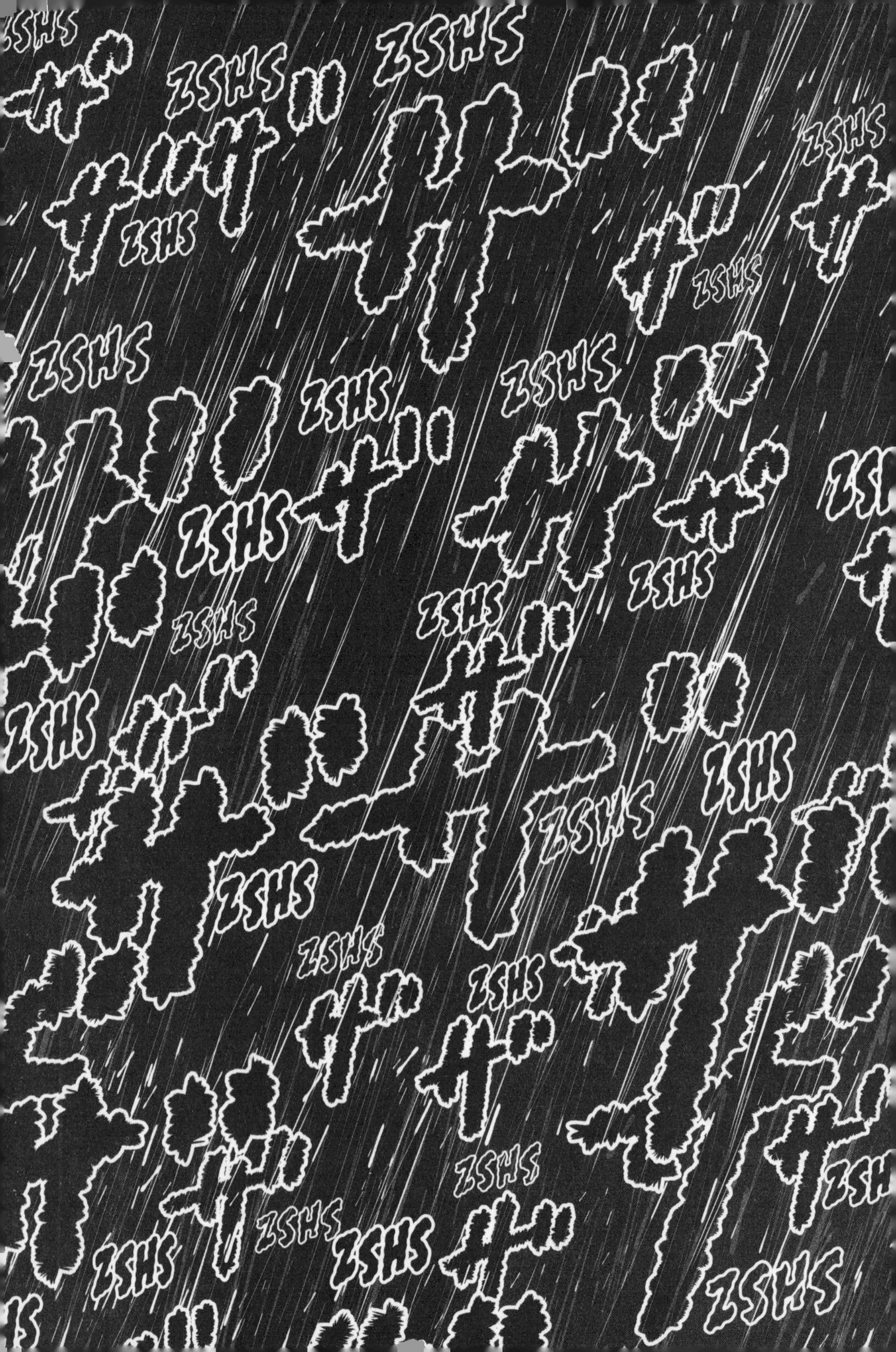
ZSHS
ZSHS
ZSHS
ZSHS
ZSHS
ZSHS
ZSHS
ZSHS
ZSHS
ZSHS
ZSHS
ZSHS
ZSHS
ZSHS
ZSHS
ZSHS
ZSHS
ZSHS
ZSHS
ZSHS
ZSHS
ZSHS
ZSHS

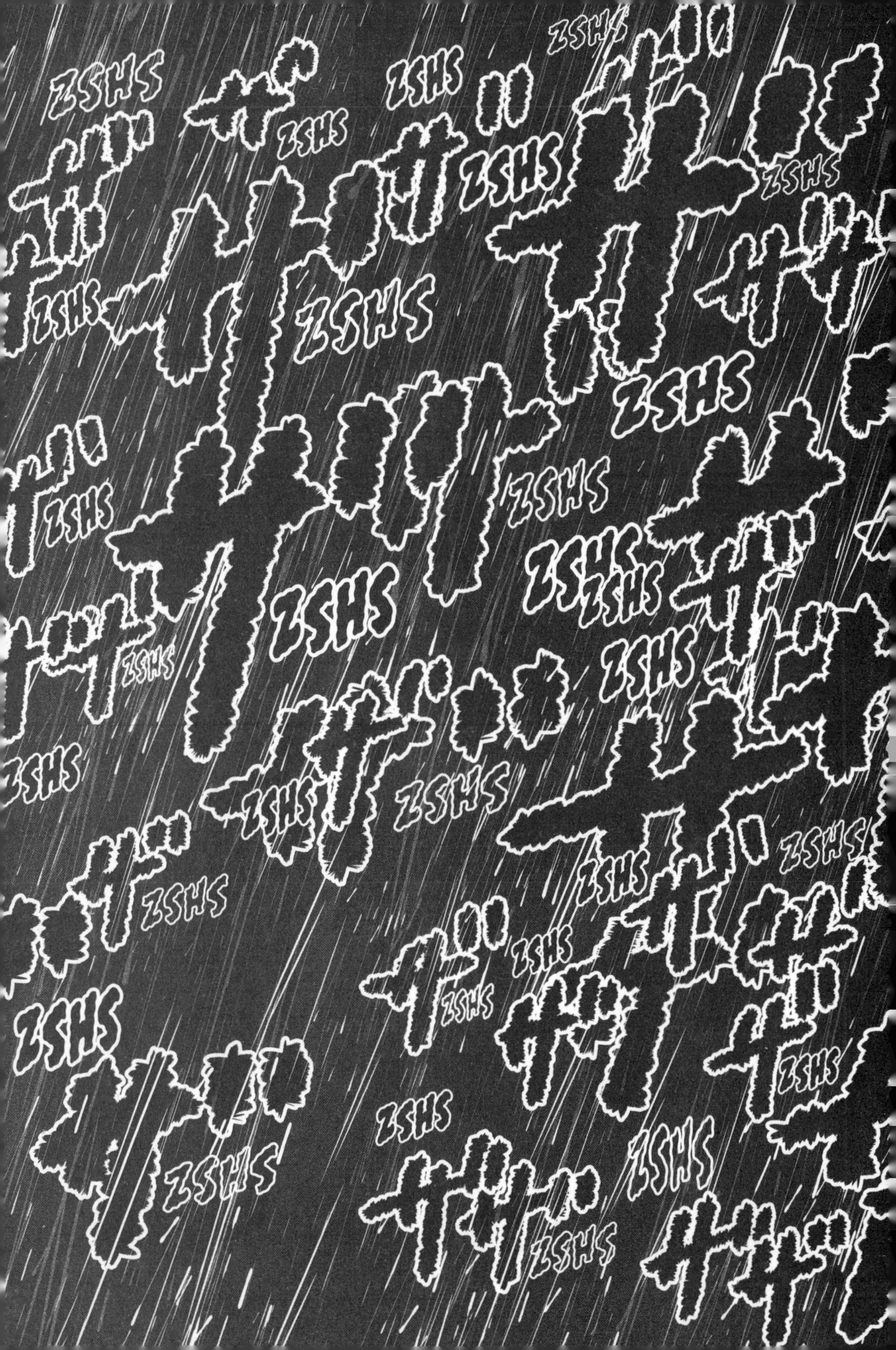
ザーッ
ZSHS

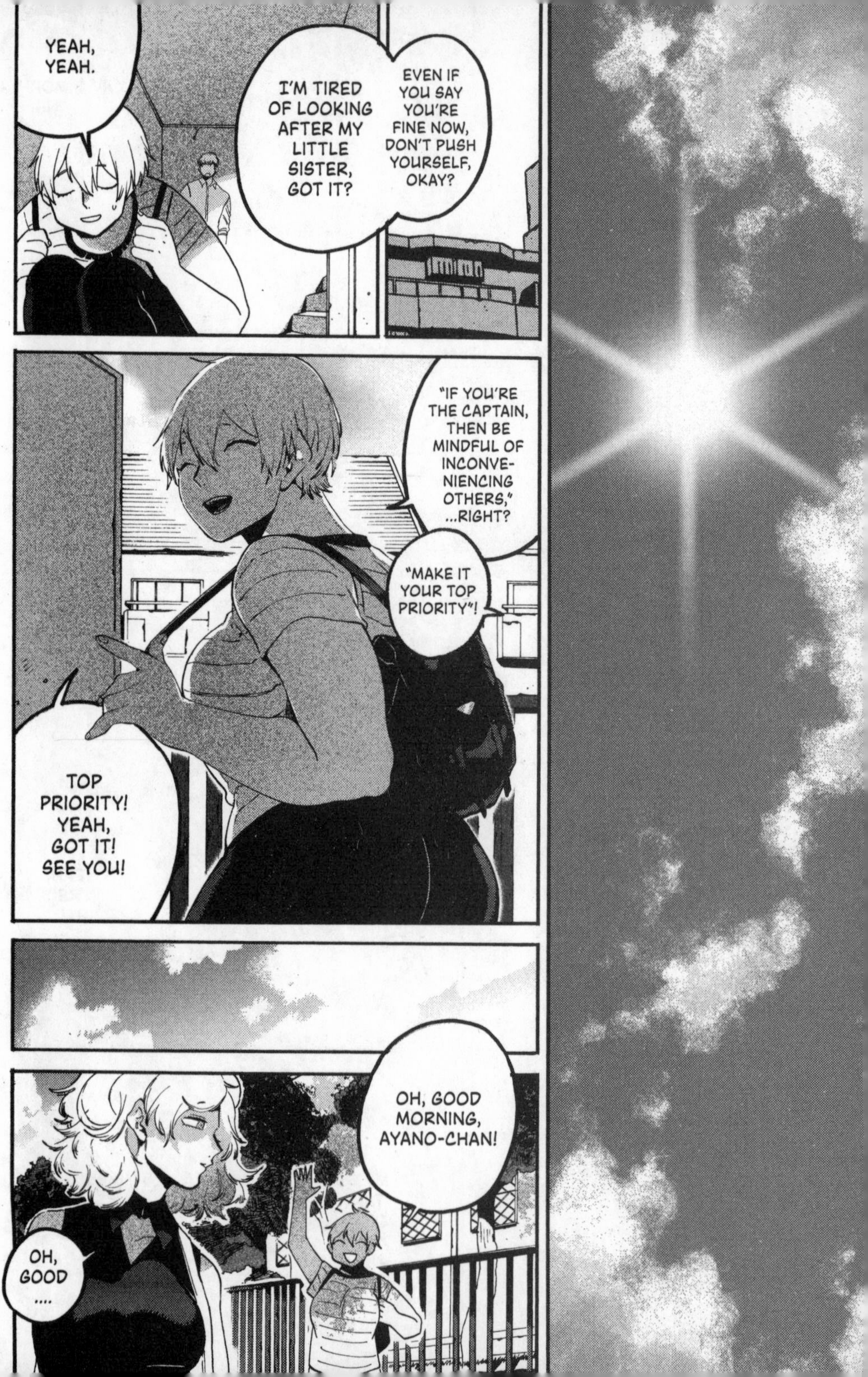
EVEN IF YOU SAY YOU'RE FINE NOW, DON'T PUSH YOURSELF, OKAY?
I'M TIRED OF LOOKING AFTER MY LITTLE SISTER, GOT IT?
YEAH, YEAH.
"IF YOU'RE THE CAPTAIN, THEN BE MINDFUL OF INCONVE-NIENCING OTHERS," ...RIGHT?
"MAKE IT YOUR TOP PRIORITY"!
TOP PRIORITY! YEAH, GOT IT! SEE YOU!
OH, GOOD MORNING, AYANO-CHAN!
OH, GOOD ....

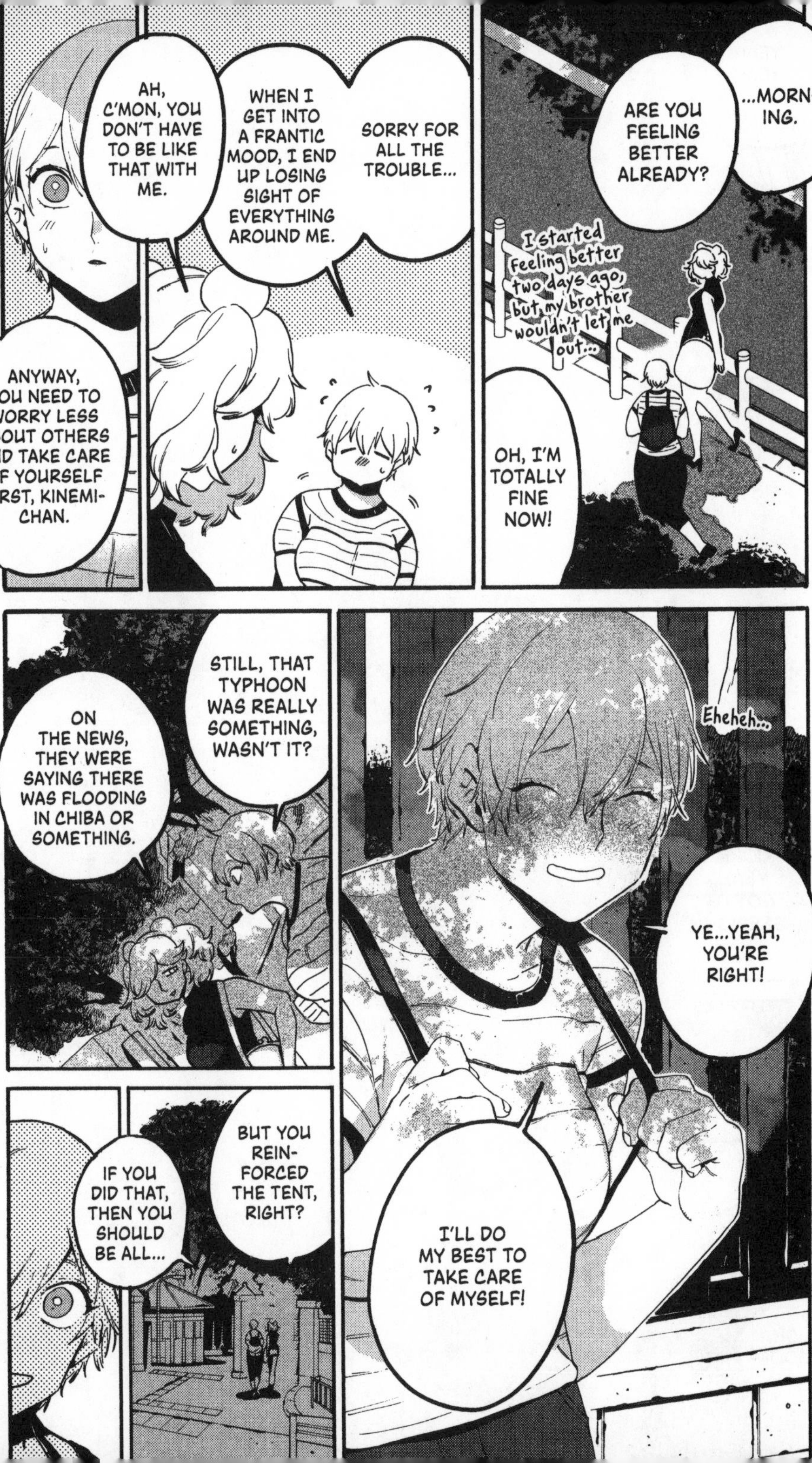
...MORNING.
ARE YOU FEELING BETTER ALREADY?
I started feeling better two days ago, but my brother wouldn't let me out...
OH, I'M TOTALLY FINE NOW!
SORRY FOR ALL THE TROUBLE...
WHEN I GET INTO A FRANTIC MOOD, I END UP LOSING SIGHT OF EVERYTHING AROUND ME.
AH, C'MON, YOU DON'T HAVE TO BE LIKE THAT WITH ME.
ANYWAY, YOU NEED TO WORRY LESS ABOUT OTHERS AND TAKE CARE OF YOURSELF FIRST, KINEMI-CHAN.
Eheheh...
YE...YEAH, YOU'RE RIGHT!
I'LL DO MY BEST TO TAKE CARE OF MYSELF!
STILL, THAT TYPHOON WAS REALLY SOMETHING, WASN'T IT?
ON THE NEWS, THEY WERE SAYING THERE WAS FLOODING IN CHIBA OR SOMETHING.
BUT YOU REINFORCED THE TENT, RIGHT?
IF YOU DID THAT, THEN YOU SHOULD BE ALL...

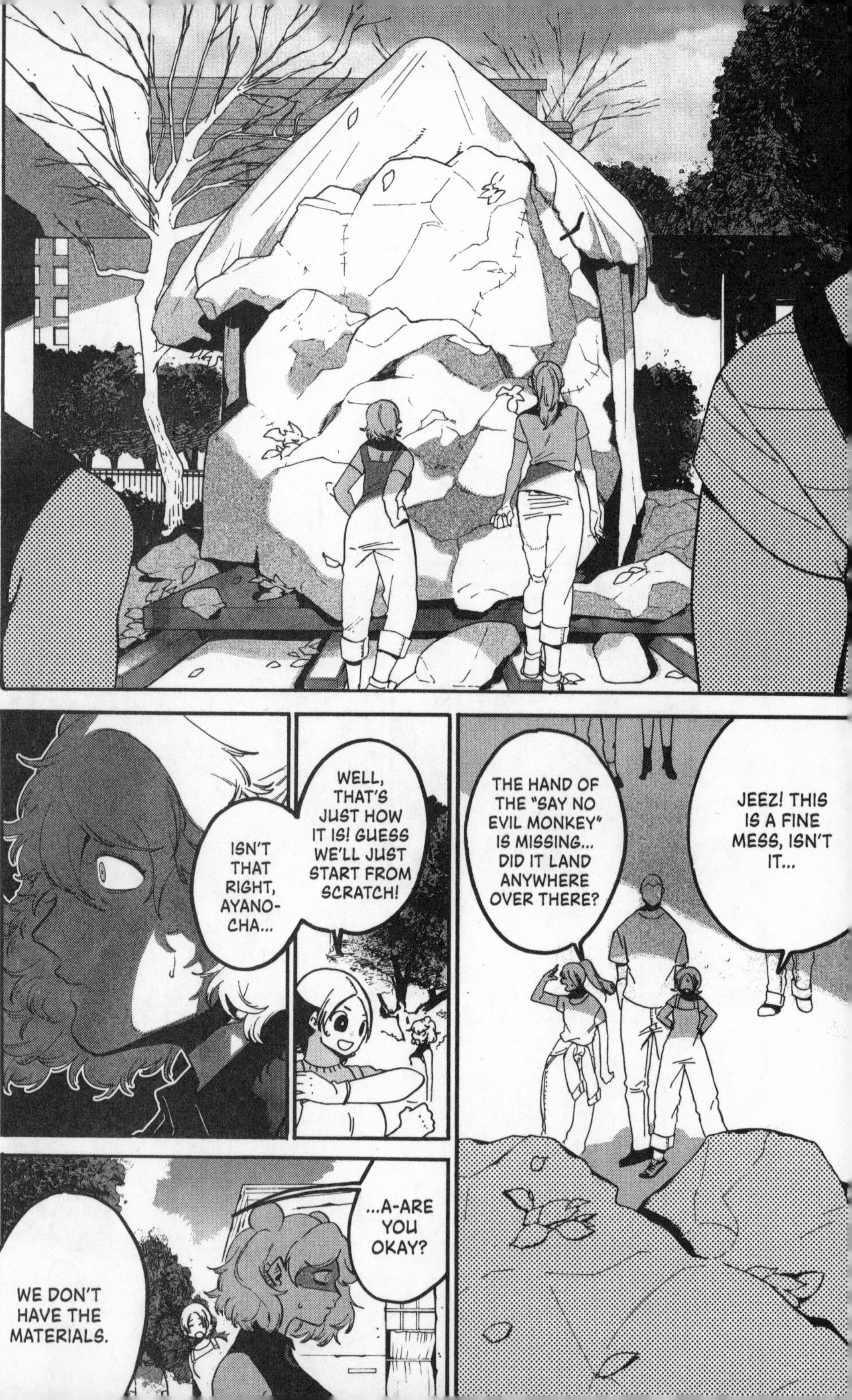
JEEZ! THIS IS A FINE MESS, ISN'T IT...
THE HAND OF THE "SAY NO EVIL MONKEY" IS MISSING... DID IT LAND ANYWHERE OVER THERE?
WELL, THAT'S JUST HOW IT IS! GUESS WE'LL JUST START FROM SCRATCH!
ISN'T THAT RIGHT, AYANO-CHA...
...A-ARE YOU OKAY?
WE DON'T HAVE THE MATERIALS.

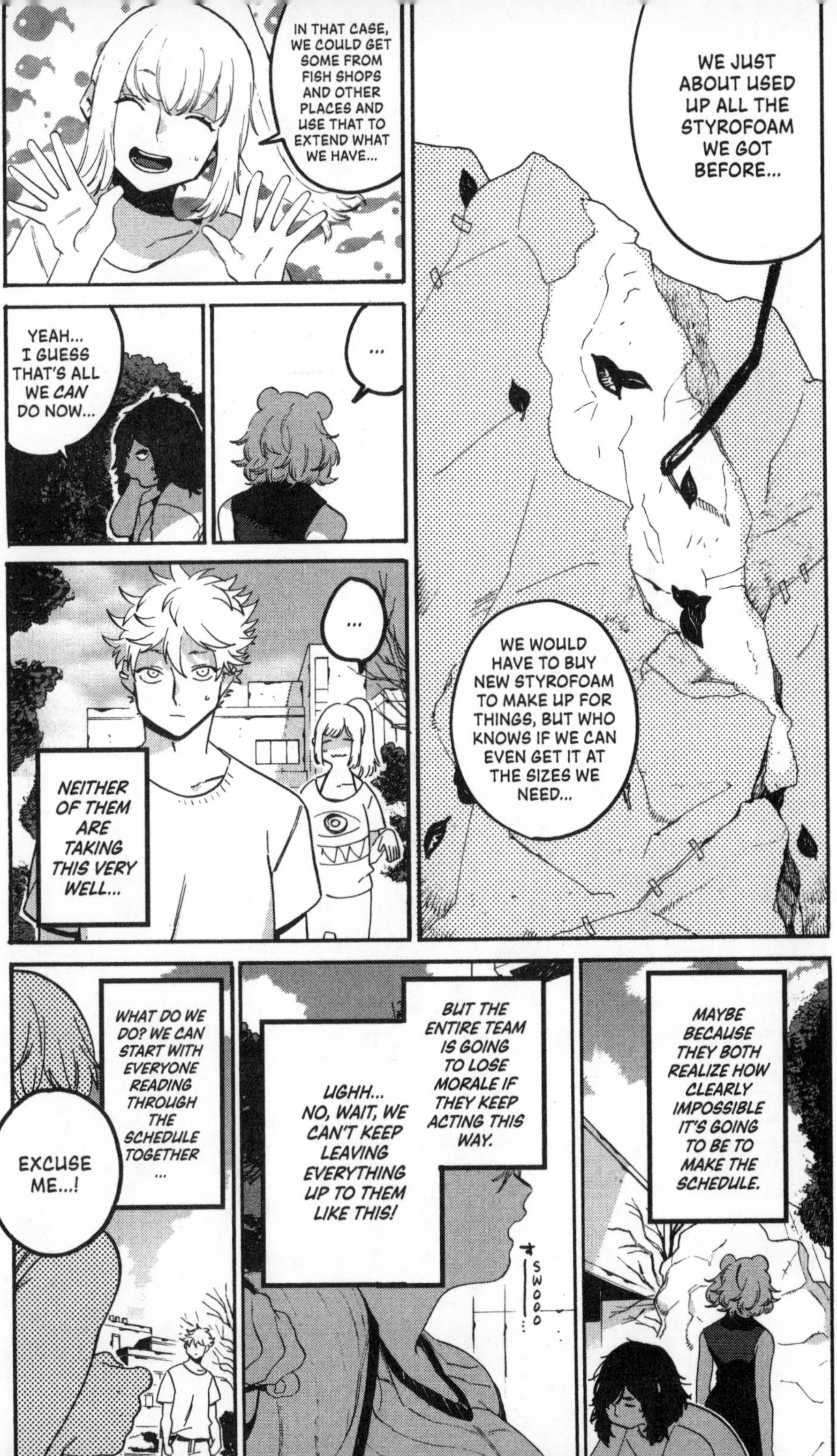
WE JUST ABOUT USED UP ALL THE STYROFOAM WE GOT BEFORE...
WE WOULD HAVE TO BUY NEW STYROFOAM TO MAKE UP FOR THINGS, BUT WHO KNOWS IF WE CAN EVEN GET IT AT THE SIZES WE NEED...
IN THAT CASE, WE COULD GET SOME FROM FISH SHOPS AND OTHER PLACES AND USE THAT TO EXTEND WHAT WE HAVE...
...
YEAH... I GUESS THAT'S ALL WE *CAN* DO NOW...
...
NEITHER OF THEM ARE TAKING THIS VERY WELL...
MAYBE BECAUSE THEY BOTH REALIZE HOW CLEARLY IMPOSSIBLE IT'S GOING TO BE TO MAKE THE SCHEDULE.
BUT THE ENTIRE TEAM IS GOING TO LOSE MORALE IF THEY KEEP ACTING THIS WAY.
UGHH... NO, WAIT, WE CAN'T KEEP LEAVING EVERYTHING UP TO THEM LIKE THIS!
SWOOO...
WHAT DO WE DO? WE CAN START WITH EVERYONE READING THROUGH THE SCHEDULE TOGETHER...
EXCUSE ME...!

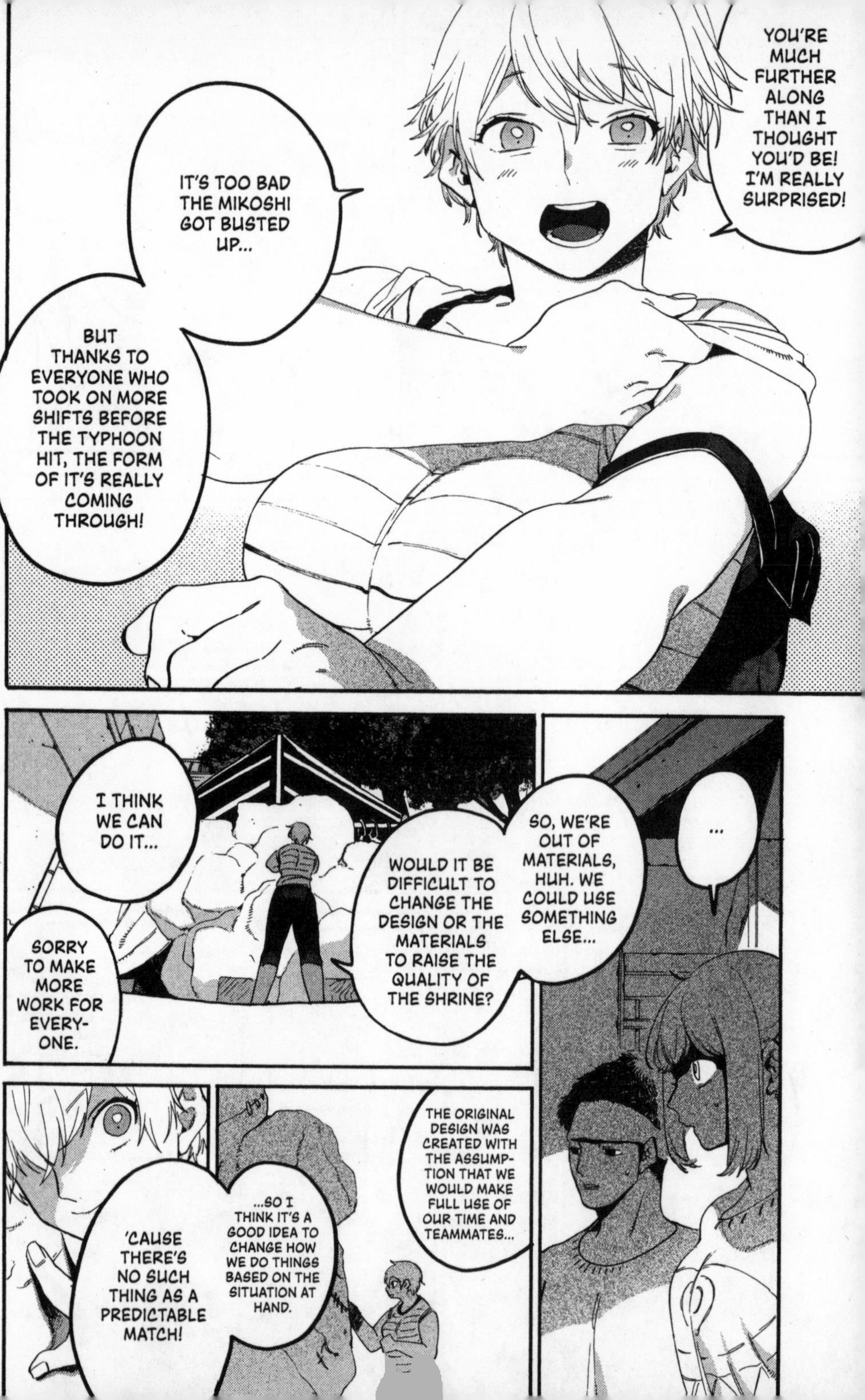
YOU'RE MUCH FURTHER ALONG THAN I THOUGHT YOU'D BE! I'M REALLY SURPRISED!
IT'S TOO BAD THE MIKOSHI GOT BUSTED UP...
BUT THANKS TO EVERYONE WHO TOOK ON MORE SHIFTS BEFORE THE TYPHOON HIT, THE FORM OF IT'S REALLY COMING THROUGH!
...
SO, WE'RE OUT OF MATERIALS, HUH. WE COULD USE SOMETHING ELSE...
WOULD IT BE DIFFICULT TO CHANGE THE DESIGN OR THE MATERIALS TO RAISE THE QUALITY OF THE SHRINE?
I THINK WE CAN DO IT...
SORRY TO MAKE MORE WORK FOR EVERY-ONE.
THE ORIGINAL DESIGN WAS CREATED WITH THE ASSUMP-TION THAT WE WOULD MAKE FULL USE OF OUR TIME AND TEAMMATES...
...SO I THINK IT'S A GOOD IDEA TO CHANGE HOW WE DO THINGS BASED ON THE SITUATION AT HAND.
'CAUSE THERE'S NO SUCH THING AS A PREDICTABLE MATCH!

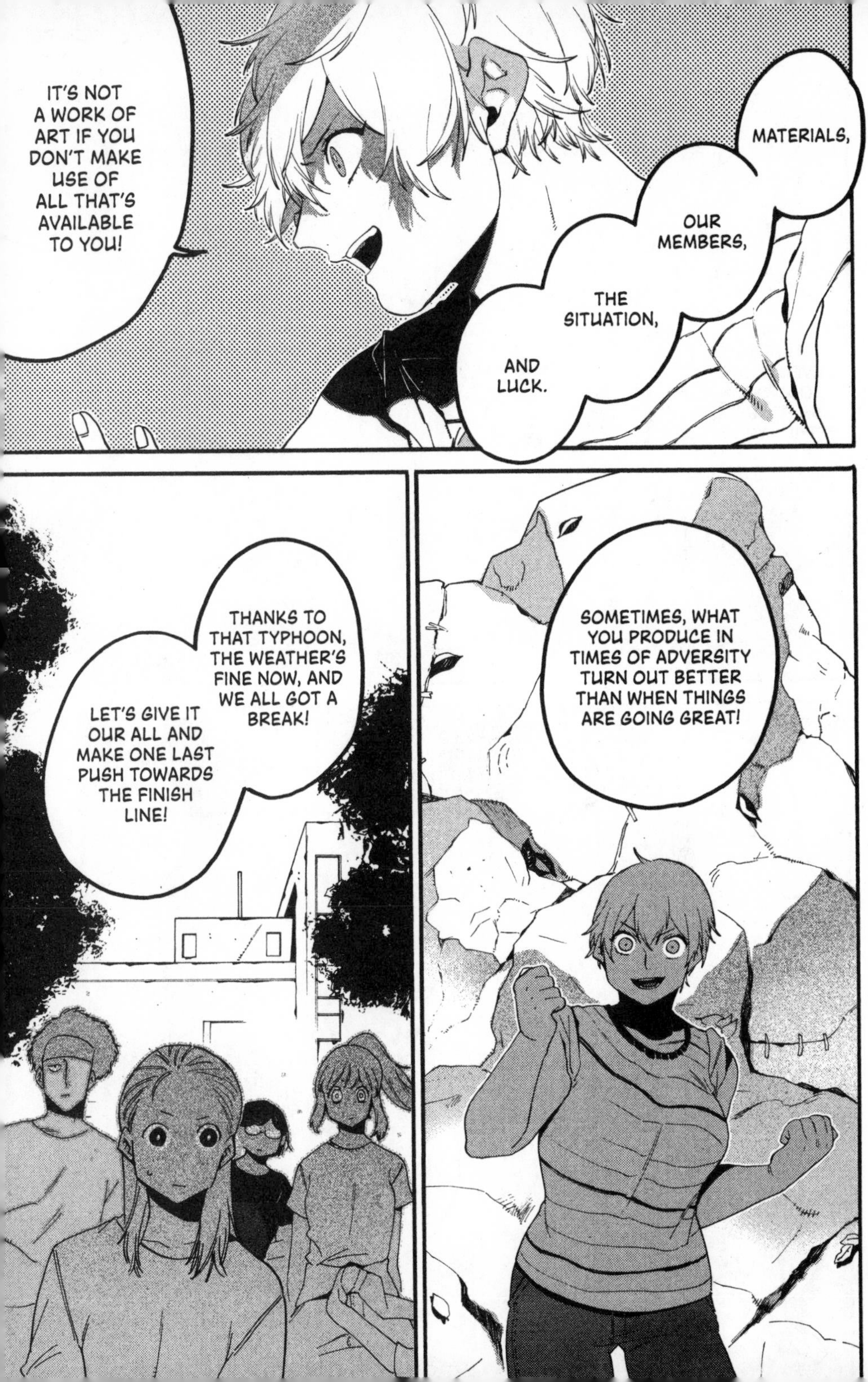
MATERIALS,
OUR MEMBERS,
THE SITUATION,
AND LUCK.
IT'S NOT A WORK OF ART IF YOU DON'T MAKE USE OF ALL THAT'S AVAILABLE TO YOU!
SOMETIMES, WHAT YOU PRODUCE IN TIMES OF ADVERSITY TURN OUT BETTER THAN WHEN THINGS ARE GOING GREAT!
THANKS TO THAT TYPHOON, THE WEATHER'S FINE NOW, AND WE ALL GOT A BREAK!
LET'S GIVE IT OUR ALL AND MAKE ONE LAST PUSH TOWARDS THE FINISH LINE!

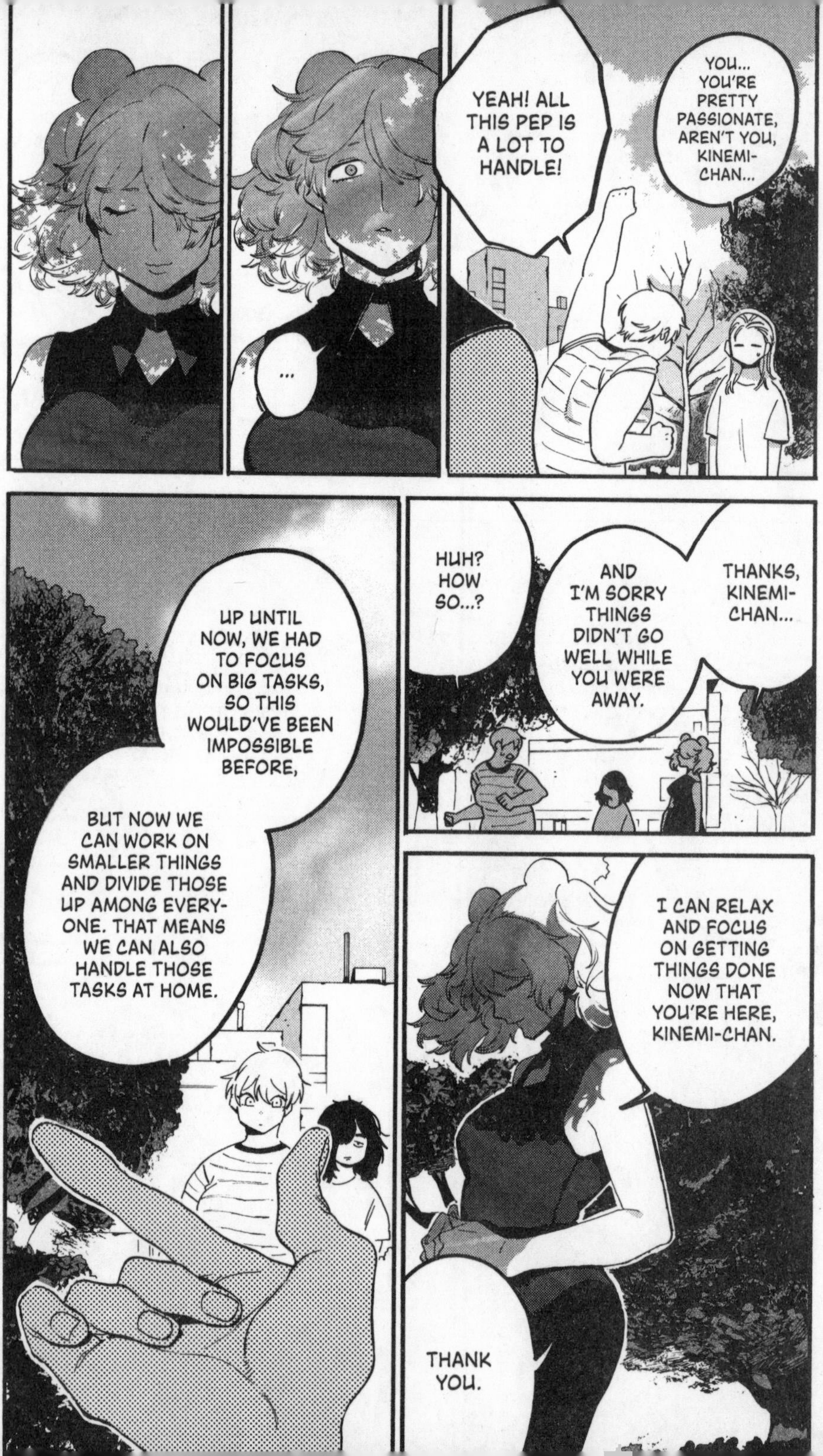
YOU... YOU'RE PRETTY PASSIONATE, AREN'T YOU, KINEMI-CHAN...
YEAH! ALL THIS PEP IS A LOT TO HANDLE!
...
THANKS, KINEMI-CHAN...
AND I'M SORRY THINGS DIDN'T GO WELL WHILE YOU WERE AWAY.
HUH? HOW SO...?
I CAN RELAX AND FOCUS ON GETTING THINGS DONE NOW THAT YOU'RE HERE, KINEMI-CHAN.
THANK YOU.
UP UNTIL NOW, WE HAD TO FOCUS ON BIG TASKS, SO THIS WOULD'VE BEEN IMPOSSIBLE BEFORE,
BUT NOW WE CAN WORK ON SMALLER THINGS AND DIVIDE THOSE UP AMONG EVERYONE. THAT MEANS WE CAN ALSO HANDLE THOSE TASKS AT HOME.

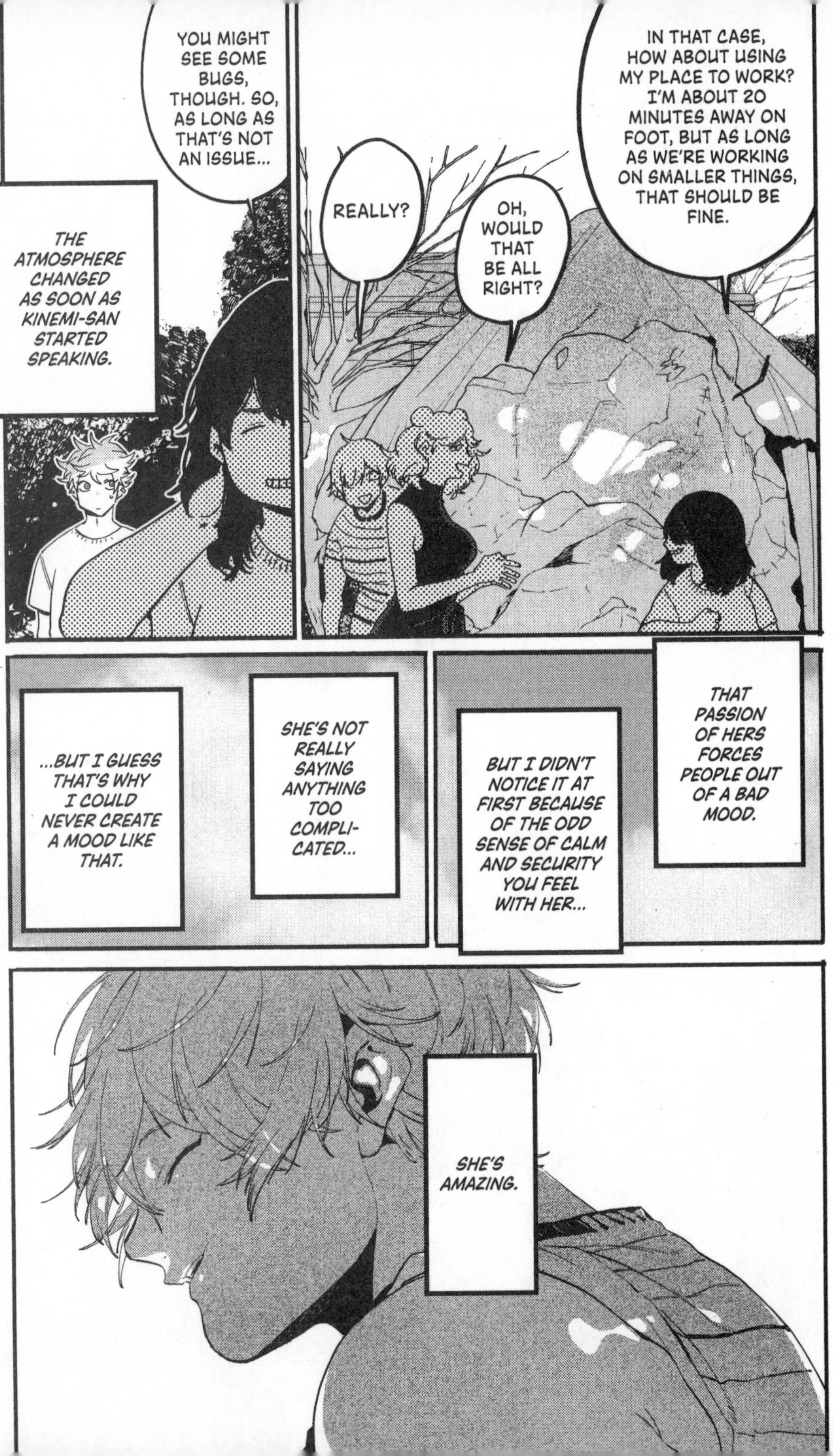

IN THAT CASE, HOW ABOUT USING MY PLACE TO WORK? I'M ABOUT 20 MINUTES AWAY ON FOOT, BUT AS LONG AS WE'RE WORKING ON SMALLER THINGS, THAT SHOULD BE FINE.
OH, WOULD THAT BE ALL RIGHT?
REALLY?
YOU MIGHT SEE SOME BUGS, THOUGH. SO, AS LONG AS THAT'S NOT AN ISSUE...
THE ATMOSPHERE CHANGED AS SOON AS KINEMI-SAN STARTED SPEAKING.
THAT PASSION OF HERS FORCES PEOPLE OUT OF A BAD MOOD.
BUT I DIDN'T NOTICE IT AT FIRST BECAUSE OF THE ODD SENSE OF CALM AND SECURITY YOU FEEL WITH HER...
SHE'S NOT REALLY SAYING ANYTHING TOO COMPLI-CATED...
...BUT I GUESS THAT'S WHY I COULD NEVER CREATE A MOOD LIKE THAT.
SHE'S AMAZING.

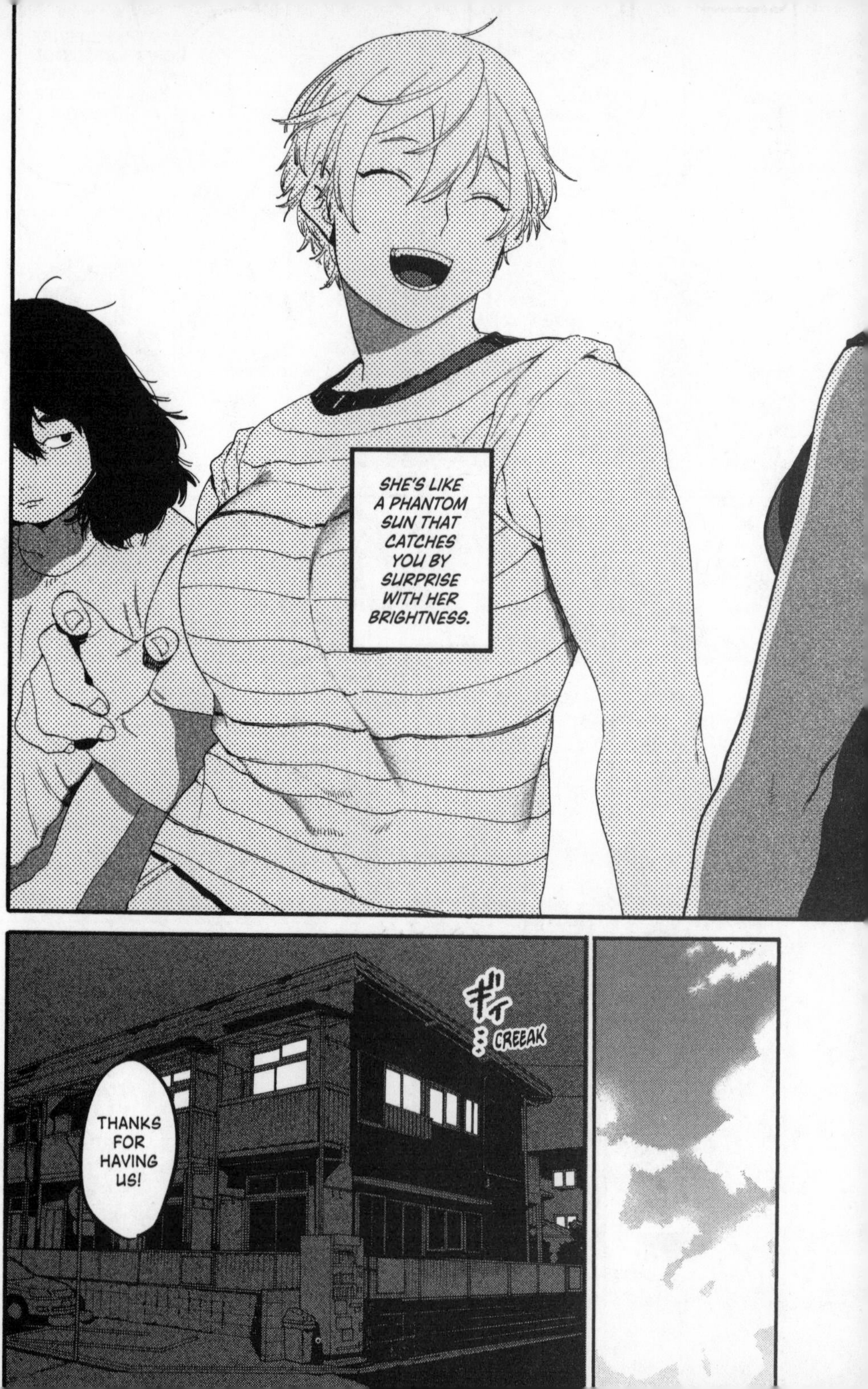
SHE'S LIKE A PHANTOM SUN THAT CATCHES YOU BY SURPRISE WITH HER BRIGHTNESS.
ギィ
CREEAK
THANKS FOR HAVING US!

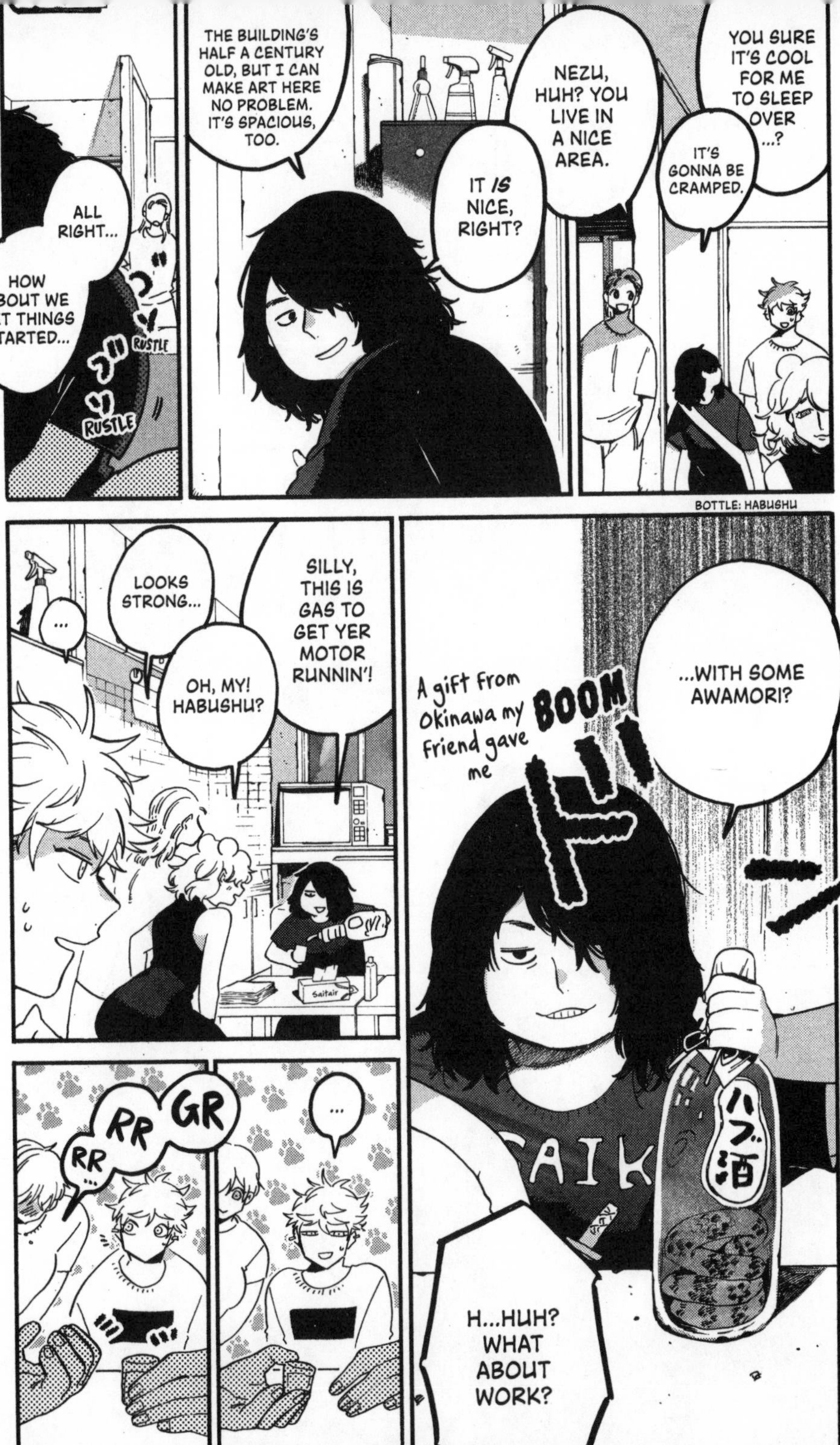
YOU SURE IT'S COOL FOR ME TO SLEEP OVER ...?
IT'S GONNA BE CRAMPED.
NEZU, HUH? YOU LIVE IN A NICE AREA.
IT IS NICE, RIGHT?
THE BUILDING'S HALF A CENTURY OLD, BUT I CAN MAKE ART HERE NO PROBLEM. IT'S SPACIOUS, TOO.
ALL RIGHT...
HOW ABOUT WE GET THINGS STARTED...
RUSTLE
RUSTLE
BOTTLE: HABUSHU
...WITH SOME AWAMORI?
A gift from Okinawa my friend gave me
BOOM
ハブ酒
H...HUH? WHAT ABOUT WORK?
OH, MY! HABUSHU?
LOOKS STRONG...
SILLY, THIS IS GAS TO GET YER MOTOR RUNNIN'!
...
...
GR
RR
RR...

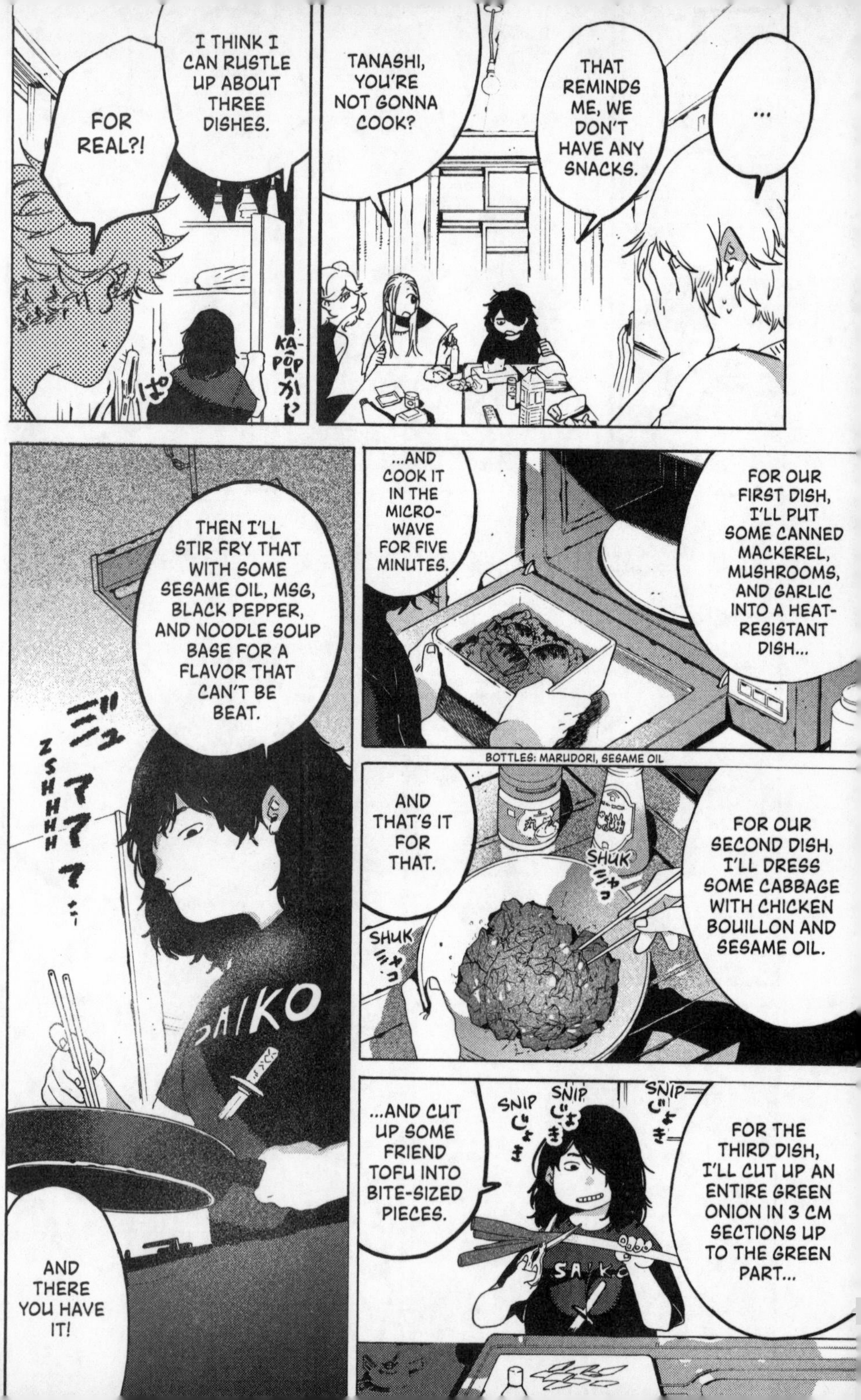
...
THAT REMINDS ME, WE DON'T HAVE ANY SNACKS.
TANASHI, YOU'RE NOT GONNA COOK?
I THINK I CAN RUSTLE UP ABOUT THREE DISHES.
FOR REAL?!
KA-POP
FOR OUR FIRST DISH, I'LL PUT SOME CANNED MACKEREL, MUSHROOMS, AND GARLIC INTO A HEAT-RESISTANT DISH...
...AND COOK IT IN THE MICRO-WAVE FOR FIVE MINUTES.
BOTTLES: MARUDORI, SESAME OIL
FOR OUR SECOND DISH, I'LL DRESS SOME CABBAGE WITH CHICKEN BOUILLON AND SESAME OIL.
SHUK
AND THAT'S IT FOR THAT.
SHUK
FOR THE THIRD DISH, I'LL CUT UP AN ENTIRE GREEN ONION IN 3 CM SECTIONS UP TO THE GREEN PART...
SNIP
SNIP
SNIP
...AND CUT UP SOME FRIEND TOFU INTO BITE-SIZED PIECES.
THEN I'LL STIR FRY THAT WITH SOME SESAME OIL, MSG, BLACK PEPPER, AND NOODLE SOUP BASE FOR A FLAVOR THAT CAN'T BE BEAT.
ZSHHHH
SAIKO
AND THERE YOU HAVE IT!

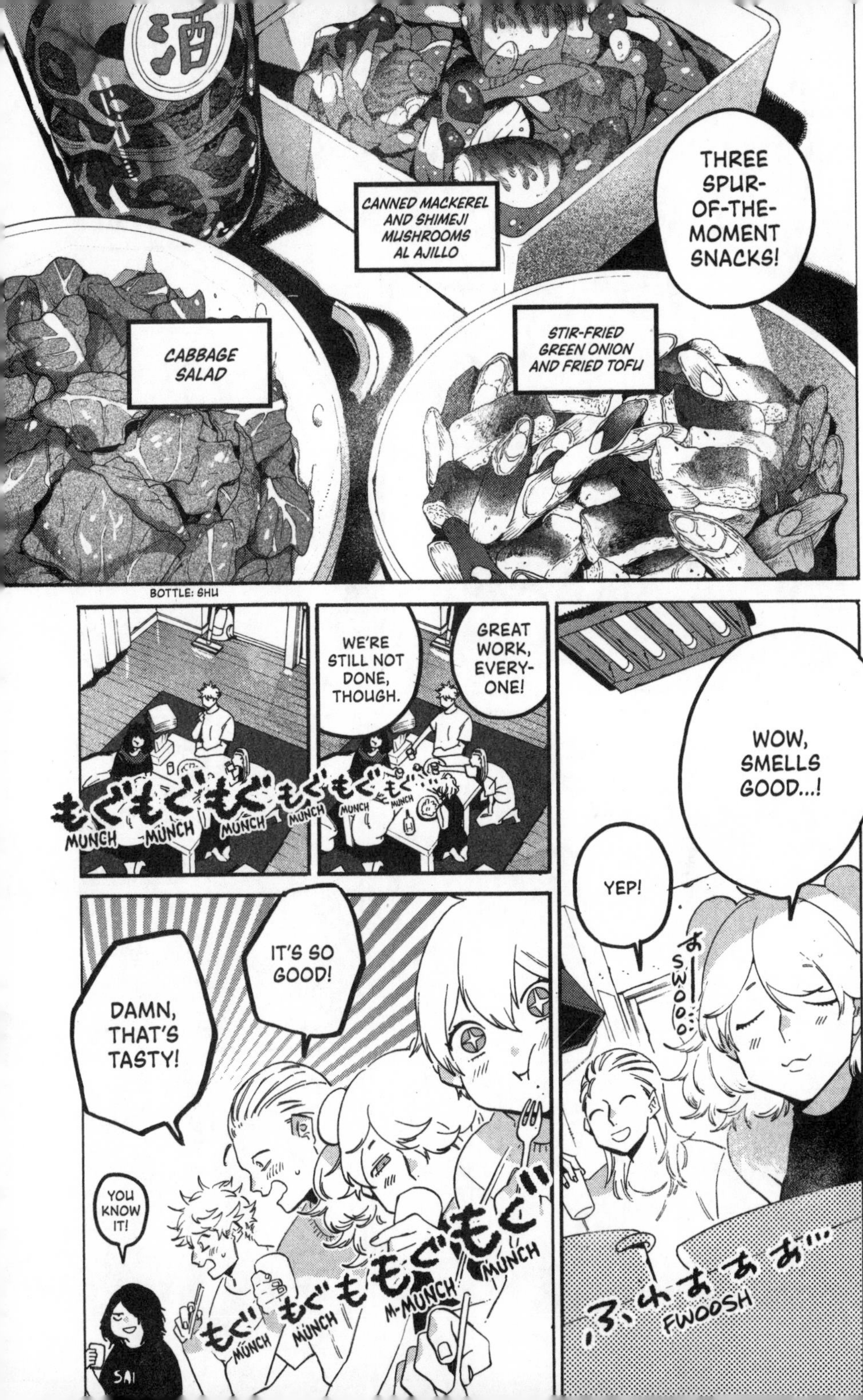
THREE SPUR-OF-THE-MOMENT SNACKS!
CANNED MACKEREL AND SHIMEJI MUSHROOMS AL AJILLO
STIR-FRIED GREEN ONION AND FRIED TOFU
CABBAGE SALAD
酒
BOTTLE: SHU
WOW, SMELLS GOOD...!
YEP!
お SWOOO...
ふわぁぁぁ… FWOOSH
GREAT WORK, EVERY-ONE!
WE'RE STILL NOT DONE, THOUGH.
もぐもぐもぐもぐもぐもぐ MUNCH MUNCH MUNCH MUNCH MUNCH MUNCH
IT'S SO GOOD!
DAMN, THAT'S TASTY!
YOU KNOW IT!
もぐもぐもぐ MUNCH
もぐもぐもぐもぐ MUNCH MUNCH M-MUNCH MUNCH
SAI

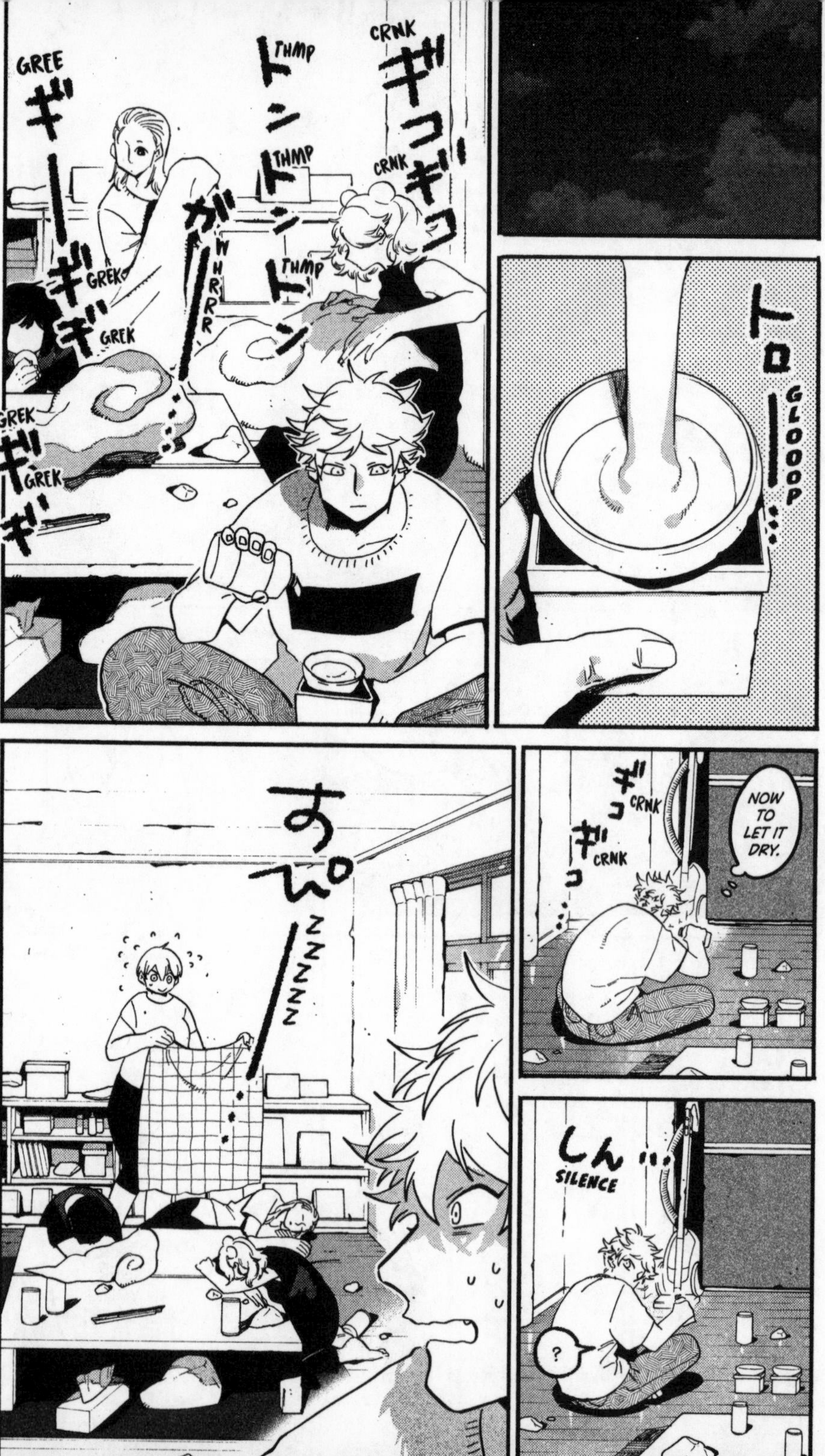
トロー…
GLOOOOP
ギコギコ
CRNK
CRNK
ドンドンドン
THMP
THMP
THMP
ガーー…
WHRRR
ギーギギギ
GREE
GREK
GREK
ギギギ
GREK
GREK
ギコ
CRNK
ギコ…
CRNK
NOW TO LET IT DRY.
しん…
SILENCE
?
すぴー…
ZZZZZZ

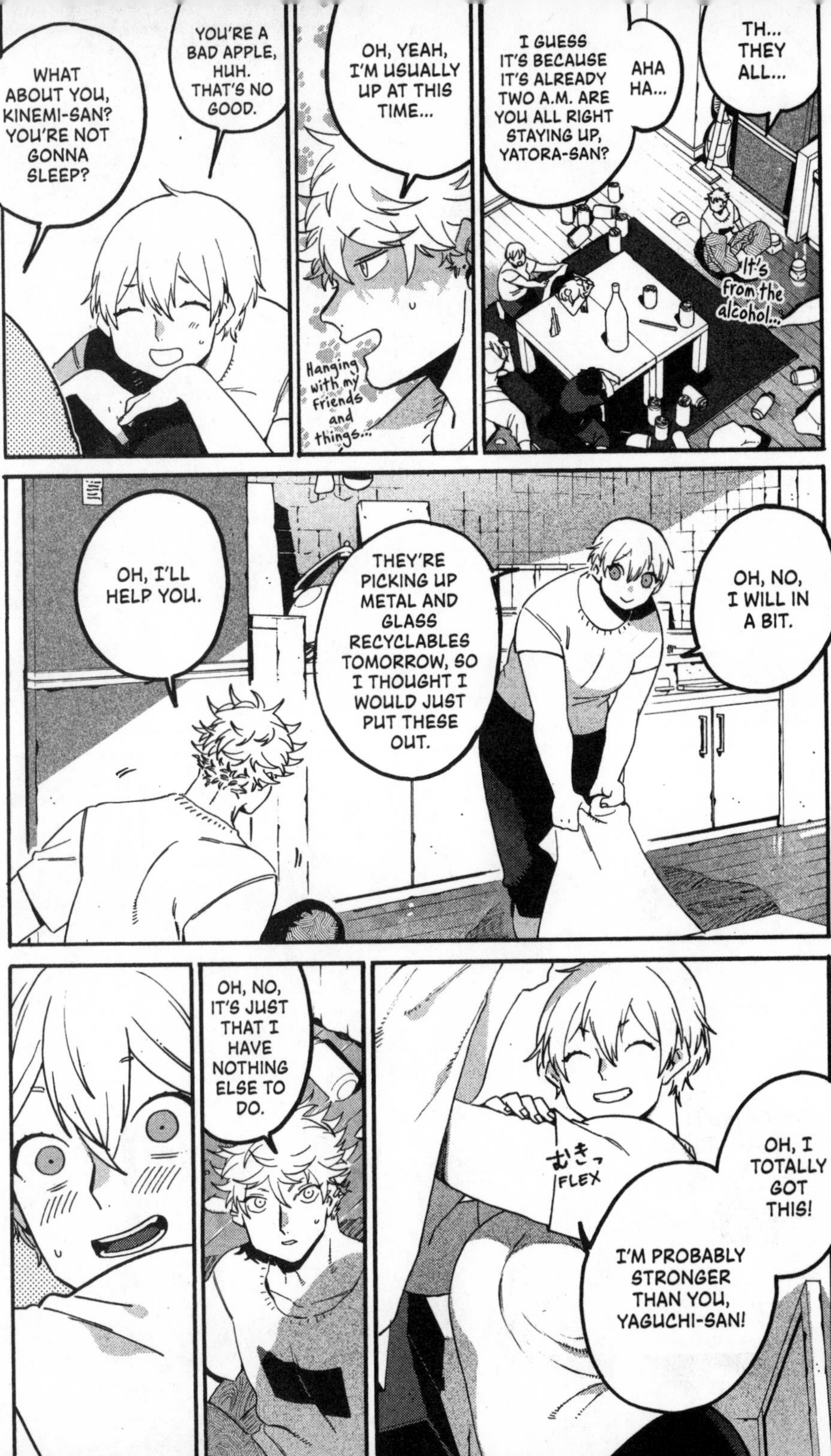
TH... THEY ALL...
AHA HA...
I GUESS IT'S BECAUSE IT'S ALREADY TWO A.M. ARE YOU ALL RIGHT STAYING UP, YATORA-SAN?
It's from the alcohol...
OH, YEAH, I'M USUALLY UP AT THIS TIME...
Hanging with my friends and things...
YOU'RE A BAD APPLE, HUH. THAT'S NO GOOD.
WHAT ABOUT YOU, KINEMI-SAN? YOU'RE NOT GONNA SLEEP?
OH, NO, I WILL IN A BIT.
THEY'RE PICKING UP METAL AND GLASS RECYCLABLES TOMORROW, SO I THOUGHT I WOULD JUST PUT THESE OUT.
OH, I'LL HELP YOU.
OH, I TOTALLY GOT THIS!
I'M PROBABLY STRONGER THAN YOU, YAGUCHI-SAN!
むきっ FLEX
OH, NO, IT'S JUST THAT I HAVE NOTHING ELSE TO DO.

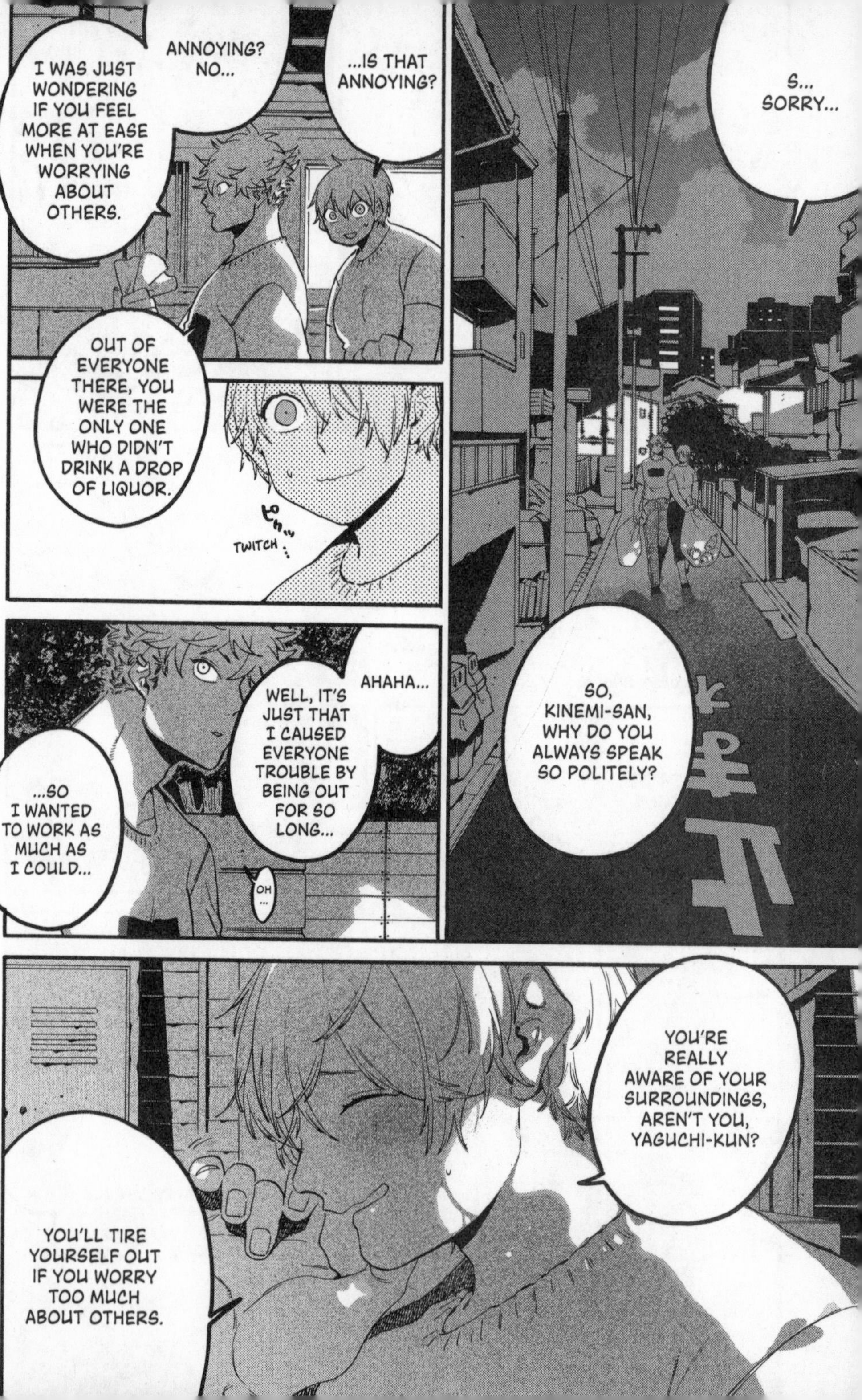
S... SORRY...
SO, KINEMI-SAN, WHY DO YOU ALWAYS SPEAK SO POLITELY?
...IS THAT ANNOYING?
ANNOYING? NO...
I WAS JUST WONDERING IF YOU FEEL MORE AT EASE WHEN YOU'RE WORRYING ABOUT OTHERS.
OUT OF EVERYONE THERE, YOU WERE THE ONLY ONE WHO DIDN'T DRINK A DROP OF LIQUOR.
TWITCH...
AHAHA...
WELL, IT'S JUST THAT I CAUSED EVERYONE TROUBLE BY BEING OUT FOR SO LONG...
OH...
...SO I WANTED TO WORK AS MUCH AS I COULD...
YOU'RE REALLY AWARE OF YOUR SURROUNDINGS, AREN'T YOU, YAGUCHI-KUN?
YOU'LL TIRE YOURSELF OUT IF YOU WORRY TOO MUCH ABOUT OTHERS.

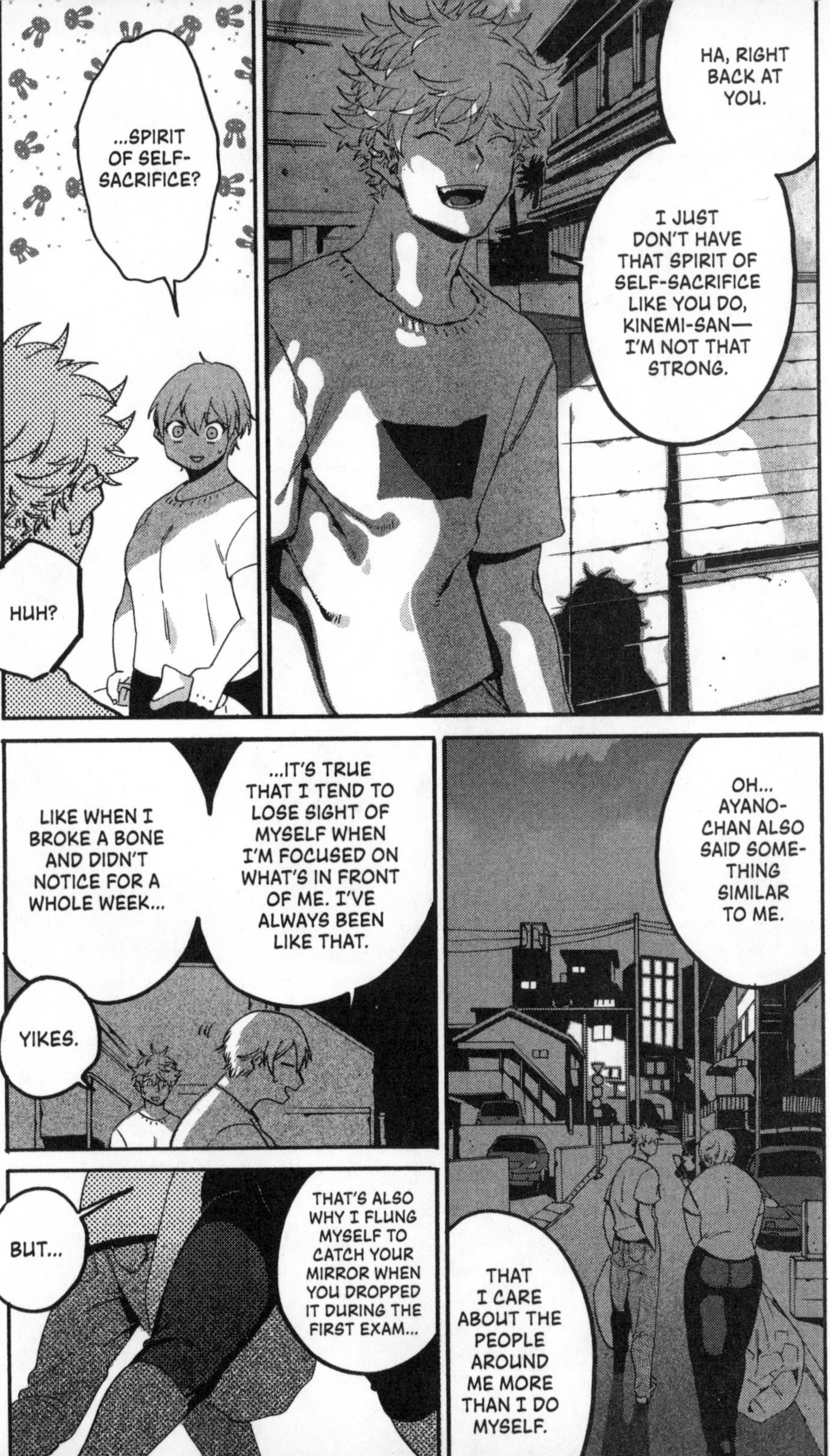
HA, RIGHT BACK AT YOU.
I JUST DON'T HAVE THAT SPIRIT OF SELF-SACRIFICE LIKE YOU DO, KINEMI-SAN— I'M NOT THAT STRONG.
...SPIRIT OF SELF-SACRIFICE?
HUH?
OH... AYANO-CHAN ALSO SAID SOME-THING SIMILAR TO ME.
THAT I CARE ABOUT THE PEOPLE AROUND ME MORE THAN I DO MYSELF.
...IT'S TRUE THAT I TEND TO LOSE SIGHT OF MYSELF WHEN I'M FOCUSED ON WHAT'S IN FRONT OF ME. I'VE ALWAYS BEEN LIKE THAT.
LIKE WHEN I BROKE A BONE AND DIDN'T NOTICE FOR A WHOLE WEEK...
YIKES.
THAT'S ALSO WHY I FLUNG MYSELF TO CATCH YOUR MIRROR WHEN YOU DROPPED IT DURING THE FIRST EXAM...
BUT...

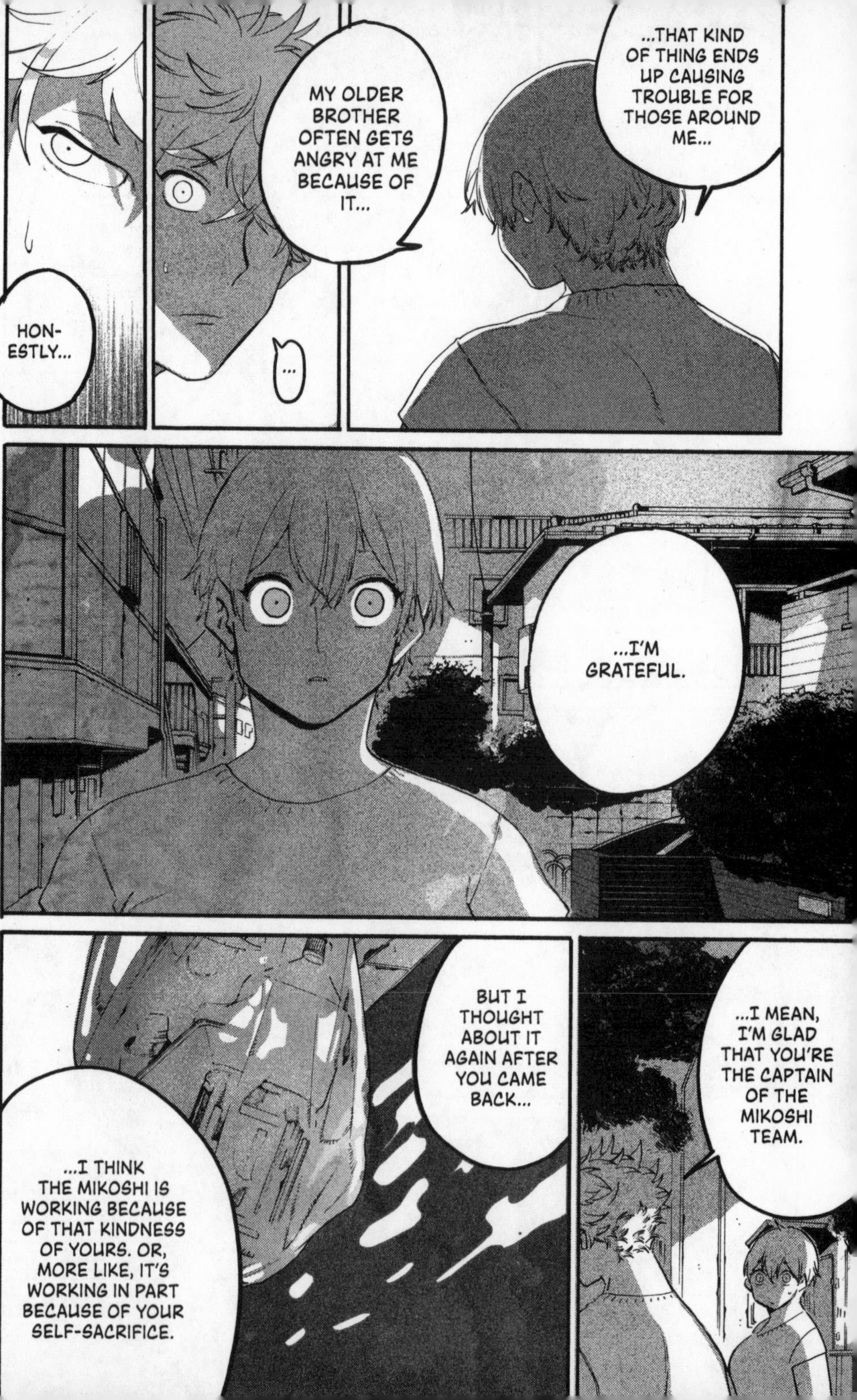
...THAT KIND OF THING ENDS UP CAUSING TROUBLE FOR THOSE AROUND ME...
MY OLDER BROTHER OFTEN GETS ANGRY AT ME BECAUSE OF IT...
...
HON-ESTLY...
...I'M GRATEFUL.
...I MEAN, I'M GLAD THAT YOU'RE THE CAPTAIN OF THE MIKOSHI TEAM.
BUT I THOUGHT ABOUT IT AGAIN AFTER YOU CAME BACK...
...I THINK THE MIKOSHI IS WORKING BECAUSE OF THAT KINDNESS OF YOURS. OR, MORE LIKE, IT'S WORKING IN PART BECAUSE OF YOUR SELF-SACRIFICE.

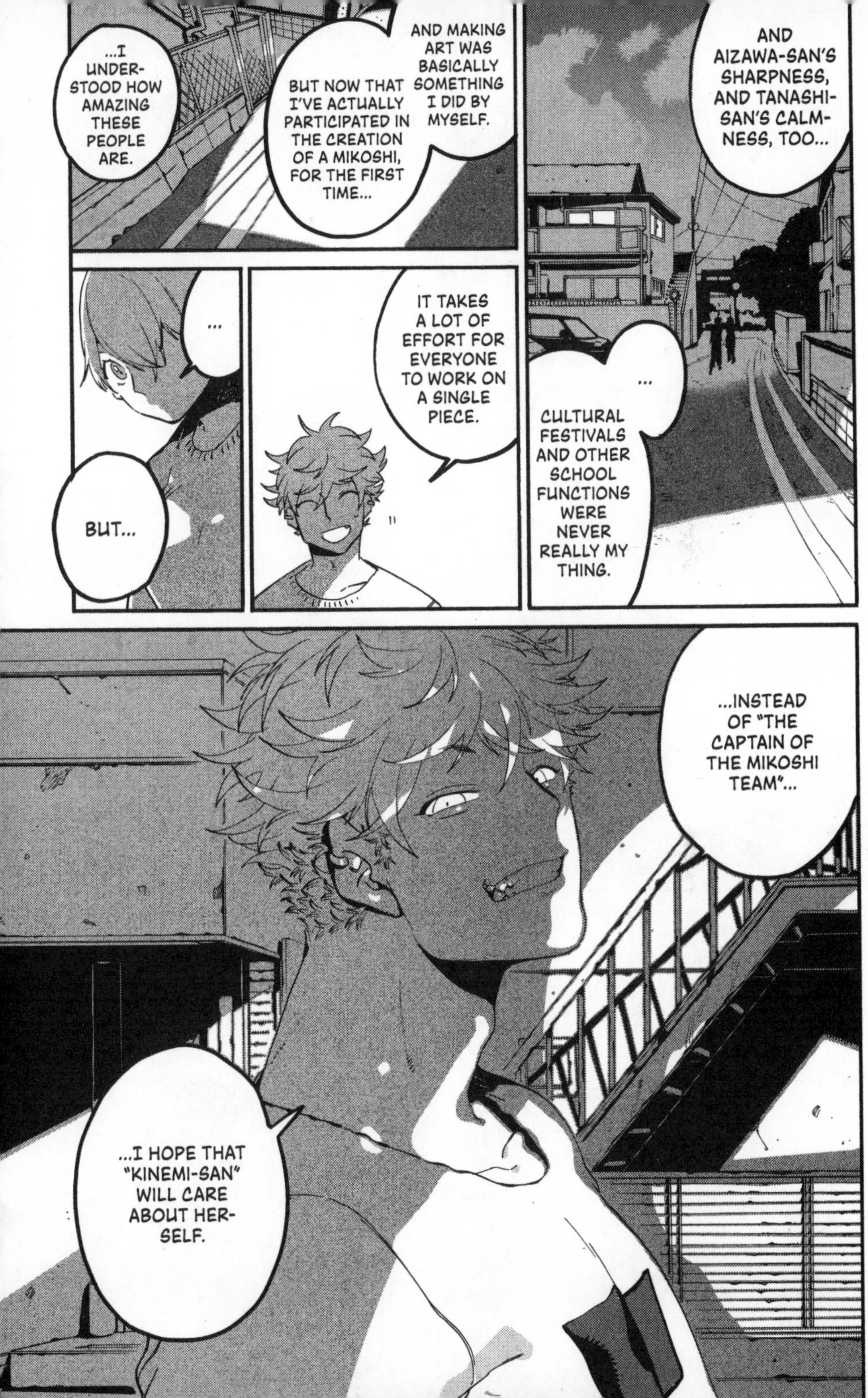
AND AIZAWA-SAN'S SHARPNESS, AND TANASHI-SAN'S CALMNESS, TOO...
...
CULTURAL FESTIVALS AND OTHER SCHOOL FUNCTIONS WERE NEVER REALLY MY THING.
AND MAKING ART WAS BASICALLY SOMETHING I DID BY MYSELF.
BUT NOW THAT I'VE ACTUALLY PARTICIPATED IN THE CREATION OF A MIKOSHI, FOR THE FIRST TIME...
...I UNDERSTOOD HOW AMAZING THESE PEOPLE ARE.
IT TAKES A LOT OF EFFORT FOR EVERYONE TO WORK ON A SINGLE PIECE.
...
BUT...
...INSTEAD OF "THE CAPTAIN OF THE MIKOSHI TEAM"...
...I HOPE THAT "KINEMI-SAN" WILL CARE ABOUT HERSELF.

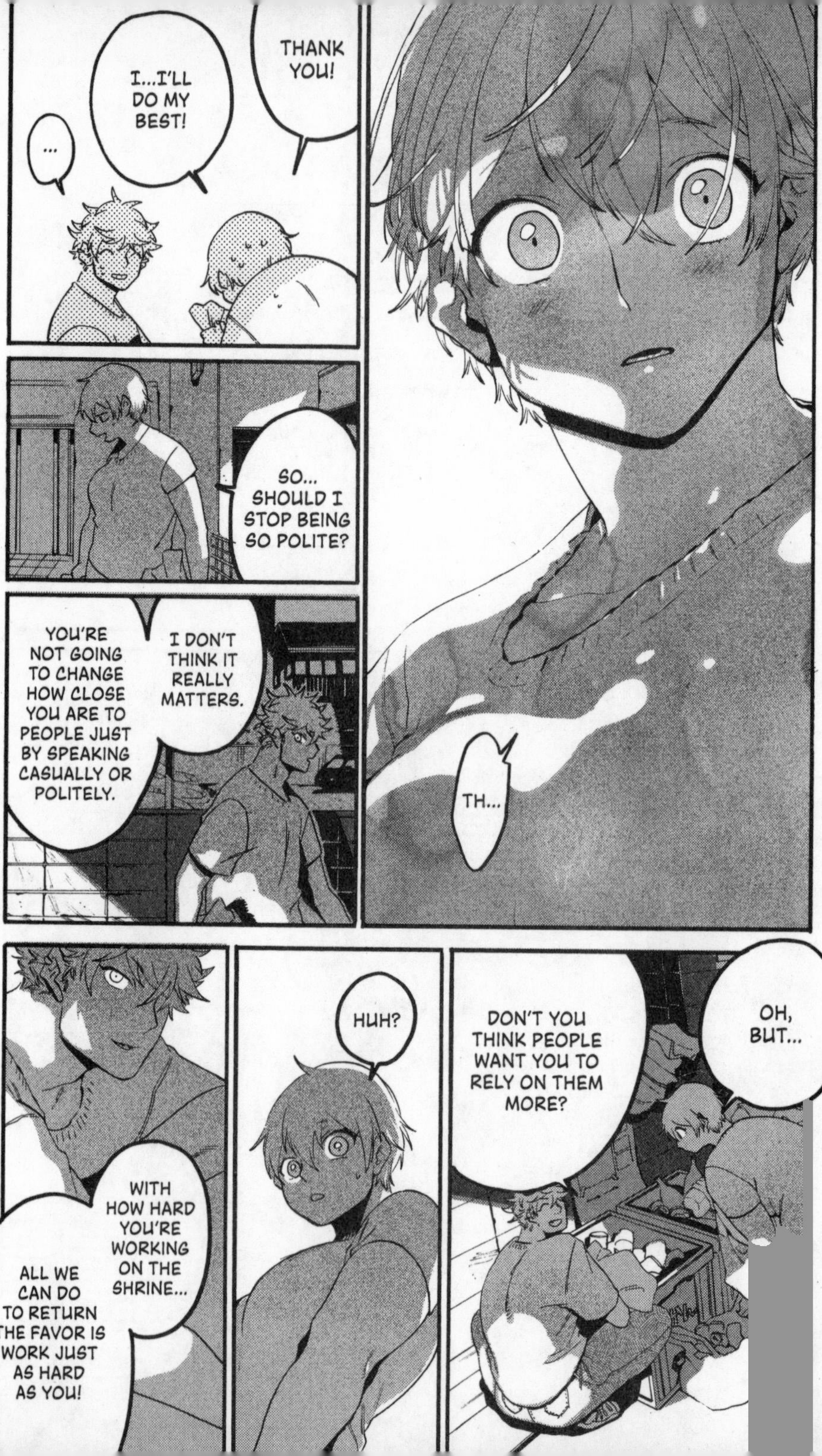
TH...
THANK YOU!
I...I'LL DO MY BEST!
...
SO... SHOULD I STOP BEING SO POLITE?
I DON'T THINK IT REALLY MATTERS.
YOU'RE NOT GOING TO CHANGE HOW CLOSE YOU ARE TO PEOPLE JUST BY SPEAKING CASUALLY OR POLITELY.
OH, BUT...
DON'T YOU THINK PEOPLE WANT YOU TO RELY ON THEM MORE?
HUH?
WITH HOW HARD YOU'RE WORKING ON THE SHRINE...
ALL WE CAN DO TO RETURN THE FAVOR IS WORK JUST AS HARD AS YOU!

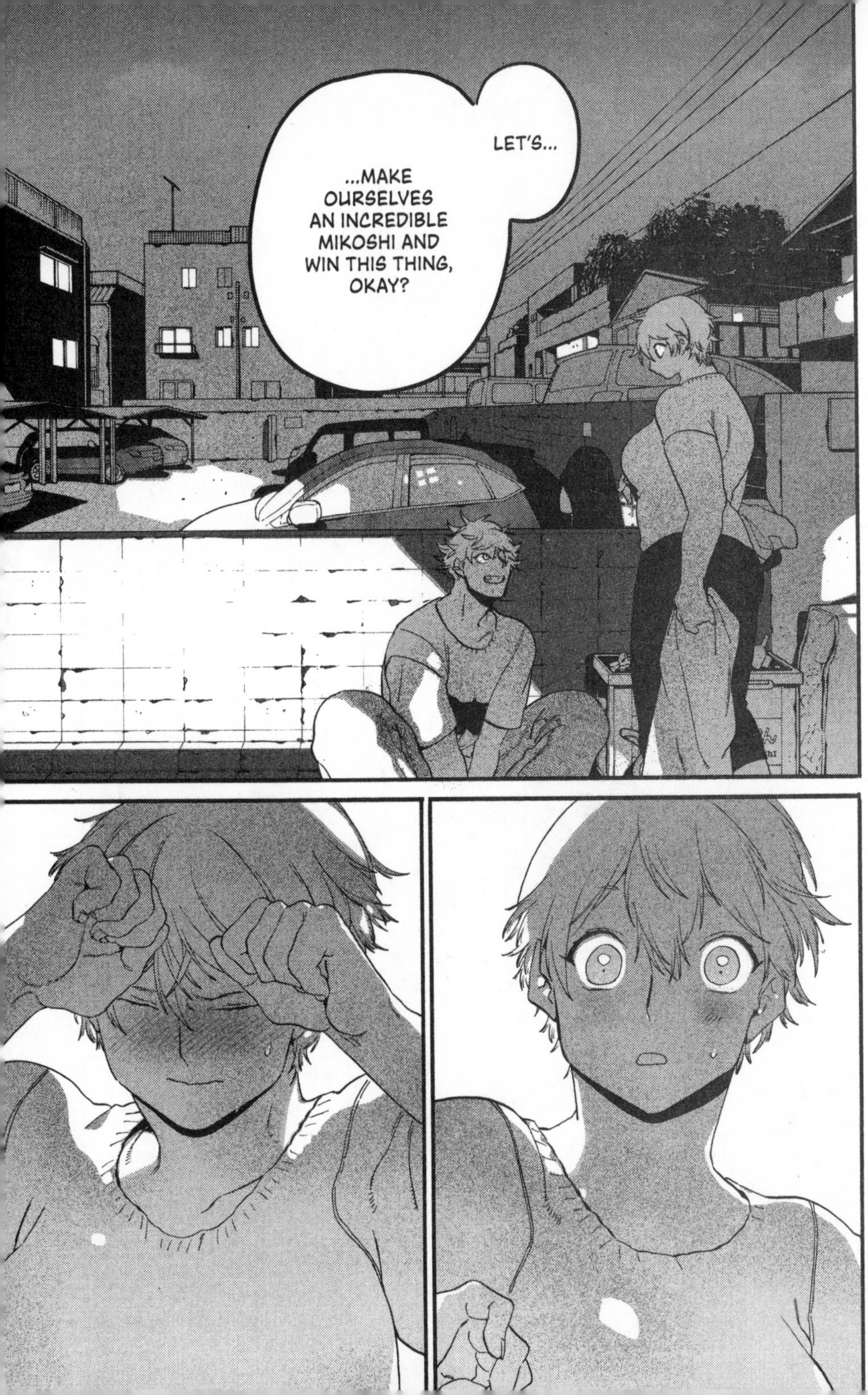
LET'S...
...MAKE OURSELVES AN INCREDIBLE MIKOSHI AND WIN THIS THING, OKAY?

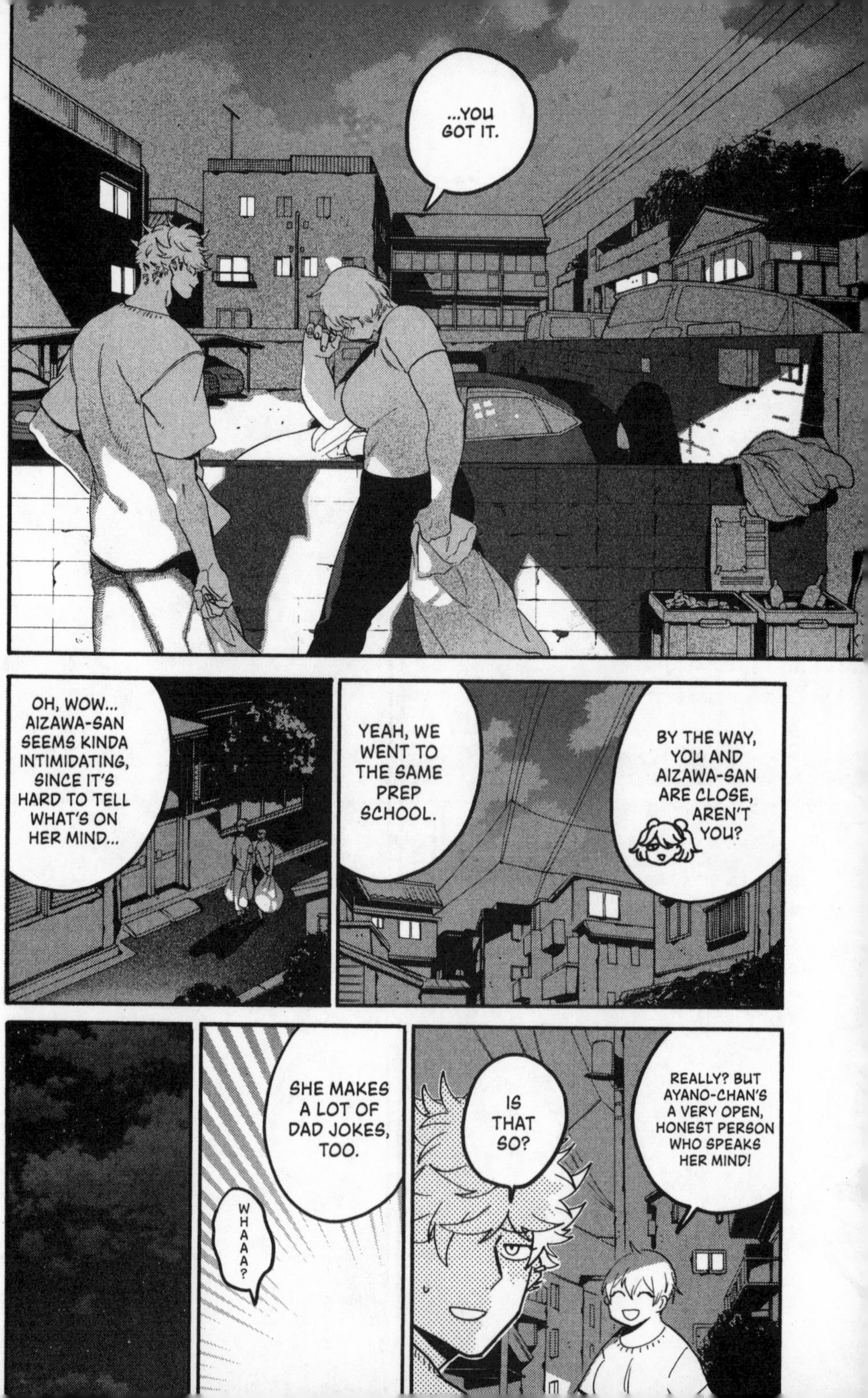
...YOU GOT IT.
BY THE WAY, YOU AND AIZAWA-SAN ARE CLOSE, AREN'T YOU?
YEAH, WE WENT TO THE SAME PREP SCHOOL.
OH, WOW... AIZAWA-SAN SEEMS KINDA INTIMIDATING, SINCE IT'S HARD TO TELL WHAT'S ON HER MIND...
REALLY? BUT AYANO-CHAN'S A VERY OPEN, HONEST PERSON WHO SPEAKS HER MIND!
IS THAT SO?
SHE MAKES A LOT OF DAD JOKES, TOO.
WHAAAA?

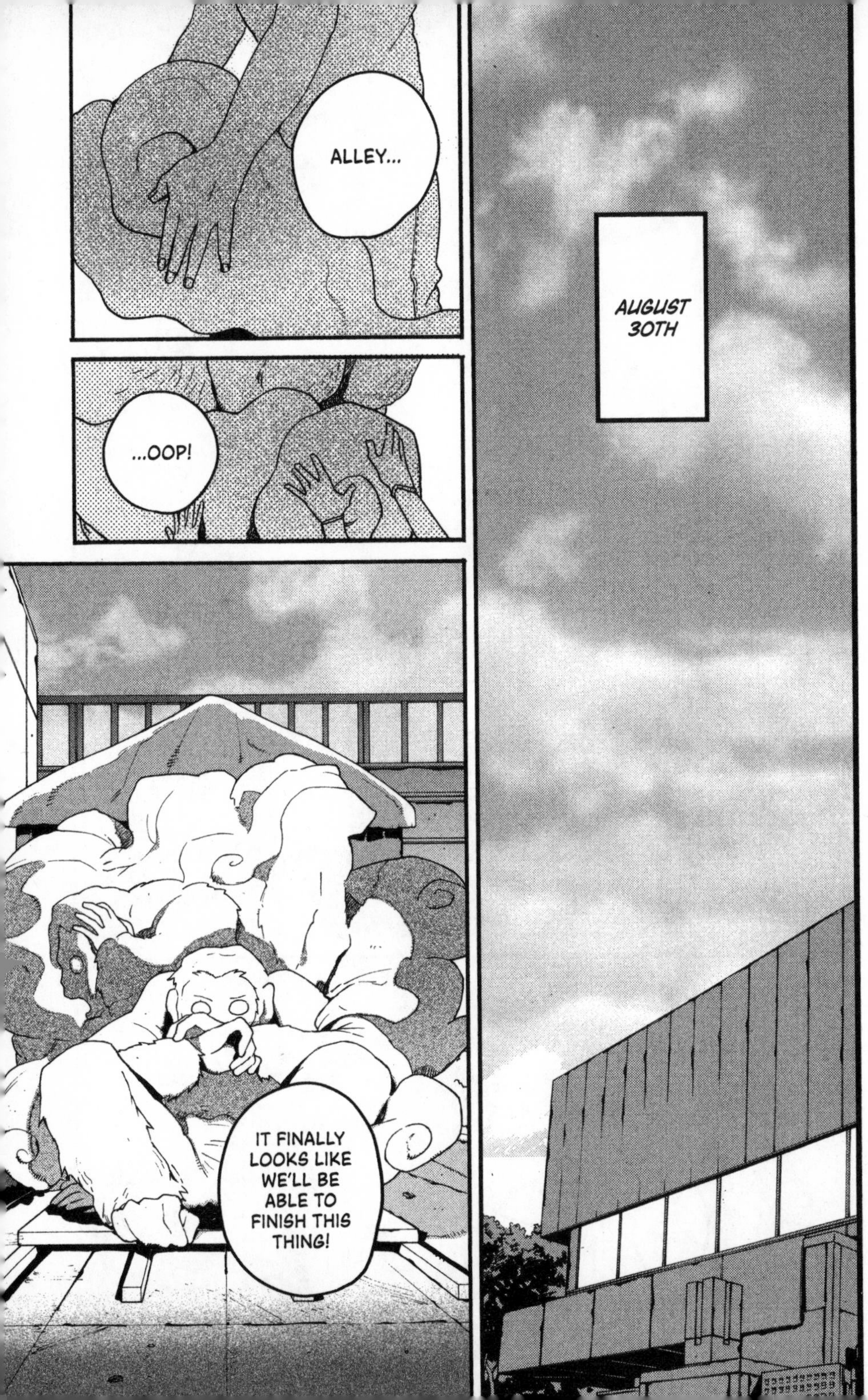
AUGUST 30TH
ALLEY...
...OOP!
IT FINALLY LOOKS LIKE WE'LL BE ABLE TO FINISH THIS THING!

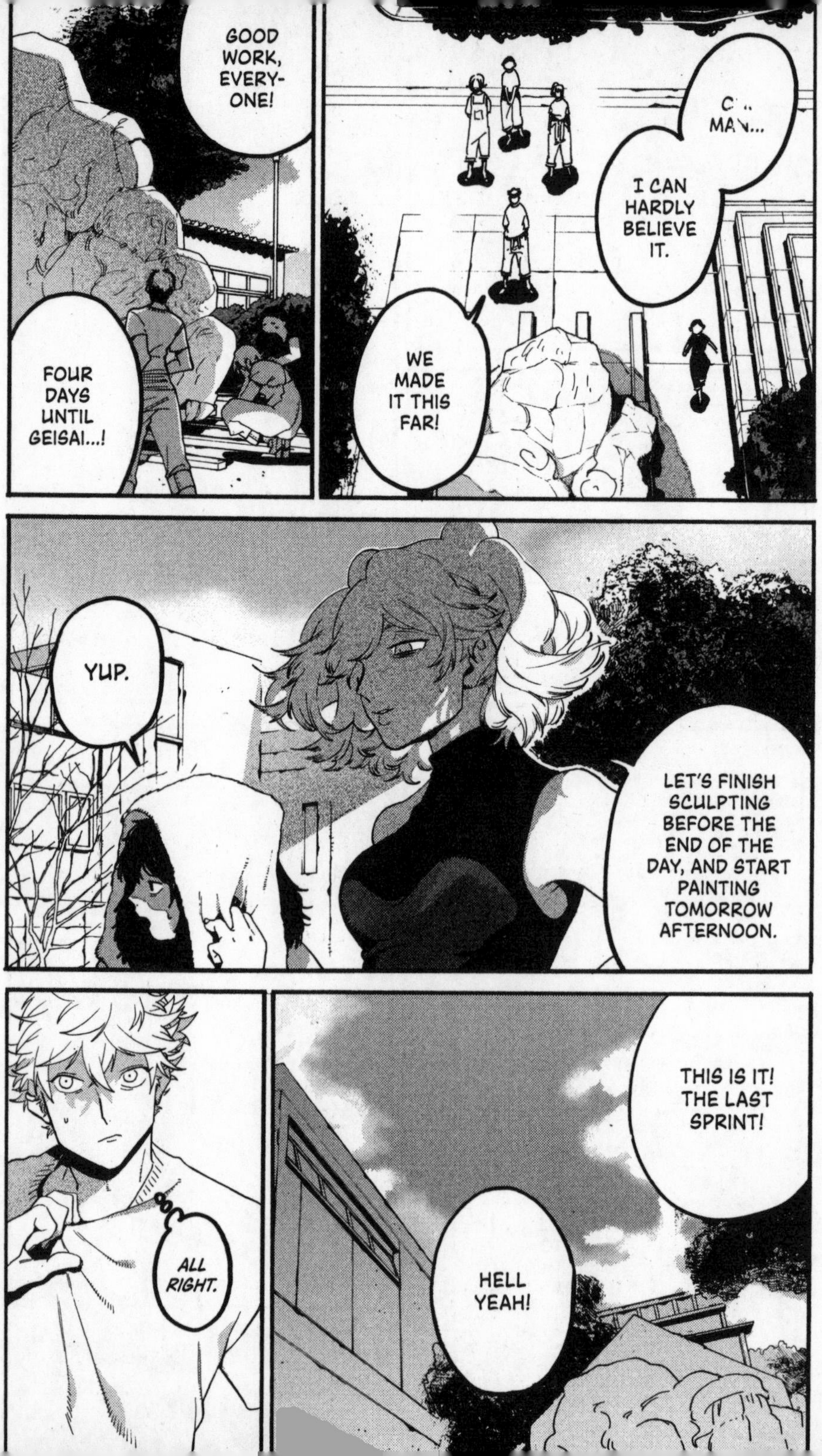
MAN...
I CAN HARDLY BELIEVE IT.
WE MADE IT THIS FAR!
GOOD WORK, EVERYONE!
FOUR DAYS UNTIL GEISAI...!
LET'S FINISH SCULPTING BEFORE THE END OF THE DAY, AND START PAINTING TOMORROW AFTERNOON.
YUP.
THIS IS IT! THE LAST SPRINT!
HELL YEAH!
ALL RIGHT.

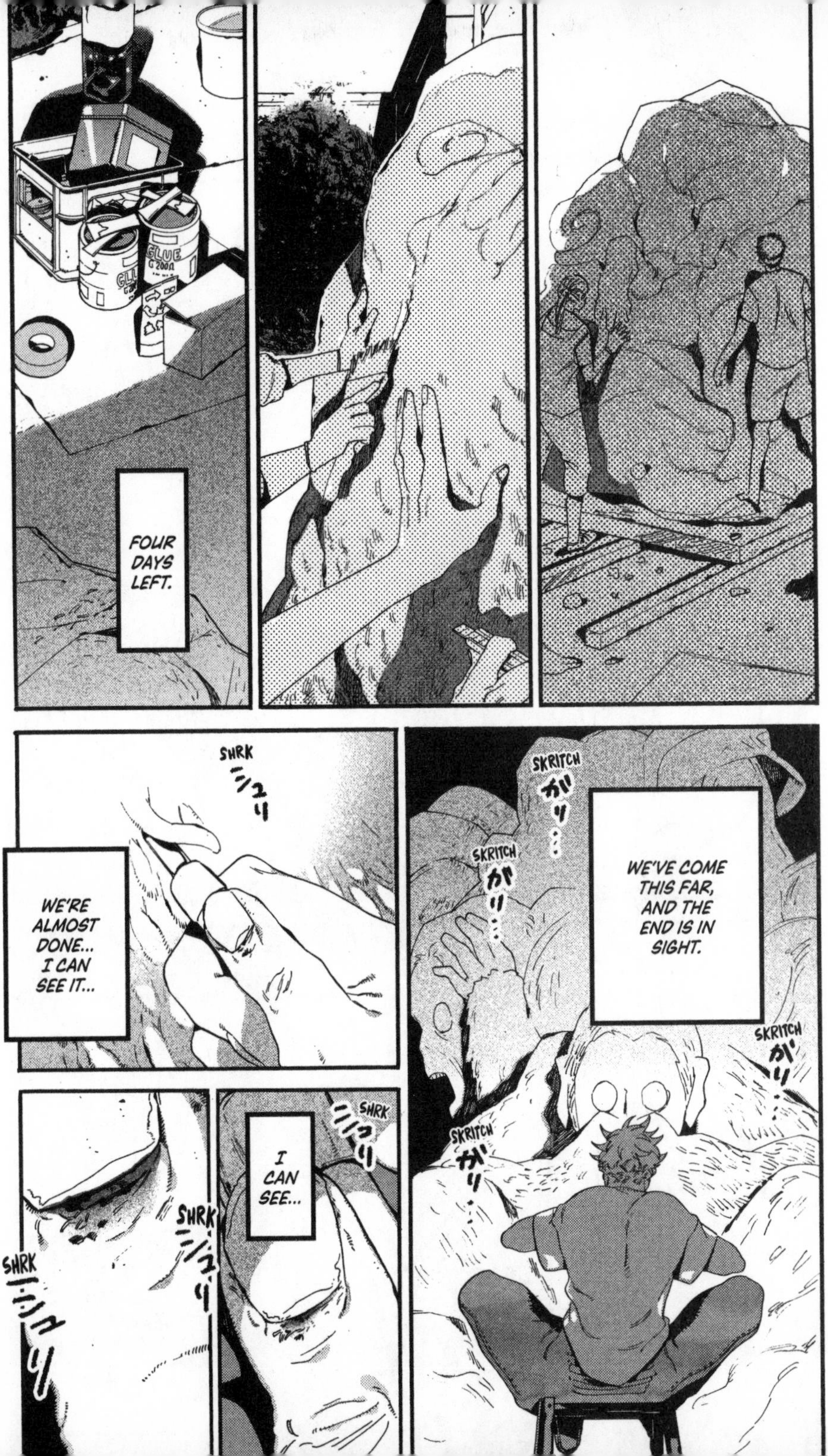
FOUR DAYS LEFT.
SKRITCH
がり…
SKRITCH
がり…
WE'VE COME THIS FAR, AND THE END IS IN SIGHT.
SKRITCH
がり…
SKRITCH
がり…
SHRK
シュリ
WE'RE ALMOST DONE... I CAN SEE IT...
SHRK
シュリ
I CAN SEE...
SHRK
シュリ
SHRK
シュリ

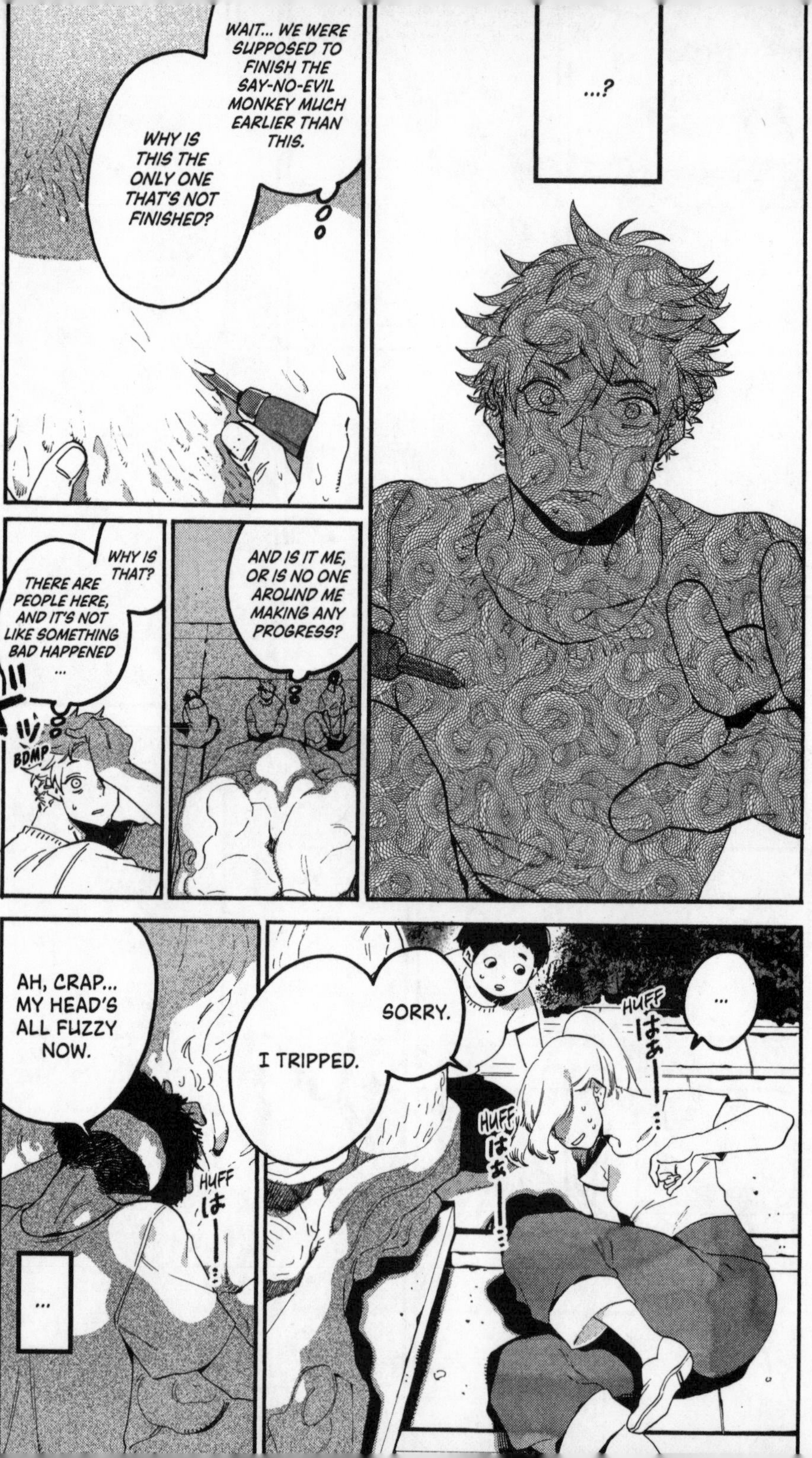
...?
WAIT... WE WERE SUPPOSED TO FINISH THE SAY-NO-EVIL MONKEY MUCH EARLIER THAN THIS.
WHY IS THIS THE ONLY ONE THAT'S NOT FINISHED?
AND IS IT ME, OR IS NO ONE AROUND ME MAKING ANY PROGRESS?
WHY IS THAT?
THERE ARE PEOPLE HERE, AND IT'S NOT LIKE SOMETHING BAD HAPPENED ...
ドッ
BDMP
...
HUFF
はぁー...
SORRY.
I TRIPPED.
HUFF
はぁー...
HUFF
はー...
AH, CRAP... MY HEAD'S ALL FUZZY NOW.
...

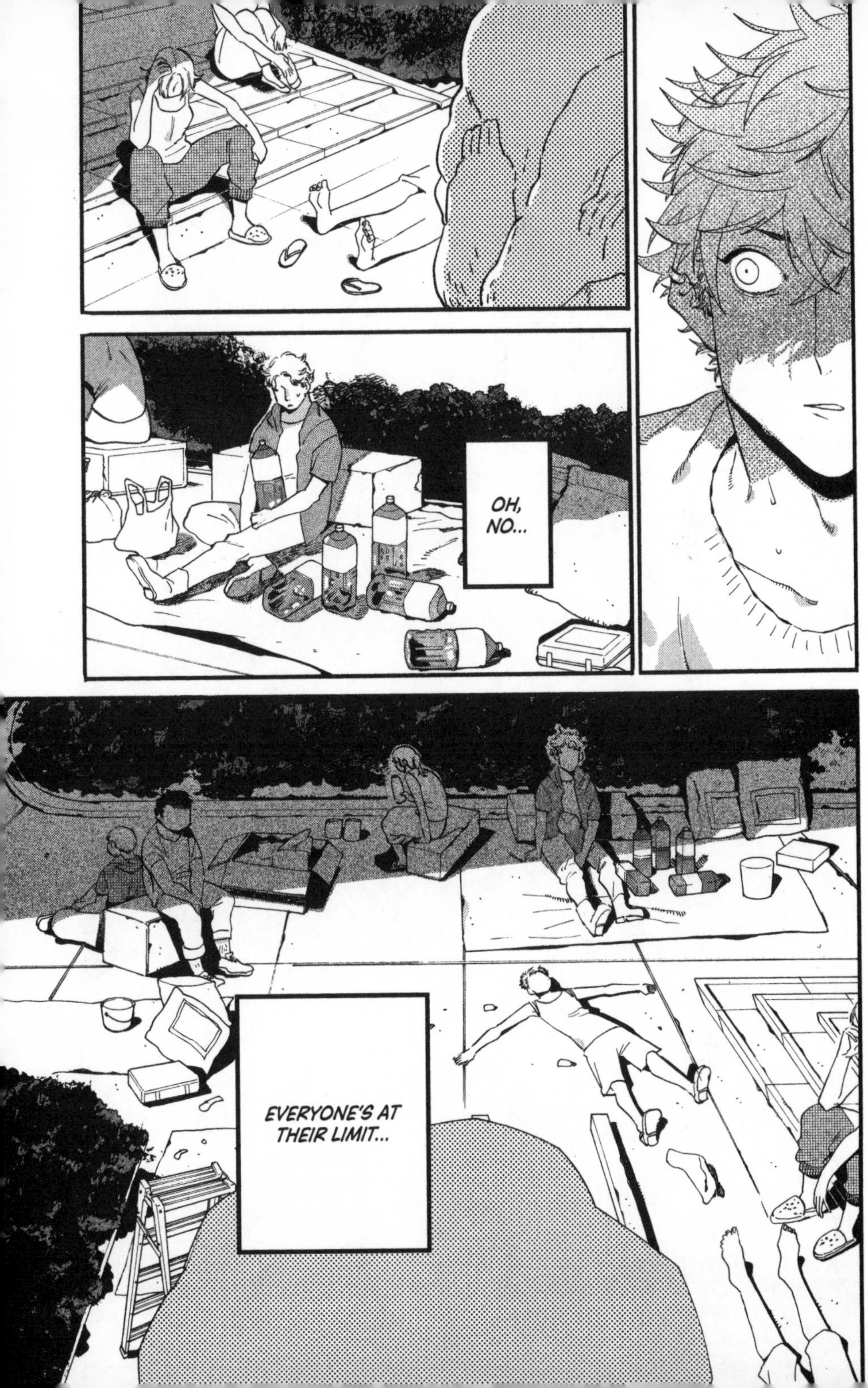
OH, NO...
EVERYONE'S AT THEIR LIMIT...

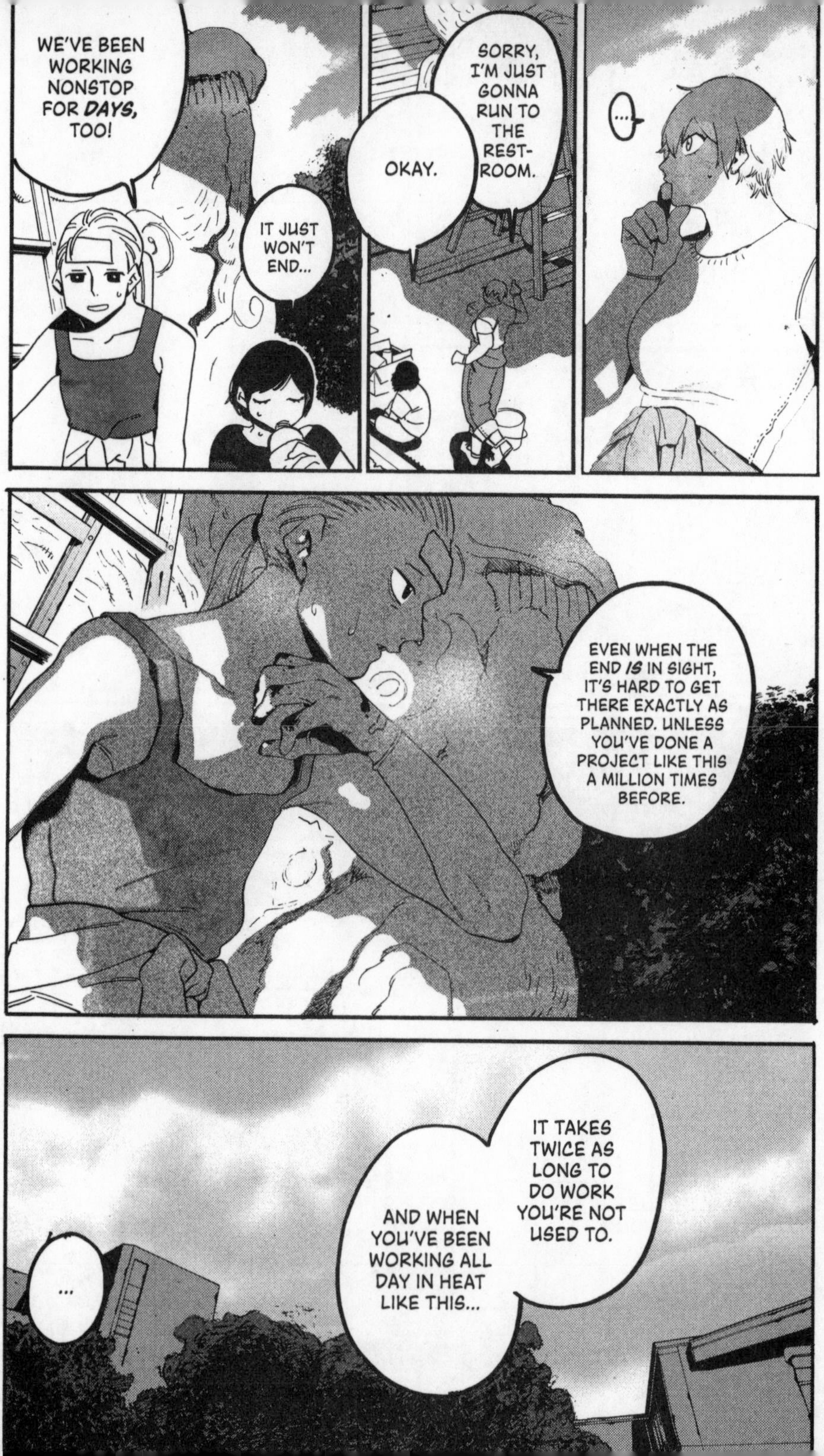
…
SORRY, I'M JUST GONNA RUN TO THE REST-ROOM.
OKAY.
IT JUST WON'T END...
WE'VE BEEN WORKING NONSTOP FOR DAYS, TOO!
EVEN WHEN THE END IS IN SIGHT, IT'S HARD TO GET THERE EXACTLY AS PLANNED. UNLESS YOU'VE DONE A PROJECT LIKE THIS A MILLION TIMES BEFORE.
IT TAKES TWICE AS LONG TO DO WORK YOU'RE NOT USED TO.
AND WHEN YOU'VE BEEN WORKING ALL DAY IN HEAT LIKE THIS...
...

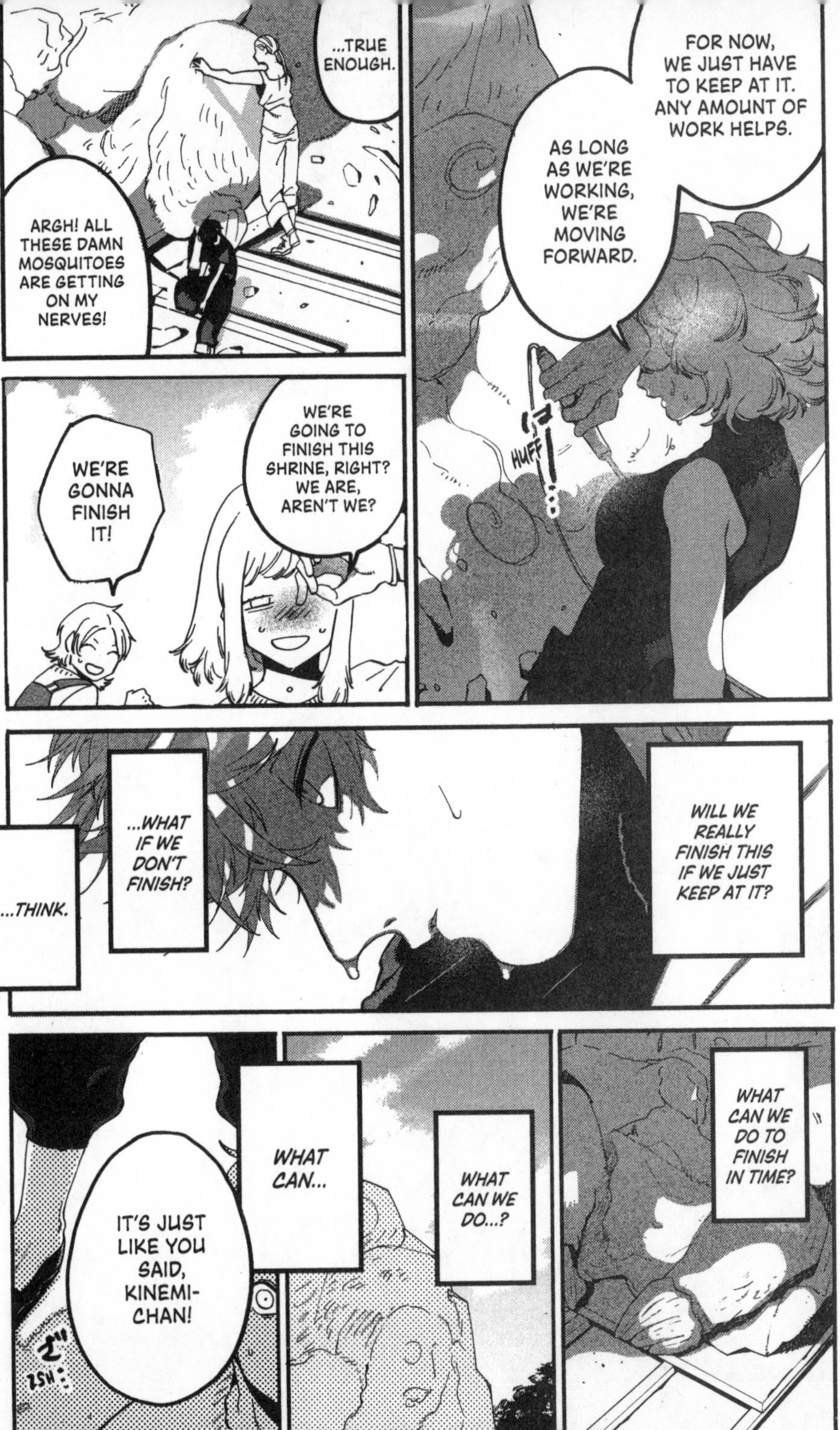
FOR NOW, WE JUST HAVE TO KEEP AT IT. ANY AMOUNT OF WORK HELPS.
AS LONG AS WE'RE WORKING, WE'RE MOVING FORWARD.
HUFF
...TRUE ENOUGH.
ARGH! ALL THESE DAMN MOSQUITOES ARE GETTING ON MY NERVES!
WE'RE GOING TO FINISH THIS SHRINE, RIGHT? WE ARE, AREN'T WE?
WE'RE GONNA FINISH IT!
WILL WE REALLY FINISH THIS IF WE JUST KEEP AT IT?
...WHAT IF WE DON'T FINISH?
...THINK.
WHAT CAN WE DO TO FINISH IN TIME?
WHAT CAN WE DO...?
WHAT CAN...
IT'S JUST LIKE YOU SAID, KINEMI-CHAN!
ZSH...

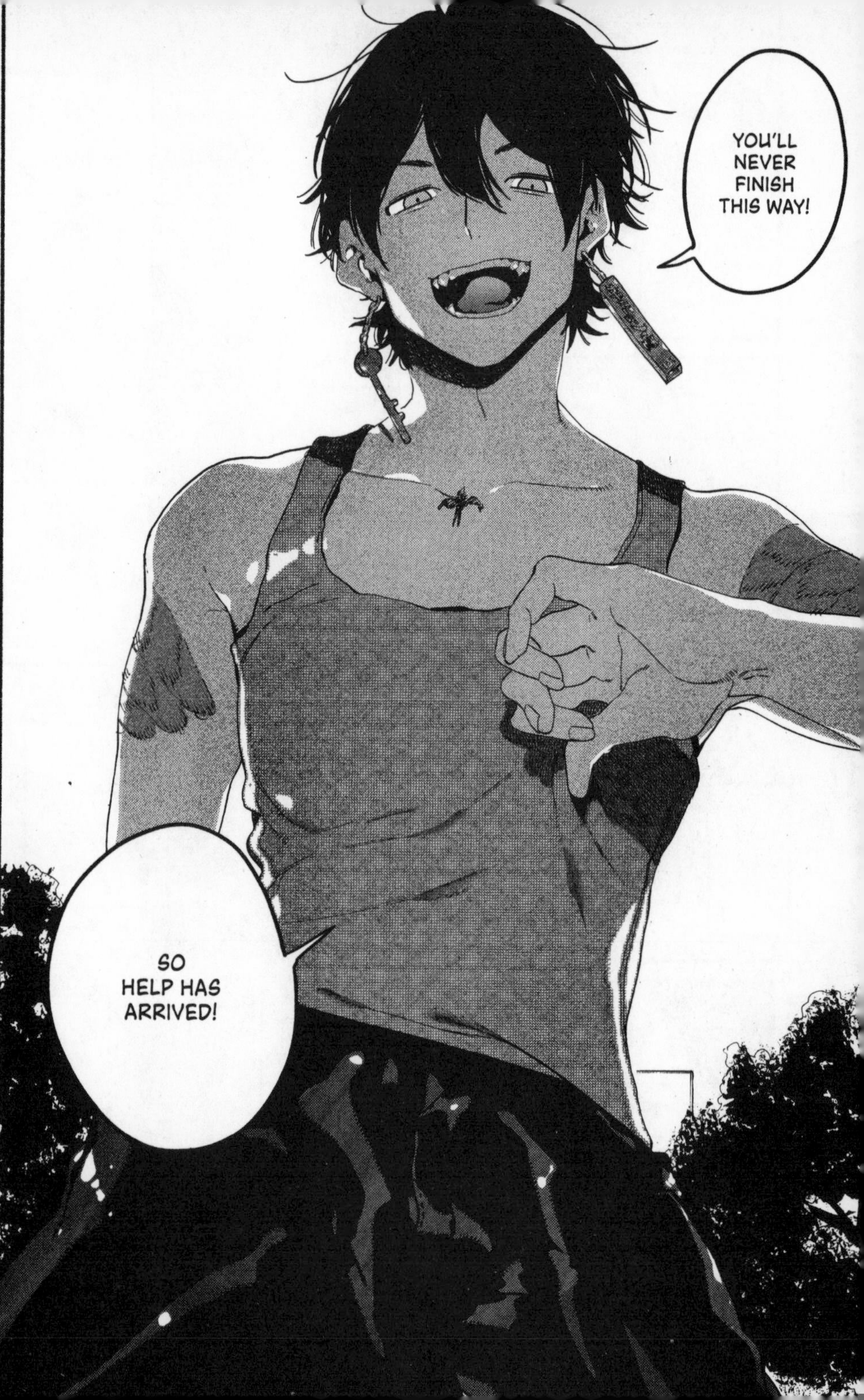
YOU'LL NEVER FINISH THIS WAY!
SO HELP HAS ARRIVED!

STROKE 33 END

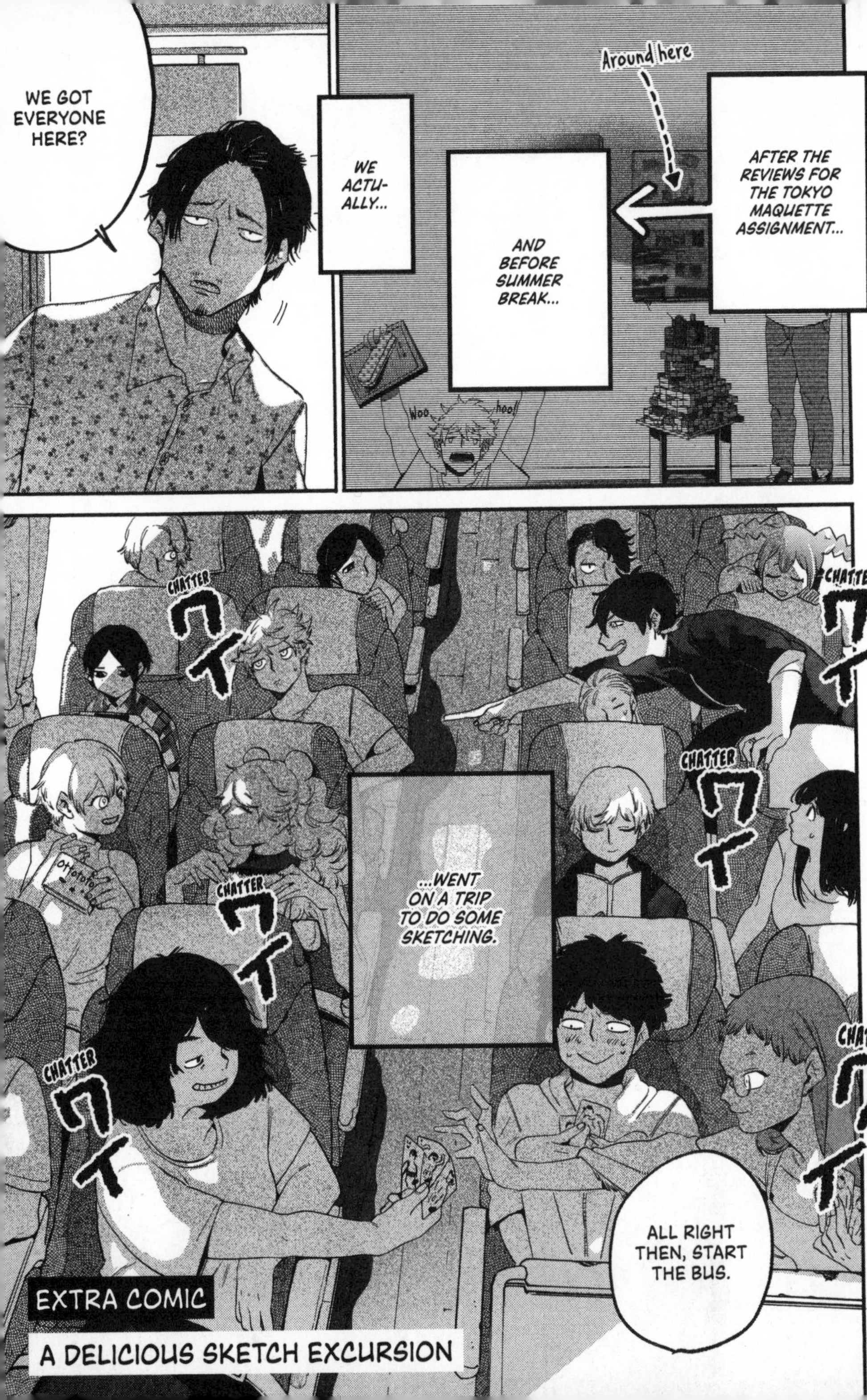
Around here
AFTER THE REVIEWS FOR THE TOKYO MAQUETTE ASSIGNMENT...
AND BEFORE SUMMER BREAK...
WE ACTU-ALLY...
Woo hoo!
WE GOT EVERYONE HERE?
CHATTER ワイ
CHATTER ワイ
CHATTER ワイ
...WENT ON A TRIP TO DO SOME SKETCHING.
CHATTER ワイ
CHATTER ワイ
ALL RIGHT THEN, START THE BUS.
EXTRA COMIC
A DELICIOUS SKETCH EXCURSION

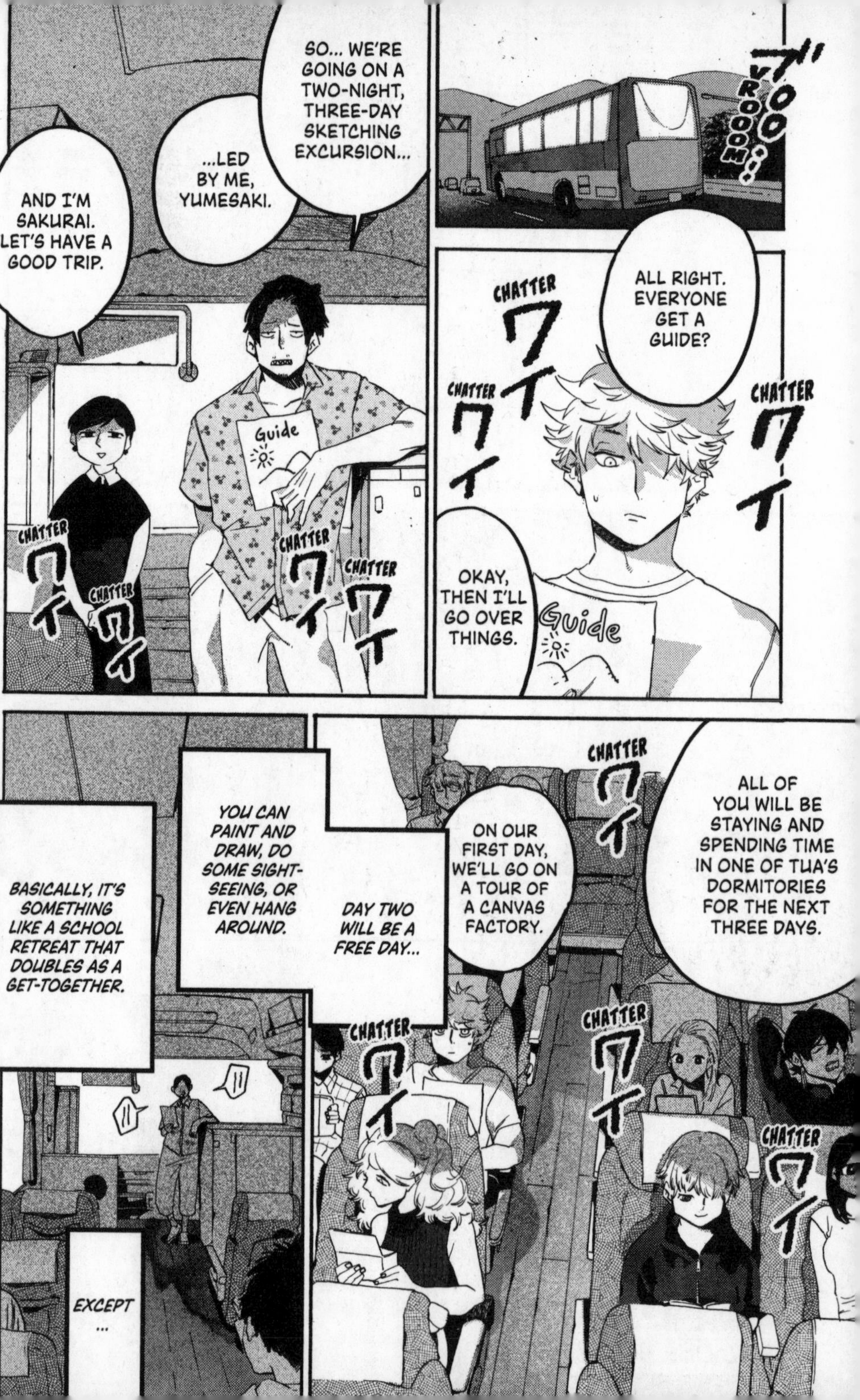
ブロロ VROOOM!
ALL RIGHT. EVERYONE GET A GUIDE?
CHATTER ワイ
CHATTER ワイ
CHATTER ワイ
OKAY, THEN I'LL GO OVER THINGS.
Guide
SO... WE'RE GOING ON A TWO-NIGHT, THREE-DAY SKETCHING EXCURSION...
...LED BY ME, YUMESAKI.
AND I'M SAKURAI. LET'S HAVE A GOOD TRIP.
Guide
CHATTER ワイ
CHATTER ワイ
CHATTER ワイ
CHATTER ワイ
ALL OF YOU WILL BE STAYING AND SPENDING TIME IN ONE OF TUA'S DORMITORIES FOR THE NEXT THREE DAYS.
CHATTER ワイ
ON OUR FIRST DAY, WE'LL GO ON A TOUR OF A CANVAS FACTORY.
DAY TWO WILL BE A FREE DAY...
YOU CAN PAINT AND DRAW, DO SOME SIGHT-SEEING, OR EVEN HANG AROUND.
CHATTER ワイ
CHATTER ワイ
CHATTER ワイ
BASICALLY, IT'S SOMETHING LIKE A SCHOOL RETREAT THAT DOUBLES AS A GET-TOGETHER.
EXCEPT ...

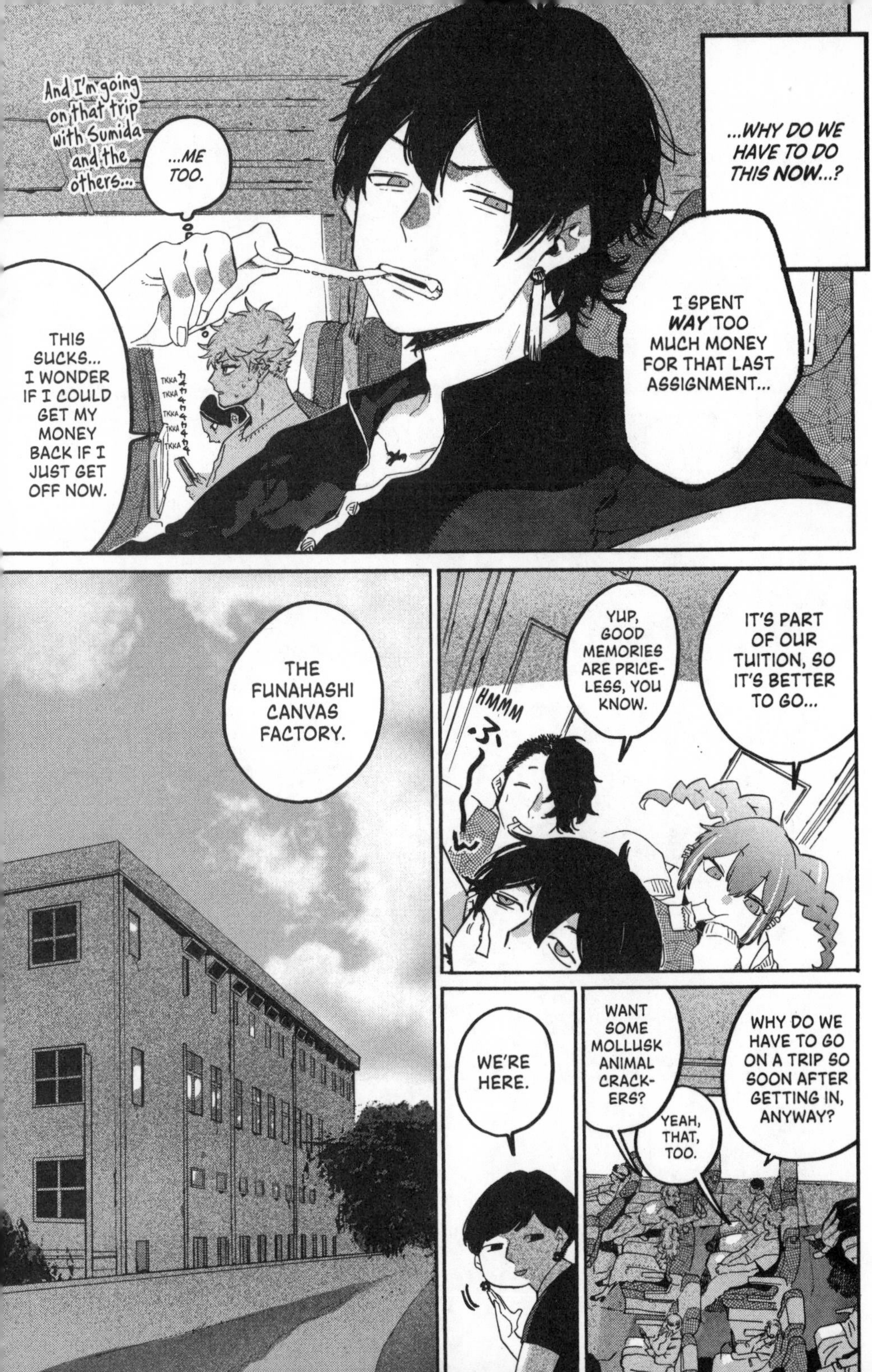

...WHY DO WE HAVE TO DO THIS **NOW**...?
I SPENT ***WAY*** TOO MUCH MONEY FOR THAT LAST ASSIGNMENT...
...ME TOO.
And I'm going on that trip with Sumida and the others...
THIS SUCKS... I WONDER IF I COULD GET MY MONEY BACK IF I JUST GET OFF NOW.
TKKA TKKA TKKA TKKA TKKA
IT'S PART OF OUR TUITION, SO IT'S BETTER TO GO...
YUP, GOOD MEMORIES ARE PRICELESS, YOU KNOW.
HMMM
WHY DO WE HAVE TO GO ON A TRIP SO SOON AFTER GETTING IN, ANYWAY?
YEAH, THAT, TOO.
WANT SOME MOLLUSK ANIMAL CRACKERS?
WE'RE HERE.
THE FUNAHASHI CANVAS FACTORY.

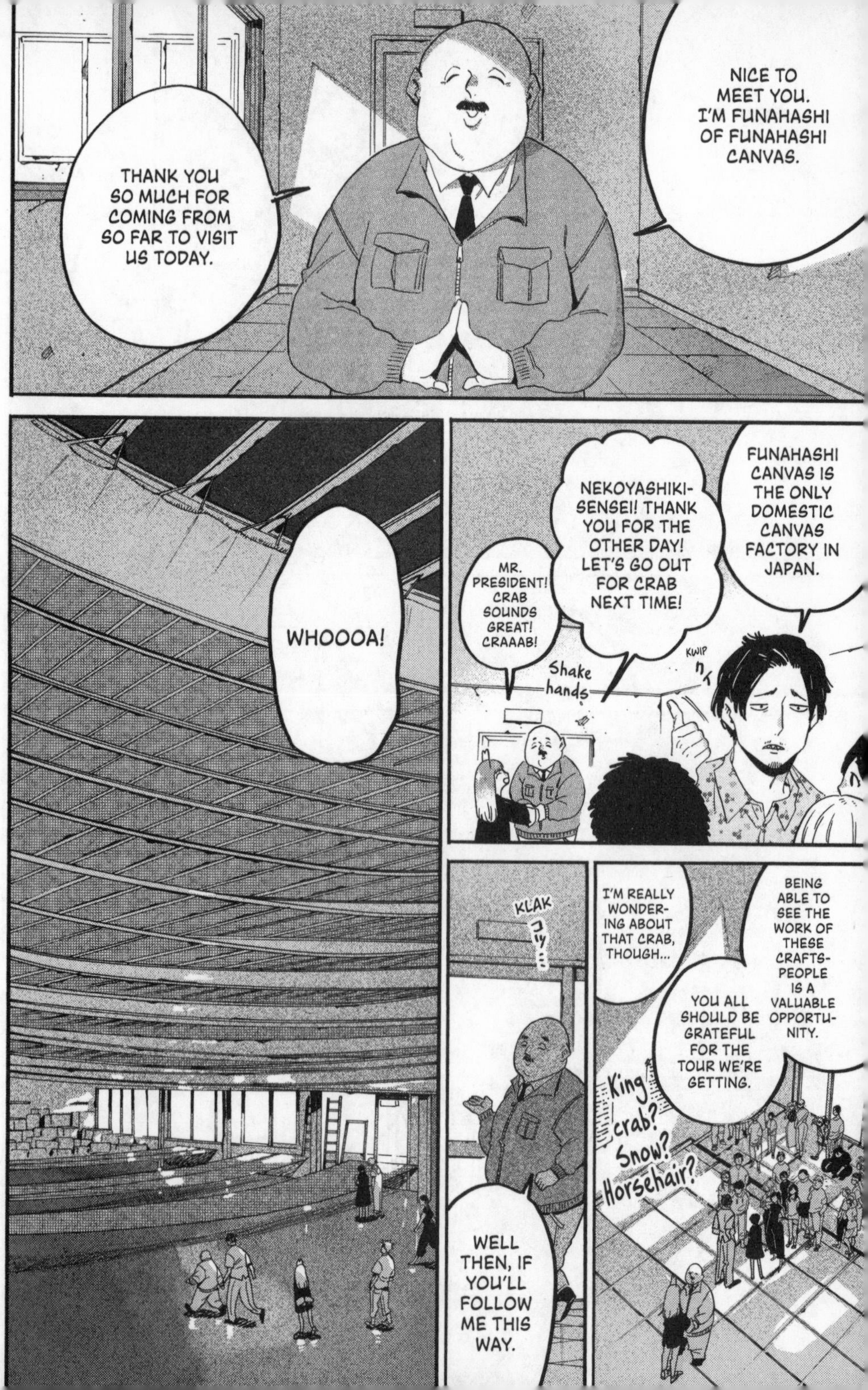

NICE TO MEET YOU. I'M FUNAHASHI OF FUNAHASHI CANVAS.
THANK YOU SO MUCH FOR COMING FROM SO FAR TO VISIT US TODAY.
FUNAHASHI CANVAS IS THE ONLY DOMESTIC CANVAS FACTORY IN JAPAN.
KWIP
NEKOYASHIKI-SENSEI! THANK YOU FOR THE OTHER DAY! LET'S GO OUT FOR CRAB NEXT TIME!
MR. PRESIDENT! CRAB SOUNDS GREAT! CRAAAB!
Shake hands
BEING ABLE TO SEE THE WORK OF THESE CRAFTS-PEOPLE IS A VALUABLE OPPORTU-NITY.
YOU ALL SHOULD BE GRATEFUL FOR THE TOUR WE'RE GETTING.
I'M REALLY WONDER-ING ABOUT THAT CRAB, THOUGH...
King crab? Snow? Horsehair?
KLAK
WELL THEN, IF YOU'LL FOLLOW ME THIS WAY.
WHOOOA!

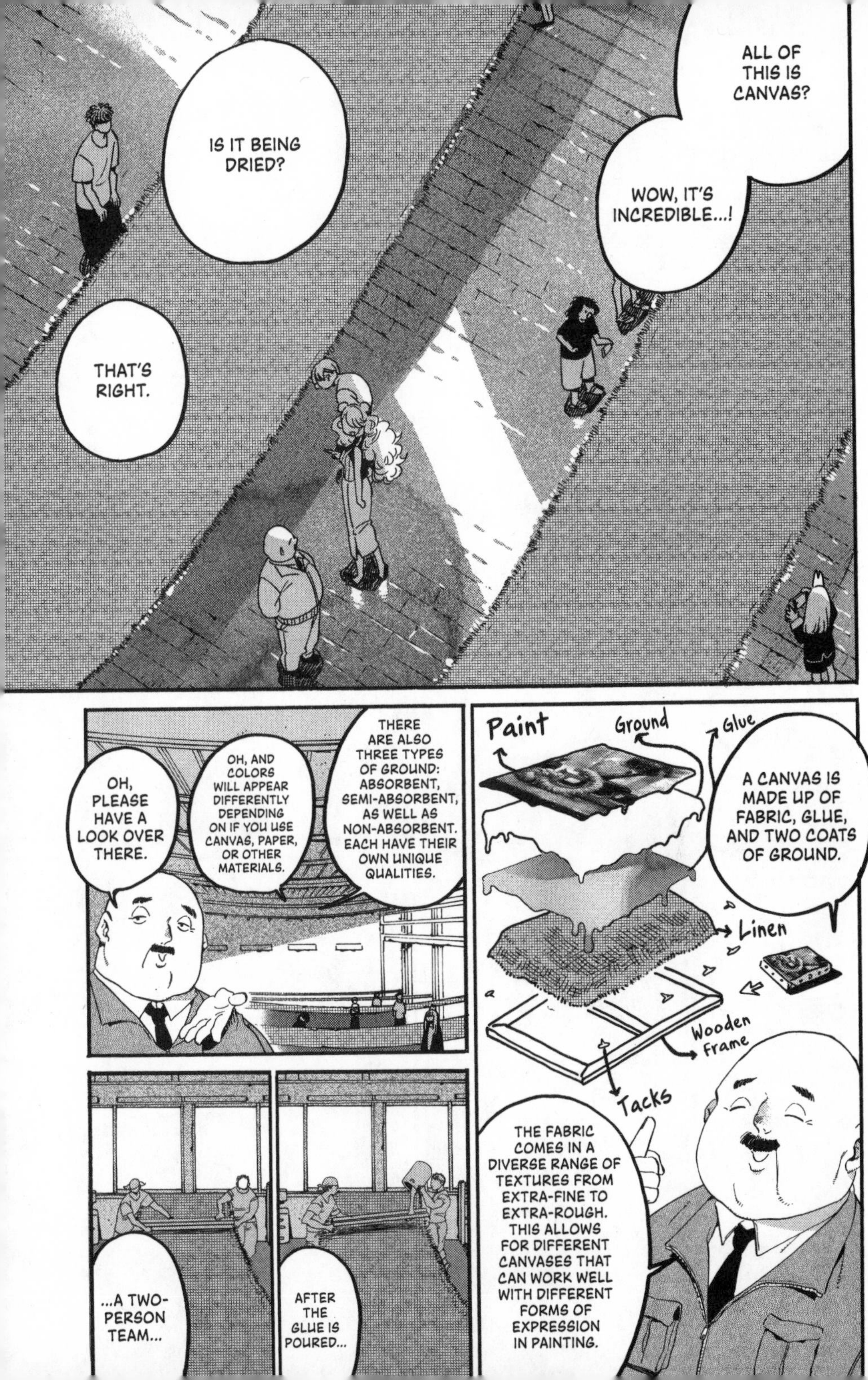
ALL OF THIS IS CANVAS?
WOW, IT'S INCREDIBLE...!
IS IT BEING DRIED?
THAT'S RIGHT.
Paint
Ground
Glue
A CANVAS IS MADE UP OF FABRIC, GLUE, AND TWO COATS OF GROUND.
Linen
Wooden Frame
Tacks
THE FABRIC COMES IN A DIVERSE RANGE OF TEXTURES FROM EXTRA-FINE TO EXTRA-ROUGH. THIS ALLOWS FOR DIFFERENT CANVASES THAT CAN WORK WELL WITH DIFFERENT FORMS OF EXPRESSION IN PAINTING.
THERE ARE ALSO THREE TYPES OF GROUND: ABSORBENT, SEMI-ABSORBENT, AS WELL AS NON-ABSORBENT. EACH HAVE THEIR OWN UNIQUE QUALITIES.
OH, AND COLORS WILL APPEAR DIFFERENTLY DEPENDING ON IF YOU USE CANVAS, PAPER, OR OTHER MATERIALS.
OH, PLEASE HAVE A LOOK OVER THERE.
AFTER THE GLUE IS POURED...
...A TWO-PERSON TEAM...

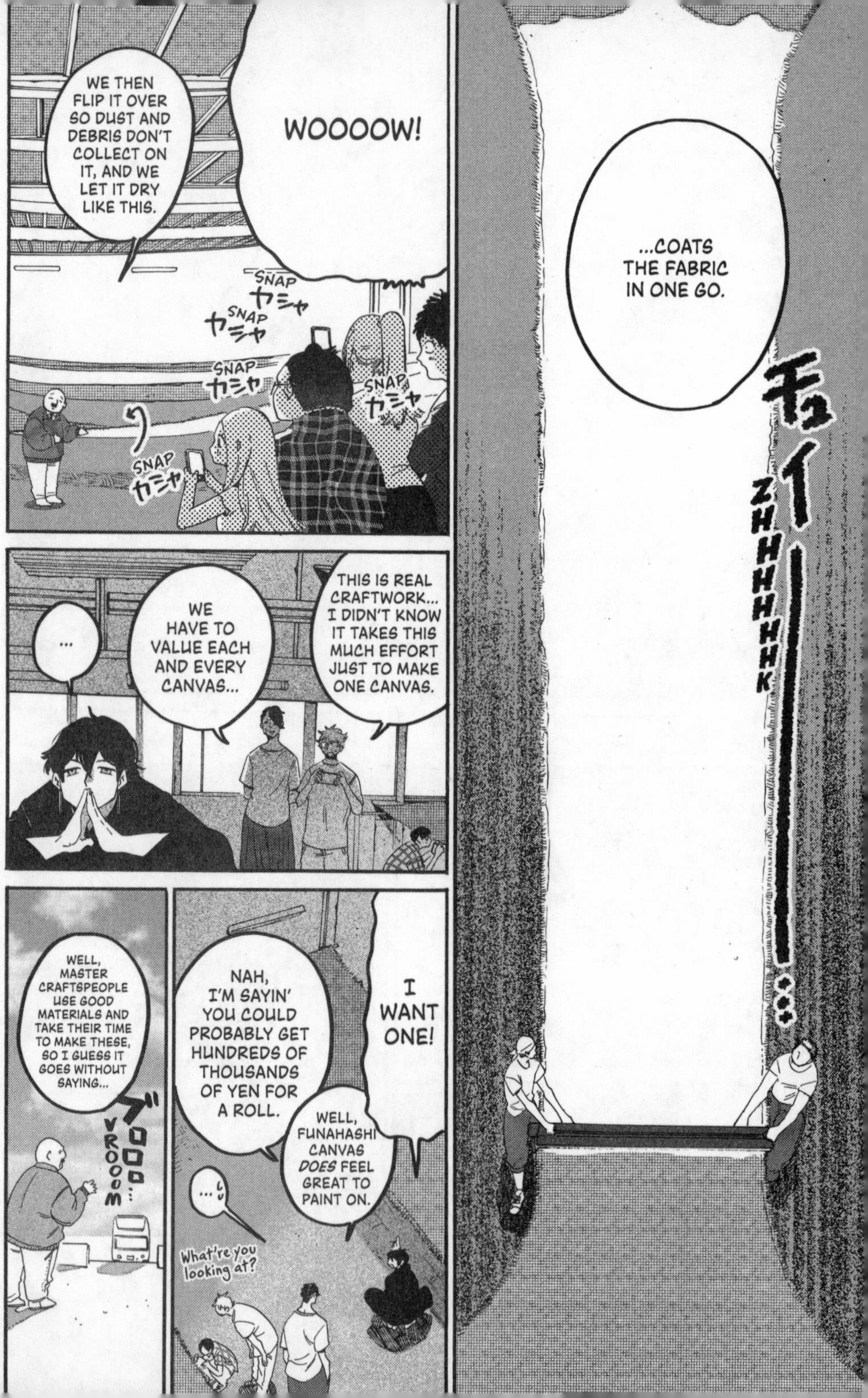
...COATS THE FABRIC IN ONE GO.
チュイー
ZHHHHHHK
WOOOOW!
WE THEN FLIP IT OVER SO DUST AND DEBRIS DON'T COLLECT ON IT, AND WE LET IT DRY LIKE THIS.
SNAP カシャ
SNAP カシャ
SNAP カシャ
SNAP カシャ
SNAP カシャ
THIS IS REAL CRAFTWORK... I DIDN'T KNOW IT TAKES THIS MUCH EFFORT JUST TO MAKE ONE CANVAS.
WE HAVE TO VALUE EACH AND EVERY CANVAS...
...
I WANT ONE!
NAH, I'M SAYIN' YOU COULD PROBABLY GET HUNDREDS OF THOUSANDS OF YEN FOR A ROLL.
WELL, FUNAHASHI CANVAS *DOES* FEEL GREAT TO PAINT ON.
...
What're you looking at?
WELL, MASTER CRAFTSPEOPLE USE GOOD MATERIALS AND TAKE THEIR TIME TO MAKE THESE, SO I GUESS IT GOES WITHOUT SAYING...
ブロロロ
VROOOOM...

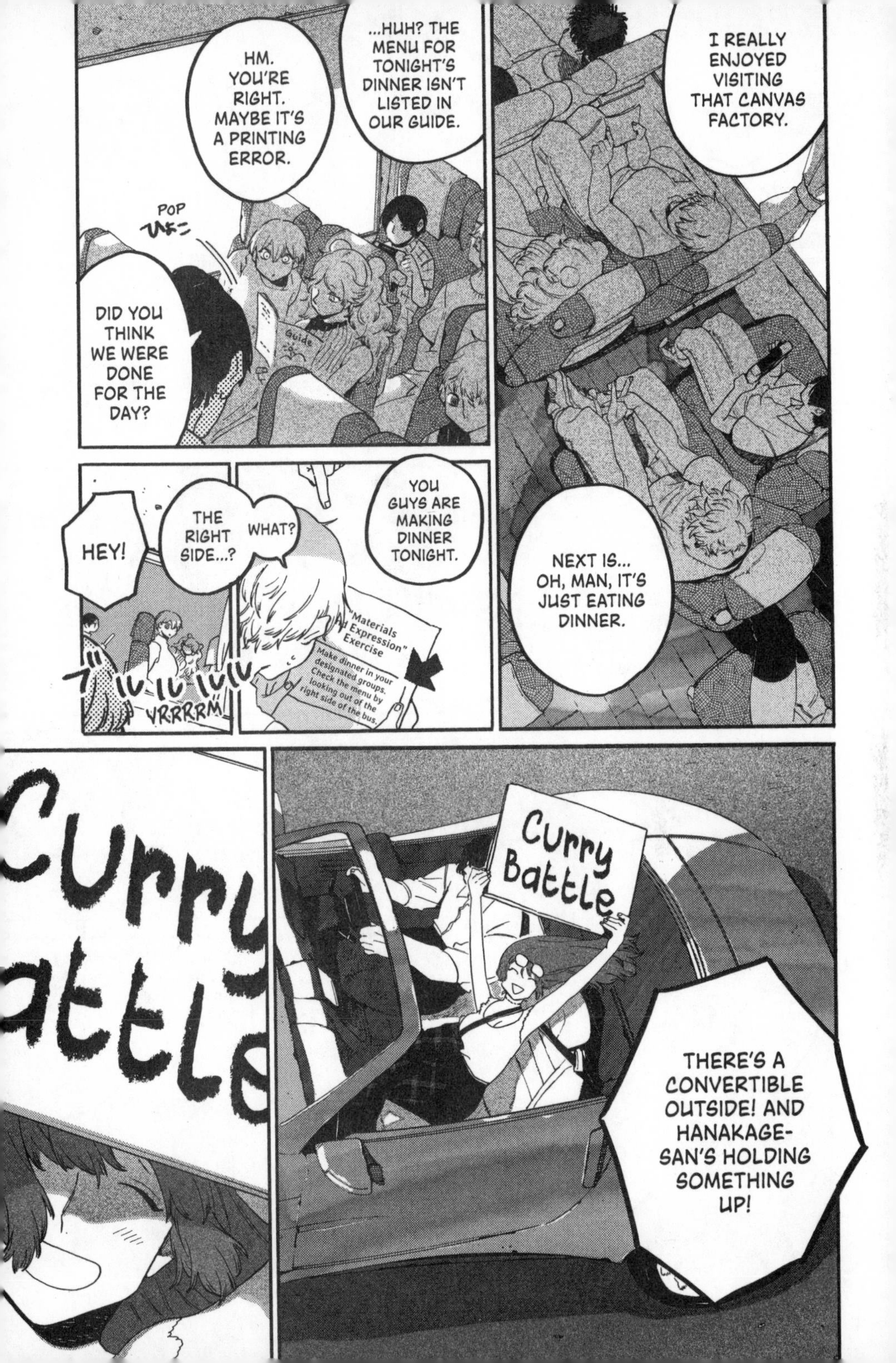

I REALLY ENJOYED VISITING THAT CANVAS FACTORY.
NEXT IS... OH, MAN, IT'S JUST EATING DINNER.
...HUH? THE MENU FOR TONIGHT'S DINNER ISN'T LISTED IN OUR GUIDE.
HM. YOU'RE RIGHT. MAYBE IT'S A PRINTING ERROR.
POP
Guide
DID YOU THINK WE WERE DONE FOR THE DAY?
YOU GUYS ARE MAKING DINNER TONIGHT.
WHAT?
"Materials Expression" Exercise
Make dinner in your designated groups. Check the menu by looking out of the right side of the bus.
THE RIGHT SIDE...?
HEY!
VRRRRM
Curry Battle
THERE'S A CONVERTIBLE OUTSIDE! AND HANAKAGE-SAN'S HOLDING SOMETHING UP!
Curry Battle

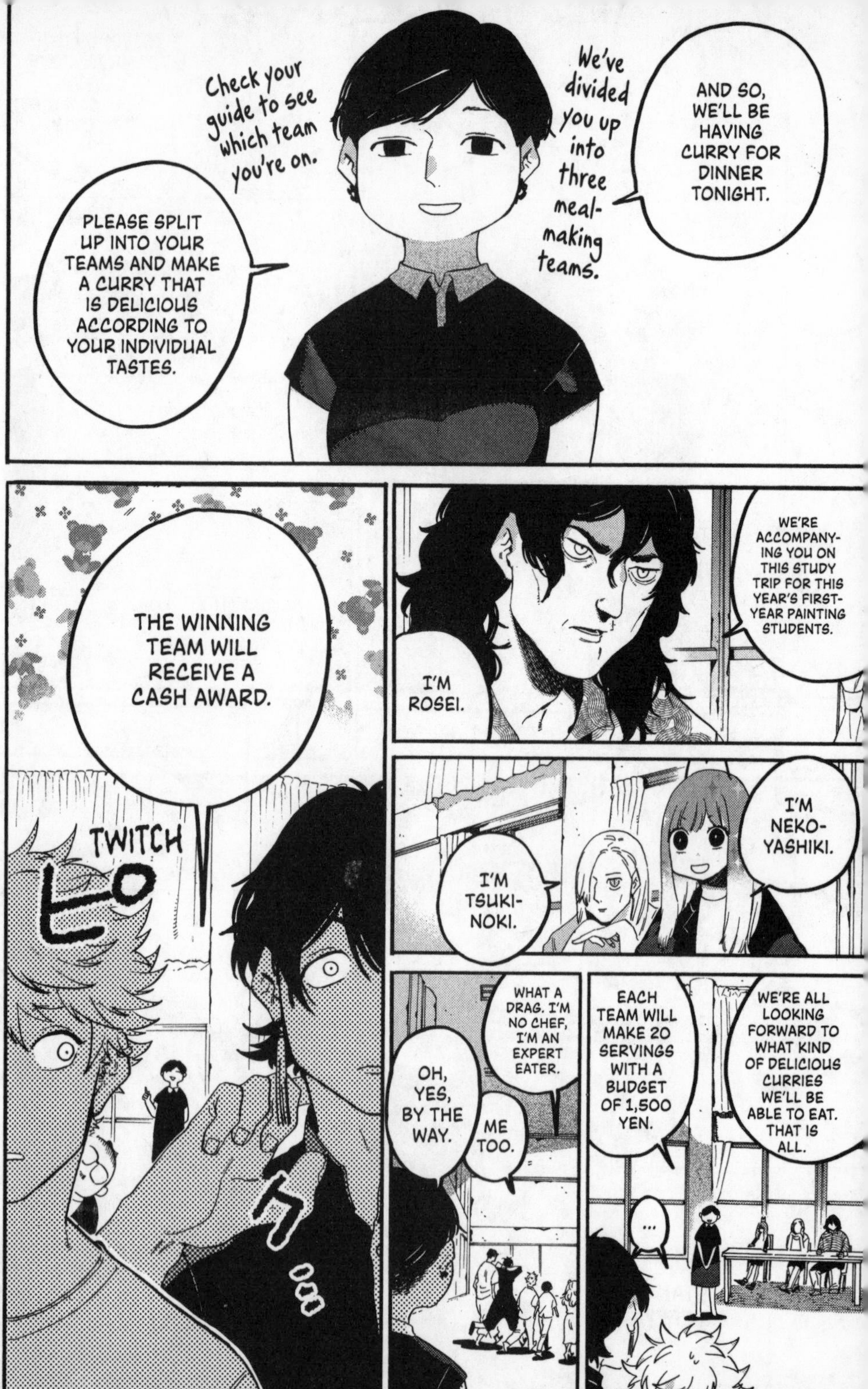
AND SO, WE'LL BE HAVING CURRY FOR DINNER TONIGHT.
We've divided you up into three meal-making teams.
Check your guide to see which team you're on.
PLEASE SPLIT UP INTO YOUR TEAMS AND MAKE A CURRY THAT IS DELICIOUS ACCORDING TO YOUR INDIVIDUAL TASTES.
WE'RE ACCOMPANYING YOU ON THIS STUDY TRIP FOR THIS YEAR'S FIRST-YEAR PAINTING STUDENTS.
I'M ROSEI.
I'M NEKO-YASHIKI.
I'M TSUKI-NOKI.
WE'RE ALL LOOKING FORWARD TO WHAT KIND OF DELICIOUS CURRIES WE'LL BE ABLE TO EAT. THAT IS ALL.
...
EACH TEAM WILL MAKE 20 SERVINGS WITH A BUDGET OF 1,500 YEN.
WHAT A DRAG. I'M NO CHEF, I'M AN EXPERT EATER.
ME TOO.
OH, YES, BY THE WAY.
THE WINNING TEAM WILL RECEIVE A CASH AWARD.
TWITCH

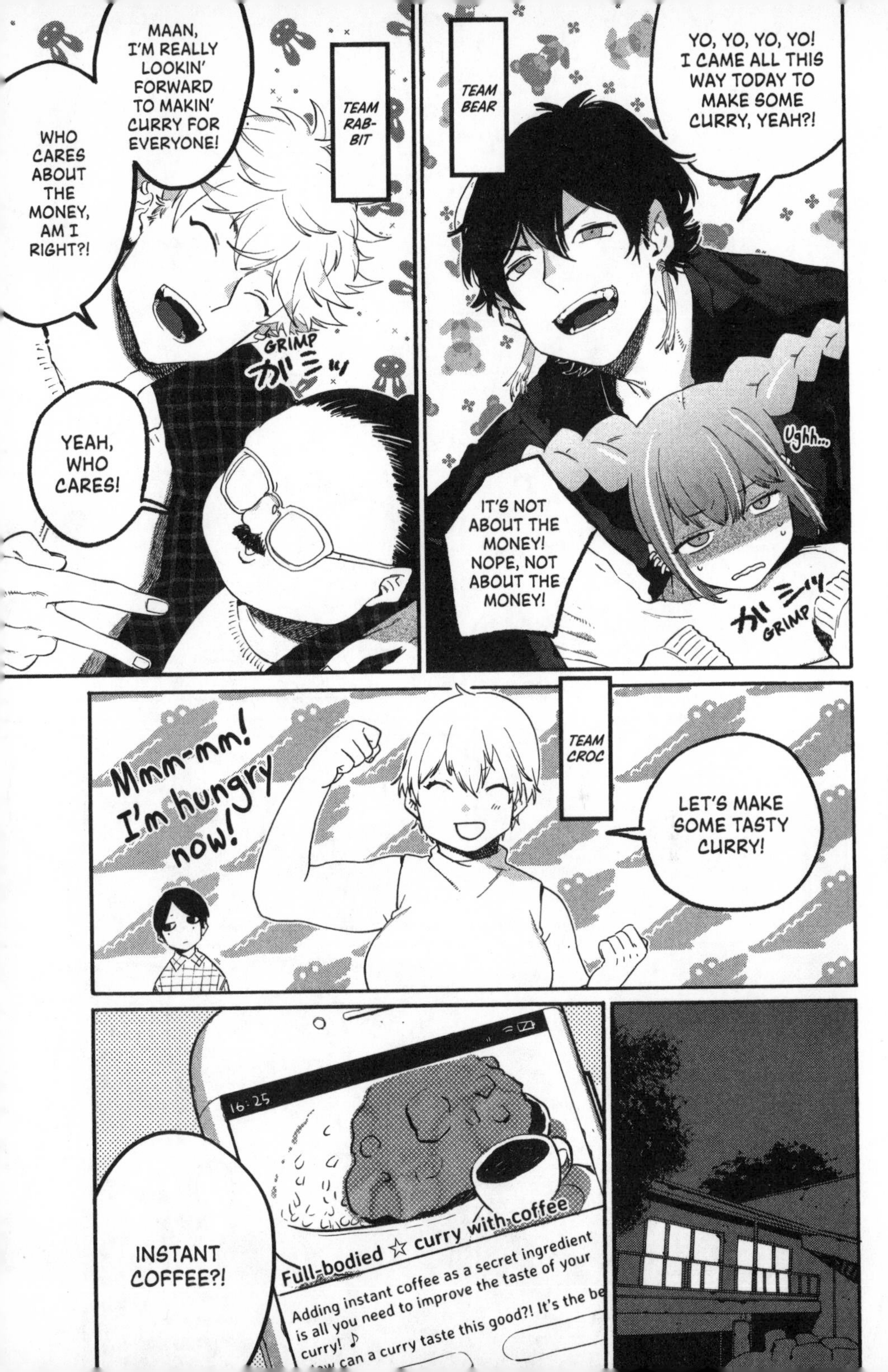
TEAM BEAR
YO, YO, YO, YO! I CAME ALL THIS WAY TODAY TO MAKE SOME CURRY, YEAH?!
Ughh...
IT'S NOT ABOUT THE MONEY! NOPE, NOT ABOUT THE MONEY!
GRIMP
TEAM RABBIT
MAAN, I'M REALLY LOOKIN' FORWARD TO MAKIN' CURRY FOR EVERYONE!
WHO CARES ABOUT THE MONEY, AM I RIGHT?!
GRIMP
YEAH, WHO CARES!
TEAM CROC
LET'S MAKE SOME TASTY CURRY!
Mmm-mm! I'm hungry now!
16:25
Full-bodied ☆ curry with coffee
Adding instant coffee as a secret ingredient is all you need to improve the taste of your curry!
curry! ♪
INSTANT COFFEE?!

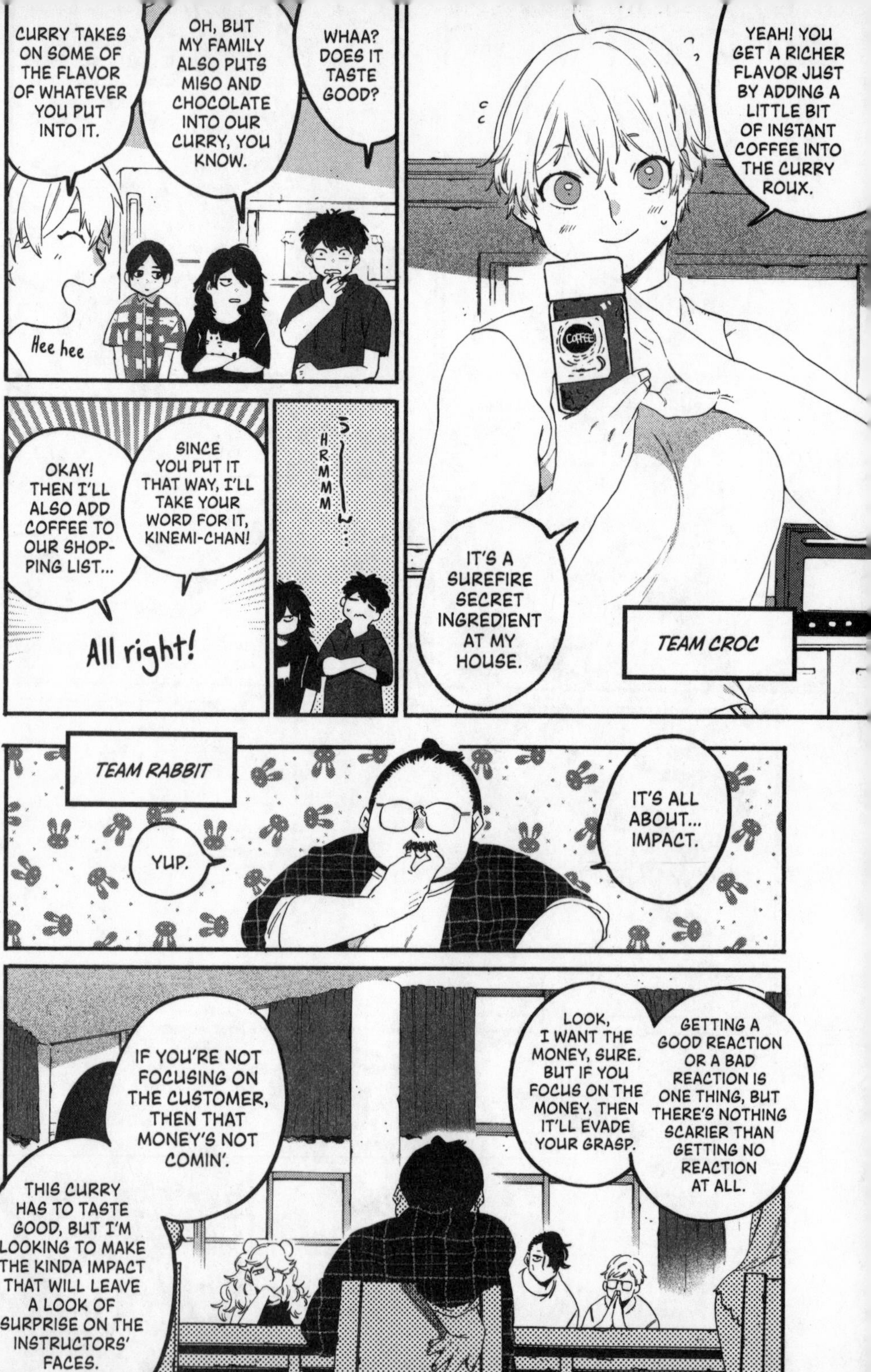
YEAH! YOU GET A RICHER FLAVOR JUST BY ADDING A LITTLE BIT OF INSTANT COFFEE INTO THE CURRY ROUX.
COFFEE
IT'S A SUREFIRE SECRET INGREDIENT AT MY HOUSE.
TEAM CROC
WHAA? DOES IT TASTE GOOD?
OH, BUT MY FAMILY ALSO PUTS MISO AND CHOCOLATE INTO OUR CURRY, YOU KNOW.
CURRY TAKES ON SOME OF THE FLAVOR OF WHATEVER YOU PUT INTO IT.
Hee hee
HRMMM...
SINCE YOU PUT IT THAT WAY, I'LL TAKE YOUR WORD FOR IT, KINEMI-CHAN!
OKAY! THEN I'LL ALSO ADD COFFEE TO OUR SHOP-PING LIST...
All right!
TEAM RABBIT
IT'S ALL ABOUT... IMPACT.
YUP.
GETTING A GOOD REACTION OR A BAD REACTION IS ONE THING, BUT THERE'S NOTHING SCARIER THAN GETTING NO REACTION AT ALL.
LOOK, I WANT THE MONEY, SURE. BUT IF YOU FOCUS ON THE MONEY, THEN IT'LL EVADE YOUR GRASP.
IF YOU'RE NOT FOCUSING ON THE CUSTOMER, THEN THAT MONEY'S NOT COMIN'.
THIS CURRY HAS TO TASTE GOOD, BUT I'M LOOKING TO MAKE THE KINDA IMPACT THAT WILL LEAVE A LOOK OF SURPRISE ON THE INSTRUCTORS' FACES.

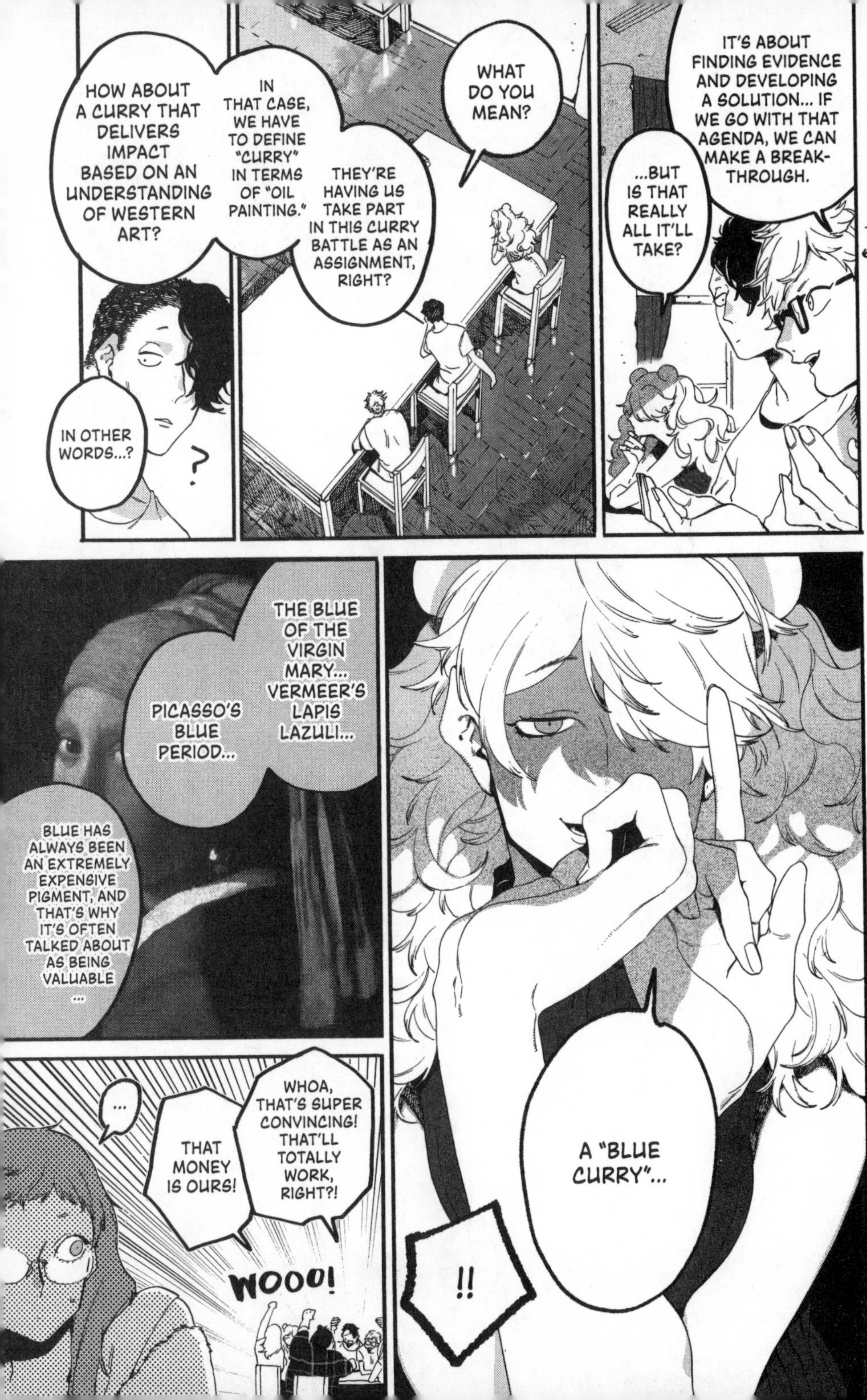
IT'S ABOUT FINDING EVIDENCE AND DEVELOPING A SOLUTION... IF WE GO WITH THAT AGENDA, WE CAN MAKE A BREAK-THROUGH.
...BUT IS THAT REALLY ALL IT'LL TAKE?
Yatora
WHAT DO YOU MEAN?
THEY'RE HAVING US TAKE PART IN THIS CURRY BATTLE AS AN ASSIGNMENT, RIGHT?
IN THAT CASE, WE HAVE TO DEFINE "CURRY" IN TERMS OF "OIL PAINTING."
HOW ABOUT A CURRY THAT DELIVERS IMPACT BASED ON AN UNDERSTANDING OF WESTERN ART?
IN OTHER WORDS...?
A "BLUE CURRY"...
!!
THE BLUE OF THE VIRGIN MARY... VERMEER'S LAPIS LAZULI...
PICASSO'S BLUE PERIOD...
BLUE HAS ALWAYS BEEN AN EXTREMELY EXPENSIVE PIGMENT, AND THAT'S WHY IT'S OFTEN TALKED ABOUT AS BEING VALUABLE...
WHOA, THAT'S SUPER CONVINCING! THAT'LL TOTALLY WORK, RIGHT?!
THAT MONEY IS OURS!
WOOO!
...

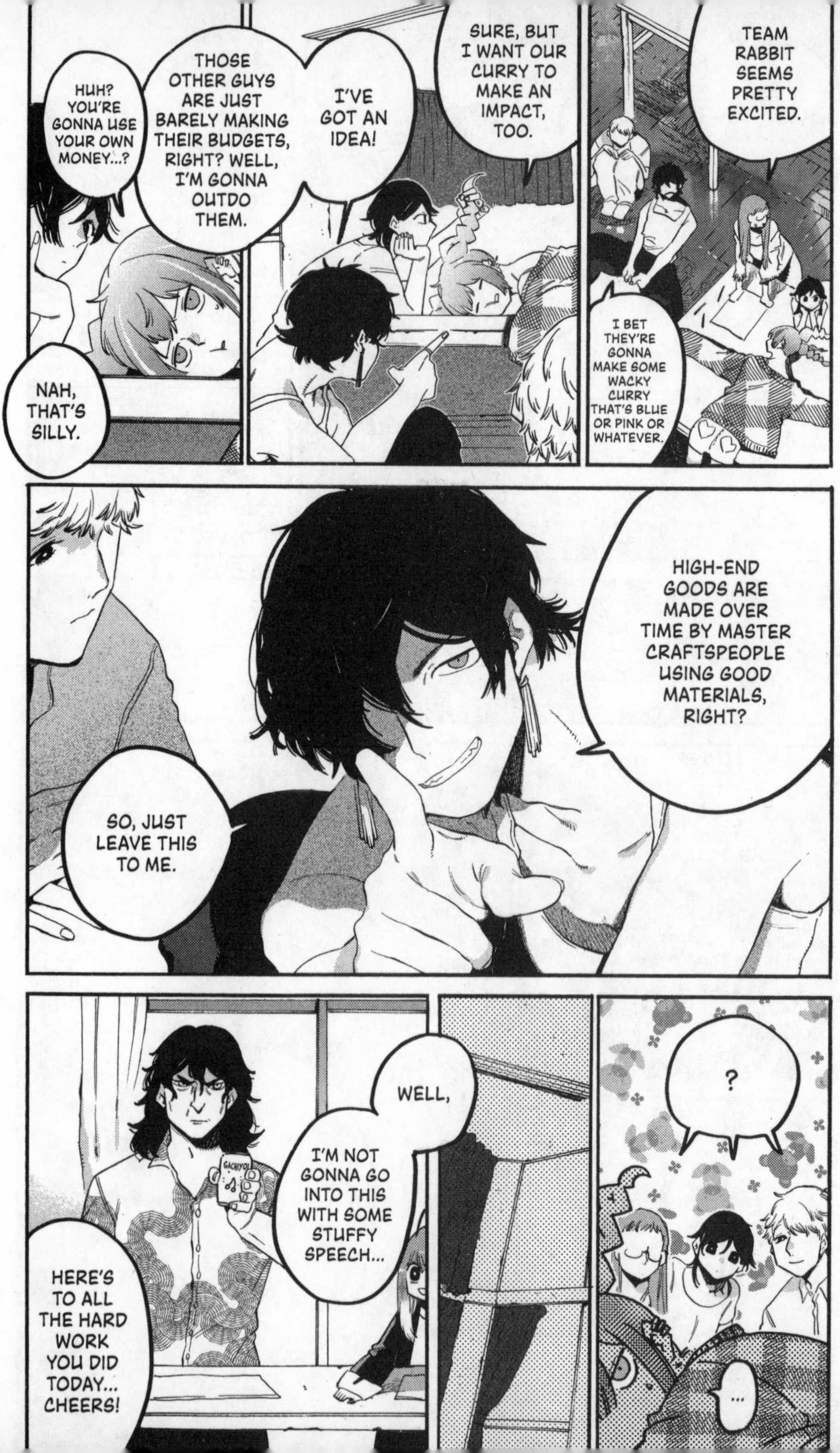
TEAM RABBIT SEEMS PRETTY EXCITED.
I BET THEY'RE GONNA MAKE SOME WACKY CURRY THAT'S BLUE OR PINK OR WHATEVER.
SURE, BUT I WANT OUR CURRY TO MAKE AN IMPACT, TOO.
I'VE GOT AN IDEA!
THOSE OTHER GUYS ARE JUST BARELY MAKING THEIR BUDGETS, RIGHT? WELL, I'M GONNA OUTDO THEM.
HUH? YOU'RE GONNA USE YOUR OWN MONEY...?
NAH, THAT'S SILLY.
HIGH-END GOODS ARE MADE OVER TIME BY MASTER CRAFTSPEOPLE USING GOOD MATERIALS, RIGHT?
SO, JUST LEAVE THIS TO ME.
?
...
WELL,
I'M NOT GONNA GO INTO THIS WITH SOME STUFFY SPEECH...
GACHIYO!
HERE'S TO ALL THE HARD WORK YOU DID TODAY... CHEERS!

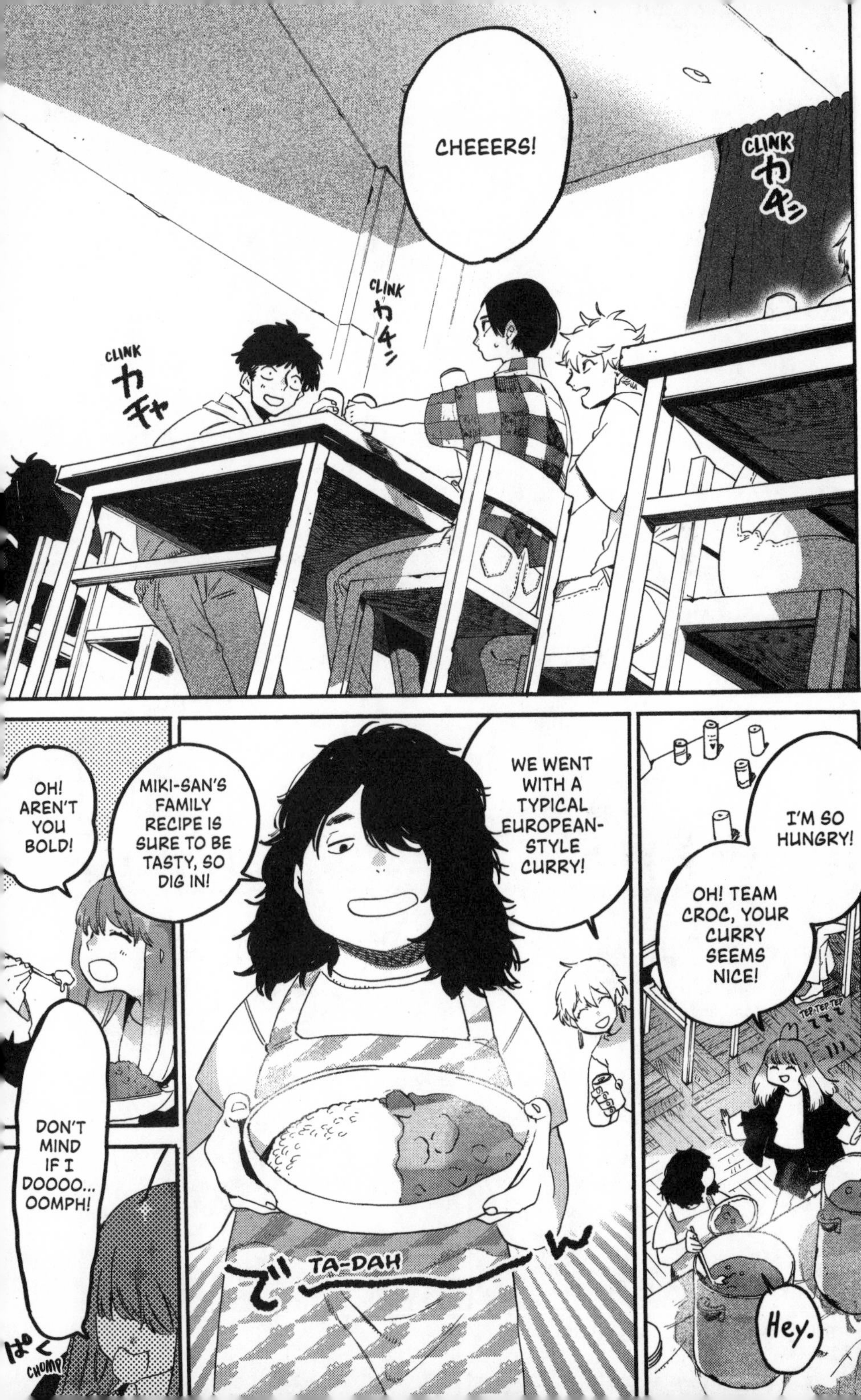
CLINK
カキン
CHEEERS!
CLINK
カキン
CLINK
カチャ
I'M SO HUNGRY!
OH! TEAM CROC, YOUR CURRY SEEMS NICE!
TEP TEP TEP
Hey.
WE WENT WITH A TYPICAL EUROPEAN-STYLE CURRY!
MIKI-SAN'S FAMILY RECIPE IS SURE TO BE TASTY, SO DIG IN!
TA-DAH
でーーん
OH! AREN'T YOU BOLD!
DON'T MIND IF I DOOOO... OOMPH!
ぱく
CHOMP

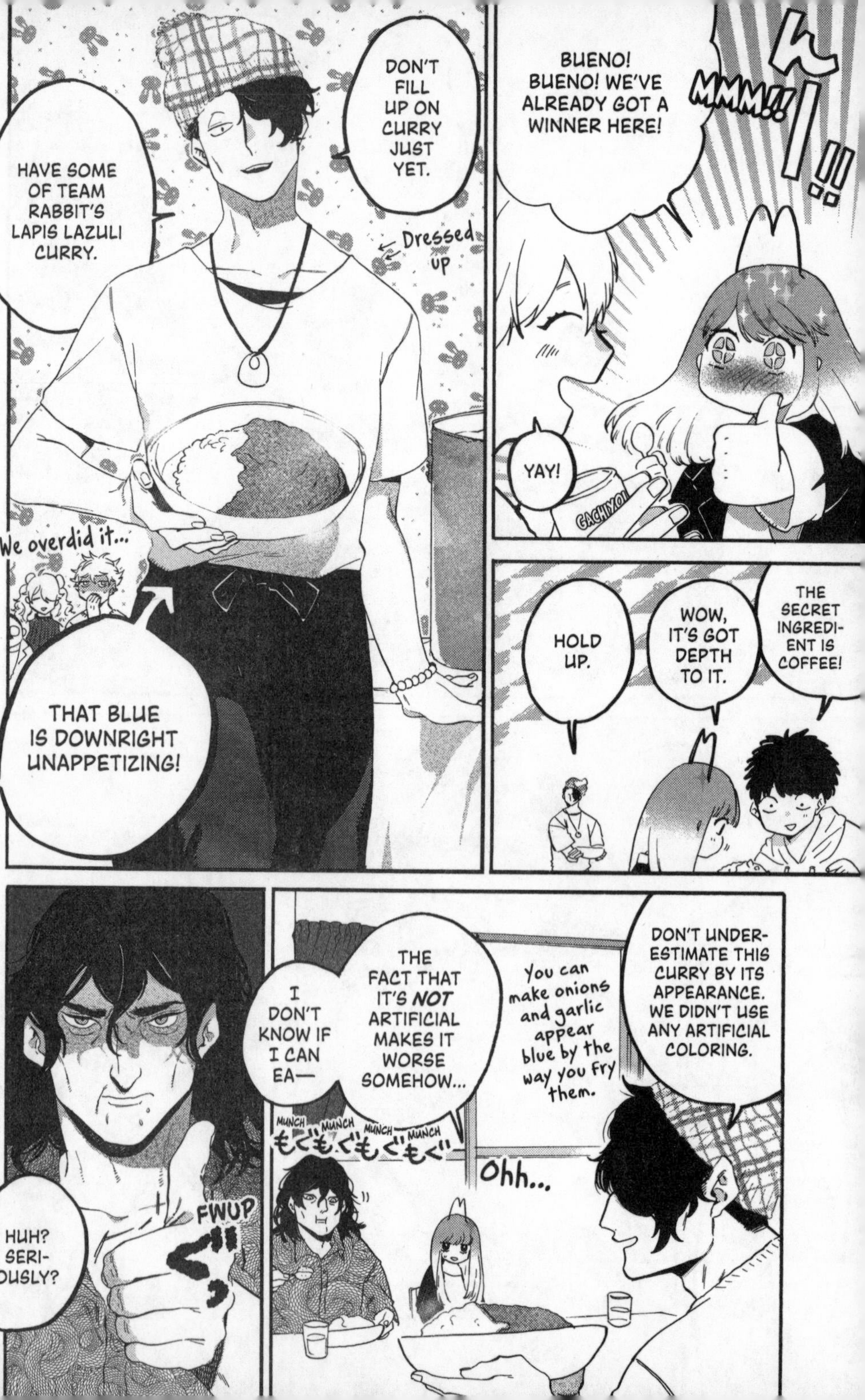
んーー!!!
MMM!!
BUENO! BUENO! WE'VE ALREADY GOT A WINNER HERE!
YAY!
GACHIYOI
THE SECRET INGREDI-ENT IS COFFEE!
WOW, IT'S GOT DEPTH TO IT.
HOLD UP.
DON'T FILL UP ON CURRY JUST YET.
HAVE SOME OF TEAM RABBIT'S LAPIS LAZULI CURRY.
Dressed up
We overdid it...
THAT BLUE IS DOWNRIGHT UNAPPETIZING!
DON'T UNDER-ESTIMATE THIS CURRY BY ITS APPEARANCE. WE DIDN'T USE ANY ARTIFICIAL COLORING.
You can make onions and garlic appear blue by the way you fry them.
THE FACT THAT IT'S ***NOT*** ARTIFICIAL MAKES IT WORSE SOMEHOW...
I DON'T KNOW IF I CAN EA—
MUNCH MUNCH MUNCH MUNCH
もぐもぐもぐもぐ
Ohh...
FWUP
HUH? SERI-OUSLY?

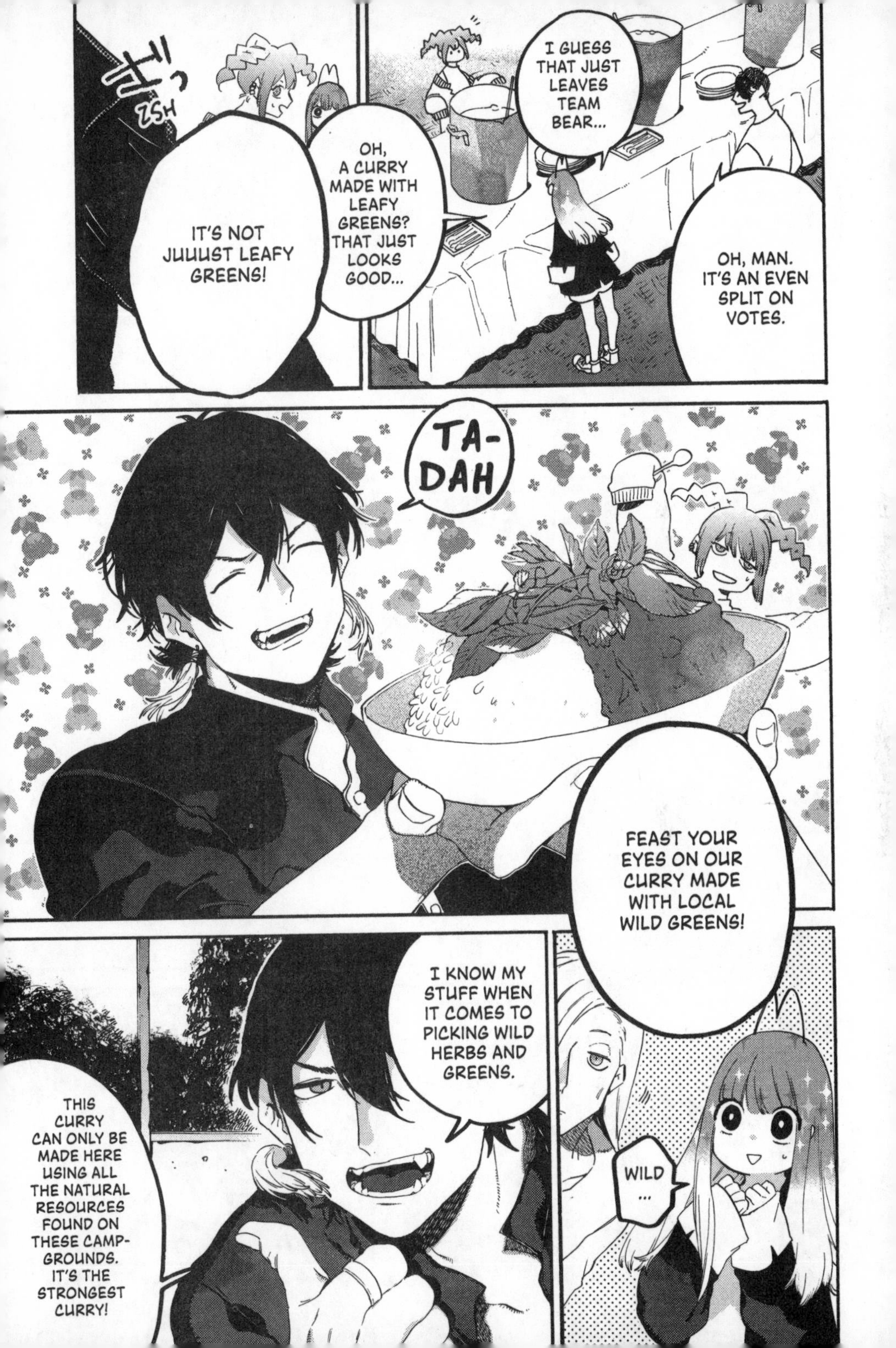
OH, MAN. IT'S AN EVEN SPLIT ON VOTES.
I GUESS THAT JUST LEAVES TEAM BEAR...
OH, A CURRY MADE WITH LEAFY GREENS? THAT JUST LOOKS GOOD...
ZSH
IT'S NOT JUUUST LEAFY GREENS!
TA-DAH
FEAST YOUR EYES ON OUR CURRY MADE WITH LOCAL WILD GREENS!
WILD ...
I KNOW MY STUFF WHEN IT COMES TO PICKING WILD HERBS AND GREENS.
THIS CURRY CAN ONLY BE MADE HERE USING ALL THE NATURAL RESOURCES FOUND ON THESE CAMP-GROUNDS. IT'S THE STRONGEST CURRY!

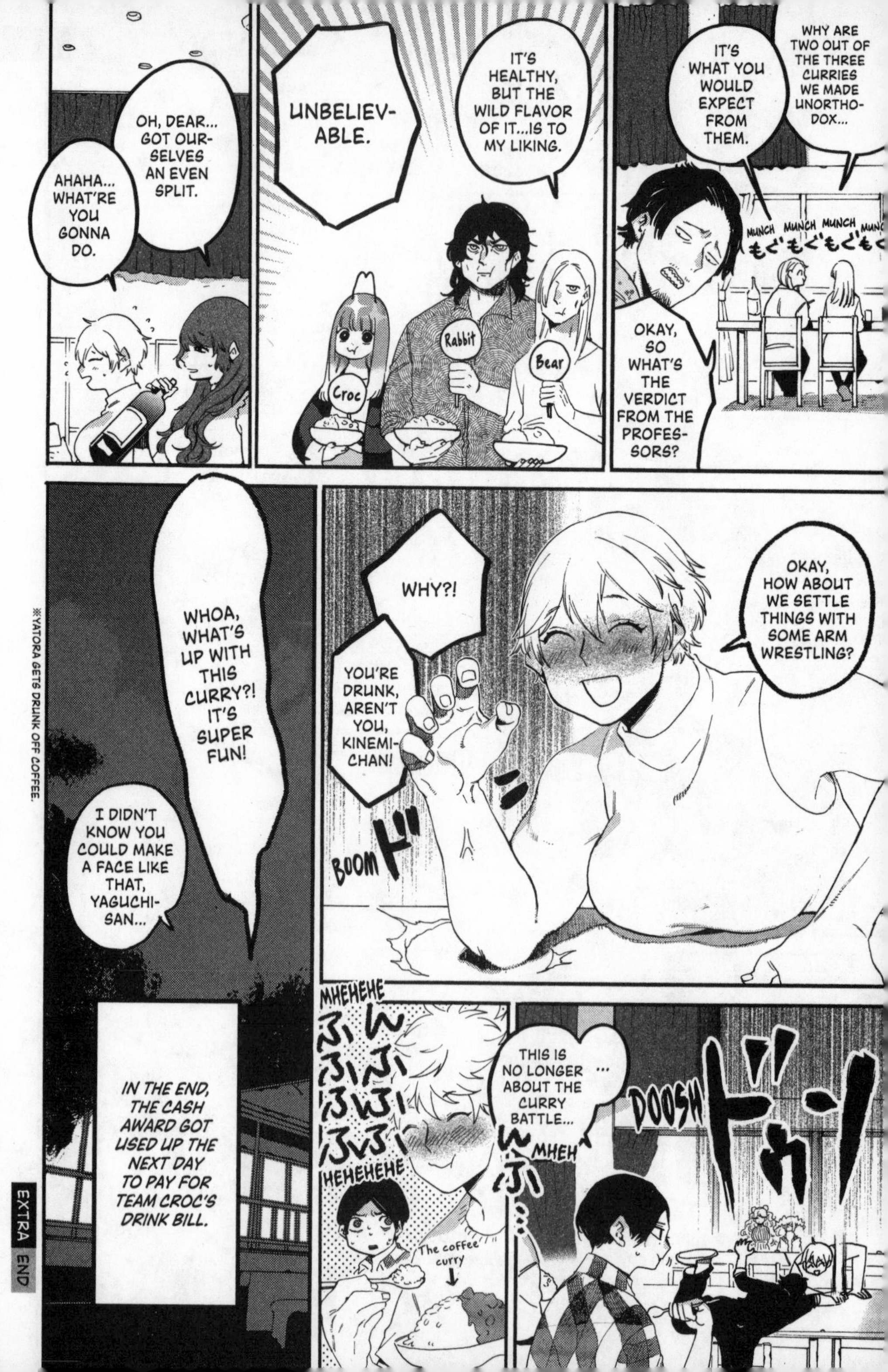
WHY ARE TWO OUT OF THE THREE CURRIES WE MADE UNORTHODOX...
IT'S WHAT YOU WOULD EXPECT FROM THEM.
MUNCH MUNCH MUNCH MUNCH
もぐもぐもぐもぐ
OKAY, SO WHAT'S THE VERDICT FROM THE PROFESSORS?
IT'S HEALTHY, BUT THE WILD FLAVOR OF IT...IS TO MY LIKING.
UNBELIEVABLE.
Rabbit
Bear
Croc
OH, DEAR... GOT OURSELVES AN EVEN SPLIT.
AHAHA... WHAT'RE YOU GONNA DO.
OKAY, HOW ABOUT WE SETTLE THINGS WITH SOME ARM WRESTLING?
WHY?!
YOU'RE DRUNK, AREN'T YOU, KINEMI-CHAN!
BOOM ド
WHOA, WHAT'S UP WITH THIS CURRY?! IT'S SUPER FUN!
I DIDN'T KNOW YOU COULD MAKE A FACE LIKE THAT, YAGUCHI-SAN...
※YATORA GETS DRUNK OFF COFFEE.
DOOSH
THIS IS NO LONGER ABOUT THE CURRY BATTLE...
...
MHEH
MHEHEHE
HEHEHEHE
The coffee curry
IN THE END, THE CASH AWARD GOT USED UP THE NEXT DAY TO PAY FOR TEAM CROC'S DRINK BILL.
EXTRA END

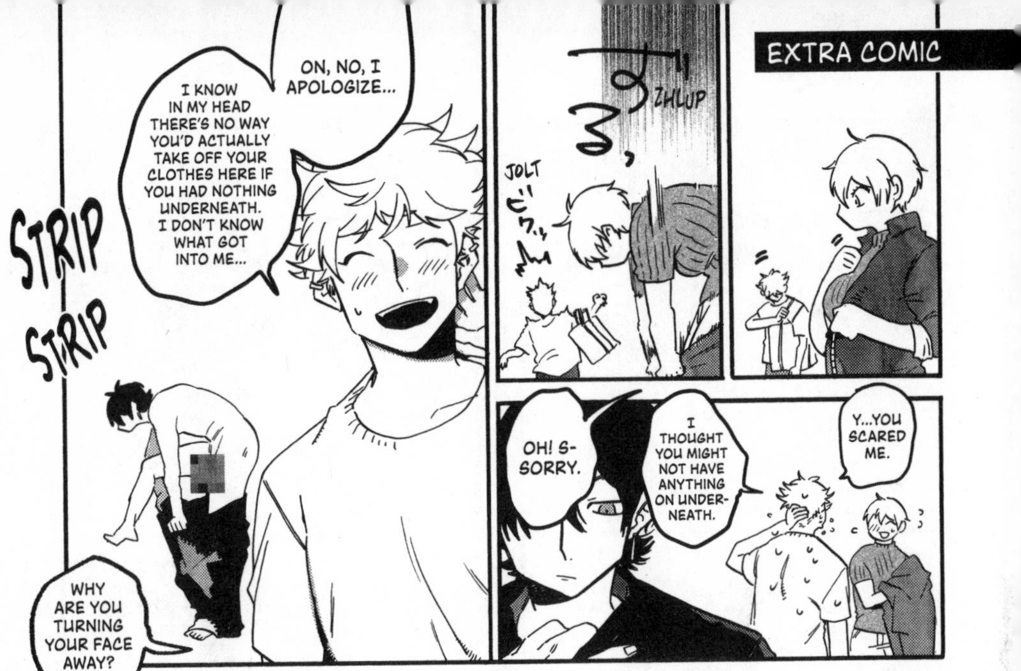
EXTRA COMIC
ZHLUP
JOLT
Y...YOU SCARED ME.
I THOUGHT YOU MIGHT NOT HAVE ANYTHING ON UNDER-NEATH.
OH! S-SORRY.
ON, NO, I APOLOGIZE...
I KNOW IN MY HEAD THERE'S NO WAY YOU'D ACTUALLY TAKE OFF YOUR CLOTHES HERE IF YOU HAD NOTHING UNDERNEATH. I DON'T KNOW WHAT GOT INTO ME...
STRIP
STRIP
WHY ARE YOU TURNING YOUR FACE AWAY?

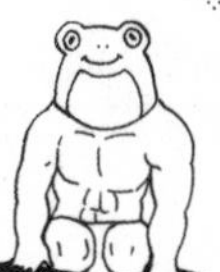

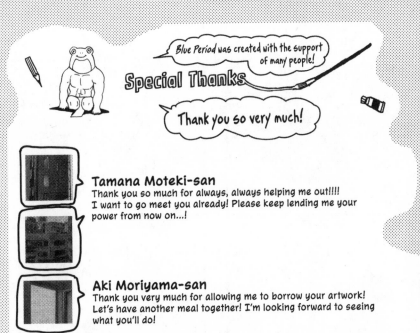

*Blue Period* was created with the support of many people!

## Special Thanks

Thank you so very much!

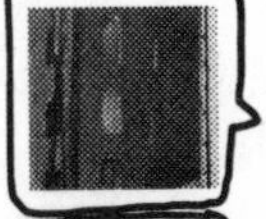

**Tamana Moteki-san**
Thank you so much for always, always helping me out!!!! I want to go meet you already! Please keep lending me your power from now on...!

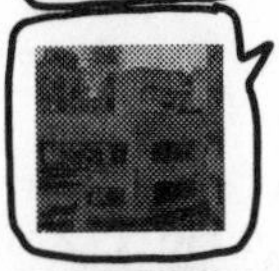

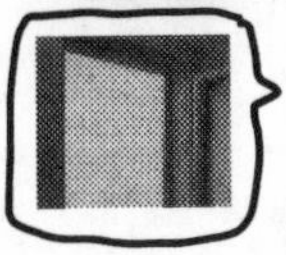

**Aki Moriyama-san**
Thank you very much for allowing me to borrow your artwork! Let's have another meal together! I'm looking forward to seeing what you'll do!

Special thanks: **Yoichi Umetsu-san**
Thank you so much for lending me your valuable knowledge...!

## UNIVERSITY FRIENDS (1)

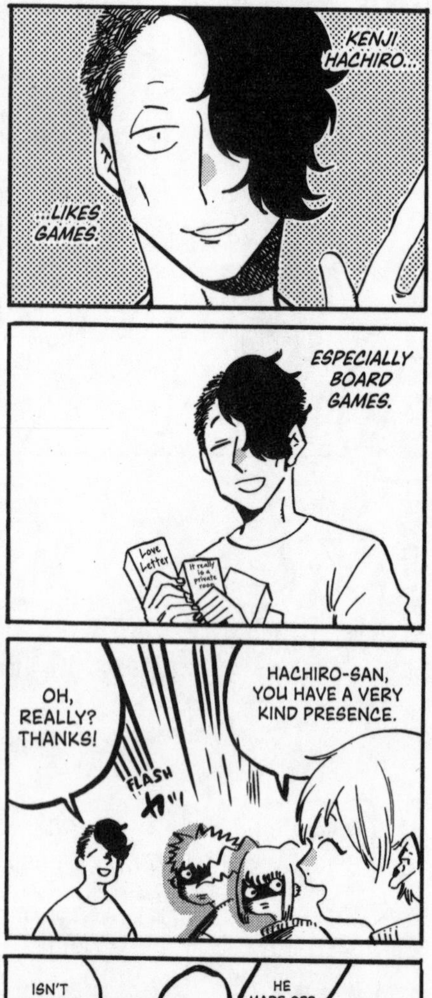
KENJI HACHIRO...
...LIKES GAMES.
ESPECIALLY BOARD GAMES.
Love Letter
HACHIRO-SAN, YOU HAVE A VERY KIND PRESENCE.
FLASH
OH, REALLY? THANKS!
NO, NO, NO! THAT GUY'S HORRIBLE! SERIOUSLY!
HE MADE OFF WITH MY LUNCH MONEY MULTIPLE TIMES!
HUH?
ISN'T IT YOUR FAULT FOR LOSING, THOUGH?

## UNIVERSITY FRIENDS (2)

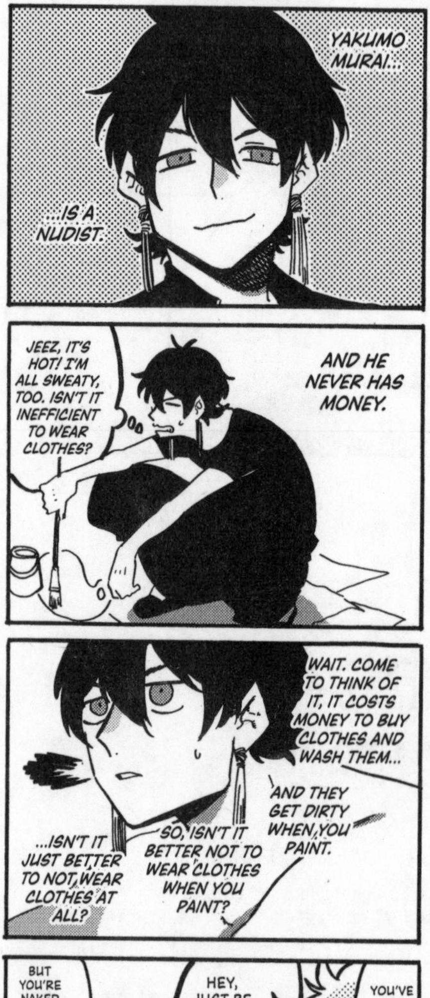
YAKUMO MURAI...
...IS A NUDIST.
AND HE NEVER HAS MONEY.
JEEZ, IT'S HOT! I'M ALL SWEATY, TOO. ISN'T IT INEFFICIENT TO WEAR CLOTHES?
WAIT. COME TO THINK OF IT, IT COSTS MONEY TO BUY CLOTHES AND WASH THEM...
AND THEY GET DIRTY WHEN YOU PAINT.
SO, ISN'T IT BETTER NOT TO WEAR CLOTHES WHEN YOU PAINT?
...ISN'T IT JUST BETTER TO NOT WEAR CLOTHES AT ALL?
YOU'VE GOT SOME WILD IDEAS...
HEY, JUST BE GLAD THAT I'M EVEN WEARING COVER-ALLS.
They got mad at me for painting in the atelier while nude, so this isn't by choice...
BUT YOU'RE NAKED UNDER-NEATH YOUR CLOTHES, TOO, AREN'T YOU, YATORA?
...but I have to wear it.
WELL, YEAH, BUT...

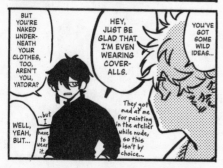

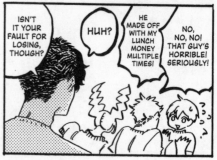

## UNIVERSITY FRIENDS (3)

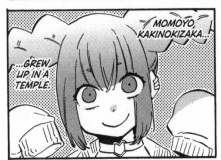

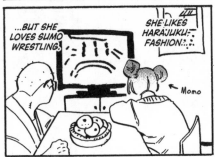

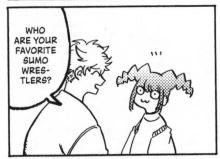

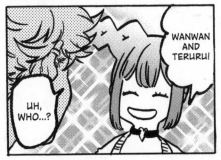

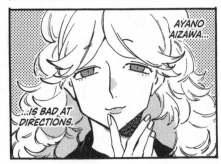

AYANO AIZAWA...
...IS BAD AT DIRECTIONS.
OH, THAT REMINDS ME, AYANO-CHAN USED TO BE A YANKII, YOU KNOW.
WHAT?
OH, DID YOU USED TO BE A YANKII, AYANO-SAN?
WHA-AAT?
IT'S NOT THAT I USED TO BE A YANKII, I JUST USED TO GO TO A SCHOOL THAT HAD A LOT OF YANKII THERE.
...

## UNIVERSITY FRIENDS (4)

MOMOYO KAKINOKIZAKA...
...GREW UP IN A TEMPLE.
SHE LIKES HARAJUKU FASHION...
...BUT SHE LOVES SUMO WRESTLING.
Momo
WHO ARE YOUR FAVORITE SUMO WRES-TLERS?
WANWAN AND TERURU!
UH, WHO...?

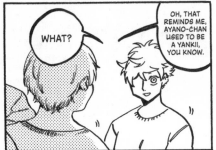

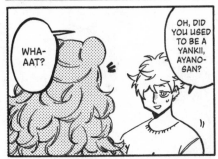

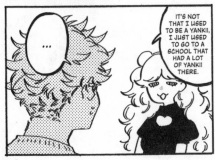

# TRANSLATION NOTES

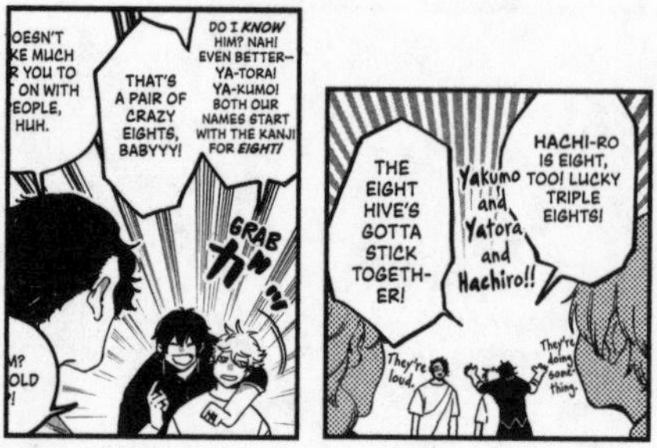
THAT'S A PAIR OF CRAZY EIGHTS, BABYYY!
DO I KNOW HIM? NAH! EVEN BETTER—YA-TORA! YA-KUMO! BOTH OUR NAMES START WITH THE KANJI FOR EIGHT!
GRAB
HACHI-RO IS EIGHT, TOO! LUCKY TRIPLE EIGHTS!
Yakumo and Yatora and Hachiro!!
THE EIGHT HIVE'S GOTTA STICK TOGETHER!
They're doing something.
They're loud.

## Crazy Eights and Lucky Triple Eights, page 11

The "Ya" in Yatora and Yakumo's name, as well as the "Hachi" in Kenji's last name can all mean "eight" in Japanese. In Japanese, three eights can have some significance as a pun on the word for "honeybee." A triple eight also has meaning as an angel number (repeating numbers that are seen as divine messages) that represents spiritual connection.

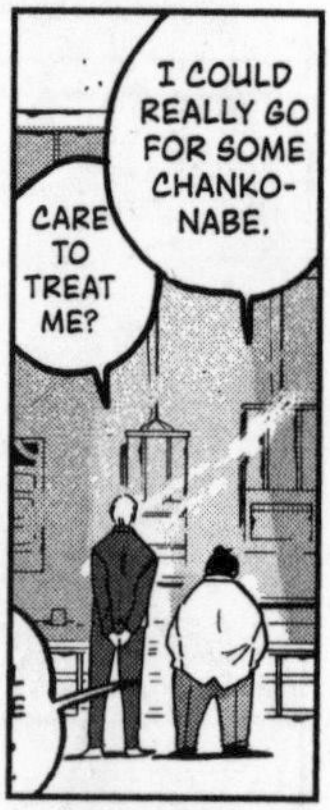
I COULD REALLY GO FOR SOME CHANKO-NABE.
CARE TO TREAT ME?

## Chankonabe, page 15

Chankonabe is a hearty one-pot dish that is associated with sumo wrestlers. The dish is a staple of the sumo wrestler's diet as a way to bulk up. Outside of the basic dashi soup base with Japanese flavorings like sake or mirin, chankonabe usually includes whatever is available to the person cooking it. Since chankonabe is typically used as a means of gaining weight, it often contains a lot of protein, such as chicken, fish balls, and beef. It may also include vegetables like daikon and bok choy.

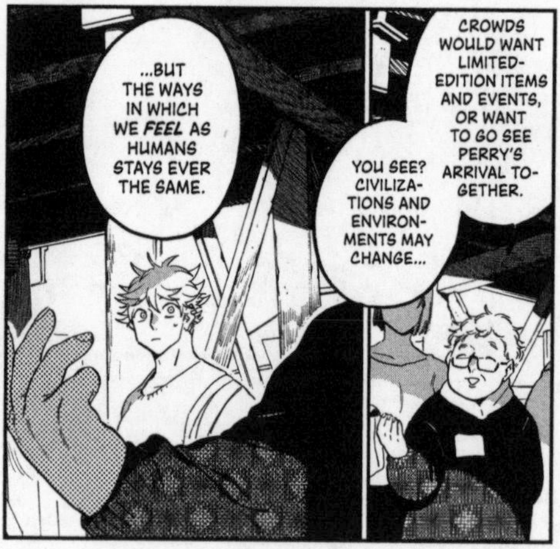
CROWDS WOULD WANT LIMITED-EDITION ITEMS AND EVENTS, OR WANT TO GO SEE PERRY'S ARRIVAL TOGETHER.
YOU SEE? CIVILIZATIONS AND ENVIRONMENTS MAY CHANGE...
...BUT THE WAYS IN WHICH WE FEEL AS HUMANS STAYS EVER THE SAME.

## Perry, page 23

In this scene, the tour guide is referring to Commodore Matthew Perry, who is famous for opening Japan to international trade during the final years of the Tokugawa shogunate. Around the time of Perry's arrival, Japan had taken an isolationist policy, and Perry was charged with forcing Japan to open up its ports. In 1853, Perry arrived in Edo Bay with his "Black Ships" and set off a chain of events that would eventually lead to the Convention of Kanagawa. This treaty opened up the ports of Shimoda and Hakodate to American ships, ending 220 years of Japanese seclusion.

**Kasha yokai, page 135**

In Japanese folklore, yokai are essentially supernatural creatures, and kasha are one type of yokai. Kasha directly translates to "fire cart" or "fire chariot." There are different interpretations of what they look like, but the most typical one places them in the class of yokai known as bake-neko (monster or transforming cats). Bake-neko usually begin as normal cats and turn into yokai after growing very, very old. Kasha are known to come surrounded by flames or in a burning cart/chariot, and steal corpses.

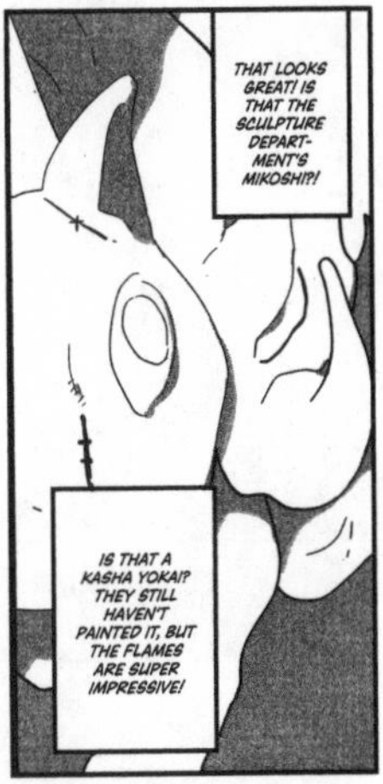
THAT LOOKS GREAT!! IS THAT THE SCULPTURE DEPART-MENT'S MIKOSHI?!
IS THAT A KASHA YOKAI? THEY STILL HAVEN'T PAINTED IT, BUT THE FLAMES ARE SUPER IMPRESSIVE!

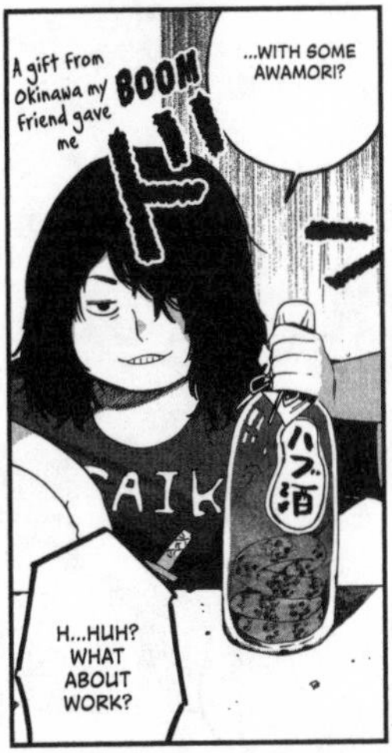
...WITH SOME AWAMORI?
BOOM
A gift from Okinawa my Friend gave me
ハブ酒
H...HUH? WHAT ABOUT WORK?

**Habushu, page 155**

Habushu is a type of liquor from Okinawa that is made with a venomous snake known as habu. The drink is a type of awamori (distilled rice liquor), and the bottles will often contain a whole habu that was drowned or killed in a way to give it a striking appearance. Habushu is said to enhance virility and help with male sexual dysfunction, but there is no evidence to back up these claims.

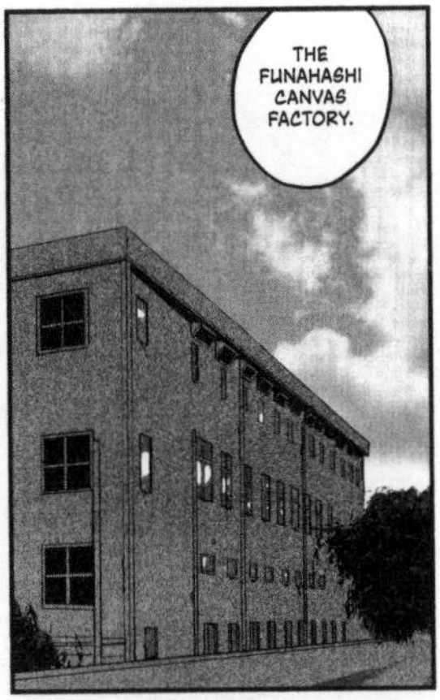
THE FUNAHASHI CANVAS FACTORY.

**The Funahashi Canvas Factory, page 177**

The Funahashi Canvas factory seems to be based on the Funaoka Canvas factory in Fukushima, Japan. Funaoka Canvas was produced by Nihon Gazai Kogyo, which had been the only domestic producer of canvas for art/painting in Japan since 1918. Unfortunately, many factors, including the economic aftereffects of the Fukushima Earthquake and Fukushima Daiichi Nuclear Disaster, resulted in the company filing for bankruptcy and closing in 2015.

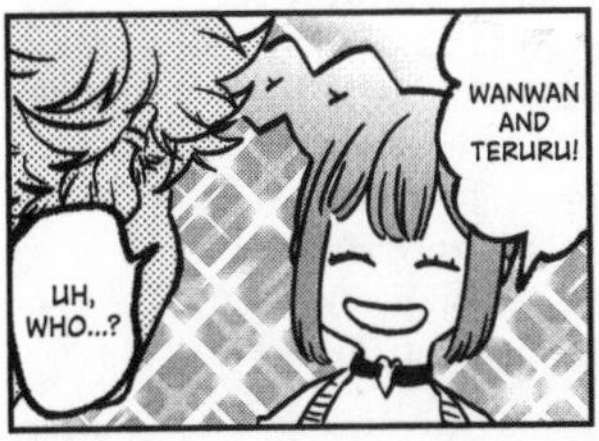
WANWAN AND TERURU!
UH, WHO...?

**Wanwan and Teruru, page 193**

Wanwan and Teruru are the nicknames for Kakuryu Rikisaburo, and Terunofuji Haruo, respectively. "Teruru" is more or less an affectionate form of "Terunofuji," but apparently, "Wanwan" got its start on the famous Japanese bulletin board, 2ch, where someone commented that Kakuryu Rikisaburo "looked like my family dog." People then took notice of his resemblance to a typical Japanese shiba, and the end result was his nickname, "Wanwan," which is equal to "bark bark" in English, or a childish way to refer to a dog, like "doggie."

# Magus of the Library

Mitsu Izumi

## MITSU IZUMI'S STUNNING ARTWORK BRINGS A FANTASTICAL LITERARY ADVENTURE TO LUSH, THRILLING LIFE!

Young Theo adores books, but the prejudice and hatred of his village keeps them ever out of his reach. Then one day, he chances to meet Sedona, a traveling librarian who works for the great library of Aftzaak, City of Books, and his life changes forever...

# Young characters and steampunk setting, like *Howl's Moving Castle* and *Battle Angel Alita*

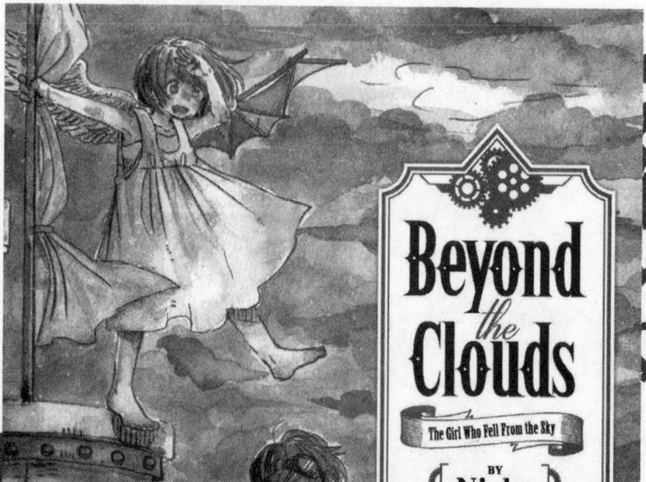
Beyond the Clouds
The Girl Who Fell From the Sky
BY
Nicke
VOLUME
01

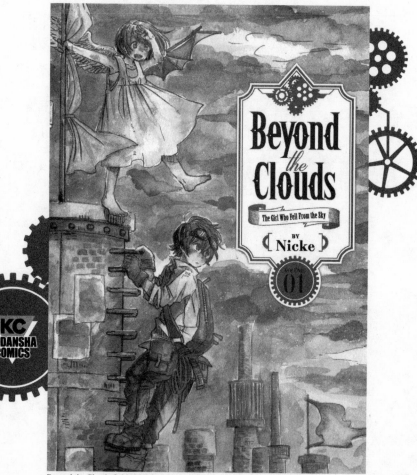

Beyond the Clouds © 2018 Nicke / Ki-oon

A boy with a talent for machines and a mysterious girl whose wings he's fixed will take you beyond the clouds! In the tradition of the high-flying, resonant adventure stories of Studio Ghibli comes a gorgeous tale about the longing of young hearts for adventure and friendship!

KC KODANSHA COMICS

*New action series from Hiroyuki Takei, creator of the classic shonen franchise Shaman King!*

In medieval Japan, a bell hanging on the collar is a sign that a cat has a master. Norachiyo's bell hangs from his katana sheath, but he is nonetheless a stray — a ronin. This one-eyed cat samurai travels across a dishonest world, cutting through pretense and deception with his blade.

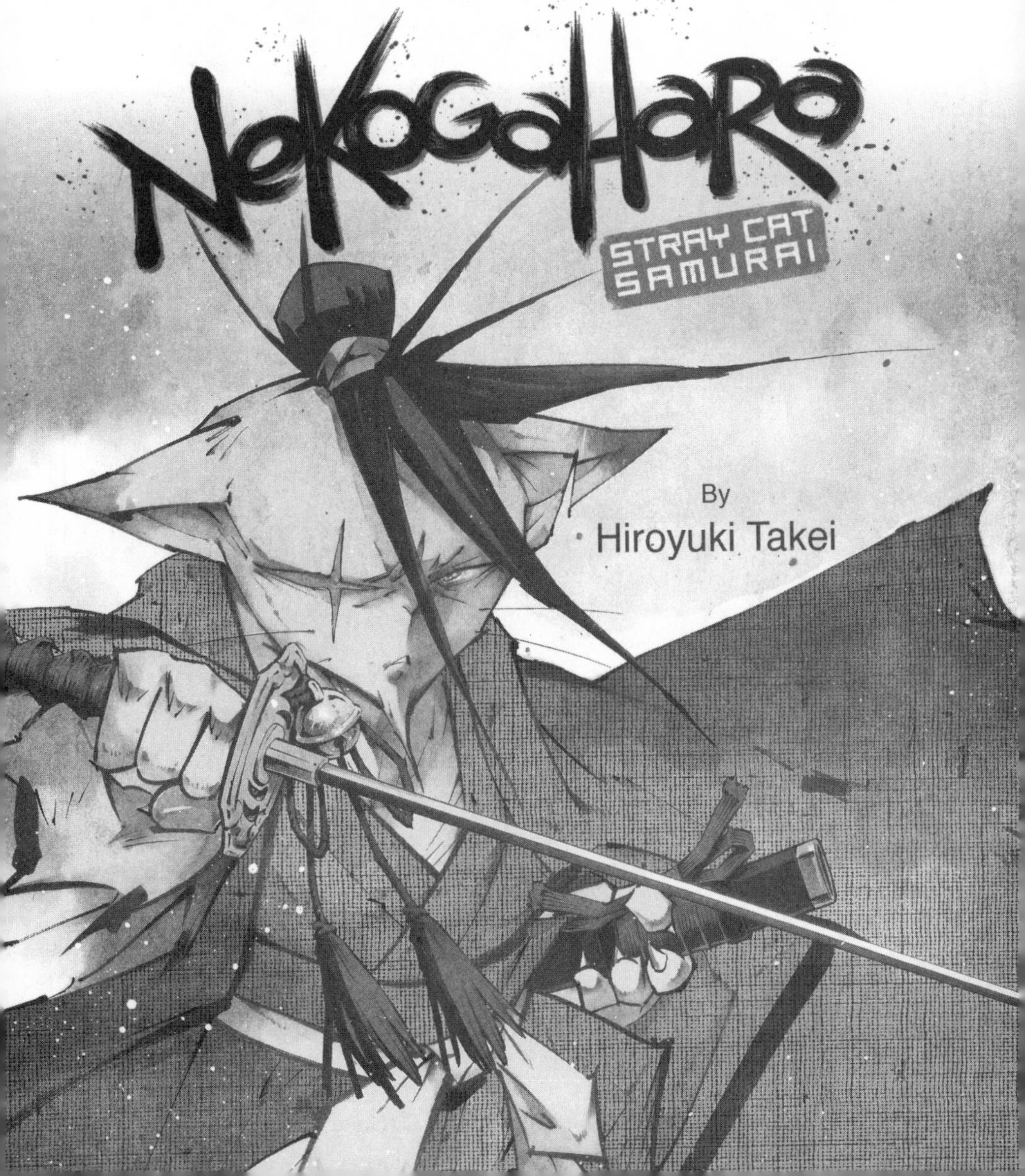
NEKOGAHARA
STRAY CAT SAMURAI
By
Hiroyuki Takei

# SAINT☆YOUNG MEN

**A LONG AWAITED ARRIVAL IN PREMIUM 2-IN-1 HARDCOVER**

After centuries of hard work, Jesus and Buddha take a break from their heavenly duties to relax among the people of Japan, and their adventures in this lighthearted buddy comedy are sure to bring mirth and merriment to all!

KC KODANSHA COMICS

"Brilliant…the physical comedy and facial expressions will make you literally LOL."
—Sam Humphries (host of *DC Daily*; writer, *Green Lanterns, Legendary Star-Lord*)

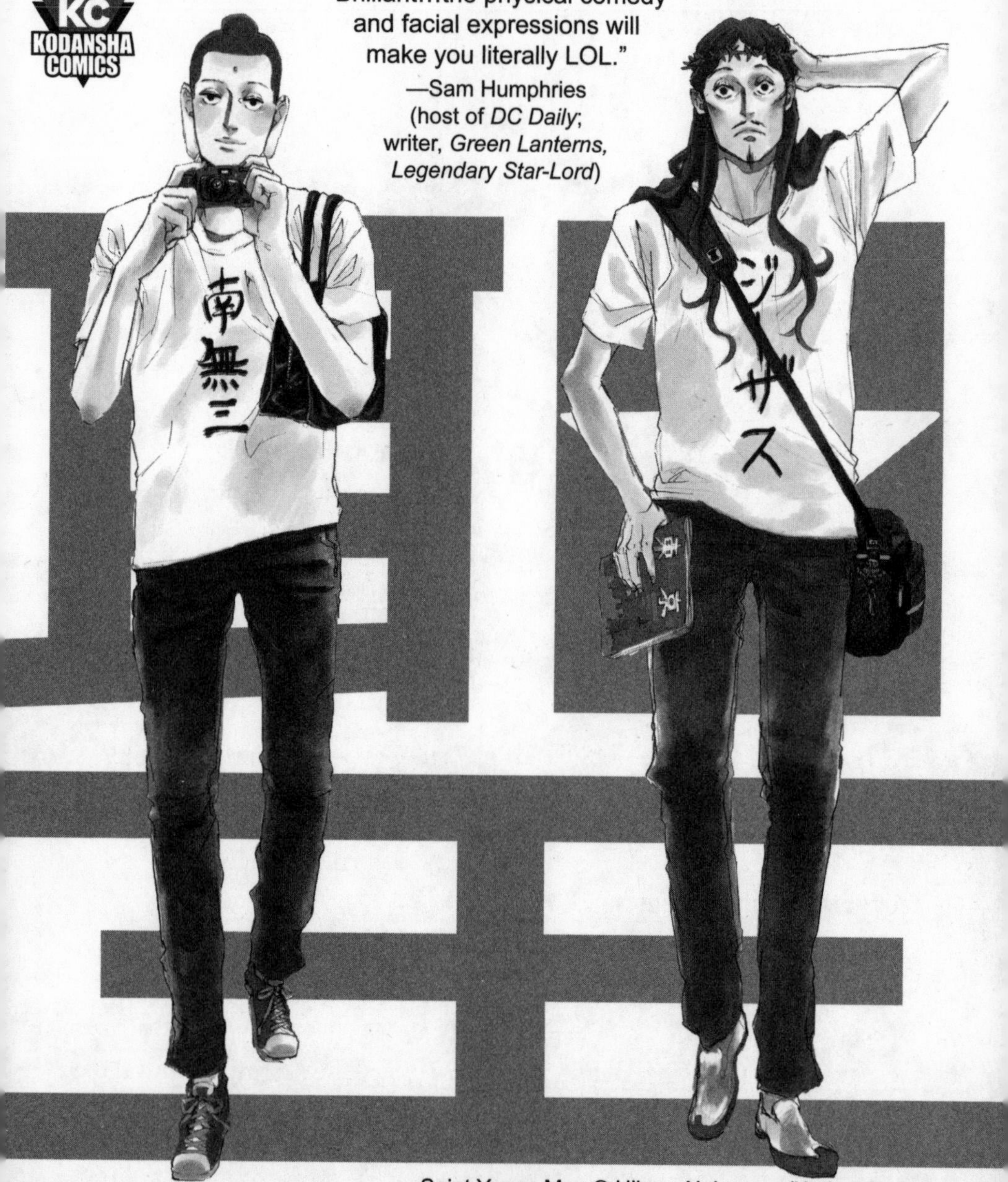
南無三
ジーザス

# Princess Jellyfish

### Akiko Higashimura

**ALSO AN ANIME!**

"One of the best manga for beginners!"
—*Kotaku*

Tsukimi Kurashita is fascinated with jellyfish. She's loved them from a young age and has carried that love with her to her new life in the big city of Tokyo. There, she resides in Amamizukan, a safe-haven for geek girls where no boys are allowed. One day, Tsukimi crosses paths with a beautiful and fashionable woman, but there's much more to this woman than her trendy clothes...!

# PERFECT WORLD

### Rie Aruga

A TOUCHING NEW SERIES ABOUT LOVE AND COPING WITH DISABILITY

An office party reunites Tsugumi with her high school crush Itsuki. He's realized his dream of becoming an architect, but along the way, he experienced a spinal injury that put him in a wheelchair. Now Tsugumi's rekindled feelings will butt up against prejudices she never considered — and Itsuki will have to decide if he's ready to let someone into his heart...

KC KODANSHA COMICS

Knight of the Ice ©Yayoi Ogawa/Kodansha Ltd.

# SKATING THRILLS AND ICY CHILLS WITH THIS NEW TINGLY ROMANCE SERIES!

A rom-com on ice, perfect for fans of *Princess Jellyfish* and *Wotakoi*. Kokoro is the talk of the figure-skating world, winning trophies and hearts. But little do they know... he's actually a huge nerd! From the beloved creator of *You're My Pet* (*Tramps Like Us*).

Chitose is a serious young woman, working for the health magazine *SASSO*. Or at least, she would be, if she wasn't constantly getting distracted by her childhood friend, international figure skating star Kokoro Kijinami! In the public eye and on the ice, Kokoro is a gallant, flawless knight, but behind his glittery costumes and breathtaking spins lies a secret: He's actually a hopelessly romantic otaku, who can only land his quad jumps when Chitose is on hand to recite a spell from his favorite magical girl anime!

KC KODANSHA COMICS

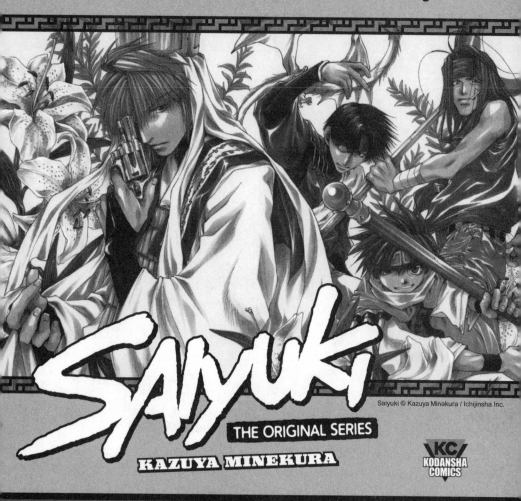

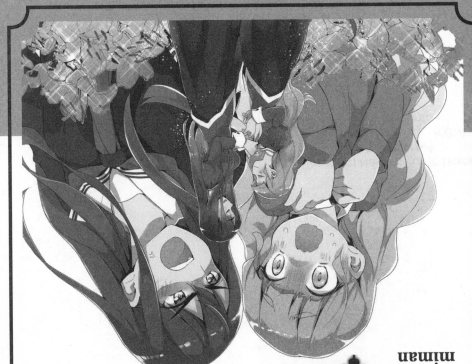

miman

# Yuri Is My Job!

❖

**JOIN US FOR AFTERNOON TEA WITH EQUAL PARTS YURI, ROM-COM, AND DRAMA!**

❖

Hime is a picture-perfect high school princess, so when she accidentally injures a café manager named Mai, she's willing to cover some shifts to keep her façade intact. To Hime's surprise, the café is themed after a private school where the all-female staff always puts on their best act for their loyal customers. However, under the guidance of the most graceful girl there, Hime can't help but blush and blunder! Beneath all the frills and laughter, Hime feels tension brewing as she finds out more about her new job and her budding feelings....

# OTOMO 大友克洋

## A GLOBAL TRIBUTE TO THE MIND BEHIND AKIRA

Prospect Heights Public Library
12 N Elm Street
Prospect Heights, IL 60070
www.phpl.info

A celebration of manga legend Katsuhiro Otomo from more than 80 world-renowned fine artists and comics legends
With contributions from:
- Stan Sakai
- Tomer and Asaf Hanuka
- Sara Pichelli
- Range Murata
- Aleksi Briclot
And more!
168 pages of stunning, full-color art

KC
KODANSHA COMICS

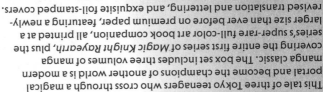

A Kodansha Comics Trade Paperback Original
*Blue Period* 8 copyright © 2020 Tsubasa Yamaguchi
English translation copyright © 2022 Tsubasa Yamaguchi

Published in the United States by Kodansha Comics, an imprint of
Kodansha USA Publishing, LLC, New York.

Publication rights for this English edition arranged through
Kodansha Ltd., Tokyo.

First published in Japan in 2020 by Kodansha Ltd., Tokyo.

ISBN 978-1-64651-292-8

Printed in the United States of America.

www.kodansha.us

1st Printing
Translation: Ajani Oloye
Lettering: Lys Blakeslee
Editing: Haruko Hashimoto
Kodansha Comics edition cover design by Matthew Akuginow

Publisher: Kiichiro Sugawara

Director of publishing services: Ben Applegate
Director of publishing operations: Dave Barrett
Associate director, publishing operations: Stephen Pakula
Publishing services managing editors: Madison Salters, Alanna Ruse
Production managers: Emi Lotto, Angela Zurlo
Logo and character art ©Kodansha USA Publishing, LLC